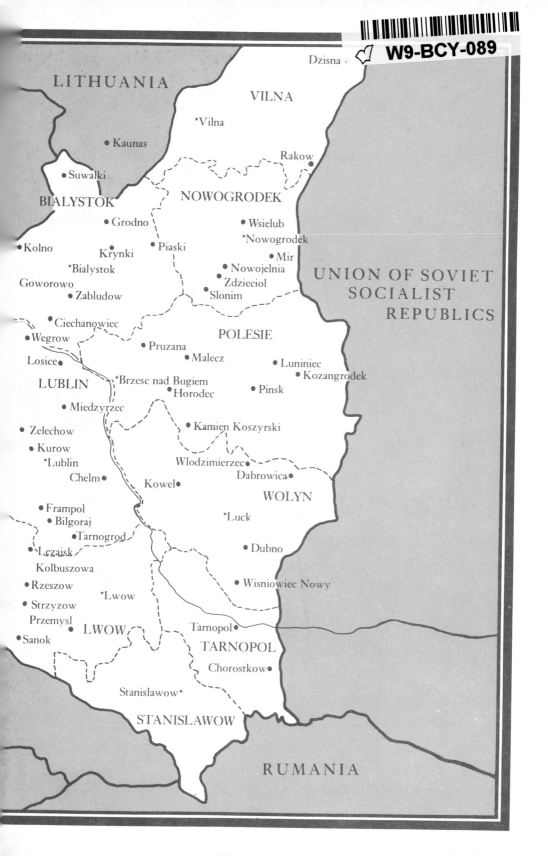

W9-BCY-089

LITHUANIA

VILNA

Dzisna

*Vilna

• Kaunas

Rakow

• Suwalki

BIALYSTOK

NOWOGRODEK

• Grodno

• Wsielub

*Nowogrodek

•Kolno

Krynki

• Piaski

• Mir

*Bialystok

• Nowojelnia

Goworowo

• Zdzieciol

• Zabludow

Slonim

UNION OF SOVIET
SOCIALIST
REPUBLICS

• Ciechanowiec

POLESIE

•Wegrow

• Pruzana

Losice•

• Malecz

• Luniniec

• Kozangrodek

LUBLIN

*Brzesc nad Bugiem

• Horodec

• Pinsk

• Miedzyrzec

• Zelechow

• Kamien Koszyrski

• Kurow

*Lublin

Wlodzimierzec•

Chelm•

Kowel•

Dabrowica•

WOLYN

• Frampol

*Luck

• Bilgoraj

•Tarnogrod

•Lezajsk

• Dubno

Kolbuszowa

• Rzeszow

• Wisniowiec Nowy

• Strzyzow

*Lwow

Przemysl

LWOW

Tarnopol•

•Sanok

TARNOPOL

Chorostkow•

Stanislawow*

STANISLAWOW

RUMANIA

From a Ruined Garden

TRANSLATED AND EDITED BY
Jack Kugelmass
AND
Jonathan Boyarin

WITH GEOGRAPHICAL INDEX
AND BIBLIOGRAPHY BY
Zachary M. Baker

SCHOCKEN BOOKS
New York

FROM A RUINED GARDEN

The Memorial Books
of Polish Jewry

First published by Schocken Books 1983
10 9 8 7 6 5 4 3 2 1   83 84 85 86
Copyright © 1983 by Jack Kugelmass and Jonathan Boyarin
All rights reserved

Library of Congress Cataloging in Publication Data
Main entry under title:
From a ruined garden.
Bibliography: p.
1. Jews—Poland—Social life and customs—Addresses,
essays, lectures.   2. holocaust, Jewish (1939–1945)—
Poland—Addresses, essays, lectures.   3. Poland—
Ethnic relations—Addresses, essays, lectures.
I. Kugelmass, Jack.   II. Boyarin, Jonathan.
DS135.P6F77   1983   305.8'924'0438   83–42717

Designed by Jacqueline Schuman
Manufactured in the United States of America
ISBN 0–8052–3867–0

We would like to thank the following organizations and individuals for granting their permission to publish the English translation of selections originally published in Yiddish:

Kupat gemilat hasadim shel yotsei Bezoyn for "The Transport from Auschwitz" by Eliahu Shimon Hifka in *Sefer ha-zikaron le-kedoshei Bezoyn.*

Kupat gemilot hasadim be-Yisrael olei shel Khelm ve-haseviva for "The Ancestors Merit the Blessings of Laughter" by Yisroel Ashendorf in *Yizker-bukh Khelm.*

Irgun yotsei Khmelnik be-Yisrael for "The Dispute over the Succession to the Rabbinate," by Mordkhe Fridnzon, and "The Ruined Wedding" by Moyshe-Leyzer Mintz in *Pinkas Khmelnik.*

Chorostkow Society for "In Khorostkov during the First World War" by S. Ansky in *Sefer Khorostkov.*

Irgun yotsei Tshekhanovits for "The Blind Cantor" by Motl Rosental in *Tshekhanovits: mehoz Bialystok sefer edut ve-zikaron.*

Irgun yotsei Dubno for "Three Parables of the Dubner Magid" by Leyzer Shtaynman in *Dubno; sefer zikaron.*

Frampol Landsmanshaft Organization of Israel for "How I Hid Twelve Jews" by Stanislaw Sobczak in *Sefer Frampol.*

Bukh komitet Horodets for "The Burial Society" by A.S. Horodetser and "Girls Kheyders" by Ami in *Horodets; a geshikhte fun a shtetl.*

· Permission Acknowledgments ·

Yigal Plot for "The Town's New Torah Scroll" by Yaakov (Ben-Moshe) Plot and "A Communist Assembly Elects a Zionist as Representative by Yaakov (Ben-Moshe) Plot in *Sefer ha-zikaron le-kehilat Kamin-Koshirski ve-ha-seviva.*

Shalom Muhlstein for "At the Market" by Shalom Muhlstein in *Pinkas Kolbishov* from the story "Kolbuszov Saturday and Weekdays."

Ha-vaad le-hantsahat sefer zikaron le-yehudei ha-ir Kolno for "My Grandmother Sews her own Burial Shroud" by Blume Goren-Malovany in *Sefer zikaron le-kehilat Kolno.*

Tala Maskal-Shults for "The Capture of Girls" by Tala Maskal-Shults in *Sefer Kolo.*

Irgun yotsei Kovel be-Yisrael for "What Is a Pinkes" told by Leybl Shiter and recorded by B. Baler in *Pinkas Kovel.*

Irgun yotsei Krinki for "Anarchist Activities" by Betsalel (Alter) Potshebutsky in *Pinkas Krinek.*

Irgun yotsei Koriv Lubelski for "I Was a German 'Soldier'" by Nekhemye Vurman in *Yizker-bukh Koriv.*

Independent Kutno Young Men's Benevolent Society for "The Last Meeting of the Community Council in Kutno" by Nosn Moskovitsh in *Kutno ve-ha-seviva.*

Irgun yotsei Lizhensk be-Yisrael for "The Twenty-first of Adar: the Great Day" by Yeshaye Kirshnboym and "Concerning Opponents of Hassidism in Lizhensk by Volf Raykhntal in *Lizhensk; sefer zikaron le-kedoshei Lizhensk she-nispu be-shoat ha-natsim.*

Irgun yotsei Loshits for "A Strike in Kheyder" by Yoysef Fridman in *Loshits; lezeykher an umgebrakhte kehile.*

Irgun yotsei Luninyets ve-Kozhanhorodok be-Yisrael for "The First Yiddish Library" by Dvoyre Kutnik in *Yizkor kehilot Luninyets Kozhanhorodok.*

Hitahadut olei Mezritsh for "How I Read Yiddish Literature to an S.S. Captain" by Berl Manperl in *Mezritsh; zamlbukh.*

Irgun yotsei Mir be-Yisrael for "From American Universities into the Polish Yeshivas" by Khayim Semyatitsky in *Sefer Mir.*

Kupat gemilat khesed shel olei Navaredok for "Novoyelne" by Khane Kamin (Kaplan), "A Disrupted Seder Night" by Yitkhok Gurvits, "Dear God!" by Dovid Kahan in *Pinkas Navaredok.*

Irgun yotsei Pyesk ve-Most be-Yisrael for "Reb Moyshe-Yudl, the Travelling Tailor" by Oyzer Shevakh in *Pyesk ve-Most sefer yizkor.*

Chaim Plotkin for "An Escape from Certain Death" by Khayim Raytshik in *Sefer zikaron le-kehilat Rozhan.*

Sandzer Landsmanschaft "A Purim in the Region of Sants" in *Sefer Sants.*

Irgun yotsei Sanok ve-ha-seviva be-Yisrael for "Ayzikl the Bachelor" by Berl Robakh and "The Death of the Bukovsker Rebe, Dovid Shapiro" by A. Sharvit in *Sefer zikaron le-kehilat Sanok ve-ha-seviva.*

Josef Weinberg for "Kol Nidre in Auschwitz" by Josef Weinberg in *Sefer Strizhuv ve-ha-seviva.*

Irgun yotsei Vengerov be-Yisrael for "Customs, Symbols, and Ceremonies" by Sh. Zabludovitsh in *Kehilat Vengerov; sefer zikaron.*

Vad sefer ha-yizkor shel ha-ir Vyerushov for "A Murder in the Forest" by Yehoshua Aybeshits in *Vyerushov; sefer yizkor.*

Irgun yotsei Vladimirets for "My Escape from the Ditches of Slaughter" by Mordkhe Vaysman in *Sefer Vladimirets*.

Dovid ben Zelig Gersht for "Khayim-Yisroel Melamed and the Kozhenitser Magid" by Dovid ben Zelig Gersht in *Vurke; sefer zikaron*.

Louis Pave, Pres. and G. Tabak Rec. Sec. Zembrov Society for "The Angry Dance" by Yom-Tov Levinsky in *Sefer Zambrove*.

Club Zyrardow for "The Butchers of Zhirardov Commission a Torah Scroll" by K. Grushka in *Pinkas Zhirardov*.

Irgun olei Zlotshev for "Zabalye the Coachwoman" by Ayzik Fayvlovitsh in *Sefer Zlotshev*.

Irgun Yotsei Belkhatov for "The Struggle for the Right to Work" by Hershl Goldmints; "Belkhatov without Jews" by Yoseph Raykh in *Belkhatov yizker-bukh*.

Kalushiner Landsmanshaft in Yisroel for "Alter the Village Peddler" by Yosl Sukenik; "The Righteousness of Revolutionaries" by Borukh Shtulman in *Sefer Kalushin*.

Vad Yotsei Opatov for "The First Suicide in Town" by Mendl Nisnboym in *Opatow; sefer zikaron le-ir-va-em be-Yisrael*.

Czenstochauer Young Men, Inc. for "Reb Dvoyre Mash" by A. Khrobolovsky; "Jewish Fighters in Spain" by Gina Medem in *Tshenstokhover Yidn*; "A Hasidic Demonstration" by Avrom Litman in *Nayer tsugob-materyal tsum bukh Tshentokhover Yidn*.

Irgun Yotsei Vishkov for "Sports Clubs and Self Defence" by Borukh Yismakh in *Sefer Vishkov*.

Irgun Yotsei Vishnevits for "Terror in Vishnevits" by One Who Was Saved in *Vishnevits; sefer zikaron*.

Zhelekhover Redaktsye Komitet for "When Anti-Semitism Raged" by Yisroel Vaysman; "The Typhus Epidemic and a Wedding at the Cemetary" by Moyshe Borukhovitsh in *Yizker-bukh fun der Zhelekhover Yidisher kehile*.

Through a miracle, I have been rescued from Nazi bondage. Yet I feel like a solitary twig from a ruined garden.

Binyomin Orenshtayn
Khurbn Otvotsk, Falenits, Kartshev.

. . . you should also recreate your speech in letters. That will be the greatest revenge you can take on the evil ones. In spite of them, the souls of your brothers and sisters will live on, the martyrs whom they sought to destroy. For no one can annihilate letters. They have wings, and they fly around in the heights . . . into eternity.

Pesakh Markus
Lite, band eyns

Contents

EVENTS

LEGENDS AND FOLKLORE

HOLOCAUST

RETURN

Acknowledgments

We would like to thank the following people for their generous assistance: Anne Gilhully, Pearl Morrell and Marilyn Stern provided much needed technical advice and assistance. Danny Boyarin, Deborah Dash Moore, Lucjan Dobroszycki, Nancy Erlich, Janet Hadda, David Roskies and Beatrice Silverman-Weinreich all read drafts of the manuscript and suggested changes. Dina Abramowicz, Malka Herbstman, Miriam Hoffman, Shlomo Noble and Marek Webb helped us to determine the meaning of terms not found in any Yiddish dictionary. We are particularly grateful to the YIVO Institute which has, among other great treasures, an extensive collection of *yizker-bikher*. We would like to thank the staff of the YIVO archives for generous access to its photographic collection; YIVO's library staff for taking a strong interest in the project; and Rosaline Schwartz and Susan Milamed of the Landsmanshaft project for helping us track down the publishers of the *yizker-bikher*.

Special thanks go to our agent, Edy Selman and our editor, Bonny Fetterman for their excellent advice and to Zachary Baker whose many contributions to this book will make the *yizker-bikher* accessible to a broad range of people.

We are eternally grateful to our parents, Fay and David Kugelmass and Sidney and Alice Boyarin for supporting Jewish scholarship and to our wives, Sharon Kugelmass and Elissa Sampson who offered critical and emotional support throughout the research and writing of this book.

—Jack Kugelmass and Jonathan Boyarin

From a Ruined Garden

Introduction

From *Sefer Kalushin*, a Polish Jewish memorial book:

> Near the river, on the square nearby the old study house, stood the old
> wooden synagogue. In town it was said that the synagogue had been there for
> four hundred years. Terrifying legends about it were circulated.
>
> People were afraid to pass by the cemetery at night, for the dead call people
> up to the Torah, and woe to the one who refuses the summons of the dead.
> Upon hearing oneself thus called, one is bound to enter the synagogue, stand
> up on the podium by the open Torah, and most important of all—walk out
> backwards, facing the Torah. . . . It was said that someone had once walked
> past the synagogue late at night, and heard a voice calling him to the Torah.
> This Jew indeed entered, found an open Torah lying on the podium, read a
> certain portion correctly, and forgot only to walk out backwards. He was
> stricken and fell dead then and there . . .
>
> Four centuries the old synagogue stood, and it was burned at the end of the
> nineteenth century. The place stood empty; only the terror and the legends
> remained.[1]

The dead have a power over the living. There are rituals to placate them and
prayers to succor them. Sometimes the living can supplicate the dead, requesting
help in this world and intervention from the powers above. Wherever the dead
reside, in some heavenly kingdom or in earthly graves, their presence is felt by
the living, and it is through the living that they find a measure of eternal life.

Completely overlooked in recent writing about the Holocaust is the single
most important act of commemorating the dead on the part of Jewish survivors.
These are the hundreds of *yizker-bikher*, memorial books devoted to the lives and
deaths of entire Jewish communities in Eastern Europe. Four hundred such
books have been written by survivors and émigrés from Polish-Jewish communities alone. These books range in size and format from now crumbling, thin
paperbound volumes produced in D.P. camps shortly after World War II, to the
four large-format volumes devoted to every aspect of the history and daily life of
the Jews of Slonim. Even now, almost forty years after the end of the war, new
memorial books are being published each year.

The selections which make up *From a Ruined Garden*, drawn from over sixty

---

*Full citations are given only for those works which do not appear in the Bibliography of Eastern
European Memorial Books (see Appendix I). Citations for memorial books are consistent with the
Bibliography except in one respect. Here, the transliterated (either Yiddish or Hebrew) name of the
town is followed by the official (Polish) name. In the bibliography, the official name and spelling are
used wherever it would not distort a correct citation (i.e., Tshenstokhover *Yidn* as opposed to
Czestochowa Yidn; the official spelling cannot have the adjectival ending that the book's title has). A
transliterated Yiddish or Hebrew is used whenever the official name varies from the name used by
the town's former Jewish inhabitants (i.e., Navaredok as opposed to the official Nowogrodek).

1. Moyshe Frukht, *"Tsu naye tsaytn," Sefer Kalushin (Kaluszyn)*.

---

memorial books, are unique historical documents that offer English readers glimpses into a previously locked storehouse of information on the traditions and transformation of everyday life in the *shtetl*, the small towns in Eastern Europe where the majority of Polish Jews lived.

The memorial-book writers were not constrained by the size of the Jewish community in their town. The town of Chorostkow (Khorostkov), with 350 Jewish families, was as likely to have a memorial book as Lodz, with its 200,000 Jews. As a result, the preponderance of memorial books are for *shtetlekh* rather than major cities, and cannot be taken to reflect accurately the demographics of prewar Polish Jewry, over one-third of whom lived in Poland's three largest cities.

The titles of the books reveal much about their origins and intent. Sometimes the name of the town alone suffices. Usually, however, it is preceded by words such as *yizker-bukh*, indicating that the book is intended to serve as a substitute for the traditional memorial service; *sefer*, suggesting that the book is to be regarded as a holy text; *pinkes*, meaning that the book is a substitute for the lost town chronicle, or *le-kedoshei*, marking its dedication to the town's Holocaust martyrs.

The inside covers of many books bear maps. Sometimes these are regional, showing the relation of the town to neighboring locations. Others are free-style, schematic representations of the town's layout. For smaller communities, these may show each house and be numerically coded to match a listing of each homeowner's name. Others show cows, crosses, gravestones and the like to represent the locations of pastures, churches, and cemeteries.

The volumes typically open with a frontispiece featuring symbols of mourning as well as symbols of life destroyed: a talis (prayer shawl) draped over a tombstone; a ghostly figure rising from the grave, his eyes covered by his hands and tears falling; a menorah overturned, its candle flames igniting the entire town; a tree cut down at the height of vitality, with a small green shoot growing from its stump.

The books' tables of contents reflect both thematic and chronological principles of organization. Given that the topics of most selections reflect the authors' choice rather than an editor's assignment, it is understandable that the chapter divisions are less than clear-cut. Whereas books are frequently divided into pre–World War I, interwar, and Holocaust sections, they also include chapters and individual selections on town characters, rabbis, or political parties that contain references to all three periods. For example, the story "Dear God!" describes peaceful traditional life, the Russian revolution, and the Holocaust in the space of a few pages. Generally the constellations that exist in memory prevail, rather than a particular chronological or historical sequence.

In making our selections, we have tried to span the range of subject matter that finds its way into memorial books. The practical considerations of time and space set limits on what could be included, and the chance discovery of particularly strong pieces sometimes caused one topic rather than another to be represented. We have tried to strike a balance between what struck us as most interesting and what demanded inclusion for the sake of a fair representation of Polish-Jewish life. Although we opted for a combination of strong narrative and unusual information, in some cases one or the other became the overriding reason to include a particular piece. In our search for narrative we turned to the most modest memorial book as well as the more celebrated; very fine pieces sometimes come from very unassuming books. The translations in this collection are only some of the hundreds of pieces we initially considered.

Although the selections reflect what surviving townspeople considered the most important features of their home communities, they also reflect what we as anthropologists found most compelling. Trained to interpret cultures, we were drawn to reminiscences that reveal the underlying themes of everyday life, particularly at times when the rhythms of that life were disrupted, as in "The Ruined Wedding." Some of these topics—such as the variety of roles played by women, and the instances of deep mutual trust between Jews and peasants— may strike readers as not at all what they have come to regard as characteristic of shtetl life; and to some extent we have favored themes treated almost nowhere outside of the memorial books.

The present book, then, is an interpretation and personal selection based on a perusal of the Polish-Jewish memorial book literature in Yiddish. It is not a statistically representative sample of each type of entry found in the books. Most of the books, for instance, begin with a substantial account of the history of the town from the time of its first Jewish settlement. Frequently these accounts are largely based on articles found in general publications such as the Polish encyclopedia (Encyclopedia Powszechna.) Others are original works of value to contemporary scholars interested in the early history of Jews in Poland. These essays do not share the sense of immediacy so characteristic of memorial books. In contrast, articles such as "The Court of the Plyaters," detailing the dealings of successive generations of a Jewish community with successive generations of a noble Polish landowning family, are much more arresting. The world of secular historiography—from which academic historians writing in Yiddish drew their principles of analysis—has a Greek heritage, harking back to Thucydides' accounts of numbers and strategies. But there is a Biblical model for "The Court of the Plyaters," epitomized by Exodus 1:8, "Now there arose a new king over Egypt, who knew not Joseph." This attitude toward history views relations with non-Jewish rulers in the Diaspora in the context of paradigmatic events such as the sojourn in Egypt; and personal relations, individual morality, and memory are all pivotal.

Another type of material found in the yizker-bikher is folkloric and linguistic: collections of customs relating to particular holidays, sayings characteristic of the town, even lists of particular individuals' nicknames, and explanations of how they had acquired them:

At the time for the Torah portion "Shemini," the stork comes flying from the warm countries. It was a sign for those who leased orchards to finish making arrangements with noblemen and priests. At the same time a Jew used to come from far away, from deep Russia, to lease fields in Zembrove. We called him "the stork."[2]

One book contains a description of the cryptic language used by a tavern owner's wife who would substitute Hebraicisms for common Yiddish terms when she didn't want a gentile customer to understand what she was saying to her husband. The book for Bendin (Bedzin) describes the different chronological strata of Yiddish phonology used in different parts of town.[3] One of the several books for Tshenstokhov (Czestochowa) contains a glossary of Yiddish slang of the Nazi era.[4] Such material, however, frequently loses much in translation, and in this case all we can do is to urge those who do read Yiddish or Hebrew to turn to the originals.

Soon after the war, memorial books became the major cultural focus of *landsmanshaftn*, mutual aid and fraternal societies of Jewish emigrants from East European towns now living in America, Israel, Argentina, and elsewhere. Before the war, the landsmanshaftn had been the immigrant's chief tie to the community he left behind. Landsmanshaftn collected money and sent representatives to distribute relief funds to destitute townspeople. After the war, the landsmanshaftn were still involved in relief work, providing funds for the emigration and resettlement of survivors and for the new State of Israel. Together with survivors who joined the landsmanshaftn, members looked for suitable ways to commemorate the dead, such as the annual memorial meetings generally held on the anniversary of the liquidation of the town's ghetto by the Nazis. Several landsmanshaftn set up communal tombstones for their towns' dead in local cemeteries—a phenomenon that began in Poland in the late 1940s and at Yad Vashem in Jerusalem, as well as in North America and Western Europe. The books, however, are an international effort, making it possible for the now widely dispersed survivors and émigrés to create an international memorial.[5]

The landsmanshaftn were remarkably suited to the task of creating these symbolic burials. By the time World War II ended, their provision of funeral benefits for their members was an integral part of immigrant life. They were the functional descendants of many of the shtetl's communal institutions, in-

2. Yom-tov Levinsky, *"Fun mayn kindhayt" Sefer Zembrove (Zambrow)*, p. 375.

3. Dovid Liver, *"Bendin dialekt," Pinkas Bendin (Bedzin)*, pp. 156–57.

4. Dr. B. Orenshtayn, *"Tshenstokhover folklor in der Natsi-tsayt," Tshenstokhov (Czestochowa); Nayer tsugob tsum bukh "Tshenstokhover Yidn,"* pp. 66–67.

5. It is worthwhile noting that when *landslayt* from the town of Zwolen set out to produce a memorial book, their expressed intention was "to create a monument."

cluding the *khevre kedishe*-the burial society—one of the most prestigious of those institutions.[6]

Thus memorial books emerged as a genuinely collective response to the Holocaust.[7] So compelling was the urge to participate in this collective voice that many contributors wrote for the first time in their lives. The memorial-book literature for all of Eastern Europe consists of more than five hundred volumes, and individual volumes contain dozens of vignettes and articles written by different people.

Why this compulsion to write? Terrence Des Pres has argued convincingly that "the need to bear witness" became a motivating force for many survivors.[8] Yet the events of the Holocaust are only part of the experience depicted in the memorial books. Survivors felt obligated not only to bear witness to the Nazi destruction, but to the world the Nazis sought to destroy. In response to this mandate, the circle of survivors grew in proportion to the size of the task, and came to include *landslayt*-townspeople—who had left Europe long before the Holocaust.

Most concentration camp survivors were young, and therefore had not been included in the initial selections for extermination. They looked healthier, were more able to survive the rigors of camp food and labor details, and had stood a better chance of foiling the Nazis' intent. The older townsfolk of their parents' age provided descriptions of a time too distant to comprise a well-defined region of their own memories. The collective voice that thus emerged blurred the line of demarcation between survivors and émigrés, ultimately imposing on all, as Lifton notes, "a series of immersions into death which mark [even] our existence."[9]

From a Ruined Garden is designed to introduce the memorial-book genre to the English reader. Since the selections included are based on perusal of hundreds of volumes for Polish towns, even those already familiar with individual books may be surprised by the consistent quality and uniform texture of the selections.

The memorial books are the result of a spontaneous effort. They were produced by independent landsmanshaftn without the urging or financial support of a government or any other agency. Yet if there were no precedent for them in Jewish history and culture, they would never have appeared as a distinct genre so soon after the war nor taken hold in such a massive way. The consistency of structure from book to book demands explanation.

6. In his study of Ashkenazic Jewry from the sixteenth to the eighteenth centuries, Jacob Katz indicates that members of the *khevre kedishe* "formed something of an elite in the kehilla; they were so considered both by themselves and the general public." *Tradition and Crisis: Jewish Society at the End of the Middle Ages* (New York: Schocken, 1971), p. 159.

7. In his study of Holocaust literature, Alvin Rosenfeld suggests that Holocaust literature in general has a fragmentary quality, "more impressive in the sum of its parts than as a separate statement." *A Double Dying: Reflections on Holocaust Literature* (Bloomington: Indiana University Press, 1980), p. 34.

8. Terrence des Pres, *The Survivor: An Anatomy of Life in the Death Camps* (New York: Pocket Books, 1977).

9. Robert J. Lifton, *Death in Life: Survivors of Hiroshima* (New York: Random House, 1967), p. 479.

There are probably as many contributing elements in the shaping of memorial books as there are in the culture of East European Jews. Three elements which stand out, however, are the Nazi Holocaust; the emergence of modern Yiddish literature; and the long tradition of Jewish mourning literature, evident as early as the Book of Lamentations. Although the latter two shaped the overall form of the memorial books long before the Nazi rise to power, only the extent of the Holocaust and the nature of the experience imposed by its perpetrators could generate the massive response represented by the memorial books.

Jews have always looked to their history for confirmation of the belief that in time all enemies are vanquished. The unequal struggle between Nazis and Jews was a struggle between those attempting to obliterate history and those holding on to it as a guarantee of eternity. Even during the war, historians such as Simon Dubnow, Emmanuel Ringelblum, and Chaim Kaplan saw that the Jewish future— if there was to be any—would depend on a valid transmission of Jewish history. As the historian Yitskhok Schipper told Alexander Donat in Auschwitz, "everything depends on who transmits our testament to future generations . . ."[10] Those who worked with Schipper in the kitchen at Majdanek recognized what was at stake in transmitting their history, and did everything they could to save him from the gas chamber.[11] The memorial books are the fruit of the impulse to write a testament for future generations. They constitute an unprecedented, truly popular labor to record in writing as much as possible of a destroyed world.

Although the scope of this catastrophe was in many ways unprecedented, there already existed a history of communal disasters, and of culturally patterned responses to them. The phrase, "If I forget thee, O Jerusalem" set the pattern of Jewish martyrology and commemoration in fundamental ways. Wherever Jews migrated, the world they experienced became a synthesis drawn from the everyday life they shared with gentiles and from the realm of Jewish tradition. This synthesis was achieved partly through an active involvement in the non-Jewish and physical world around them, and partly through an emotional disengagement from that world by means of Bible and Talmud study, prayer, and retelling of the oral tradition. For the exiled Jew, the mingling of symbols from the present and ancient past was a typical mode of discourse. Thus, as Max Weinreich notes in his *History of the Yiddish Language*, the Ashkenazic Jew tended to picture King David celebrating the Sabbath by eating a festive meal of fish and meat—appropriate fare for the courts of the hasidic rebes.[12]

The same "panchronistic" logic that brought ancient tradition closer to home also bequeathed to contemporary history a share in the Biblical aura. Symbols of

10. Alexander Donat, *The Holocaust Kingdom* (New York: The Holocaust Library, 1978), p. 211.

11. Y. Likhterman, *"Di letste teg fun doktor Yitskhok Shipper," Torna (Tarnow): Kyuma ve-hurbana shel ir Yehudit*, pp. 876–78.

12. Max Weinreich, "The Language of the Way of the SHaS," in *History of the Yiddish Language*, (Chicago: University of Chicago Press, 1980) p. 208.

both glory and tragedy were applied to the everyday world of each Jewish generation. Vilna, the focus of Jewish intellectual and religious life in the Jewish pale of settlement, was known as "the Jerusalem of Lithuania," whereas both the Chmielnicki massacres of the seventeenth century and the Holocaust are sometimes referred to as *khurboynes* (catastrophes)—the paradigmatic *khurboynes* having been the ruin of the First and Second Temples.

Panchronism originated through an existential need to observe Jewish rituals originally intended for the Temple in Jerusalem after the First Temple had been destroyed and the Jews went into exile in 586 B.C.E. When the Jewish exiles in Babylonia confronted the problem of observing biblically prescribed rituals in a foreign land and in the absence of the Temple, their solution consisted essentially of remembrance through repeated symbolic reenactment. The intense valuation of historical memory as a vital act incumbent upon every Jew became a cornerstone of Jewish consciousness. A similar impulse lay beneath the custom of Ashkenazic Jews during the Middle Ages to keep *Memorbücher*, which contained the names of important communal and religious leaders as well as the names of martyrs, and which were read during memorial services.[13]

Closer to our own time, the anti-Jewish massacres of the late seventeenth century, in the course of Bogdan Chmielnicki's Ukrainian uprising against the Polish nobility, were crystallized for historical memory in a work by Nathan Nata Hannover known as *Yeven Metzulah (The Abyss of Despair)*. The work prefigures twentieth-century memorial books in crucial ways. It contains narrative description of the pogroms (albeit in highly stylized fashion), rather than formulaic martyrologies, and it includes a section detailing the greatness of the Jewish life that was destroyed. The work's continuing hold on Jewish consciousness is attested to by the fact that it was reprinted following the pogroms during the Russian civil war, and again shortly after the Holocaust.[14]

The first modern memorial books emerged as a response to the Ukrainian pogroms between the end of World War I and the early 1920s. In the volume *Khurbn Proskurov*, published in 1924, several motifs stand out. Some are unique to the book. Each page in the book is bordered in black. The chronicle of the pogrom is printed in parallel columns of Hebrew and Yiddish, calling to mind the format of traditional Jewish Bibles, with their original Hebrew and parallel Aramaic translations. Other motifs became mainstays of the memorial-book genre: thus, the pages bearing the table of contents, and a title page following, have drawings of gravestones as their backgrounds. The title page carries the injunction, "Each year on the anniversary [of the pogrom] you shall read this aloud to your children and grandchildren."

13. Yosef Hayim Yerushalmi, *Zakhor: Jewish History and Jewish Memory* (Seattle: University of Washington Press, 1982), p. 46.

14. Abraham J. Mesch, trans., *The Abyss of Despair (Yeven Metzulah)* (New York: Bloch, 1950), pp. 11–12.

Most significant for our purposes, the book contains what may be the genre's first true anecdote, in an article on the Bazilyer Rebe by the folklorist A. Rekhtman, who may have first heard it when he accompanied the Yiddish writer S. Ansky's ethnographic expedition to the Ukraine:

> One of his followers, a very wealthy estate manager from a village near Nikoleyev, came to his court. If my memory serves me, he was from the village of Tshipilifke. Together with his note requesting the Rebe's blessing, the man included a valuable coin. It was the Rebe's custom to read out his follower's requests at the top of his voice. When he finished reading the note, he also read the signature, which ended with the words, "and all the children of my family." But by changing the vowels in the last word, he read the phrase, "and all the children of my female servant." At this a tumult broke out among the Hasidim present, and after intense inquiries it turned out that the estate manager had indeed had relations with a female servant, who had borne him children.[15]

The story points out the Rebe's almost unnatural insight into his followers. The point of retelling it in the memorial book, however, is to provide a "narrative vessel" to fix the Rebe's memory in the reader's mind. This defining component of the memorial-book genre—narrative as a means of preserving and establishing living memory—is a point we will return to later. The fact that the article on the Bazilyer Rebe was written by a folklorist who had worked with the author of *The Dybbuk* suggests a related theme: the development of Yiddish narrative in connection with the ethnographic preoccupation of the classic Yiddish writers.

Not only the pogroms following the First World War, but the Great War itself, led residents and émigrés from East European towns to believe that the world they had known was fast disappearing. "An individual can ultimately find a place to exist and come to feel at home," wrote the émigré writer and journalist A. S. Zaks in his book *Khoreve veltn* (*Ruined Worlds*) in 1917. "The whole, however, cannot transport its traditions and customs to another place."[16]

The ruin of the Polish countryside in the course of the war hastened the dislocation of East European Jewish life which had been in process since the freeing of the serfs and the Polish rebellion in the 1860s. Adult Jewish males, religious and secularist alike, were conscripted en masse into the armies of the various nations among which Poland was divided. The Jewish population of entire towns migrated to large cities for the duration of the war.

One such town was Sanok, which lay within the boundaries of the prewar Austro-Hungarian Empire. It was situated on the river San, the historical border between Galicia and the Ukraine, and hence a likely battleground. Most of its

15. A. Rekhtman, *"Bazilyer Rebe," Khurbn Proskurov*, pp. 50–51.
16. A. S. Zaks, *Khoreve veltn* (New York: Literarishe Farlag, 1917), p. 7.

Jews spent the war years in Vienna and Prague. When they returned, many had shed their traditional caftans forever, and those who still wore them responded to the new situation in their own way:

> Rabbi Shapiro, fearing that he would miss the funeral, demanded a special train from the government to take him to Sanok. This was one of his privileges as a deputy of the Polish parliament. . . . The Railroad Ministry immediately announced to all of the station masters between Pyetrkov and Sanok that a special train bearing a V.I.P. would be passing through. They were all sure that one of the leaders of the state would be on board, and they were stunned to see a Jew with a fur hat on his head instead.[17]

The great Russian and Austro-Hungarian empires were broken up in the aftermath of the war, when Poland and other nations regained their independence. The Treaty of Versailles, which resulted in that independence, also included clauses guaranteeing cultural rights to ethnic minorities. And the huge Russian market for Polish textiles, upon which Jews had been so dependent as workers, agents, and manufacturers, was cut off. Until the Holocaust, East European Jews considered World War I to be one of the great traumatic events in Jewish history.

The war brought not only destruction; it also brought change and hope. If it is possible to specify a point at which traditional institutions gave way to labor unions, religious and secularist political parties, and secular cultural organizations as the basic structures of Jewish life in Polish towns, that point is the First World War. The memorial books frequently fall into a basic tripartite division: the period prior to World War I, the interwar years, and the Holocaust. In the book for the town of Pshemishl (Przemysl), these three sections were each edited by a different person.

Every culture, writes George Steiner, needs a sustaining and guiding myth of a golden age.[18] The memorial books create an image of a time when life was spiritually satisfying and emotionally warm, if physically precarious. The book for Rudki refers to the town as " 'The Anatevke' of our youth and childhood dreams."[19] Anatevke, of course, is one of the most famous towns in Sholem Aleichem's fictional geography, and its evocation points us toward the ironic yet affectionate image of the shtetl sketched by the classic writers of modern Yiddish literature. The classic writers gave Yiddish literature an ethnographic focus. Like Sholem Aleichem's work, the memorial books explore a distinct universe in

---

17. A. Sharvit, *"Undzere rebeyim un zeyere khasidishe 'heyf,' " Sefer zikaron le-kehilat Sanok ve-ha-seviva,* p. 499.

18. George Steiner, *In Bluebeard's Castle: Some Notes Towards the Redefinition of Culture* (New Haven: Yale University Press, 1971), pp. 3–4.

19. *Rudki: sefer yizkor le-yehudei Rudki ve-ha-seviva,* p. 371.

which the different stars and planets—the townspeople—related to one another by unique laws of gravity and repulsion.

Sholem Aleichem's autobiography *Funem Yarid* (*At the Fair*), begun just before the First World War in his adopted home in New York, betrays a sharp nostalgia along with an eye for the shtetl's catalog of social types. His account of being separated from a beloved childhood friend draws the reader into the book, and his friend into the present:

> What do you think: Is he still alive somewhere, that curious Shmulik? . . .
> Whoever knows something, whoever has heard of him—please reply.[20]

Of course, Sholem Aleichem was a master of the literary illusion of direct address. But here, it seems that he was actually hoping for news of Shmulik. If the greatest writer in Yiddish could thus call openly to his reading public to help him find a single lost childhood friend, it is not difficult to see how the memorial-book writers could express such unashamed nostalgia in commemorating the whole of their lost communities.

Yet, for all their outpouring of feeling, the books are not blind to the seamier aspects of life, although those aspects are invariably subsumed within a positive image of the Jewish community. That image is the product of a retrospective solidarity more evident in an overall perusal of yizker-bikher than in individual volumes. Remarkably, the joining of ranks is accomplished without the expedient of passing over social conflict in silence. Strife within the Jewish community is anything but ignored. Many of the landsmanshaftn that sponsored memorial books were oriented toward the Zionist and non-Zionist Left. Yet their erstwhile rivals, the towns' anti-Zionists, hasidic groups, or Jewish Communist party organizations are seldom banished from the community depicted in the books they published. There is a generosity at work here (in principle, if not invariably in fact) which is commensurate with the scope of the catastrophe.[21] It seems that those people who worked together on the books recognized that every religious and political faction, every individual from the town rabbi to the assimilationist lawyer to the ragtag water carrier, had been an essential part of the town's genius. "Every shtetl had its madman," reads one account. "Our town was small, so our *meshugener* was only half-crazy."[22]

A photograph in the memorial book for the town of Koriv (Kurow) may help to explain why this is so. It shows the funeral procession of a young female Communist party organizer passing through the town square. The men in the crowd are all dressed in modern suits and fedoras. The corpse, however, is being

20. Sholem Aleichem, *At the Fair*, trans. Tamara Kahana (New York: Collier, 1970), p. 25.

21. The essay concerns itself only with an overall evaluation of memorial books. In-depth studies of what took place behind the scenes in creating individual books will undoubtedly reveal a good deal of wrangling between political factions and individual personalities. Indeed, some *yizker-bikher* are undisguisedly partisan. See, for example, *Pinkes Varshe*.

22. Khayim Shabakh, *"Zamke der meshugener," Pyesk (Piaski) ve-Most; sefer yizkor*, p. 493.

carried on a plain board; essentially, it is a photograph of a traditional Jewish funeral. The woman being buried, though a Communist, was still a Jew, and hence required proper burial according to Jewish law.[23] The same was true, of course, with respect to the survivors' relation to all those in their communities who had perished. Over and over again, introductions to the memorial books assert: "We have now, finally, fulfilled our last obligation to the dead." That obligation consists of remembrance and burial, a reversal of the normal order of the two processes.

Various Jewish symbols of death and mourning are employed as analogies for the Holocaust and/or the memorial books themselves. The catastrophe is occasionally referred to as "the Hitlerite flood." The survivors who gather to reminisce about the dead are said to be "sitting *shive*," observing the seven-day period of ritual mourning for deceased family members. Sometimes the book is called a *ner tomid*, an eternal light. The most frequent symbol employed is that of a *matseyve*, a gravestone.[24] Few Holocaust victims were ever given a proper burial. They were burned in the crematoria, thrown into mass graves when local ghettos were liquidated, starved or shot as fugitives in the forests. Most memorial books include descriptions of attempts just after the war to locate the remains of those killed when local ghettos were liquidated, to exhume their remains, and to give them a proper burial. In the shtetl, membership in the burial society had been an indication of communal trust. In the town of Vyerzhbanik (Wierzbnik), it was a member of the burial society, Leybish Herblum, who "took upon himself the holy task of gathering the bones of the martyrs and setting them in the common grave."[25]

Although similar efforts are reported in many memorial books, the task of proper burial often proved beyond the capacity of the handful of survivors who returned. Often the location of the common graves was not known. Even when it was known, the violent hostility of Gentile Poles sometimes prevented Jews from traveling to isolated areas to exhume bodies. The violence was motivated in part by fear that returning Jews might demand the return of their homes and belongings. Or it was the product of superstition. To their non-Jewish neighbors, returning Jews were ghosts:

> The next morning, I returned to the gravestone at the cemetery. . . . And as I
> stand stiff with pain and sorrow, a gentile suddenly appears. His cows have

23. Shimen Vaynberg, *"Undzere profesyonele fareynen," Yizker-bukh Koriv (Kurow)* p. 78.
24. "The memorial book which will immortalize the memories of our relatives and friends, the Jews of Pshaytsh, will also serve as a substitute grave. Whenever we will pick up the book we will feel we are standing next to their grave, because even that the murderers denied them. The bones of our relatives were crushed and scattered to fertilize the earth after their tortured bodies were burned in the crematoria." "Forwort," *Sefer yizkor le-kedoshei ir (Przedecz), Pshaytsh khurbanot ha-shoa*, p. 130.
25. Simkhe Mintsberg, *"Nokh der bafrayung," Sefer Vyerzhbanik-Starakhovits (Wierzbnik-Starachowice)*, pp. 345–48.

wandered into the graveyard, and he after them. Turning among the graves, he suddenly saw me, and crossed himself in terror. . . . His appearance roused me and tore me away from my mental journey through a lost world.[26]

The problem of exhumation and proper burial was not merely an obligation to the dead; it had critical implications for the living. How were the survivors to reestablish any connection with the memory of the martyrs? How were they to locate and communicate with the dead, to obtain the ancient comfort of mourning? Some survivors were not even aware of the extent of the catastrophe until after the war ended:

> While being repatriated from Russia, on the way back to Poland, we still had faith that in our old home of Torne a new task of construction, the Jewish community, Jewish schools, the Jewish library, and all the other national, social, and philanthropic institutions awaited us. We knew that a terrible storm had passed through Torne. But unextinguished within us burned the last ray of hope that it had merely broken branches, and the tree still stood.[27]

All this contributed to what Lifton refers to as the problem of the "homeless dead" (what others have called the "missing grave" syndrome), and the resultant "impaired mourning."[28] Elsewhere in the description of the visit to the Wierzbnik cemetery cited above, Sore Pustavski Shtaynhart writes:

> Here I stand thinking. . . . I thought that I'd come here and weep my heart out, pour out a sea of tears, for I stand not only before my father's grave, but at the grave of all Jewish Vyerzhbanik. But not a tear falls. . . . The spring of my tears is exhausted. . . . I stand as if petrified, frozen and I cannot even bring a sigh from my throat. I am struck mute. Perhaps it is because I don't know whom to weep for first? For my father, who died "in his time" and received a Jewish burial; or for my mother, sister, and brother together with their families who were murdered, whose very bones have disappeared?[29]

The memorial books came to be seen as substitute gravestones. Frequently they contain lists of the names of the dead; one man said of his participation in the creation of the Lublin memorial book that his role had been to "bring in the names." These names are the core of the entire commemorative effort. The

26. Sore Pustavski Shtaynhart, *"Kay Vyerzhbanik af keyver-oves," Sefer Vyerzhbanik-Starakhovits (Wierzbnik-Starachowice)*, pp. 368–69.

27. *"Forvort funem redaktor," Torna (Tarnow): Kyum ve-hurbana shel ir Yehudit*, p. xviii.

28. Robert J. Lifton, *Death in Life: Survivors of Hiroshima* (New York: Random House, 1967), pp. 492–94. See also Joost Meerloo, "Delayed Mourning in Victims of Extermination Camps," in *Massive Psychic Trauma*, Henry Krystal, ed. (New York: International Universities Press, 1968), p. 74. According to Meerloo, the greatest complaint of those who had gone through concentration camps 'was that they had not been permitted to mourn over their dead, those they had lost in these very camps. Not the torture, not the famine, not the humiliation kept them down now, but this lack of cathartic ceremonial."

29. Sore Pustavski Shtaynhart, *"Kay Vyerzhbanik af keyver-oves," Sefer Vyerzhbanik-Starakhovits (Wierzbnik-Starachowice)*, pp. 368–69.

extended descriptions of individuals focus on the towns' notables, on the one hand, and the towns' eccentrics, on the other. But vignettes, descriptions of local institutions, and even extended narratives are stones with many names inscribed. Some are merely implied by the phrases "and wife," "and children," or "and family," listed after the name of a murdered householder. Others are mentioned in the context of a particular institution or event, sometimes with a single phrase of physical description. Many faces are found on group and individual photographs, but here as well, the captioned names are all-important.

The memorial books are structured on a continuum from simple acts of naming to highly elaborated narrative. The most abbreviated entries—the lists of names of the dead that conclude most books—suffice to fulfill the commandment to remember. But those acts of naming contained within narratives also observe a time-honored precedent in Judaism. The teachers of the Talmud had enjoined Jews to "build a fence around the Torah": that is, to go beyond the requirements of Biblical law and thus assure that the Torah could not be violated. Likewise, the elaboration of individuals' names with descriptions and characteristic stories are narrative vessels that both preserve and transform the essence of the person:

> When I review in thought my life in Rozhan, events, splinters of half-forgotten memories, appear before my eyes. People, formerly flesh-and-blood and everyday Jews, were transformed by the tragic events into figures similar to heroes in the dramas one reads. Of all the people of that time, individuals stand out whose names stick in my memory. . . . And to these people, most of whose remains lie in no cemetery, may my humble words about them serve as an eternal monument and redeem them from merciless oblivion. With trembling and fear of God I write my modest words, which are no more than a pale reflection of what was in reality.[30]

Shlomo Pultusker, who wrote these lines, was conscious that the events separating him from those he wrote about had inevitably colored his memory. Nevertheless, he captured something of their souls, which could now be passed on from generation to generation and from land to land. Narrative not only confirms human existence; it is the core of human culture. It establishes bonds of friendship between individuals. It solidifies the ties of kinship. And it unifies people separated by decades, centuries, even millenia of time.

In the living world of East European Jewry, the time for storytelling was "*tsvishn minkhe un mayriv*," between late afternoon and early evening prayers, when yeshiva students and old men gathered around tables in the study houses and synagogues to entertain each other and ward off the melancholy of dusk.[31]

---

30. Shlomo Pultusker, "*Merkvirdike tipn*," *Sefer zikaron le-hehilat Rozhan (Rozan)*, p. 233.

31. Barbara Kirshenblatt-Gimblett, "The Concept of Varieties of Narrative Performance in East European Jewish Culture," in Richard Bauman and Joel Sherzer, eds. *Explorations in the Ethnography of Speaking* (New York: Cambridge University Press, 1974), p. 286.

The German-Jewish critic Walter Benjamin wrote of the "aura" that surrounded storytellers in earlier times.[32] Even though the story may be no more than a legend, its telling by a living person makes possible a vibrant connection between the characters and events of the story and the audience that listens to it. That living connection between story and audience was broken with the rise of the less communal, more private novel form.

The memorial books occupy an anomalous position with respect to this dichotomy of the told story and modern fiction. The books are almost always printed in editions of less than a thousand; their audience is the community of survivors and émigrés from the town itself.[33] Many readers would know the author of a piece personally. The connection, therefore, between the teller and the audience is immediate. The audience is drawn into the narrative to experience events that they or people they know have already witnessed. Since author and reader frequently reverse roles in memorial books, the genre bears some similarity to a storytelling round.

Although burial and commemoration are the dominant motifs within the memorial books, several of them mention the desire to pass along something of the East European Jewish heritage to coming generations. The process of committing these narratives to print is evidence that the oral link between generations has been severed. We who were not born in Eastern Europe are excluded from the storytelling round; we arrive too late. It is quite dark already; the study house is almost deserted. A book lies on the table, written in a language few of us can read. We open the book, and flip through its pages. Pictures of town characters, village peddlers, coachmen catch our eye. Who are they? Who are all these common people who found their way into the book?

One should not confuse the memorial books with the towns they commemorate. The reality depicted in the memorial books is distorted, because it is all seen—and can *only* be seen—through the prism of the Holocaust. Stories which ostensibly have nothing to do with the Holocaust conclude with one-line epilogues, such as the story of a poor but honest father in Bendin (Bedzin) who won the lottery, and whose family might have lived happily ever after, "if not for the terrible chaos which cut him down together with his entire family."[34] The Holocaust is evidenced less directly in other stories from the prewar years, sometimes only modulating their tone. The account of "Anarchist Activities" in Krinek (Krynki) includes no reference to the Holocaust, yet the violent conflict between the anarchist terrorists and the Jewish manufacturers is overshadowed by a retrospective consciousness of the community they all belonged to and the fate they all shared.

32. Walter Benjamin, "The Storyteller," *Illuminations* (New York: Schocken, 1969).
33. The *Yizker-bukh fun der Zhelekhover (Zelechow) yidisher kehile* was printed in 550 copies. Other books cite a somewhat lower figure.
34. Motek Hamfel, *"Dos groyse gevins," Pinkas Bendin (Bedzin,)* p. 149.

We read the memorial books through that same prism. There is nothing included in this book, and very little in the memorial books in general, which we do not find plausible. In large measure this is due to the foresight of editors and contributors, who wanted future scholars to turn to the books.[35] The book for the town called Oshpitsin in Yiddish—which has gained infamy under its German name of Auschwitz—contains a bibliography of five hundred entries in Yiddish on the topic of the Auschwitz death camp. Some books contain substantial essays by Jewish academic historians such as Raphael Mahler, Isaiah Trunk, and N. M. Gelber.

Notwithstanding the value of scholarly pieces, the more "casual" articles are even more revealing on occasion. Thus, an article on a typical market day in the town of Markushov (Markuszow) describes a hapless class of Jewish traders who will deal in whatever merchandise they can get from the wagons of peasants on their way to town. Another memoir of a town market details the exchange of slaps on the hand that served as a means of bargaining between peasants and Jews who did not share a common language. A third story, whose basic theme is the growth of Polish anti-Semitism in the countryside between the wars, records the attitudes of a substantial peasant family on the one hand, and of a Polish priest on the other, toward a Jewish peddler who visited their village each week. These accounts indicate some of the subleties that flowed from the net of trade relations between Jews and Polish peasants—including the role Jewish innkeepers played as bearers of "information:"

> In the evening, the peasants would gather, tie the horses to the fence, have a drink, and hang around and stare with open ears, ready to hear and find out what was happening in the world and at the front. I was the one who brought Yoshe the news from the front and he was asking me the names of our generals. He wanted to know all the names—so I would think up Christian-sounding names from my head. I don't know whether Yoshe really believes me and he accepts my generals as real, but he relays the names to the peasants with particular reverence; Ivan Petrovitsh, Nikolai Yermovits form in his mouth the shape of formidable heroes who throw themselves, swords raised, on the German generals, who are forced to retreat. The peasants listen, cross themselves, and ask for another glass and more information; Yoshe strokes his beard, feeling very pleased.[36]

Unlike Yoshe, most memorial-book contributors are deeply concerned with the accuracy of what they set down. Although the Holocaust and the passage of time have distorted memory, the collective voice tends to mitigate distortion and favor accuracy of detail. Overly apologetic or ameliorative urges the writers may

35. Jacob Shatzky's reviews of *yizker-bikher* in *YIVO Bleter*, 1955 and 1956, point out both the value and deficiencies of twelve volumes published during the two years. Like any source, memorial books require careful critical evaluation to be used in reconstructing the history of a given locality.
36. D. Kahan, *"Yoshe der Horodetshner," Pinkas Navaredok (Nowogrodek)*, pp. 149–50.

have felt were checked by the fact that their editors and intended audience had their own memories of the person or event being described. Reading memorial books will never be an adequate substitute for the classic anthropological method of participant observation. Still, we have much to learn from them about the nature of Jewish life in Polish towns. The books make it clear, for example, that the Polish-Jewish shtetl, in the first half of the twentieth century, was more than just an impoverished backwater. The great modern European writers were read in Russian, German, and Yiddish, and liberal and socialist European political currents found partisans there as well. Not every woman was restricted to kitchen and children, nor even to the store in front of the kitchen. There were women who taught school, women who prayed three times a day, and women who drove wagons. Nor did the life of the shtetl end entirely with the Nazi invasion. Jews responded to their persecutors with whatever means were at their disposal, trying to the end to establish some semblance of meaning and order out of the chaos into which they had been thrust.

Despite the public's lack of familiarity with the memorial books, more and more people are making use of them. Most of these are genealogists, who profit from the profusion of names in the books. Others are scholars concerned with local history, or the history of certain movements and periods.[37]

The accounts included here, though, are intended to convey the outstanding memories of individuals. "Sometimes we have to wait for years," writes the poet Edmond Jabes, "before the minute which marked us finds its voice again."[38] These are the moments that marked certain lives. Not until the writing of the books could these moments find their voice; and until then, their muteness tormented the survivors.

Survivors' experiences were so similar to the experiences of those who had died that their feelings of torment are hardly surprising. "One thought filled me: I was running after I was already dead, I had certainly been killed, and neverthe-less I was still running," wrote one man who escapted from a ghetto liquidation at the last possible moment.[39] In retelling the story of how they survived, and in memorializing the lives of those who remained on the other side of the abyss, the survivors were drawing a line to separate themselves from the dead. Writing about the dead helped them to establish their own continuous existence among the living.

The guilt and self-doubt that plagued survivors was mirrored in the world's

37. See, for example, Rachel Ertel, *Le shtetl: la bourgade juive de Pologne* (Paris: Payot, 1982); William Glicksman, *Jewish Social Welfare Institutions in Poland: As Described in Memorial (Yizker) Books* (Philadelphia: M. E. Kalish Folkschul, 1976); Isaiah Trunk, *Judenrat: The Jewish Councils in Eastern Europe Under Nazi Occupation* (New York: Macmillan, 1972).

38. Edmond Jabes, *The Book of Questions II*, trans. Rosemarie Waldrop (Middletown: Wesleyan University Press, 1977), p. 29.

39. Mordkhe Vaysman, *"Mayn antloyfn fun di mord-griber,"* *Sefer Vladimerets (Wlodzimierzec)*, pp. 443–49.

attitude toward them. Immediately after the war, and throughout the 1950s and 1960s, survivors were largely seen as an embarrassment. They were a reminder that while for Americans, the war had ended in the triumph of good over evil, for Jews there could be no recompense for the evil that had reigned for twelve years.[40]

The image of "the survivor" has had its own peculiar history. Soon after the war, psychiatrists began to identify the guilt and numbness of survivors associated with the "missing grave" syndrome and the resulting inability to mourn. In 1975, Terrence Des Pres, a literary scholar, published a study of survivor literature in which he attempted to isolate the salient characteristics that enabled certain individuals to survive in Nazi and Stalinist death camps. Des Pres' study had considerable impact, changing the connotation of the word "survivor" from "one who happened to remain alive" to "one who has the capacity to survive," and who actively resists his persecutors in doing so.[41]

Perhaps the changed image of the survivor also reflects increasing realization that we may all die ingloriously and senselessly. We are all too familiar with random terror, and with the constant threat of extinction. The reevaluation of the survivor reflects a general change in the Western attitude toward history since the Holocaust. Where a less cynical age saw the successive accumulation of contributions to civilization, we have come to see a precarious and ultimately indeterminate struggle to preserve a measure of human dignity.

The memorial books tell us a great deal about the culture of survivors. Although most of the books contain accounts of brief returns to the towns shortly after the war, the ultimate impossibility of return is always evident, as in this incident recounted in the book for Pshemishl (Przemysl):

> Whoever passed through the place where the [Nazi-adminstered] ghetto had been saw a bizarre scene. Almost all the houses which had once belonged to Jews had sunk and collapsed. Perhaps this was because Christians came every night looking for treasure; but the survivors saw in this the sign of a curse hanging over the quarter.[42]

The same earth that is hallowed in memory is cursed in the present, a reversal so utterly inexplicable that those who lived through the destruction felt torn between dream and reality. A writer in the Suvalk (Suwalki) memorial book felt compelled to reassert that even though the town's past seems like a dream, in fact "the 'now' is a dream—a terrible, inhuman nightmare."[43]

40. As George Steiner suggests in *Language and Silence: Essays on Language, Literature and the Inhuman* (New York: Atheneum, 1970), p. 144, "By its very finality, the Holocaust justified every previous impulse of immigration. The Jewish soldier who went to the Europe of his fathers came better armed, technologically more efficient than his murderous enemy. The few Jews he found alive were out of a hideous but spectral world, like a nightmare in a foreign tongue."

41. Terrence Des Pres, *The Survivor: An Anatomy of Life in the Death Camps* (New York: Pocket Books, 1977).

42. Dr. M. Shatner, *"Khurbn Pshemishl," Sefer Pshemishl (Przemysl)*, p. 536.

43. Kalmen Abramovitz, *"Nito mer Suvalk," Yizker-bukh Suvalk (Suwalki)*, p. 652.

The creation of a historical record is an outgrowth of the past intended to order the present. But the fact that the retellings did not remain solely oral, that the thousands of contributors to memorial books were willing to commit pen to paper at all, should not be taken for granted as a natural response to the destruction. The alternative of silence was always available and had its advantages: survivors' stories are rarely pleasant and were often difficult for others to credit immediately after the war. Also, in a crime as massive as the destruction of six million persons, the line between perpetrator and victim inevitably becomes blurred, as indeed the Nazis intended it to be.[44] By setting down their memories on paper, the survivors refused to collaborate with the silence and dehumanization of totalitarianism, and insisted on their right to rejoin the chain of generations. Robert Lifton has pointed out that the psychic numbing that was a key to survival in a concentration camp could degenerate into "an absolute loss of the sense of human continuity."[45] The memorial books represent the antithesis of this syndrome: a resurgence of feeling, an assertion of belief in the existence of community, however fragmented, and an insistence on the need and possibility for communication.

The entire possibility of the survivors' fulfilling their debt to the dead seems contingent on acceptance of the present and belief in the future. The importance of holding onto the promise of liberation during the Holocaust is attested to by accounts of Passover seders in Nazi ghettos and concentration camps. The writers of the books never rail against God for having abandoned the covenant made with Abraham; nor do they claim that God is dead. At most, they speak of the "deaf heavens." Nor do they take the approach of saying that the Holocaust constituted God's punishment for Israel's myriad sins. The memorial books are not theological. Their concern is primarily with human experience in history. The covenant sealed by the publication of a memorial book is with the dead: to sustain their memory, and to be sustained by their memory in turn.

The Book of Genesis tells us that God left to Adam the task of naming things; that was to be the human share in divinity, in creation. For the memorial-book writers, the act of writing is an act of re-creation. This act is an emphatic denial of the Nazi search for what Hannah Arendt termed "holes of oblivion" in which to hide both the memory of Jewish existence and the memory of the Nazis' own evil deeds.[46] On the verge of irony, several accounts in the memorial books bear the authors' camp numbers as titles. And the Oshpitsin memorial book mourns,

44. As Hannah Arendt argues in *The Origins of Totalitarianism* (New York: Harcourt Brace Jovanovich, 1973), p. 452, "The S.S. implicated concentration camp inmates—criminals, politicals, Jews—in their crimes by making them responsible for a large part of the extermination, then confronting them with the hopeless dilemma whether to send their families to their death, or to help murder other men who happened to be strangers, and forcing them, in any event, to behave like murderers."

45. Robert J. Lifton, *Death in Life: Survivors of Hiroshima* (New York: Random House, 1967), p. 500.

46. Hannah Arendt, *Eichmann in Jerusalem: A Report on the Banality of Evil* (New York: Penguin, 1979), p. 232.

"The Nazi murderers . . . twisted and changed the respected and time-honored name of Oshpitsin into the terrifying name Auschwitz."[47] In writing the book, the town's survivors gave it back its Jewish and human name, along with the most fitting burial they could think of for an annihiliated community. They erected a stone, and on it they wrote all they could remember about a time and place that now exist only in memory. In so doing, they and others fulfilled an ancient and solemn obligation:

> Koriv Jews spoke to one another only a few moments before they were shot, and agreed that if even a single one survived the massacres he would come to the graves of the others and shout down to them, proclaiming the end of Hitler.
>
> No graves have been left of all those who were slain. And the surviving Koriv Jews will not be found on Koriv soil in Poland. That is why the surviving Koriv folk . . . cry out to you, to your wailing, wandering, never-resting souls: "Beloved and precious martyrs of Koriv, we bring you to burial today! In a yizker-bukh, a memorial volume! Today we have set up a tombstone in memory of you!"[48]

---

47. Yankev Zeyfter, "*Di shtot Oshpitsin,*" *Sefer Oshpitsin (Oswiecim)*, p. 361.
48. M. Grossman, "A keyver un a matseyve," *Yizker-bukh Koriv (Kurow)*, unnumbered.

Our Towns

What Is a *Pinkes*?

TOLD BY LEYBL SHITER AND RECORDED BY B. BALER
Pinkas Kovel (Kowel)

I remember hearing the word *pinkes* several times when I was a small child.

For instance, when an unusual event took place in town, the adults, while commenting among themselves on the events, used to say: "Such a terrible story should be recorded in the pinkes!" On other occasions when things happened that weren't quite as unheard of, but were nevertheless curious, even the women used to finish their accounts with: "It was something to write down in the pinkes!"

But what this thing called a pinkes was, what it looked like, and where it was to be found, this pinkes which was mentioned in tones of such respect, as though it were something holy—I had no idea, and even in my imagination I couldn't picture it.

More and more I was driven by the desire to see the pinkes with my own eyes and touch it with my own hands. Good fortune was mine, and my wish was fulfilled. This is how it happened.

The pinkes in our town, and probably in other towns as well, was kept by the burial society (which was called "The Society of the Concerned" in Kovel). When a new trustee was chosen for the society—on Simkhes Toyre, as was done in other small towns—the pinkes was given to him to hold.

One year my father, may he rest in peace, wanted to become the trustee of the society. My father Mikhl Zaygermakher was an excellent candidate. Why not? Of course! However, there was a hitch: my father couldn't become the trustee, because his name was Mikhl.

Why did the name, Mikhl, bar him from being trustee of The Society of the Concerned? It was a custom in our town—and no doubt it was thus recorded in the pinkes itself—that any Jew whose name began with an *M* was forbidden to occupy the trusteeship, because the word for "corpse," *mes*, begins with an *m*.

What could my father do to circumvent this custom? It wasn't even the trusteeship itself that drew my father, but the desire to show the likes of Reb Yankev Fudl and Reb Osher Shvarts, that this year he, Mikhl Shiter, a congregant of the "municipal" study house, would be the trustee, instead of one of the congregants of the Great Synagogue.

Finally something was hit upon. I imagine there was a quiet meeting of congregants from the study house, at which it was decided to nominate Reb Shimen Zokner as trustee. He was a candidate with all the proper credentials for the post. However, being the owner and operator of a tannery and a mill, he had no time to fulfill the trustee's duties. It was arranged that Shimen Zokner would turn over actual responsibility to my father.

On Simkhes Toyre Reb Shimen Zokner was led from the study house to his home with great fanfare, where the crowd drank hot whiskey with honey and ate dumplings also fried with honey, and everyone had a wonderful time.

Shortly after the holiday, the whole town knew that my father was the real head of the society. It was as though my father were Shimen's secretary—no one complained about it.

As soon as the previous trustee handed over the pinkes and the other belongings of the society to Shimen Zokner, he immediately brought everything to our house, where I finally had an opportunity to see the pinkes.

My father put the pinkes in a safe place in our store. One day, when no one was around, I approached the closet where it lay, my steps slow and my heart pounding, opened the doors and looked at it. I saw a large, old book, the size of a volume of the Talmud, with ribbed, leather covers torn in the corners. Out of them peeked the tops of yellowed, inscribed pieces of paper.

I grew terrified just looking at it. I myself don't know why I was so afraid, but at that moment images flew into my mind of awesome, horrifying events that had taken place in our town, events I had been told about and which were certainly recorded in the pinkes. The book seemed especially holy to me, and I was afraid even to touch it.

Yet I still didn't know what the book was needed for, or precisely what it contained. My childish mind burned with the desire to find out the secret.

Once I went up to my mother, may she rest in peace, just when she was busy with housework, and asked her: 'Mama, what's a pinkes? What's it used for?"

My mother gave me a strange look and said, "Go away, and don't annoy me with your questions!"

Another time I went to my grandmother Khaye-Rokhl, may she rest in peace, and asked her the same question. She listened to my question attentively, caressed my head and said, "Leybele, when, God willing, you grow up, you'll understand what a pinkes is and what's written down in it. You can't understand yet. Go, my child, go play with the children. Go . . ."

I decided to ask my teacher. He used to come to our house to tutor me, since I attended gymnasium and couldn't go to kheyder. The teacher whom my parents hired was Reb Artshe Karliner, a very fine scholar but, he should forgive me for saying so, a man with an awful temper.

How could I ask him? I had to figure out the right way to approach the matter, since he was always angry and grouchy. If one dared to try to speak to him of a matter that had nothing to do with study, one's life was in danger.

I set upon a plan: I knew that he was dearly fond of a hot glass of tea. Once, when he came to tutor me and my mother was out of the house, I stood up and said, "Rebe, would you like me to pour you a glass of tea?"

"Certainly, bring me a glass of tea. But be careful not to burn yourself!" he warned.

With trembling hands, I brought him the tea, and carefully asked him, "Rebe, what is a pinkes? What's written in it?"

The teacher, without raising his eyes from the glass, above which he was bent over, holding it in both hands and sipping from it with great pleasure, emitting a loud "Aaaaaah" after each sip, answered me with measured words in his Lithuanian dialect:

"A pinkes, Leybele, is a book in which all of the unusual events and occurrences that take place in a town are recorded, both good things and, God forbid, not such good things." He continued slowly, sipping after each phrase: "The good things are recorded, so that the generations that follow us will learn to behave well and will also perform good deeds. The bad things that happen, may we be spared, are recorded so that people may know not to do them, and also so that the One Above will pity us and see that no evil harms us in the future. Amen."

Now, in connection with the publication of the *Pinkas Kovel*, I remembered this episode from my childhood. I remembered the old pinkes of our town, which I saw in my parents' house, and which they so carefully and lovingly guarded. I am sure that we, the people of Kovel, wherever we may find ourselves, will know how to judge the value of this pinkes which we have published. We will preserve it as a dear and holy possession, with the same importance and even holiness with which the Jews of Kovel preserved through so many generations the pinkes of our town.

For, to our immense loss and sorrow, this *Pinkas Kovel* is the only remnant that remains of our beloved hometown.

The Court of the Plyaters

YITSKHOK FEYGLSHTAYN
Sefer Dombrovits (Dabrowica)

Our description of Dombrovits' early days would be incomplete without an account of the Polish noble family Plyater, with whom the Jews of Dombrovits were closely connected for over three hundred years. Various stories were told about this period, describing good and bad counts and countesses, those who did favors for the Jews and those who cruelly beat them.

In the Seventeenth and Eighteenth Centuries

About two hundred twenty years ago, Anton Plyater wrote up a statute instituting special rights for the Jews of Dombrovits. His lands were spread throughout all of Volhynia, as well as in the regions of Vilna and Cracow. Jews were scattered everywhere on his lands. However, he was particularly fond of the Jews of Dombrovits; this was explained by the fact that the Jews had supported the counts when they were threatened by Chmielnicki's bands, or by other Haidamak chieftains, who burned Polish estates and murdered Polish nobles in the seventeenth and eighteenth centuries.

During the rampage of Chmielnicki's forces in our region, they slaughtered all of the Jews in the surrounding towns: Berezhnits, Stepan, Berezene, Tshartorisk, and others. Only the Jewish community of Dombrovits was delivered from their hands. A legend grew up around that event: it was said that the attackers wandered around outside Dombrovits for an entire night, but God blinded their eyes and it seemed to them that they were lost in a huge oak forest. On the other hand, Polish sources say that there was a large Jesuit monastery on the outskirts of town, surrounded by fortifications and occupied by a Polish military garrison, which put up a strong resistance to the marauders and prevented them from forcing their way in. After the invaders withdrew, the Poles, led by the Plyaters, left town through an underground tunnel, together with the Jews, and attacked the marauders in open battle. Later the Poles and Jews made their way through to Kolk and eventually reached the Ozeryer forest, where they joined forces with the soldiers of the Polish Prince Mankiewicz. Thus the Jews of Dombrovits fought alongside the Plyaters against Chmielnicki's bands, and remained alive.

Old Jews remembered and retold how, in the struggle for Polish independence throughout the course of the nineteenth century, the court of Dombrovits was deeply involved. The Jews of the town had fought for the count, and several had fallen in battle. After the Poles were defeated, the Plyaters were forced to flee to Italy, and the court was ruined. For several decades it was impossible for the Jews to make a living, and they were forced to live in dire want. During the revolt in 1863, the next-to-last Plyater declared his loyalty to the Russian tsar, and the imperial powers gave him back his economic freedom. With this restoration, the material situation of the Jews in Dombrovits also improved significantly.

The Old Countess

Older Jews also loved to speak warmly about the old countess (who died around 1850 or 1855). At every opportunity, she expressed her gratitude to the Jews for having participated in the uprising of 1830. She remained trustee of the estate, after her nephew, an active rebel, fled across the border. His aunt, the countess, then moved into town, and lived in close contact with the local Jews. It was said that she had a Jewish messenger, who used to make trips on foot from Dombrovits to Warsaw: he kept her in contact with the Warsaw Polish Resistance Committee, and brought money for the countess. She distributed the money she received among the Jewish poor, because she herself didn't need much. Her sole expenses were related to maintaining the house, and feeding the six old chestnut horses, with which she rode twice a year to church in Berezhnits: on New Year's day and Easter; the church in Dombrovits had been confiscated and closed by the Russians, as a nest of rebels. When all of Dombrovits burned to the ground during the 1840s, the countess placed her forests at the disposal of the Jewish victims for free. The great synagogue was rebuilt with the countess's money at that time.

The Next-to-Last Count

After the death of the countess, the father of the last count arrived in Dombrovits. He brought along engineers, and divided his lands up into lots. The land was surveyed, and the forest was divided into quadrants and sections, and ditches were dug. Steady work began in the forest, which continued until the Holocaust. Jewish entrepreneurs built pitch refineries, distilling pitch and turpentine for many years. Count Plyater built a factory to make clay pipes for drawing water away from low areas. Trees were chopped down, and the lumber was floated to Danzig. That aspect, too, was managed by Jewish entrepreneurs. Water mills were built and leased out to Jews. New buildings were built, and Jews worked as carpenters, tinsmiths, and so forth. Milk was transported from the barns by Jewish lessees; Jews leased the orchards, and bought grain and vegetable crops. Count Plyater's houses in town were inhabited by Jews. At the brewery, by the liquor distillery, stood Jewish oxen. The Dombrovits estate included several separate holdings; the lands were spread out across dozens of kilometers. All sorts of enterprises were operating everywhere, and the Jews, directly or indirectly, made their livings from them. An important source of livelihood for Jews were the many tons of animal pelts, the tens of thousands of pounds of mushrooms, herbs, berries—in short, all trade both local and for export.

When Plyater settled his difference with the Russian Empire and got the church back, he rebuilt the large church on Vorobiner Street for the local gentiles. Here as well Jewish merchants and workers found employment. It was said that the church took a very long time to be built, because it kept sinking into the ground. Then a respected Jew is supposed to have prayed, saying: "Lord, if the *goyim* don't have churches, things will be even worse"—and the church stopped sinking.

Nevertheless, there was no love affair between the Jews and this noble Polish "brave gentleman." Was the old count an anti-Semite? No one could give a clear answer to this question. It is a fact, though, that among his hundreds of major and minor officials, there wasn't a single Jew. The sole exception was the one winter that Noyekh Burshteyn spent working as a shipping clerk in the lumber export operations. Jews were traders, customers, lessees, and workers, but never officials. The count never sold his forests to Jewish merchants, even though the lumber trade in Polesie lay in Jewish hands. The count himself exploited his forest, that is to say: there were Jews who supervised the harvesting of the forest, and Jews who bought up the milled boards, but no Jews who brought up the entire forests.

In short, the old count was an odd fish, both in his opinions and in his relations with non-Jews as well as Jews. In addition, he was extremely stingy; he used to say, "Anyone who can't hang on to a penny isn't worth a nickel." When a beggar somehow found his way into the main office, the count himself unlocked the cash box and handed him a penny.

Once, when he had come from Pinsk by way of the Pinsk–Sernik train, he decided to make himself incognito and hired a non-Jewish coachman to take him to Vorobin. The driver rode all night, and beat his thin horse until he broke his whipping stick. He cut an oak sapling from Plyater's forest, and made himself a new whip. The count asked him: "What are you doing? It's not your forest, it's Count Plyater's forest!" The driver replied, "It won't kill Plyater."

When they arrived in Vorobin, Count Plyater paid the coachman two rubles and said: 'I'm deducting three rubles, because a large oak worth three rubles would have grown from that sapling you cut."

When he used to come to the forest, he always poked around while the work was going on, inventing reasons to fine the Jewish contractors in order to cover the costs of his trip. There were also times when he personally beat Jews whom he had decided he didn't like. Shmuel the carpenter, for example, got a solid beating from the count when he protested against being fined for an imaginary error. He broke one of old Antigonus' ribs with his stick, because it seemed to him that the shingles were being laid too far apart on the roof. Yosl Ezra's was badly beaten by him, along with many other Jewish workers.

Plyater even went so far as to bring Polish carpenters from Radom, but they refused to stay. No gentile would stand for his brutality; more than one Jew, on the other hand, silently bore curses and blows. Plyater struck the old man Yisroel Genzer, who leased his water mills, in the presence of a large crowd.

Once, while Plyater was sitting in his main office together with some of his gentile officials and several Jewish contractors and merchants, his five-year-old son came in. Plyater took his child up to each of the gentiles in turn, and instructed him to offer his hand and say, "Good morning." Then he took the child's hand, "made a fig (fayg)" with it, and said to the boy, "My son, give this to each of the Jews." Of all the Jews present, only one reacted, a representative of Brodsky's sugar refineries in the Kiev region. As an expression of protest, this Jew tore up the contract he had signed with the count, and demanded the return of the deposit he had made toward a large transaction.

When he was forty-five, Plyater married the heiress of a huge estate, a daughter of Count Potocki. When they arrived in Dombrovits, the Jews put up a beautiful arch they had made, and the whole town went out to meet them, bearing bread and salt. Jewish musicians from Dombrovits played marches, the cantor sang a Psalm, and everyone shouted, "Long may he live!" The young bride, the countess, received the reception with gratitude, but the count asked, "Which one of you *zhidkes* organized this beautiful reception?"

Zalman Slutzky, Plyater's most important contractor, a rich Jew and a respected person, bowed and said, "I made the arrangements."

In the presence of the bride and the noble in-laws, the Jewish community of Dombrovits received this answer: "*Zhidek*, you probably stole enough from me already, if you thought it was worthwhile to arrange such a fancy reception."

Nevertheless, the Jews of Dombrovits knew that many of their number depended on the count for their livelihoods. His death sent a tremor through the entire town, and, genuinely grieving, the Jews of Dombrovits followed his funeral procession, as the cantor and his choir sang psalms.

The Fate of the Last Count

After his death, the countess managed the financial affairs of the estate, and there were no economic problems between her and the Jews, even though she drove a hard bargain. The Jews continued to trade with her and to earn money. Outside of business, she had nothing to do with Jews, with the exception of the wife of the government rabbi, Shaynpraysh, who had come from the same town as the countess. Mrs. Shaynpraysh was received by the countess at her palace.

After the countess died, her three sons ran the estate. Relations between the Jews and the lords continued as before; their attitude toward the Jews was liberal and humane.

In late 1918, when Dombrovits was declared a "Red Republic," all of the mistreated peasants from the surrounding hamlets came to take revenge. They surrounded Vorobin and stormed the palace for a day and a night, until the beleaguered noble family surrendered. The peasants captured the two elder sons, along with twenty-seven of their higher officials, and shot them. By chance, the youngest son was away from Vorobin at that time, and he remained living.

When the Polish state was established in November 1918, the surviving son was given exclusive control over Plyater's possessions. He stayed somewhere in central Poland, and his estates and enterprises were supervised by a manager. The count's estate remained a source of livelihood for dozens of families in Dombrovits and the surrounding settlements until the outbreak of the Second World War.

At the Market
A JEWISH TOWN'S STRUGGLE FOR BREAD

SHALOM MUHLSTEIN
Pinkas Kolbishov (Kolbuszowa)

One needs no particularly rich imagination to picture the chaos and uproar of the Jewish camp in the desert on that Friday morning when Moses the lawgiver announced that no manna would descend from heaven on the Sabbath, and that everyone should therefore collect enough to last until Sunday. Men and women of all ages hurried to their tents with all the vessels they'd brought along from Egypt, to grab the heavenly bread before the sun came up and it dissolved: a race, a noise, a confusion and above all, the voices and shouts of those-well known screamers, Dathan and Abiram. This image swims into consciousness as an apt comparison to the feverish commotion on a Tuesday morning, when a townful of Jews had to obtain its livelihood not only for two days, but in most cases for an entire week.

The fair at Kolbishov constituted a colorful, bustling spectacle, which took place both on Commerce Street (where the trading in cattle was held) and the market square, where a lively trade in all sorts of merchandise went on. The air was filled with a grating mixture of shouting voices. All the voices flowed together into a chorus expressing one word and one word only: *Par-no-se* (livelihood)!

The center of town was organized in precisely the same way as the tribes in the desert. Four lines of low houses surrounded the big square, with the well and street light right in the middle. Most of these stone houses consisted of three rooms, the foremost of which served as a place of business. These shops contained everything to satisfy the minimal needs of the peasants who came to the fair en masse every Tuesday, in order to sell their agricultural produce and bargain for city goods with the money they obtained. These stores commanded only part of the trade, however; all day long the huge marketplace was covered with wagons, booths, and wooden setups laden with all sorts of merchandise.

This is what it is like on a Tuesday, market day in Kolbishov.

The first rays of God's sun meet with signs of preparation for a busy day. Shutters open. Jews with their *tefillin* bags under their arms hurry home from early services. The Biale vegetable growers, who had arrived the previous night in order to secure their accustomed spots, creep out from underneath the wagons where they've spent the night, and begin to sort out their produce. The "Bialer goyim" are well-acquainted with the things Jews need for their Sabbath table. Onions for fish, parsley for soup, little cucumbers with dill for pickling, and carrots for *tsimes*. A growing human stream, together with containers and merchandise, pours forth from all of the back streets, Jews bearing crates, poles, and boards get ready to build their "pavilions" at the Great Weekly Exhibition.

Trains of peasant wagons bearing every sort of produce from the surrounding villages arrive endlessly. At the side of the road are masses of barefoot peasants and peasant women in colorful peasant clothes with baskets of eggs, butter, cheese, and poultry under their arms. Those who are too elegant to walk around barefoot in town carry their shoes dangling from their shoulders in order to spare the soles, and only put them on as they come into the market.

After selling their produce, the peasant men and women wander around the Jewish shops and stalls to do their own shopping. They go in groups, families and neighbors, mothers with children, whom they've brought along to show them the wonders of town and let them sample its humble luxuries. Here's a mother with six daughters, one smaller than the next, all in seven-layered petticoats. Large kerchiefs with floral designs on their heads, and their feet bare; each tastes long sour pickles, or white braided challahs baked by Jewish hands. Thus they go from shop to shop, from stall to stall, looking for the best bargains.

Every trade has its set place at the exhibition and its trademark, so to speak, with which those who make their living at it are associated. Fruit, for example, is sold here as in every Jewish town by *mark-zitsers*, who are famous for their unique form of invective. Here this trade is mainly in the hands of a Jewish family from the nearby town of Glogov, who buy up entire orchards and distribute the fruit at the surrounding fairs.

Binem, the head of the fruit merchants of Glogov, is an important figure at the market, giving it added tone and atmosphere. Standing on the wagon of fruit, he hawks his merchandise in a strong basso which drowns out other voices. "It heals the heart," he praises his wares. And when business is poor, he begins to argue with his relatives on the next wagon, shrieking so loudly that they are quickly surrounded by curious peasants. Then, as curses pour out of their mouths, apples pass through their hands as if they were going out of style.

Binem's voice is accompanied by the barrel organ of the lottery-ticket seller, the harmonica and pious Christian songs of the Polish beggars, and—to make a distinction—Meyer Gersheles' Psalm melody, "Before birth your destiny is sealed."

Right in the middle of the square are the woodworkers. Jews from nearby Sokolov are represented by the furniture they've manufactured. Among piles of wooden vessels, sieves, and strainers, strides the grizzled and venerable Reb Matisyohu, the patriarch of the industry.

Not far away are the textile dealers, hasidic youths in velvet hats and long black overcoats, who sell striped and flowered percales and muslins for peasant dresses and kerchiefs, and speak to the women in Polish mixed with Hebrew: "Well, then, how much will you offer?"

Textiles are the most common item sold. The competition in this business is especially fierce, and earnings small: a group of merchants stand in a circle, discussing the lamentable business situation. Motl, a progressive businessman whose clean-shaven face, sleek figure, and years of living in Vienna have earned him the title "Herr," rather than the usual "Reb," is the discussion leader. Motl argues that despite all of the failed attempts so far, it is time to try once again to organize a merchants' society, to introduce sound business practices. Others claim that such an undertaking has no chance of success whatsoever, because too much of the trade is in the hands of teachers. As an example of how teaching and trading go hand in hand, the anecdote about Betsalel the town magnate is retold. When he had wanted to take his son out of *kheyder* and allow him to engage in secular studies, Yisroel Isser Melamed had argued with him: "Why does he need to be a lawyer, Reb Betsalel? Let the lad study with me, he'll grow up to be a merchant."

A good deal of the blame is placed on Getsele Bentsh. Getsele's is the most important name in the textile market, and this is regarded as a disaster. Getsele is a shrunken little Jew, an experiment in frugality on the part of the Creator. The name *Bentsh* refers to the blessing after eating meals with bread, and testifies to his stinginess: "Even before he washes himself before eating, his wife reminds him to say the after-meal blessing. So it's no wonder that Getsele can get by on the lowest profits and murder the prices," argues a Jew half-joking and half-serious. The argument is picked up by a young man studying at the bes-medresh, who describes Getsele's stinginess in his own way: "Getsele can sit down to eat less than the minimum portion necessary to say the blessing afterward, and finish with enough left over for saying the blessing."

With quick, agile steps, bearing cackling hens in both arms, Perl drifts by. Perl is the head of an enterprising family. They export grain overseas, they ship poultry to Cracow, they have a textile shop, they set up a booth at the market-place, and Perl stands at the head of it all. Perl stops awhile by the circle of merchants and sums up the stagnation in the textile business in her own fashion: "It's a real curse. When you buy a bit of fabric in Raysha, it's for a girl, and when you bring it home, she's already a matron." And people with experience in both business and married life testify that Perl's assessment of the situation is quite accurate.

Nearby the textile wares is the exhibit of the needle industry. The head of the underwear industry is Mendl Shnayder. Mendl certainly deserves a medal for productivity: a tailor's workshop for men's clothing, an underwear factory, and eight children. God only knows where there's room for all that in his one-room dwelling on Shendishover Street. But tall, proud noblemen and government officials have to bow their heads crossing the threshold of his low room, and prospective grooms think it risky to be presented in clothes made by any other tailor, because Mendl has a reputation as a first-class master of his craft.

Mendl is always buried in work. If someone wants a garment for summer, he has to order it in winter. A piece of goods that enters Mendl's workshop goes through a whole series of transformations before it fights its way onto the sewing table. First it is spread out on the floor to protect the finished work, then it's a tablecloth, and then it's placed under pieces of ironing. Mendl explains that this procedure is very good for the material, making it sturdy and stain-resistant. Mendl is a pleasant, calm person. He pronounces each word slowly, sucking a hard candy meanwhile. When someone comes to try something on, Mendl always has a finished garment—sometimes too big, sometimes too small—but always reassurance that he's working on the order. Sometimes the customer sees his order laid out as a bedspread. Mendl smiles, in a bit of a dilemma, eats a grape and recovers, measures the customer once again, and cuts the material right then and there, and the client goes away reassured. But Mendl's tempo is quite different before market day. Then the workshop is organized according to principles of mass production. Actually, before market day it is Mendl's wife who determines the pace. The mother of his eight children can be seen every morning on top of a loaded wagon, on her way to a market in another town. In short, the Jewish clothing industry occupies a major role in the market.

In the cattle trade on Commerce Street, Jews also play an important role. The trade in horses lies in the hands of Jews from the neighboring town of Maydan. An old horse trader named Treytl once lived there, and Treytl has remained the generic name of the Jewish horse traders of Maydan. It's even said that in the old days, when a market day fell during the intermediate days of a festival, they used to come from Maydan in their silken overcoats, bare feet, and fur hats on their heads.

Here is also the place where Jewish butchers get their meat. Only the trade in swine is "Judenrein." The trading is carried on in a very crude fashion. Every proposed price is accompanied by a heavy slap of one fleshy paw on another and loud comments from the onlookers, reminding the observer of a sporting match. When the transaction is finished, everyone goes to have a drink in a Jewish tavern.

As day goes on, the pace of the market increases. It becomes jammed with people. The trading grows more and more intense. The peasant women, the principal shoppers, who have already made a tour of all the shops to see what's available at what price, have now made up their minds and haggle for the merchandise they've decided on. Compromises are reached. Hands are slapped. Hands reach out. Bundles of coins are untied from different corners of the kerchief. People count on their fingers, then their money is counted. Shimek the policeman bangs on his drum. Everyone comes running, and it is announced that a horse and wagon are to be sold at auction for back taxes. On the way from church, the priest rides his carriage, ringing a bell. Throngs of peasants on both sides of the road kneel in the mud and cross themselves.

"*Yaftiru besafa yaniun rosh*" (They move their lips and sway their heads), sings Meyer Gersheles.

"Ten cents a pound," calls out Binem from his wagon, and the barrel organ plays and the blind beggar sings.

Not only did the Jews at the market play an important role as middlemen, buying up raw products for export and selling factory products, but a good deal of the manufactured goods that were sold were made by Jewish artisans. Jewish artisans sat and worked on sieves, strainers, and other wooden items, and distributed their products throughout the entire region. Families of Jewish bakers spent entire nights at troughs full of dough. There were Jewish tinsmiths, capmakers, coatmakers, shoemakers, Jewish porters, even Jewish peasants, but at the time when the Polish pogroms broke out, most of the Jews left the villages, where life was less safe than in town.

Jews bought factory goods in the big cities and sold them at the market. They were far from being parasites, as the anti-Semites depicted them, for they served the peasant, who received everything he needed for a minimum price. Under normal conditions no businessman would be contented with the low margin of profit that the Jew received for his effort and worry. In their attempt to take away from the Jews their livelihoods, the Poles organized cooperatives, hoping thereby to drive the Jewish middlemen from the marketplace. These cooperatives, with all the privileges that the government gave them, couldn't exist at the low profit margin that the Jewish merchant had maintained. Peasants found that the merchandise was cheaper in Jewish businesses than in the cooperatives. The same was true of the Jews who bought up the peasants' produce. The markup they received barely covered the physical labor expended in packing and loading. The Jewish grain dealer used to carry the sack from the wagon himself, as the peasant followed, whip in hand.

The earnings were so minimal because of the terrible poverty in which the peasant lived. The wide fields and all of the villages around belonged to Count Tishkyevitsh, for whom masses of peasants worked at starvation wages. The produce from the fields was exported overseas while the count himself, like many other noblemen, spent entire years at Monte Carlo, gambling away the income from his holdings.

The Polish political leaders, instead of correcting these unjust conditions, found it easier to point to the Jewish stores as a solution to their situation. This is how the great enmity between Jew and non-Jew came about, which prepared Polish soil to be the great Jewish cemetery. But the struggle went on for many years, and the Jews didn't give up their economic positions easily.

The economic and political struggle of the small Jewish community between the liberation of Poland in 1918 and the Hitlerite invasion reflects in miniature the "parliamentary anti-Semitism" which characterizes that period in Poland. Government-supported Christian cooperatives were the mildest of the means taken by the Polish government in its determination to take away the livelihood of Jews. The attempt to hold markets on the Sabbath was a heavy blow to the Jews; it was a sad time for the Jews in town. Not a single Jew in Kolbishov opened his store on the Sabbath. Most of the peasants boycotted the Sabbath market, believing there could be no effective market without the Jews. The community council, whose main source of income consisted of fees for wagons and stalls at the fair, finally had to give up the plan.

The Jews comprised a clear majority in town and the Jewish representatives in the town council naturally worked against the Poles' attempt to administer the city against Jewish interests. For years the Poles tried to artificially increase the Christian population of the town by including parts of neighboring villages within the town's boundaries. The Jewish community was well represented in court by Shloyme Zontag, Betsalel Grinshteyn, and Yekhezkl Dershovits.

The struggle against the anti-Semitism of both the government and town officials was supported by the cooperative bank under the leadership of Grinshteyn and Dershovits, and later by the free loan society which distributed smaller loans, and which was directed by representatives of all of the Jewish parties in town; they were important resources in the Jewish struggle for a bit of bread.

The traditional Jewish free loan society also played a very important role. Kivtshe Leystner, for instance, a Jew who always sought to do good, had a sort of private free loan society, running around the market borrowing from one Jew and lending to another. These were all means of economic self-defense, as the Polish bosses of the country, with the help of taxes and assorted restrictions, drew the rope tighter and tighter around the Jewish merchant's throat.

The Poles lived to see their hopes realized much quicker and more thoroughly than they could have expected. There are no more Jewish businesses and traders. The market in Kolbishov is planted with potatoes. Whether this made the Polish residents much happier remains in doubt.

Evening falls.

The pace of the fair grows slower and more relaxed. Housewives who are themselves merchants come to the grocers of Biale to shop for the Sabbath. Binem climbs down from his wagon, the anger disappears from his face, and he begins to joke with the Jewish women. A girl hurries to the slaughterer with a goose; its liver will be prepared for tonight's dinner. A tall young Hasid walks with a list in his hand and a pen stuck behind his ear; he's going to collect a little honest capital so that the next day he'll be able to travel to Raysha and pick up some merchandise for his store. Bit by bit, the marketplace is emptied of wagons and stalls. A group of drunkards leave a tavern; they embrace, kiss, weep, start arguing, beat, and bloody each other. The peasant women tear them away from each other, drag them off to the wagons, and drunken voices are drowned out by the clatter of the wheels on the highway.

Jews hurry to the synagogue. The church bell chimes, paying its last respects to a dying day. Kapuste the water carrier sets down his tanks, tugs off his cap, and crosses himself. Jews hurry to the synagogue. On the Bes-medresh Street, on the pavement not far from Leyzer-Meyer's fence, a drunken peasant lies snoring. Next to him stands his wife, wrapped in a shawl, with a box under her arm. She pulls him by his dirty clothes, damns him with massive Polish curses, insults with him obscene peppery comments that impugn his mother's modesty. The peasant lies snoring, and Jews hurry to the synagogue.

In the bes-medresh it is warm and bright. Jews pray with feeling: "Who distinguishes times and changes seasons . . . rolls away the light before the darkness, and the darkness before the light . . . makes day to pass and brings the night . . ." And the warm murmur flows from one corner of the bes-medresh to the other, until the congregation is rocked in a silent and grateful *Shmone esrey*—grateful for what fate has brought them today, for their earnings at the fair.

After the evening service, people turn their attention back to the day's business. The market is now brought inside the big bes-medresh. Little groups of merchants talk over the results of the day. Grain merchants make deals, and rye, oats, and lupines go from one hand to another. Money is counted, dollars exchanged. A restrained slap of one butcher's hand on another, at the long table near the door, tells that a sterile cow or a young ram has changed ownership, and it has been decided on whose cutting board the animal will serve to honor the Sabbath. The butchers quench their thirsts with a glass of apple brandy from Yankev-Borukh's jug, snack on a jar of salted beans, and turn toward the crowd that stands around the big table near the clock, where Leybtshe-Leyzer is reading a chapter of the Mishnah. They listen to catch a good Jewish word.

On their way out of the big bes-medresh, they stop a few minutes at the doorway of the little bes-medresh to catch a look at one of their boys, who diligently sways over the Talmud. After all, what is it that a Jew works for? The Lithuanian Preacher, just recently, clearly expressed the insight that the whole world is like a fair. The difference between one person and another lies in how each manages at the fair, and how each is able to answer when called to task at the Heavenly Court: Have you traded faithfully? Brother, what did you obtain at the fair?

Novoyelne

KHANE KAMIN (KAPLAN)
Pinkas Navaredok (Nowogrodek)

Novoyelne was a little *shtetele*, but nevertheless a town fondly remembered not only by the Jews who lived there, but by everyone in the area.

First of all, Novoyelne was known because of its railroad station, the only connection between Navaredok and the world. Between Navaredok and Novoyelne ran a little train which rode so slowly, especially in the snows of winter, that it was faster to go on foot. As it moved, passengers could get off the little train, play in the snow and throw snowballs, run a bit to warm themselves up, and still manage to get back on the train. The railroad station in Novoyelne was the heart of the town: there one could meet merchants, relatives, and friends. There one did all sorts of business. During the winter total stillness reigned, broken only by the piping of the locomotive. Jewish life in Novoyelne centered around the main street, where a couple of dozen families made their living from trade. Once a week, on a market day, the peasants from the surrounding hamlets came to do their shopping and trade their produce. The rest of the week everything was quiet, and the rabbi, the cantor, and several householders (my father, may he rest in peace, among them) had time to study a portion of the Talmud even in midafternoon. The youngsters studied in Navaredok, for the most part, and only came home for vacations. Right next to the town there was a large pine forest; in winter it stood lonesome and forlorn, but in the spring it revived and awoke. As soon as Passover ended, the Jews of Novoyelne began to prepare for the *datshnikes*, the summer people. Novoyelne was a summer resort for the entire region. People from all of the surrounding cities and towns spent the summer there. The pine trees and the little river attracted young and old, great and small from all over. The "TOZ" summer camp was there; retired people on pensions were there; people rented houses for the entire summer. The *datshnikes* stretched out, regained their health and forgot about their cares. The forest was alive! Late at night one could hear the laughing and singing of the young folk strolling along its paths. Each one of us remembers pleasant hours spent in the shade of the pines. But all at once this life was eradicated by the Nazi butchers, and many near and dear ones lost their lives.

The Twenty-first of Adar: The Great Day

YESHAYE KIRSHNBOYM
Lizhensk (Lezajsk); sefer zikaron le-kedoshei Lizhensk she-nispu be-shoat ha-natsim

For us youngsters Purim was an unforgettable experience, a genuine holiday that we waited for from Hanukkah on.

The most obvious thing that was special about the day was the large number of visitors. A town of six hundred families was suddenly filled with thousands of new faces from all parts of the world. From within the Austro-Hungarian Empire, even non-Hasidim came from far and wide. A drowning man will grasp at a straw; Jews never lacked for troubles and Rebe Elimelekh had written that none who came to his grave with a request on the anniversary of his death would go away disappointed. Some asked for a decent livelihood. Others had arranged marriages for their children, and were afraid that the agreement might collapse before the wedding. One had a defect, which doctors had despaired of healing. Another had children who had fallen into evil ways, becoming Zionists and starting to read [Micah Yosef] Berdichevsky, [J. L.] Gordon and [David] Frischmann, and only the Rebe was capable of exorcising the demon. Rich Jews came as well, praying that the Messiah might soon come and redeem them to a Jewish kingdom, along with their money.

Huge crowds of Hasidim from other countries came, dressed in modern, "German-style" clothes, which we found bizarre and made us suspect them of being disguised evil spirits. When we spoke to them, however, we found out that they were genuine, kosher Hasidim. They were from Holland, England, and even America. They, too, knew of the Rebe's will. All of the Hasidim came with their own, living rebes.

The largest number came from Russia. Traveling from Russia to Austria on that day meant taking a great risk for *kidesh haShem*, the sake of the Name. It was impossible for a Jew to receive a passport to leave Russia, so people simply stole across the border. Once they had left the Russian gehenna and had arrived in Franz Josef's liberal land, the way was eased for them, especially when they were known to be illegal arrivals for the twenty-first of Adar. Thus people came riding and on foot, with great faith and with heavy hearts, to Lizhensk.

But as far as we younsters were concerned, the guests of honor were the Umaner Hasidim, the so-called "Dead Hasidim" of Reb Nachman Bratslaver, who, following Reb Nachman's will, had had no rebe since his death. Yet they did allow themselves to visit Rebe Elimelekh's grave en masse. They crossed the border somewhere near Ulanov, some twenty-eight kilometers from Lizhensk, and they rode the Rozvadov train from Niska. We knew more or less when they would arrive, and we used to run to the station, about a kilometer from town, to await them.

Long before the train pulled in we could hear voices, and when the train approached the voices grew stronger and joined together, blending into an endless song. Dancing and singing they descended from the train, and as soon as they poured out they joined shoulder-to-shoulder in rows of six and eight, and thus woven into bands they arrived in town dancing and singing.

They sang well. The Rebe, while he was still alive, had said, "Serve the Lord gladly." It was a delight to hear their song—sweet, sad, and ecstatic all at once. We children used to join their rows, and dance with them into town. The Umaner didn't only use the sidewalks. With our willing help they flooded the streets. More than once a terrified horse turned tail and ran off without its master.

In addition, the twenty-first of Adar afforded us a day off from kheyder. Our teacher was even more involved than we were in the holy day—attending to guests, to rebes, and to collection boxes. Above all, every child's home was more festive than usual. There were guests everywhere, and food was served all day. While some of the guests were setting off for the cemetery, others were already on their way back. They came and went until midnight, bearing candles and lanterns to light their way.

Mothers had begun baking three days previously. They made all the best things: egg cookies, *rogelekh*, fresh pastries, and, most important, fruitcake. I can still taste that delicious fruitcake. Wherever my mother hid it, I managed to find it and promptly do justice to it.

Each of the guests had acquaintances with whom they left their bags until they returned from the cemetery. When they returned from the grave, tired from the press of the crowd, they were certain of their "room and board" until their departure.

The twenty-first of Adar was also a day for family get-togethers in Lizhensk. Choice wines which had been set aside especially for that day were brought from the cellar, and there was also esrog jelly, which had been made right after Sukkes.

Among the great rebes who came were the Sandzer, the Radomishler, the Dzhikever, the Plantser, and the Rozvadover. I remember that even the Belzer Reb Yisekher used to come. Many of his Hasidim lived in town, and upon his arrival and departure the train was unable to move, because crowds of Hasidim surrounded it and there was a serious danger of an accident.

I remember an episode from my childhood connected with that day. In 1910 or 1911, my mother and I went off to see the Tutshner Rebe, of whom it was said that he didn't know the difference between one coin and another. When my mother handed him a donation, he handed her in return a handful of coins for good luck. The press there was so great that she mixed the sacred charms together with the everyday coins in her pocket. Unable to tell which were the Rebe's coins later on, she put all the coins together in a little purse, tied it up, and set it aside for the generations.

The mausoleum over Rebe Elimelekh's burial "cave" was right at the entrance to the cemetery. It was a small, old building, already somewhat tilted, with a low entranceway; in order to go inside, one had to bend over and descend a step or two. I believe that the "cave" had already fallen in. Inside, there were two rooms. In the first there were three or four stones, the first for a certain Reb Naftali [the Rebe's grandson—ed.] The gravestones were set quite close to each other. In the second room lay the great Rebe Elimelekh himself. The grave was surrounded by a wooden barrier with crossbars on all four sides.

At the head of the grave several of the crosspieces were missing. Over the years people had squeezed in to bemoan their troubles right next to the remains of the Rebe's holy head, and the boards hadn't long withstood the pressure. After thus pouring out his troubles, each of the visitors pushed in a slip of paper on which he had written his request, trying to slip it in at the bottom of the mountain of paper so that it would be as near to the Rebe as possible.

When one shift finished, another throng pushed its way in, continuing until late at night. Candles that people had brought with them burned in both rooms. More than once the slips of paper caught fire, which was barely extinguished in time. Although the smoke burned everyone's eyes, no one was dismayed by it. The main thing was to reach the holy Rebe.

After reaching the entrance, one immediately began saying Psalms. Once inside, the anxiety lessened, and it was easier to wait one's turn. Most of the Jews first went to the bath, in order to be ritually pure when they came to the Rebe.

In the study house, men sat all day studying the Mishnah together along with the Rebe's work, *Noam Elimelekh*. It was a day different from all other days; the people and the town were different as well.

A day to remember.

The Burial Society

A. S. HORODETSER
Horodets (Horodec): a geshikhte fun a shtetl

One of the oldest, most influential and wealthiest societies in town was the burial society. It was a great honor to belong to the burial society, not to mention becoming one of its officers. Very few people achieved the distinction of being a *gabay* in the burial society, which was somewhat like being a president. Only outstanding individuals, the scholars of the town, such as Reb Yisroel Mazursky, Reb Hillel, and Reb Sholem Kastrinsky, merited that honor.

The burial society did not limit its affairs to burial plots and the dead. It also included other community activities within its functions. All of these activities were inscribed in the chronicle of the burial society.

To our sorrow, the old chronicle, containing descriptions of many remarkable events, was destroyed, while the new chronicle, which only concerned the affairs of the burial society, no longer exists. The chronicle was lost during the First World War, when the residents of Horodets evacuated the town, and many houses were burned down.

Whenever someone wanted to join the society, he had to pay an initiation fee of twenty-five rubles, and also make the annual feast on the night before the beginning of the month of Shevat. And if the feast wasn't sufficiently lavish, the new member was liable to be forced to give a second and better one.

The new member also had to serve as the society's *shames* for a period of three years. The role of this shames was to call the members of the society to do their duty whenever someone died. The members received burial rights for free, but when someone who didn't belong to the society had a death in his family, the burial society, together with the gabay, decided on the fee on an ad hoc basis.

The burial society in Horodets was unusual in the number of unique traditions and customs it observed, such as praying together in the synagogue every year before Rosh Hashanah, observing the "little" Yom Kippur together, and making annual feasts.

The most famous tradition was the winter feast before Rosh Khoydesh Shevat. Before the feast was celebrated, all of the members fasted and said penitential prayers in the study house.

The feast took place at the home of the gabay. If there was no new member to make the feast, the society paid for it out of its own funds, as stipulated in its by-laws. It was just like the feasts of King Solomon in his day. Special challahs were baked, large pieces of fish were served, along with meat, chicken, tsimes, and compote. There was no shortage of wine and brandy, either. The mood was quite festive. Various tunes were loudly sung. At this annual feast, new officers would be chosen for the coming year. Almost always, the same officers were reelected. The crowd went home happy, carrying in their pockets leftovers for their wives and children.

A second, smaller feast was also held on Simkhes Toyre, again at the gabay's house. It began on the evening of Shemini Atseres, and went on until late in the evening. The feast consisted of fruits, tarts, and brandy. The atmosphere was filled with the joy of Simkhes Toyre. After the feast, everyone went out into the street, and the gabay was led into the synagogue. People carried burning candles in their hands and loudly sang hasidic and misnagdic tunes. The children of the town walked in front and sang along. Inside the synagogue the celebration continued with song and dance, as everyone circled around the podium in a procession. Everyone in town, both Hasidim and misnagdim, came to the synagogue to take part in the procession.

The burial society had fairly high expenses: maintaining the cemetery, paying the gravedigger, feasts that were considered very important because of the prominence of the society, and so forth. But where was the money to pay for all of this? The society attempted to cover its expenses by charging a fee for each burial, based on the financial situation of the family. A committee was appointed to determine how much to charge in each case. The committee saw to it that the society had all of the money it needed. In fact, it must be said that the committee's calculations were not very precise.

This was during the years when the revolutionary movement in tsarist Russia began to grow. The struggle for freedom spread all across the land, and found its way inside Horodets as well. The first signs of this movement appeared in the burial society, which was characterized by a strong bureaucratic tendency. A revolt was raised against the society. People came out in public with criticisms of the society's organization. They demanded justice in the determination of burial fees. But the society had its own legitimate motives, and was unwilling to concede to the "revolutionaries." Thus began a full-scale feud in town, the famous "burial society feud."

A group of young, strong, and capable men united to form a new burial society, and began to compete with the older society. When someone died, they would arrive first and grab the corpse, carry it off to the cemetery, and bury it for free. The old society didn't have a bit of work to do: no dead people, no money. On the other hand, they didn't remain silent. When they realized that they were in a bad spot, that they were about to go bankrupt, they woke up and began to hurry up themselves. It sometimes even happened that both societies stood around waiting for the corpse. It was a matter of ambition: who would defeat whom, which society would go away and which would stay?

This anarchic situation lasted for three years. Both sides became exhausted. When the feud cooled down, both sides agreed to a rabbinical hearing.

Rabbis were brought in from Kobrin and Antipolye to sit in judgment along-side the old town rabbi, Rabbi Reb Yoshua Yankev of blessed memory. After hearing the claims of both sides, the rabbis pronounced the following verdict, consisting of four points: the old burial society was to remain in office, while the newer society was to be disbanded; a standard price of three rubles was to be charged for each corpse, and no more; the poor were not to be charged at all; and wealthier people could be charged more, but at the rabbi's, not the society's, discretion.

Both societies were content with the verdict. The old society was happy to remain intact. The new society was pleased to have won a moral victory and carried through its program. Peace and harmony returned to our town.

Girls' Kheyders

AMI
Horodets (Horodec); a geshikhte fun a shtetl

The following questions are often asked: "Where did our mothers and grand-mothers learn to pray, to read the Yiddish Bible, to write a Yiddish letter? Where did some of them even learn to write addresses in Russian? Who were the teachers that taught many of them to understand the prayers, even to a limited extent?"

True, girls were not taught to read the Bible in the original Hebrew in Horodets, but every Sabbath they used to read the *Tsene-rene*, the Yiddish adaptation of the Bible. If Grandmother didn't finish the weekly portion before the end of the Sabbath, she read it during the week. Every mother went to the synagogue to pray on the Sabbath. If she wasn't quite competent at reading the prayers or keeping her place in the prayer book, she would sit next to someone who knew better, and follow along.

Who implanted this religious sentiment in the hearts of Jewish women? Who lit the flame of piety in our grandmothers' souls, so that they came to the afternoon and evening services? And from where came the elderly Jewish women's fear of God, so strong that they used to stand throughout an entire day of prayers on Rosh Hashanah and Yom Kippur?

First of all, it must be said that the prevailing atmosphere in which such mothers and grandmothers grew up was permeated with spirituality; but their character was also due in no small part to the female teachers who devoted themselves to their education. These women were themselves quite pious and observant, and they shaped the lives of Jewish mothers-to-be.

The *melamdeke* or *rebetsin*, as she was called, was different from the male *melamed*. Most of the male teachers worked at this profession all of their lives, until their deaths. The women, however, held their positions only temporarily. Often they saw it as a means of earning extra income to help out their husbands.

For example, one hundred years ago there was a rebitsin in Horodets named Miriam. She was Yermye Zerekh's wife. Yermye Zerekh's was a slaughterer and teacher, and Miriam taught girls who used to come to her home to study. It is said that she was a genuine scholar. And what did she teach her "girls"?

She taught them how to pray, how to read the Yiddish Bible, how to write a letter to their future husbands. And the rest was taught to the girls by their mothers: how to make meat kosher and the other obligations of a Jewish woman.

When Vishke, Ayzik's wife, became a widow, she opened a kheyder in her home and taught the girls of Horodets the same Torah that Miriam the rebetsin had taught.

Apparently, the above-mentioned curriculum didn't satisfy the younger generation. New birds, new wings. When the demand that girls be taught how to write addresses in Russian became widespread, a man who was a bit more modern and knew a little Russian was needed. Vishke was unable to teach this subject.

The young man who took the job was Avrom Moyshe, the son of Itshe Silke's, a young man who was familiar with secular literature and was known as a semi-intellectual. He used to visit the girls at home and teach them there. He brought along a book of sample letters, and tutored the girls in how to write letters to their bridegrooms, their in-laws, and so on.

Almost every girl in Horodets received this sort of education. The daughters were happy, and their parents were also satisfied. For only a little bit of money their girls grew up to be proper Jewish women.

Yet the march of progress continued; new winds began to blow, and they found their way into Horodets as well. No longer were the girls satisfied with just an address in Russian and the Yiddish alphabet; they wanted to be able to read books in Russian, and some of them wanted to learn the holy tongue as well. This demand was fulfilled by another young man from Horodets, Shimshon Alter Visotsky's. Shimshon stemmed from a prestigious family, the Mazurskys, and had a fine reputation of his own: he knew Hebrew and Russian, and was an expert at arithmetic.

Shimshon established a girls' kheyder in which he taught how to write Russian and Yiddish, as well as arithmetic. It didn't last long, however. As mentioned above, teaching girls was a means of gaining a temporary livelihood, until something better came along. Shimshon went off to Vilna and became a bookkeeper.

What was to be done for the girls of Horodets who thirsted for education? Into the breach stepped Yudl Khaye-Miriam's, a youngster who stemmed from the other prestigious family in town, the Kastrinskys, and was himself quite learned. Yudl continued with Shimson's curriculum, but not for long, because Yudl died quite young.

God did not forsake Horodets; Khane Tsodek's, the daughter of a teacher, established a new girls' kheyder. Khane introduced the girls to the Bible in the original, in addition to spoken Russian and letter writing. No matter that they didn't understand some of the fancy German words in the letter-book—they survived. The girls of Horodets were thoroughly versed by the time they finished this kheyder.

But even Khane's kheyder didn't last long. A total stranger, Hershl Pomerants, appeared in town, and a new epoch in the history of schooling in Horodets began with him. Khane's kheyder declined, until she herself left Horodets and settled in America.

Much has happened since then, and we glance backward and say: "Thank you, pious and honest teachers, both male and female, who taught our mothers and grandmothers. May the merit of your deeds sustain you!"

Anarchist Activities

BETSALEL (ALTER) POTSHEBUTSKY
Pinkas Krinek (Krynki)

Anarchist Article of Faith

The anarchists of Krinek occupied a distinct place among the fighters for a new and liberating regime. As is well known, they didn't recognize domination in society or the state, which they believed was based on the force and compulsion of law.

The anarchist movement in Krinek was divided into various tendencies. Discussions of Proudhon's work, *What Is Property?*, were conducted in town; and the concepts of "federalism" and "mutualism" were daily expressions among the youngsters of Krinek. There was no lack of followers of Kropotkin's anarcho-communism or of Bakunin's teachings on the use of terror to destroy the mother of all oppression, the state. Even those who deified the German Max Stirner with his extreme individualism and instinctive egoism, and the Russian nihilist Nechaev with his justification of the most brutal methods of terrorism against the ruling regime were to be found among the anarchists of Krinek. In addition, there were the so-called anarcho-syndicalists and "ethical" and "philosophical" anarchists.

The anarchist group in Krinek was founded by Yankl "Professor" (the writer Yankl Kreplyak). Active among this group were Nyome Yoyne the Carpenter's, Moyshele Rive's and Avrom-Yitzkhok Vilner, their leader.

Terrorist Acts

In practice the majority of anarchists approved of terrorist acts directed personally against the tsarist authorities and against oppressors and exploiters of workers. They also approved of and carried out expropriations, or *x's*, as they were called in their lingo. If it was impossible to improve wages legally, and thus return to the worker the stolen surplus value of his labor, so they argued, they would take it back from the exploiters by other means.

And serious actions really were carried out in Krinek. The industrialist Shmuel Vayner "Amerikaner" was shot. He was called by that name because he had once been in America. He was very proud of the fact that he had permission to carry a revolver. He even teased the youngsters, showing them his weapon. The last day of Passover, when Shmuel Amerikaner left the synagogue with a group of well-known citizens, he was attacked on Tanners' Street. The attackers were between the ages of seventeen and nineteen.

The Jewish population of Krinek hadn't had time to calm down after the attack on Shmuel Amerikaner before rumors of a planned attack on a meeting of industrialists at the large bes-medresh made the rounds. A bomb made in Horodok was supposed to be thrown. The group in Krinek delegated Moysheke to go pick it up.

On his way Moysheke was wounded. He was brought to Sislevits for medical treatment. The doctor who tended him gave word to the police. Moysheke was arrested and he was held in the prison in Grodno.

Later it was discovered that his trial was to be held in Warsaw. His mother Rive did everything she could to have the trial moved to Vilna. Every attempt was made to turn the matter over to lawyers. But Moysheke, true to his ideals, decided to confess to carrying the bomb and simultaneously make a political declaration against the regime of slavery and tyranny. He intended to announce that he was attempting to use the bomb to murder the minions of the autocracy. His mother threatened to take her life if he did that. Finally the Jewish child in him, his mother's son, was aroused, and the revolutionary Moysheke denied his guilt and was released. A short time later he was again arrested, and sentenced to four years in prison.

Anarchist Demonstrations

There were anarchist demonstrations in Krinek on several occasions. The demonstrators wore black overshirts, black tassels, black overcoats, and black caps. They marched along the road to the church, singing the anarchist hymn in unison. When the quiet small-town population began to sense that things were about to get rowdy, the shopkeepers locked up, pedestrians hid in their houses, and the town notables, headed by Nokhum-Anshl, behaved very calmly toward the irresponsible, stormy youth.

Nyomke "Anarchist"

I recall a meeting of industrialists in Krinek. It was heavily guarded by armed Cossacks, including the sergeant. Suddenly there was a shot, and the sound of breaking glass. The sergeant took off after Hershl's son Nyomke, the "mangy one" and threw him down.

As it turned out, the bomb was thrown by Moysheke Siderer. It exploded, but no one was hurt. Nyomke was sentenced to eight years at hard labor at the court in Slonim.

On the way from jail, Nyomke took out a revolver which had been hidden in a loaf of bread, shot the guard, and escapted to Krinek. Several days later he was arrested again, and led off to the Grodno prison under heavy guard.

When he was called out for questioning, he tore the weapons out of the guards' hands, and attacked and shot them. Then he barricaded himself at the nearby home of a tailor, and continued the shootout with the police. When Nyomke saw that he had only one bullet left, he shot himself.

When the police entered the room, they saw an inscription in blood: "Long live anarchy! You'll never take me alive!" (Another account of Nyomke's end was written for this volume by his brother.)

There were attacks on Krinek sergeants long after they had left the town. The "minor" sergeant was shot while staying with Kapelyushnik in Sokolke. The attack was carried out by Aproytshik, Yosl Moyshe the Tailor's, and Moysheke Siderer. Aproytshik was sentenced to be hanged. The sentence was eventually commuted to twenty years at hard labor. In 1917 it was rumored in Krinek that Aproytshik had been seen free in Moscow, and that he held an important position there.

Activities of Krinek Anarchists Outside of Town

There were instances of Jewish anarchists from Krinek who died while carrying out secret orders. Thus Yisroel Isser the Slaughterer's and Meyer Yankl-Bunim's paid with their lives while riding to Bialystok on a droshky. There was the sound of an explosion, and both were killed instantly.

The activity of Aron-Velvl Yankl-Bunim's made a strong impression among the anarchists in Bialystok. It was said that when a group of arrestees were led from the Bialystok prison along Vashilkover Street to the regional police commander, the guard was attacked and the arrestees freed. This action was carried out by Aron-Velvl, who was then one of the leaders of the Bialystok "battle group."

Sometime later, in 1897, the same Aron-Velvl carried out an attack on a textile manufacturer named Nokhum Kolner, and was sentenced to four years' imprisonment in Irkutsk, Siberia. Aron-Velvl's lover accompanied him in his wanderings and they were married in prison. While in exile, they had children, and the family later returned to Krinek. Boys from Krinek were often called on to help "make the revolution" in other towns. For example, Yankl "Tshayne" was delegated by Yankev Kreplyak to help "make the revolution" in Sislevits. Both of them spoke before the large crowd. Suddenly it was announced that the police were coming. Everyone quickly dispersed, and Yankl Tshayne came back to Krinek. He was one of the most capable agitators.

It was said in town that Yankl Tshayne had gone over to the anarchist movement because he was dissatisfied with the Bund, finding it too moderate. This was brought about by the following coincidence: Yisroel Isser the Slaughterer's took him away to Bialystok and brought him into the ranks of the fighters. There was a rally on Factory Street. Someone came up and handed Yankl "The ABCs of Anarchism." Just then there was a tumult; the police had surrounded the meeting place. They shouted, "So you're one of the rebels from Krinek!" and beat him. Yankl Tshayne tried to take revenge, but the ranks of the Bund weren't ready for it, so he went over to the more extreme anarchists.

The anarchists of Krinek were also active in other cities. In Sidre (a town in the region of Sokolke) anarchists from Krinek attacked the post office. One of them, Dovid the Mason's, was killed by a postal official.

In 1905 an anarchist group that included several boys from Krinek planned an attack on the mayor of Odessa. Active in the preparations were Avrom-Yitskhok the Vilner, Moysheke Rives, and Nyomke Rive the Carpenter's.

The Struggle for the Right to Work

HERSH GOLDMINTS
Belkhatov (Belchatow) yizker-bukh

In the early 1920s, with the revival of the Polish textile industry, the machines in the factories of Belkhatov were set in motion after having sat idle during the entire First World War. The youth of the shtetl, and even some adults, gaped at the machines as if they were magical. Before then the factories had been lifeless; their windows—especially those of Perets Fraytog's factory, which stood on the new road—had been targets for the stones hurled by children playing at war.

The noise of the machinery was something new for most of the young people. Before, we had only heard our parents describing what it was like before the war, when all the factories had been in operation.

The workers who sat at the mechanical looms were Poles, along with a few ethnic Germans. There were no Jewish workers, with the exception of one or two, in the mechanized factories. Jews worked in the factory administration; also, most of those who did the manual preparatory work were Jews. For members of bourgeois or Hasidic families, whose fortunes had declined, becoming a cutter was no shame. Indeed, many young Hasidim did become cutters. A young cutter stood a good chance of obtaining a fine bride with a dowry.

Just as before, Jewish weavers were employed at the hand looms, rather than the mechanical ones. On Pobyanets Street, which was inhabited almost exclusively by Jews, not one house lacked a hand loom. Children whose feet barely reached the pedals were set to work by their parents.

Beginning on Sunday morning (and often on Saturday night immediately following the end of the Sabbath) and continuing until Friday afternoon, one heard the monotonous clatter of the hand looms, accompanied by the tones of a nostalgic love song, a workers' anthem, or simply a hasidic melody, which carried through the open windows out into the street.

The hand-weavers' situation grew worse and worse. They were paid by the piece, and as the boss demanded larger and larger pieces, they had to work longer hours. Sometimes people had to work all through Thursday night in order to have enough money to buy food for the Sabbath.

The Jewish youth, who were already in the habit of frequenting the locals of various left-wing political parties and the textile workers' union, began to envy the legal benefits that the Polish workers enjoyed: eight-hour workdays, health and unemployment insurance, annual vacations, and so forth. The Jewish workers, who had to work halfway through the night, had no legal protection whatsoever, since they worked at home. Furthermore, it grew harder and harder to protest for better pay, because a new type of competition had arisen. These were the peasants of the surrounding villages, who installed looms in their homes and did the work much more cheaply. For them it was an extra source of income, which they did when they weren't busy in the fields; for the Jews it was their only source of income.

Beginning in 1926, on the initiative of the National Council of Jewish Professional Societies, a campaign was undertaken to struggle for the right of Jews to work. The council that started the campaign included representatives not only of the Bund (which had a decisive influence in the National Council), but also of the Labor Zionist parties and the "leftists." We in Belkhatov responded actively to the National Council's initiative. For a few zlotys one could start learning mechanical weaving from one of the local Polish or German weavers. But there was still no work, even for a Jew who knew how to operate the machines. And new troubles arose: claiming that if Jews learned mechanical weaving there would be a rise in unemployment, the textile workers' union discouraged their being taught, even though Jews belonged to the union. The restriction didn't apply to Christian working-class youngsters, because childen of employed weavers automatically had the right to work.

The Jewish members of the textile union began a bitter struggle against this measure, and against the transformation of the union into a guild. I took part in this action as the delegate of the cutters and I was supported by the hand-weavers' delegates. As the representative body of a workers' organization, the Polish majority delegation couldn't come out openly against the Jewish workers, but all sorts of chicanery were employed in order to prevent the Jews from being allowed into the factories.

Meanwhile, several Jewish workers had managed, by means of connections and bribes, to become trained at the mechanical looms. In addition, some Jews had worked the looms earlier. Yekhezkl Birntsvayg, Yisekher Feld, and others saw to it that more and more Jewish workers made the switch from hand to mechanical weaving, but since all of the jobs were occupied and no new factories were being built, most of the trainees moved to Lodz and sought work there.

A new crisis arose in the years 1927 and 1928, when the Jewish factory owners almost entirely ceased giving piecework to Jewish weavers, giving it to the peasants instead. Only a few of the older hand-weavers retained their jobs, through force of time and privilege; the rest, especially the youth, were simply thrown out of work. The situation was further exacerbated by the taxation policies of the Pilsudski government, which forced children of merchants and petty traders to look for factory work. Most of these were cutters, and those who were related to the factory owners were given jobs at the expense of the previous workers. In certain cases the expelled workers were even given severance pay.

In response to all this, attempts were made to organize the remaining Jewish hand-weavers, and to convince the peasant weavers to charge higher prices so as not to compete with the Jews. Unfortunately, the crisis in the textile industry in

1928 ruined our attempts to resolve the differences between the peasants and the Jewish weavers.

In 1930 M. Zhukhovsky built a large factory and brought about 130 mechanical looms from Pobyanets. We began to intervene in order to have Jewish workers employed as well. The manufacturer agreed, on one condition: the Jews were not to work Sabbaths or Jewish holidays, and on Friday they were to work only the morning shift. After long negotiations, the Christian workers agreed to work only the afternoon shift on Fridays and to let the Jews work the morning shift. Thus the Christian workers also benefited from the Sabbath day: the Jewish workers had no choice but to agree to all of the conditions, although they lost six hours of work every week. Finally, good relations were established between the Christian and Jewish workers.

Meanwhile new winds were blowing from Lodz. The Polish professional unions, which were dominated by the National Workers' Party, began to agitate against the employment of Jewish workers, and even went out on strike over this issue.

Good relations between Polish and Jewish workers prevailed for a long time in Belkhatov. Jewish delegates were elected alongside Poles, and we conducted economic and political actions together, because we were under the jurisdiction of the central office of the professional unions in Lodz. But bit by bit anti-Semitic influences became visible in the ranks of the Polish workers, some of whom were reluctant to accept the idea that Jews were also to be employed in the factories. Anti-Semitic agitators began to appear in Belkhatov, attacking the unified socialist spirit that reigned there, and it didn't take long for them to bring about tragic results. One day the Polish majority in the union passed a resolution saying that every worker had to work the standard eight-hour day. In other words, the Polish workers were no longer required to work for the Jews on the Sabbath, even though they received special wages for doing so. Furthermore, the Friday shifts were no longer to be switched to allow Jewish workers to work mornings only. If Jews wouldn't work on the Sabbath, the machines were to stand idle. Of course, many Jewish workers would have been willing to work on the Sabbath, but the Orthodox Jewish manufacturers would under no circumstances agree to this, nor would they allow the machines to stop.

At the initiative of the Bundist party committee, a meeting of all Jewish mechanical weavers was called. All of the Jewish workers' parties in Belkhatov sent representatives. After discussing the anti-Semitic actions of the executive council of the textile union, in which Jews had long been loyal and active members, it was decided to withhold union dues for the time being, to renew the effort to establish Jews in mechanical jobs, and to obtain equal rights for Jews and Christians in every respect.

These resolutions were immediately announced to the union executive and to the Jewish manufacturers, and a committee was elected to lead the campaign.

The members of the committee were Yekhezkl Birntsvayg, Moshkovitsh, Yisekher Feld, M. Yakubovitsh, Gedalye Shtayn, and the writer of these lines. The situation was very tense. The main struggle was conducted in Zhukhovsky's factory, where mostly Jewish workers were employed.

Thus several suspenseful weeks passed. The anti-Semitic agitators spread propaganda saying that Jews wanted to destroy the eight-hour day; meanwhile, we began an educational campaign among the more class-conscious workers. With great effort we succeeded, and the factories remained open. On the one hand we warned the Polish workers that under no circumstances would we allow ourselves to be pushed out of the factories; on the other hand, we argued that the maintenance of the previously established conditions was in the common interest of all the workers. The conflict continued for quite some time, but seeing our determination to defend our right to work, the Polish delegates eventually announced that they would accept our demands. Thus ended in Belkhatov a chapter of the struggle for the right to work of the Jewish working class.

The Jewish workers of Belkhatov continued in the avant-garde of the struggle for better working conditions. Under their influence, the textile workers of Belkhatov took part in several demonstrations against the prevailing political terror in Poland, and even on behalf of the rights of the Jewish population. In addition, several political actions were conducted in common, including those during the Vienna events of 1932 (the workers' revolution against the Dollfuss regime), during the Pshitik affair, against the institution of separate seating for Jewish students in Polish high schools, and in various other instances. True, the black shadows of anti-Semitic propaganda more than once attempted to poison the peace among the workers, but in Belkhatov, thanks to the determination of the Jewish workers, it rarely had much success.

Light and Shadow

REYZL TSEBER
Sefer ha-zikaron le-kehilat Khelm (Chelm)

Which one of us does not remember the wide Lubliner Street that ran from the Rayvitser forest, through the suburb of Pulikhanke, to the Hrubyeshover forest: Jews and Jewish life swarmed in the central street and the streets nearby. The Jewish businesses were located there: the stock market and the famous "ring" of seventy Jewish stores, which hugged the small marketplace, flanked by the Jewish butcher shops. All around stretched streets inhabited entirely by Jews.

I remember the spring of 1927. Reports flew around the town that the Radom train station was going to be transferred to Khelm. The town administration decided to build the necessary buildings on the open areas next to Hrubyeshover Street and Town Hall, and to improve the roads leading from the railroad offices to the station. The people of Khelm hoped that the transfer of the Radom station to Khelm would bring thousands of new residents and improve the town's economic situation. They hoped for business, work, and the improvement of Jewish livelihoods.

When summer came, several construction engineers along with architects and contractors arrived in Khelm, and work was begun on a major scale. Thanks to the construction work, many Jewish laborers and businessmen prospered. The Jewish Merchants' Bank, an agency of the "Joint,"* grew quickly in assets and membership. At the same time a petty traders' bank was founded. Jewish cultural life developed apace. Two Yiddish papers—the *Khelemer shtime* and the *Khelemer vokhnblat*—appeared regularly, three Yiddish libraries increased their holdings, and the best Yiddish theater groups and lecturers performed frequently.

The Jewish youth of Khelm went to Yiddish primary schools and local high schools, such as the Tarbut† Gymnasium, the trade school, the Yiddish-Polish Gymnasium, the teachers' seminary and others. Many continued their studies at the universities of Warsaw and Lemberg.

In the course of several years the railroad headquarters were built, and the town had a substantial new quarter.

Owing to the intervention of the Radom City Council in the *Sejm* (Polish parliament), which opposed the transfer of the administration to Khelm, the town administration was transferred to Khelm from Bidgoshtsh.‡ The officers were real Nazis. They moved into the beautiful, comfortable new buildings. Along with them came Christian merchants who settled right in the Jewish center of town, and did great damage to the Jewish businessmen of Khelm.

The economic condition of the Jews of Khelm began to grow steadily worse, and the tax burden became unbearable. The newly appointed tax commissioner imposed such heavy taxes on the Jewish population that several people had to go out of business. Petty traders and artisans suffered especially severely. The Jewish banks were affected as well; in 1935 the merchants' bank failed. As the crisis deepened, many young Jews left for Warsaw and other places in search of livelihoods.

In 1937 the situation grew even worse, and Jews in Khelm no longer felt free and secure. It became dangerous to walk along Christian streets at night. Pickets were set up around Jewish businesses, dissuading Christian customers from partronizing them.

---

*Officially known as the American Jewish Joint Distribution Committee, it provided, among many other relief activities, small loans at no or nominal interest to the needy.

†A Hebrew educational and cultural organization providing Hebrew language instruction and written material.

‡Bydgoszcz (formerly Bromberg), a town in western Poland outside the Yiddish-speaking sphere. Until the First World War the town was part of Germany.

Nineteen hundred thirty-nine was the worst year under the Polish fascist regime. Several months before the awful war began, bitter anti-Jewish edicts were announced, which were particularly hard on the Jews of Khelm. An urban renewal program was put into effect, the so-called "beautification action." The Khelm City Council, which joined this effort, decided that its first task would be to tear down all of the poor Jewish houses. The "ring" of Jewish stores on which hundreds of Jews depended for their livelihood also fell victim to "urbanization."

The order to tear down the "ring" threw the Jews of Khelm into a state of depression. Attempts were made to have the order canceled: delegations went to see the councilmen, the president of the council, and others, but without success.

While the attempts at intercession were in progress, the town firemen were ordered to destroy the roofs of the Jewish stores and to remove the "ring." As moral compensation, the council decided to give each Jewish businessman a symbolic zloty. This was a painful insult and a great humiliation.

The Jewish Porters of Warsaw

BEN KHAYIM
Pinkes Varshe (Warszawa)

Everyone who has lived in Warsaw is well acquainted with the many facets of the porter's occupation. In every country there are a large number of people who earn their living bearing loads. This was true in Poland, too, and especially in Warsaw. The means of transportation were underdeveloped there, and in order to move goods from one part of the city to another, or to load merchandise onto wagons, old-fashioned methods were employed. This work was performed by the porters in various ancient ways: carrying merchandise on their backs, under their arms, in their hands, or pushing or pulling small handcarts to which they were harnessed like horses.

Several tens of thousands of men, both Jews and Christians, served as porters in Warsaw. There were more Jews than Christians, however, because most of the commerical enterprises lay in Jewish hands, and Jews were more likely to be employed by them. For the Jewish merchants, it was simpler and more comfortable "to deal with a Jew than a non-Jew."

The more Jewish business developed, the more the functions and numbers of the Jewish porters expanded. There were those who worked at the railroad station unloading goods from freight cars onto carts and wagons. The coachmen themselves only drove their loads from one place to another, and did not concern themselves with loading and unloading. There were those porters who unloaded goods from the carts and carried them into stores. Those were the locally famous "back-porters," who bore the heavy crates that arrived from various cities in Poland, especially from the "Polish Manchester," Lodz. The crates sometimes weighed hundreds of pounds each. These porters would walk up to the wagons, bend over, and the coachmen would set the loads on their backs.

Another type of porter carried smaller loads, also on his back, from one store to another or from neighborhood to neighborhood. Those were porters of the second category. There were also those who transported smaller loads to distant parts of the city, and the handcart porters who moved items such as coal, wood, potatoes, fruit, and the like. These last were known as "coal-porters." A large number of porters worked in the large slaughterhouses and in the smaller poultry-slaughterhouses. These last considered themselves equal to the "back-porters," and the two groups wanted to lord it over all the porters, which caused continuous disputes.

The Christian workers were concentrated in a few specific areas, such as the area around the railroad station and in the larger slaughterhouses. Relations between the Christian and Jewish porters, especially among the "back-porters" and the slaughterhouse workers, were good, despite the antagonism caused by the power struggles. But good relations were less the result of workers' solidarity than of the brute strength of the Jewish porters, which the gentile porters sometimes felt on their own backs.

This is how the porters' work territories were divided up: the city was divided into stations, each station taking in several streets. Porters in a given station were allowed to work in that station only. The porters at each station chose someone out of their ranks to serve as treasurer; and after the end of the business day, they divided the total income. The price of work was based on the number of loads and on the weight of each load. The porters of each station took turns canvassing their territory, looking out to see where deliveries were being made. The rest sat in the taverns and restaurants, waiting until there was work to do. Work was done in rotation: while some worked, others would watch, and at the next job, they would exchange places. But all of them were present at the worksite. Virtually every station had one man who was used only when very heavy loads came in, which only he could carry. The rest were quite willing to save him for these special tasks. More or less the same organization of labor prevailed among the other categories of porters.

The chief stations at which the back-porters worked were located near the major Jewish enterprises: at the corner of Nalewki and Gesia, No. 2 Nalewki at Simon's Passage, Franciszkanska and Bonifraterska at Jaruszewski's Courtyard, Twarda and Grzybowski Place, on Krochmalna Street, Grzybowska Street and Twarda, at the Iron Gate, the Pociejow area, the Mirowska Market, Janasz Courtyard, on Przechodnia Street and Ptasia Street.

The people who served as porters stemmed from the poorer classes of Jewish Warsaw. They were children of poor storekeepers, petty artisans, and peddlers.

They had been raised in poverty, without sufficient food or rest. They had had a scant few years of schooling in kheyder or in the philanthropic *talmud-toyres*, such as the one at 63 Nowy Mila Street, which was famed in Warsaw for graduating complete ignoramuses. For these children, who had been raised in the street, it was very hard to get and keep a regular job; they had not learned any craft, and as déclassé proletarians, their only chance of employment was as porters. From their life in the street, they had come into contact with various underworld types. Thieves, pimps, hustlers, bullies, persons involved in various sorts of shady deals and illegal transactions, and "strong men"—men who were actually physically strong—all mixed together. Among the last group were porters, especially back-porters, with whom the underworld had to reckon.

The Jewish labor movement, which had shown its strength in the revolutionary uprising of 1905, counted among its tasks the displacement of the underworld and the recruitment of the porters into the movement. To some extent, the workers had been convinced of victory in the years 1904–1905, when the underworld was dealt a severe blow. But on account of the porters' constant contact with the criminal element, and on account of the fact that the workers' movement was illegal after 1905, the attempt to organize the porters was not entirely successful.

Success finally came only after the First World War, when the labor movement took on a new character. Legal trade unions were instituted and every political party, Jewish and non-Jewish, attempted to gain influence over these unions. A porters' union was created, which largely succeeded in drawing individual porters away from the influences of the "street" and in making them dependable members of the labor movement.

Still, it wasn't entirely possible to make class-conscious workers out of them. They remained under two competing influences, the labor movement and the underworld. But another reason, perhaps more crucial than this, was also a factor. This was the use of both Jewish and Christian porters by the various political parties as a physical force in the continuous struggle among the parties between the two world wars. Different groups of porters were "kept" by the political parties that had managed to win their support. This manipulation by the political parties led to splits and antagonisms between the various branches and categories of porters. Instead of the solidarity that should prevail between those who work in the same job, there was animosity. It grew into a vicious circle: if the back-porters, for instance, were influenced by one party, it was enough to make another group of porters throw its support to a competing party. No union shifted back and forth as frequently in its party loyalties as did the porters' union.

Between 1919 and 1929, for instance, the back-porters wandered from the Communists to the "Unity" Left-Zionists to the Bund. In 1929 they went over to the right wing of the PPS (Polish Socialist party), and later on they split three ways, with one group going to the Bund and one to the Communists. When the back-porters belonged to the Bund, the coal-porters belonged to the Communists. Of course, the porters became aware that the parties were eager to avail themselves of the porters' strength in the interparty struggle. As a result, it became somewhat accurate to say that the porters were not so much influenced by the parties, as that they laid their own personal stamp on party work. This was especially true of the parties' battle squads, which resulted in a number of ugly incidents for the parties in particular and for the movement in general.

What did their strength consist of? The porters displayed a good deal of wantonness and hostility. They wanted everyone to see and sense their bravery and to fear them; they wanted their peers to serve them and help them realize their ambitions. In this fashion groups arose led by self-crowned kings, whose authority derived from the boldness and abandon they had displayed in brawls. These groups constantly struggled between themselves for the upper hand. Often two groups would make an agreement, which would be sealed with a toast and a plate of roast goose. Other confrontations resulted in street battles, which concluded with several participants being led off to the hospital, and the rest going in for a drink and a meal.

There were various issues to be fought over: the desire to prove one's own group to be the strongest; attempts to get a better station, when it seemed that another group was making more money than one's own; because of a girlfriend that a member of one group had stolen from a member of another group; and finally, under the influence of the parties, because of the struggle for political dominance.

Several incidents are characteristic of the physical strength of the porters, and of their dominance of street life. During an anti-Semitic attack by the "Nara" youth (in the supposedly "democratic" Poland of the Pilsudski years) in the streets around the Iron Tower (Twarda, Grzybowska, Zabia, and Granciczna), the back-porters of that neighborhood received the hooligans with such a "welcome" that several of the "Nara" heroes had to be taken to the hospital, while others spread the word not to come back to the Jewish quarter and pick fights with Jews. Thus the back-porters showed their physical strength in the struggle against anti-Semitism in Warsaw.

The following episode in their class struggle against their employers is interesting. In 1928 they were organized into the union, which had its offices at Szczesliwa number 9. At that time all of the divisions of the porters' unions belonged to the Central General Polish Transport Union, which included every transport worker in the country, from railroad employees to handcart porters.

Shaye-Yidl was a famous man at that time: he was the "tsar" of the porters. He was a quiet, personable man, with a smiling face; it was hard to imagine him raising his hand against anyone.

Once there was a porters' strike at the Towarowa Station, where the freight trains on the major lines pulled in. The strike was aimed at the wholesalers of manufactured goods on Gesia Street, who controlled the unloading of merchandise from the freight cars onto the wagons. The merchants resisted the twofold payment for unloading goods at the station and then again at their stores. They convinced some of the coachmen who brought loads from the station to Gesia Street to unload goods at the station and bring them into the stores themselves. The porters at that station brought the situation to the attention of the union, and the union board immediately delegated Shaye-Yidl and the union secretary to take care of the matter. When Shaye-Yidl arrived at the freight yard, the coachmen had already unloaded half of a freight car. Shaye-Yidl approached the non-Jewish drivers and explained to them that the work belonged to the porters. The non-Jewish drivers, who knew him well (and actually called him by his Yiddish name, Shaye-Yidl), asked him to let them at least finish unloading the one car. Calm and smiling, Shaye-Yidl answered that they would have to reload what they had taken out of the car, and seal the doors back up. The coachmen complained to no avail; Shaye-Yidl simply asked them whether they thought the porters would so easily allow their work to be taken away. At this, the drivers and their assistants reloaded the merchandise and called over a railroad employee, who managed with some difficulty to reseal the freight car. This convinced Shaye-Yidl's companion, the union secretary, that Shaye-Yidl really was the porters' "tsar." But he still didn't entirely understand the source of the authority that had caused the coachmen and their assistants to obey Shaye-Yidl's orders. The merchants of Gesia Street likewise had no choice but to obey Shaye-Yidl and pay the porters of their local station.

Even though physical violence was avoided in the course of strikes and other union actions—simply because the union employed its authority to prevent the use of terrorist methods—and the influence of the union on the porters themselves and on their employers continued to grow, it was nevertheless difficult for the union leaders to prevent battles when there were disputes between individuals or groups of porters. One such dispute took place between the back-porters and a group of poultry porters, who belonged to the same union with offices at 9 Szczesliwa Street. One of the porters died, and all of his fellow porters came to the funeral on Sapiezynska Street. While they were waiting for the funeral cortege to arrive, they traded some words, feeling strong since they were all present. It developed into a brawl, despite the intervention of the union representatives.

Shaye-Yidl was sitting in a cafe on a side street near Bonifraterska, waiting for the funeral. The news of the fight was brought to him. Then the union officers saw why he was the "tsar": a tiger ran out of the cafe in the form of a man, and began striking right and left with his fists, feet, head, and entire body. He hugged three or four opponents close to him—who were no dwarfs themselves—and didn't let go of them. He just kept on hitting them, and they didn't have the strength to tear themselves loose. Fortunately, the funeral procession arrived. Then Shaye-Yidl released his opponents, and the funeral proceeded calmly, as though nothing had happened. Some of the mourners, following the cortege, wiped blood from their eyes. Shaye-Yidl's face was once again friendly and smiling. When the procession had gone a short distance, a large group of Warsaw police arrived, who stayed with the funeral as far as the cemetery. (The Warsaw police invariably arrived when a brawl among porters was already over.) Probably the issue was settled in a tavern after the funeral, because the two groups got along very well afterward.

Another interesting episode occurred during that same year, in connection with interparty struggles. The right-wing PPS [Polish Socialist party] had until that time been very powerful among the Christian workers, and had also had influence among the meat porters, the railroad porters, the coachmen, and others. They were unhappy with the powerful position the back-porters enjoyed within the Jewish union movement, and sought ways to win the back-porters away from Bundist influence. This wasn't very difficult to accomplish, because there were always candidates for "tsar" to replace Shaye-Yidl. One such individual was Itshe "Zavukh," who made a secret deal with the PPS to hand over the entire porters' union to them. He managed to win over a certain group who resented Shaye-Yidl's control, and there developed an open rivalry. One day both forces were mobilized: on one hand the PPS under the leadership of their battle squad with the famous leader Lokutek in the front rank, and all of the Christian unions backing Itshe Zavukh's group; and on the other hand the Bundist battle squad led by their champion "Bernard" and by Shaye-Yidl, at the head of all the porters who had remained with the Bund. The muster took place in a large courtyard on Ptasia Street among carts filled with crates of fruit. That's where the Bund gathered; the opposing "army" had its stronghold in a similar courtyard on a neighboring street. Both groups waited for the other to attack.

But the leaders of both groups realized that it couldn't be allowed to come to an actual battle, or a terrible bloodbath would result. There were discussions between the leaders of the two "battalions," and party representatives restrained the "commanders." The matter ended without a war. Itshe Zavukh and his group went over to the PPS and gradually took over the entire union. However, Shaye-Yidl and a small group, without an army, remained loyal to the Bund. Thus the porters of Warsaw, and in particular the back-porters, showed their own form of strength within the life of the Jewish community of Warsaw.

It's hard to believe that the Warsaw porters, especially the back-porters, failed to play any role in the Warsaw ghetto or in the uprising itself. But as much as the writer of these lines has searched through materials on the ghetto, he has been unable to find anything about the participation of the porters in the struggle against the Nazis, whether before or during the revolt, except for a small note in Ber Mark's book, *Ruins Retell*, about a small "wild" group of porters (meaning that they didn't belong to the general Jewish resistance organization) who took part in the uprising.

Did the porters, too, allow themselves to be seduced by Nazi lies about being sent off "to work," and thus murdered with the rest of the six million Jews? As of now, we lack material from which to learn about the role of the porters in the Warsaw ghetto.

When Anti-Semitism Raged

YISROEL VAYSMAN
Yizker-bukh fun der Zhelekhover (Zelechow) yidisher kehile

My grandfather's house stood between two wealthy homes: on one side, Sharf-harts's house, pompous and imposing as befitted the nouveau riche, and on the other side, Ber Eyger's house, whose isolation and mysteriousness filled us with the same fear as did the cemetery a bit further on. Our house, although still possessing traces of its former aristocratic grandeur, was nevertheless typical. My pious grandfather was deeply attached to the simple Jew, the artisan, but he couldn't stand the apostate upstarts with their unions and their Bund.

The personal sense of tragedy that my grandfather suffered when the Bund opened its first chapter in Zhelekhov, right across from our window, is sharply engraved in my memory. My hasidic grandfather considered the misfortune to be a punishment from God personally directed at himself. I only wish the curses he and other Jews flung at the apostates had befallen those who later slaughtered our families. I remember that when the Bund used to hold a meeting or a small performance, my grandfather drove his grown children as well as myself into the house, to prevent us from seeing and hearing what was going on there. The impression remained with me that my grandfather Hirsh Perets saw in the apostates a danger to his version of Judaism, which he saw as the only way to ensure the existence of the Jewish people.

When I think about the extermination of those near to me, of the Jews of Zhelekhov and of the six million, I see before my eyes images of Jewish persecutions, which prepared the ground for their ultimate extermination.

During my childhood, I attended Shloyme Khantshe's kheyder. It was during the First World War. Two German soldiers burst into the kheyder as our teacher was napping. On the teacher's feet the Germans saw a pair of good boots, which his son had given him when he went into the army. The soldiers quickly began pulling the boots off Shloyme's feet. A bottle of water stood near the bed; our teacher, weak though he was, grabbed it and struck one of the soldiers in the face, making blood flow. We, the "holy flock," didn't remain silent, but set up an alarm. People came running, and the soldiers left, leaving the boots behind.

Another anti-Semitic incident befell the same Shloyme Khantshe's: a gang of drunk Polish soldiers came into the kheyder and demanded that he give them horses. Otherwise they threatened to shoot us. One of the children managed to escape, shouting that out teacher was being beaten. Dashkevitsh came and led the rowdy gang out, promising to get them horses.

A final incident that I will never forget was the going-away present that Pilsudski's soldiers gave me and my mother in 1920. We were on our way to Warsaw to pick up our American visas. It was the time of Pilsudski's campaign against the Soviet Union. Together with dozens or perhaps hundreds of people, we wandered around Sobolev for weeks waiting for a train, because all of the trains were occupied bearing wounded back from the battlefield. Once a train stopped in the middle of the night. A door opened, and those inside called out in Polish: "Come in, come in, there's room for everybody." Several women, as well as my mother and myself, packed in. As soon as the door closed, we saw whose hands we had fallen into. The car was full of soldiers. As soon as the train began to move, they began to bully the women. I was picked up like a herring, and someone asked for suggestions of what to do with the "little *Zhidek.*"

It didn't require much thought. "Throw him out!" they all shouted; the door was opened, and out I went. My mother tore herself free of them and also jumped. Fortunately, the tracks were laid out on a raised embankment, and we fell into a field. In the morning, a peasant who passed by took us to Garvolin. What happened to the other women and to our baggage, God only knows.

Those outrageous acts that took place in anti-Semitic, reactionary Poland were hardly isolated cases. They happened not only in Zhelekhov, but all over Poland, where the anti-Semitism of Pilsudski and the National Democrats spread. I will always be filled with bitter enmity to that Poland, which paved the way for Majdanek and Treblinka.

Sports Clubs and Self-Defense

BORUKH YISMAKH
Sefer Vishkov (Wyszkow)

It was in 1925 that the idea of founding a sports club in town was born. Of course, this club was to be only one link in a chain of social organizations, such as morning schools, evening courses, and trade unions. The latter had begun in the lumber industry, and then spread to many other trades. There was also a movement to build up libraries. Virtually every party and organization took upon itself the initiative to start its own library. Of course, the selection wasn't that large; but people read nevertheless. The most competent member of each group was chosen to be the librarian. No book could be taken out for more than fifteen days. When a reader returned a book in exchange for another one, the librarian had the right to test him to see whether he had indeed read the book, and if so, whether he had understood it. Passionate discussions were frequently held about the hero of this or that book. The most frequently read books were those of Sholem Aleichem, Y. L. Peretz, Avrom Reisen, Perets Hirshbein, and H. D. Nomberg. We, young readers just out of kheyder, loved reading the Yiddish writers.

More advanced readers requested the works of Tolstoy, Dostoyevsky, and others. Naturally, there weren't enough copies to go around, and we often had to wait several weeks before receiving a book. The librarian suffered on account of this, since he was held responsible.

I've begun with the libraries, since the first article in the statutes of the three sports clubs that were founded then concerned the establishment of libraries.

The movement began with two clubs: Maccabi, consisting of the bourgeois element in town, with the active participation of Hechalutz* and Hashomer Hatzair;† and the united workers' sports club, Skala—although the unity only lasted for a few weeks. The main cause of dispute was ideological. All of the members of the Left-labor Zionist group left the Skala club, and immediately founded the third sports club, Gwiazda (Star). Then the spirit of competition took hold. Every club organized a soccer team, and the matches made the life of the town lively. At first the matches were only between local teams, and none won all the time. I don't have to tell you the interest that the matches aroused in town, since each victory meant "a victory of ideas" for the team that won.

I've mentioned the political affiliations of the Maccabi and the Gwiazda. The Skala club belonged to the Communists, to the Jewish division known as the Yevsektsye. They also attracted a certain element, which was politically undecided, under the slogan, "If you're a worker, you belong in our club." Thus all of the clubs were transformed into party fortresses. Although the struggle between the different Jewish clubs was bitter, certain people in them had a broader perspective. When one of the teams had a match in a different town, it borrowed players from the other teams. There were also instances of betrayal. When, for example, Gwiazda had a match against a bourgeois club from a different city and borrowed a player or two, the latter deliberately played poorly, in order that their political comrades might win. But things were different when a Polish club challenged one of ours to a match. Then Maccabi and Gwiazda were in complete solidarity, aiming to play their hearts out and win. There was also a period when two of the clubs agreed to do calisthenics together. The only club that had a whole network

*A Zionist organization whose members studied Hebrew and gained experience in manual labor in preparation for emigration to Palestine.
†A Zionist-socialist youth movement that prepared its members for settlement on kibbutzim.

of sporting groups was Gwiazda. They even had uniforms for every group. It was impressive to see the whole club march from its clubhouse to the gymnastics field. Our parents didn't like it; some of them even tried to spread rumors. Yet when we explained to them the importance of organized self-defense groups, and that gymnastics helped us develop our muscles, they sadly kept their silence.

Two moments from that exciting period remain in my memory. One is the day when Gwiazda (nearly the entire group), consisting of the men's section, the women's section, and the youth section, all in their own uniforms and bearing their sports equipment, marched from the center of town to the railroad station, from where they traveled to Poplava Station, and finally, in full uniform, into the town of Rozhan. Our arrival in Rozhan set off a virtual revolution. It was a pious town, which wasn't used to seeing gangs of young men, young women, and children, who were dressed like soldiers but weren't soldiers. The Jews ran to their rabbi to ask what was to be done about us. The rabbi decided that since it was just before the Sabbath, we were to be given a warm reception. We enjoyed ourselves that Saturday and Sunday. Monday evening, when we returned, a large crowd awaited us, and our march into town was a magnificent demonstration of Jewish strength and organization.

The second moment was when the Thirteenth Army Regiment, which was famous in Pultusk for its soccer team made up of officers, challenged Gwiazda to a match in Pultusk. The parents of our members forbade them from going. The regiment was known to be made up of the worst sort of anti-Semites. Knowing that we weren't going to grant them an easy victory, people frankly feared for the lives of our players. Yet the challenge had to be accepted. After a series of meetings, in which most of the Jews in town participated, it was decided that we would go and let them win, without disgracing ourselves.

There were also moments when the Jewish clubs had tasks in common. It was the custom in Vishkov (it is difficult to say when the custom began) for nearly all of the Jewish youth of the town to come to the marketplace and stroll back and forth in couples and groups. We chatted, debated, and gossiped about this or that. There was plenty of time. The stroll lasted from nine to eleven o'clock in the evening. The street used to be full of people. The sound of laughter and cheerful voices made the walking pleasant. Apparently, our Polish neighbors couldn't stand this; they hired some street boys, got them drunk, and sent them out to drive us away. When one of these gentiles showed up among the strollers and began shouting "Jews to Palestine!," chaos broke out in the street. People fell down and stepped on each other. In one part of town people ran, and in another part of town people shouted that Jews were being slaughtered. After this sort of panic, the marketplace would remain empty. We became afraid to step out of our houses. This began to happen more and more often. The hired hooligans were reinforced by many volunteers. They enjoyed the game, and they grew bolder each time. One gentile made a thousand Jews run.

The leaders of the Jewish sports clubs decided to get together and organize self-defense. Strong, healthy fellows were chosen to work in pairs. Their first task was to put an end to the panic, make people stop running away on account of one belligerent person, defend Jewish honor, and be on guard against possible serious attacks. And secondly, they were not to permit the delightful custom of Sabbath strolls to be repressed. It was no easy job convincing representatives of the Skala club that the first order of business was to get the hired goons off the street. Most of them were lumber workers who were members of the same union, and Skala had to explain to them not to give up their ideals for a bit of whiskey. We accomplished little along those lines, but the Jews who went out for a walk knew that there were strong hands among them, ready to ward off any attack. There were times when we had to use our fists against hooligans who refused to calm down and go home. Our procedure was to first take them in hand and suggest that they stop, since they were bound to be unsuccessful this time anyway. Sometimes we managed to avoid further struggle; other times we had to punish them, and give them a taste of the water in the gutter, where we left them to sober up.

The anti-Semitic clique didn't desist easily either. If their own forces were small, they recruited police help. Policemen always walked behind them; thus they were the just party, and we were guilty. They began a well-organized campaign against members of the self-defense group. We were warned to choose between leaving the city and a knife in the back. Several young people left, especially for Latin American countries, the only places to which emigration was possible in the years 1929–30.

The situation of the Jews grew worse; the self-defense group had to disband. We were capable of defending ourselves against hooligans, but we were no match for the police. In addition we were threatened with pogroms in retaliation for any kind of self-defense.

The Last Meeting of the Community Council in Kutno

NOSN MOSKOVITSH
Kutno ve-ha-seviva

Dust and cloying heat envelop the city. The trees languish motionless. No hint of a breeze. Only a few passersby hurry, although tired, along the shimmering sidewalk. In the distance the eye catches green pastures beyond the city, and the mirrorlike surface of the river Okhna.

The Tuesday market is ending. Leftover merchandise is already being packed up at both the old market and the new. The portable shops are pulled along on handcarts, in sacks carried on the back, and in crates. The crowd runs home to escape from the August heat.

At the corner of Zamenhof Street appears Moyshe Blank, tall and thin as a *lulav*, with the heavy copper container slung in front of him, shouting forlornly: "*Soda vaser! Woda sodowa!* [Soda Water, Soda water]." His cry is drowned out by the wheels of the horse and wagons passing by, on whose buckboard sits Moyshe Yatshe.

From a different corner the Polotkin brothers hurry home, bearing green-painted boxes on a two-wheeled wagon. They wear white aprons and white caps on their heads, and don't cease shouting: "Ice cream, ice cream."

From different directions the first representatives start arriving for the meeting of the Community Council, which is to take place in the council's own brightly lit meeting hall near the new marketplace, in Shmuel Ash's home. All of the admission cards to the meeting have been distributed, a certain number to each party. People push each other into the "gallery," that is, behind a barrier that separates the public from the Council. Among those eager to see and hear the meeting is Itshele, Pinkhes Dayen's son.

A strange character, this Itshele. Small in stature, he never has any time; he's always hurrying, but he's never busy. His needs are seen to by the community. Religiously inclined, he is full of complaints against the Almighty: Why is there so much injustice and degradation in the world? He doesn't even spare his own father, demanding to know why he wasn't taught a trade. If he had been, he could struggle together with all workers for a better world.

Together with him his neighbor Kletshevsky slips in; he regularly attends the Community Council meetings. He has barely had time to change into his Sabbath clothes after a hard day's work at quilting. This evening he wants to hear the debate over provision in the community budget for various funds dealing with Israel: the Jewish National Fund (*Keren hayesod*), and support for those who are emigrating.

Around the two long tables, which are arranged in the form of an *L*, sit the members, representatives of parties which belong to the Council. Above the presidium hangs a large portrait of Theodor Herzl; next to it, a wall calendar open to August 1939. On the table in front of each councilman lies a copy of the preliminary budget for the year 1940, and a copy of the budget for 1939, all of which have been prepared by the community secretary, Yoel Borovsky.

The keynote speech is delivered by the chairman of the Jewish community in Kutno, Shiye Falts. His well-pressed gray suit and carefully tied cravat make a fine impression. Falts begins to list the many proposals for various religions, secular, cultural and social needs such as the free talmud toyre, the Beys Yankev girls' school, "Am Ha-sefer," the V. Medem Folk School, the Y. L. Peretz and

Ahad Ha'am libraries, YIVO, TOZ, sports societies, and so forth. The speech presents a multicolored picture of diverse activities.

As soon as the chairman has finished his speech, the Bund representative, A. M. Silberberg, takes the floor. Discussing the proposed figures, he points out that some of them are altogether unrealistic. He raises the suspicion that taxes will have to be raised, which will be very hard on the masses.

Yet Meyer Lentshitsky bravely defends the proposed budget. The constantly depressed councilman, with his thin face and gray eyes, is forthright, even aggressive. Immediately after him Leyzer Zandberg, his fellow in the General Zionist party, adds his support to Falts's presentation.

Then the Orthodox councilmen, Fishl Zandberg and Yoel Shtaynfeld, take the floor. Both are of the opinion that the subsidies for religious needs are too small. To support their claim, they point out that other cities provide much larger subsidies to religious institutions.

Leybish Kam fumes and seethes. His eyes dart, his hands gesticulate, and his mouth retorts to the previous speakers' complaints: in fact, the community spends too much for religious purposes, even though part of the population does benefit.

The representative of the Labor Zionists and Zionist Youth, Shor, is the final speaker at the first (and last!) budget meeting of the Kutno community council.

The clock strikes midnight. A large moon rises in the sky, illuminating the sleeping city. From somewhere comes the sound of a dog barking, which is echoed by other dogs barking, and then it disappears. In that nocturnal stillness, many of us were thinking of the approaching storm.

The meeting was never continued.

Townspeople

The Blind Cantor

MOTL ROSENTHAL

Tshekhanovits (Ciechanowiec); mehoz Bialystok sefer edut ve-zikaron

Tshekhanovits was known as a shtetl that loved cantors. The local cantor, Reb Dovid, who was also the kosher slaughterer and a great scholar, devoted more attention to the treatise he was writing about kosher slaughter than to his cantorial duties.

He only sang in the synagogue on the High Holy Days, and on rare occasions he and his choirboys (or as others called them, his "posts," because they stood still so long) performed a new version of the prayer "*Shema Yisroel*" or of "We Will Honor Thee." In general, everything he sang belonged to his old repertoire. The audience, who knew all of his tunes inside and out, would quietly join in.

The older townspeople were quite satisfied with the cantor, because they didn't have to pay him much. In addition they felt that cantors like him were few and far between: when he prayed on Rosh Hashanah or Yom Kippur, the walls of the synagogue would tremble. But the younger congregants, particularly those who considered themselves musical connoisseurs, were dissatisfied and longed for a modern cantor.

From time to time a cantor and his choir would visit the shtetl for the Sabbath, and the town became lively. If the cantor was well-received, everyone would go around for days speaking of nothing but the cantor and his choir: "Now *that's* a cantor! *That's* what I call a choir!" And no one was more excited than the self-designated connoisseurs.

An entire winter passed by without a single performance by a cantor. Everyone was longing to hear something new.

One Friday morning after Passover, the storekeepers slowly and sleepily began to open their stores and set out their merchandise. Some just stood in their doorways and yawned, looking out into the street.

A flock of doves strolled undisturbed around the marketplace, pecking at the grain that had fallen out of the horses' feedbags at yesterday's market. All at once, they rose into the air and flew off with their wings fluttering. The clip-clop of horses' hooves against the hard stone pavement had warned them of the approach of a wagon, which stopped in front of Meyer-Tevye Shenker's inn. The coachman snapped his whip, entered the tavern, and announced that he had brought a blind cantor with four choirboys for the Sabbath.

In the wagon sat the cantor with two older boys and two younger. Meyer-Tevye came out, offered them a friendly "shalom," and invited them to come in.

Meyer-Tevye happily called out to the storekeeper Moyshe-Yosl, who stood looking into the street: "Moyshe-Yosl! We have a blind cantor with a choir for the Sabbath!" The news quickly carried across the entire shtetl, and the town waited impatiently for sunset.

The new prayer house was packed. The doors and window were open, and the sweet singing of the cantor and his choir carried through the prayer house into everyone's heart.

When the service was over, everyone pressed toward the eastern wall in order to have a look at the cantor and his choir. With considerable effort, the *shames* managed to convince the crowd to go home and let him close up.

By the time the crowd reached their homes, it was quite dark. The candles in the houses had almost gone out.

In the morning the cantor sang in the synagogue. During the Torah reading, people started streaming in from all of the prayer houses; some had already eaten and some had only made *kidesh*. People stood around in groups talking about the cantor and his choir. The largest number of people crowded around the teacher Shloyme Yagnik and the weaver Khayim Dovkes, because they were considered to be great experts on cantors.

The shames banged on the podium, shouting "Let the reading continue! It's a desecration of the Name!" But the crowd paid no attention to him, and continued to listen to the opinions of the two experts, whose praise knew no bounds.

It only became quiet when the cantor resumed praying, and the congregation listened as though bewitched to the sweet and heartfelt tones which poured out of the singers' mouths.

Long after the blind cantor had gone away, and despite the many cantors who came and went after him, his melodies continued to resound in the ears of those who had heard him but one time.

Passing by a house where workers sat at their shoemakers' workbenches, one could hear them singing the blind cantor's tune to the prayer *"Ose shalom."* And Shayele Klopot, a worker who could imitate the blind cantor down to the last little ornament, would stand up, place his hand against his throat, and sing as the blind cantor once had sung.

And the shoemakers, striking hammer against sole in rhythm, sang along: "Bring, bring, bring peace, goodness, and blessing."

Reb Moyshe-Yudl, the Traveling Tailor

OYZER SHEVAKH
Pyesk (Piaski) ve-Most; sefer yizkor

When Moyshe-Yudl the itinerant tailor woke up on that wintry Sunday morning, he didn't know that it was to be a lucky day for him; he didn't even dream that a gift had been prepared for him in Heaven. As was his habit, he performed his ablutions, packed up his tools, said "good morning" to his wife, and set off.

The cold morning air nipped at his ears and nose, the untrodden snow was soft under his feet. When he came to the Zaretsh well, he stood awhile and considered which way to proceed. To the right was the path to Bolovitsh; to the left was the way to the village of Turi. He had no time to lose, because his feet were already beginning to freeze. Without anyone's advice he set off for the compound which served the nobleman's palace at Bolovitsh. Moyshe-Yudl hoisted his heavy pack filled with pieces of leather, and began humming his morning prayers. The snow creaked under his boots, and it grew colder and colder. The fields lay covered by a pure white sheet. Snowdrifts blocked the road, making it difficult and dangerous to walk, and his burden became heavier with each step.

The traveling tailor's livelihood was a difficult one, requiring him to be away from home and from his wife and children all week. He wandered from one gentile home to another, getting by on herring and a piece of bread, sleeping on bedbug-ridden mattresses. A week's toil resulted in a few *gulden* or payment in kind—some chickpeas, beans, or potatoes. The daughters, no evil eye, were growing and turning into women; Khane the eldest was a beauty who was already married to a fine young man, and both of them wanted to become pioneers in the land of Israel. But there was no money for steamship tickets, and how could he allow them to go off without proper clothing and equipment? The smaller children had to be sent to kheyder, which meant tuition, shoes, a Bible and other books. God alone knew where Moyshe-Yudl would find the money for everything.

Thus Moyshe-Yudl prayed, asking God to have mercy on him and send him a good customer, so that he wouldn't have to be ashamed in public and would be able to obtain everything he needed for his family.

The barking of dogs awoke him from his reveries. He had already reached the compound at Bolovitsh. "Get out of here," he began to shout at the dogs. Fortunately the watchman heard him and drove the dogs away. Moyshe-Yudl entered the hut, barely managing to warm himself a bit.

He heard a voice: "*Zhidek* Moyshe! Come out, the lord is calling for you!" Moyshe-Yudl despaired, thinking that the lord was going to drive him out and set the dogs on him. "Faster, Moyshe, the lord is calling!" Brokenhearted and fearful, Moyshe-Yudl stood up and went out of the peasant house. His head bent, he approached the manor house, which stood among lofty pine trees in the forest, covered with snow. Windows hung with heavy curtains and illuminated by crystal chandeliers winked out from inside. He had never seen such luxury. The guard led him into the vestibule and told him to wait.

In less than a quarter hour, the lord himself came in. He was a tall man with a long, pointed mustache, a brown beard combed to two points, a high brow, and angry eyes. "Zhidek," he said to Moyshe-Yudl, "do you have some money? I'm playing cards with some friends of mine, and I need more money to keep playing."

"Yes, your Lordship, I have a bit, and if the lord needs more, I can go right home and get it."

"Good. Go tell Reb Avrom Shevakh the miller, who cuts lumber in my forest, to pay you in trees for the money that you give me." Moyshe-Yudl quickly took out his purse, gave his money to the nobleman, kissed his hand once more, and disappeared.

"Reb Avrom," he said as he ran into our house, "listen to what happened to me, and tell me what to do."

"First of all, here's a thousand rubles," replied my father. "Take them to the nobleman. Here's my sled, it will get you there faster. Pray to God that he doesn't change his mind, and that he continues to lose, and afterward we'll see what we have to do."

Reb Moyshe-Yudl became a lumber merchant. Reb Avrom Shevakh walked him down a forest path, explained to him which trees were useful, and how many railroad ties and boards could be gotten from a tree fifteen meters high.

After a year in the business, he decided one day in the synagogue that he was smarter than God. That Yom Kippur the Rasher Rabbi spent a little more time than usual saying the *Shmone esrey.* There was plenty to pray to God about; there were wars, pogroms, and other troubles from which Jews were suffering. He stood and begged God to grant his congregation a prosperous year, forgetting that Reb Moyshe-Yudl already had everything he needed, that Moyshe-Yudl was eager to return home, and couldn't wait for the rabbi to finish. And Moyshe-Yudl shouted that everybody shouldn't have to stand around waiting for one man.

The rabbi finished the Eighteen Benedictions. Reb Avrom Shevakh approached Moyshe-Yudl and said, "Go ask the rabbi's pardon, Moyshe-Yudl; otherwise the prices will drop, and you'll have a terrible year." Reb Moyshe-Yudl grew terribly frightened, went up to the rabbi, and said:

"Rabbi, I beg your pardon."

"My son," the rabbi answered, "pardon is asked and granted before Yom Kippur, not afterward. You have a year to wait yet."

And Reb Moyshe-Yudl the lumber merchant lowered his head, folded up his talis, and went home with a heavy heart.

Ayzikl the Bachelor

BERL ROBAKH
Sefer zikaron le-kehilat Sanok ve-ha-seviva

In Sanok there lived a pious old bachelor. His name was Ayzikl. He didn't want to get married because he was dreadfully shy. He used to say that he would get married only in a cellar, where no one could see. But he used to wear a fur hat when he went to pray on the Sabbath, which was a very rare thing for a bachelor. Ayzikl was very skillful in three areas: as an engraver, as a sign painter, and as a tombstone cutter. He was known far and wide for his talent. One time, when he was already sixty-five years old, he grew quite sick. Kindhearted people, both men and women, brought him food to eat and clean Sabbath clothes. His health returned, but he was deeply in debt, having bought on credit from several stores.

As the story goes, Ayzikl the Bachelor approached a well-known rich man with a note for fifty Austrian kroner in his hand and said: "Reb Moyshe, here's a bank note for fifty kroner; please give me twenty kroner. But I beg you not to part with the fifty, because I'm keeping it as a memento which I received from the former Countess of Linsk. You hear, Reb Moyshe? Remember! When I earn the twenty back, I want you to return my fifty." A short time later Ayzikl came back with twenty kroner and asked for the fifty kroner note, which he promptly received. But imagine the rich man's shock when Ayzikl placed the note by the flame of a candle and burned it to ashes!

Ayzikl himself had forged the bank note so accurately that the rich man couldn't even tell that it was false.

Zabalye the Coachwoman

AYZIK FAYVLOVITSH
Sefer Zlotshev (Zloczew)

She was a woman, but with her unusual habits and vulgar behavior, she might as well have been a man. She could have taught ten men how to curse, drink, and brawl. Yet she lived from honest toil. She owned a horse and wagon, and she transported assorted loads, particularly merchandise, from Sheradz to Lodz. She herself was as strong as a horse, and it was said that when part of her wagon broke down or it lost a wheel, Zabalye lifted the entire wagon up on her back and fixed what needed fixing. After driving the wagon for several years (from 1900–1906), she exchanged it for a carriage, and began taking passengers.

In Zlotshev she was the only woman in her profession, but there were several male coachmen with characters and habits similar to hers. One of them, named Dovid, had a father who was also a coachman. Dovid inherited from his father not only his profession, but his "virtues" as well; as it is said, "the apple doesn't fall far from the tree." Dovid's father had a weakness for the bottle, and Dovid himself rarely refused to join in a toast. Furthermore, Dovid's father wasn't altogether honest in his business dealings, but compared to Dovid, he was a saint. But none of these qualities prevented Dovid from catching Zabalye's eye. Quite the contrary: since their characters were so similar, she was quite impressed by them. Gradually they grew more and more close, and one fine day the news that they were to be married made the rounds of the shtetl, together with wishes for their future health and happiness.

Their families met, and couldn't get over what an appropriate match Zabalye and Dovid made for each other. In fact, the couple became business partners before long. Dovid sold his cart, and together they drove the carriage.

Time, the horses, and the partnership grew on together. Months passed, and gossips whispered that the partnership wasn't limited to business; yet no one heard of any wedding plans. It's true that the entire shtetl had a weakness for gossip, but it seems that this time the gossip was true. The couple ignored the rumors; people said what they said, and they continued living their life without the benefit of ceremony and official pronouncement.

After a time, Dovid was drafted into the army for a four-year tour of duty. Zabalye was left alone, but not for long. Misfortune struck the family of drivers: Dovid's mother grew sick and passed away after a short illness. After the seven-day period of mourning, the father realized that he was completely alone, with his son in the army and his wife gone. He started to think about his daughter-in-law-to-be: meanwhile she wasn't married, and she herself was lonely. Thus they found their way to each other, and a new partnership in driving the carriage was begun. Like the first partnership, it eventually diversified.

The father had promised to marry Zabalye, but as long as Dovid was in the army he had an excuse to put off the wedding, since he needed Dovid's consent. On the other hand, when Dovid came home and saw what the situation was, he didn't want to marry Zabalye either, and she was left with a dilemma. Both father and son were willing to be her partner, but neither wanted to marry her. She was equally ready to marry father or son. Although she was angry and cursed up and down, there was nothing she could do against a pair like Dovid and his father. For once, she was helpless.

However, her brothers eventually came to Zlotshev and brought suit against the two men in a rabbinical court. The town's rabbinical judge, Reb Moyshe Aron Natanzon, categorically refused to preside, and named a court of three judges to rule on the case. There were several comic moments in the course of the hearing, because none of the parties was inhibited, and they freely detailed their intimate circumstances. It was assumed that the court would make its ruling, and one of the men would marry Zabalye "according to the Law of Moses and Israel." The only question was, Which man it would be? But the ruling that actually came forth was completely unexpected: both men were ordered to divorce her!

Why and what for?!? They'd never gotten married, how could they be divorced? But that was the ruling, and there was nothing to be done about it. Together they went to the nearby shtetl of Vidava, on the banks of the river Warta, as the court had stipulated, and there they were divorced. Later it was said that the old coachman had married someone else, and that his son Dovid and Zabalye had both gone mad.

That was the tragic end of the story of Zabalye the coachwoman.

The Mute

DR. YESHAYAHU FAYG
Torna (Tarnow); kiyuma ve-hurbana shel ir yehudit

Here I wish to memorialize a person whose name no one knew, although he spent his entire life among the residents of the city. No one knew whether he had relatives or a family, where he came from in the morning, and where he returned at night. He was deaf, dumb, and blind, and he was simply called "the mute." He was tall, always wore a frock, and carried a stick in his hand. The painter Krestin did a portrait of him, which was later reproduced on postcards. His entire vocabulary consisted of a sound he made in his throat, which sometimes expressed anger and sometimes joy. In the course of a week, he stopped at every Jewish home in Torna. He determined which houses were Jewish by touching the doorpost and seeing if there was a mezuzah. He never stepped across the threshold of a home, and no one ever refused him alms—usually, an Austrian half-graytser, the smallest coin there was.

Even for the medical community he was an unusual phenomenon. Nowhere in the medical literature have I read of such a case of someone who was deaf, dumb, and blind at the same time. When he wanted someone to help him, he would make a noise and the person passing by would realize that he wanted to cross the street, or to have a door opened. For the latter purpose, he also knocked on doors with his stick, which was also useful in fending off the attacks of young pranksters.

He divided the Jewish quarter into six sections, and each day he made the rounds of one section. At each house, he would appear on the same day of the week and at the same time of day each time. When the mute came to one's house, one knew exactly what time it was.

Despite all of his handicaps, he was an exceptional gentleman. He refused to accept anything more than the smallest coin from everyone. If someone handed him a larger coin, he would reach into his pocket and produce exact change. There were times when he was handed an entire crown, and he would produce precisely forty-nine and a half pennies in change. If he received food, he would take no money.

Every Sabbath he came to the synagogue, sat at the Eastern Wall, and was considered one of the congregants. It's hard to imagine what he was thinking then. If he didn't appear at a Jewish home at the usual time, it was a sure sign that he was ill. When he was healthy again, he would resume begging according to his established order, showing that he knew which day of the week it was. No one knew what was in his heart or his thoughts, but it may be assumed that he more or less led his own intellectual life, despite his terrible handicaps.

Esther-Khaye the Zogerin ["Sayer"]

SHMUEL LIFSHITS
Zabludove (Zabludow) yizker-bukh

At the beginning of the month of Elul, Esther-Khaye the zogerin [sayer] appears on the scene. All year she is hardly visible. She is a quiet, modest woman with a shrunken face, who always wears a kerchief on her head, summer and winter.

Her face is the same color as her dress, the color of sand. Whenever you come across her, her lips are murmuring a prayer. She never has any time. She is always busy. Here she is baking bread for sale, there she is attending to her sickly husband, who is the *shames* of the old synagogue and also a gravestone cutter. Or she might even be running into the study house to catch the afternoon prayers, not to mention the holy prayers that women hire her to say for them. It's no trifle, at ten zlotys per prayer.

But who is like unto her at the beginning of the month of Elul: then she is a heroine. Every moment of her time is gold. Women stand waiting for her as if she were the greatest celebrity. Not only the people of Zabludove alone, but even strangers who come to visit their ancestors' graves, know her already. Who doesn't know that with her "saying" she can move a stone from a pit? No one can remain indifferent to her "saying," not even menfolk. There have been jokers who've bet that while she "says" they would stand laughing. But no one has managed to do that. It moves them so that tears pour out of them.

If a woman is having a difficult childbirth, or someone is dangerously ill, they quickly run to ask Esther-Khaye to go to the cemetery. They don't have to give her any instructions—she knows what to do. Don't worry, she can be relied on. She takes along all the necessary supplies, such as candles and wicks for spanning gravestones, and thank God, the sick person or the woman in labor pulls through.

The High Holy Days are quite different. Then she produces a new wellspring of words which the pen is quite unable to contain.

Just at daybreak before the High Holy Days, this picture is to be seen: a large crowd of women, led by Esther-Khaye bearing her book of supplications, set off for the cemetery. The way to the graveyard is not far from town, and as Esther-Khaye enters, she feels at home, among people she knows. "Good morning, God," she begins in a tragic melody, "Your servant Esther-Khaye has come . . ." And approaching the grave, she looks over at the woman on whose behalf she is supplicating, and words begin to pour from her mouth, as if from a spring.

First she calls out the name of the deceased and strikes the gravestone three times with her hand, speaking as if to a living person: "Good morning to you, Rive-Mindl the daughter of Yankev-Tsvi, your daughter Sore-Rivke has come, for she wants to see you and pour out her bitter heart before you. Look, Rive-Mindl, at what has become of your daughter, if you were to arise now and see what has become of your daughter, you would return to the grave. Request, Rive-Mindl, a good year for your daughter, a kosher year, that she may know no ill, exert yourself for her sake, why are you silent? Why do you not supplicate the Lord of the Universe?

"It is five years since the wedding, and she is still (may we be preserved from harm!) a barren woman. Be not silent, Rive-Mindl, sunder the heavens, pray to the Lord of the Universe for her and for all of Israel which now withstands such bitter troubles, and for this deed may you enter the Garden of Eden, and let us say, Amen."

Or in this version: "How can you be still, when your daughter is in need of health and livelihood? Exert yourself for her sake, pray to the Lord of the Universe, after all you're somewhat closer to Him than we sinners, be an intercessor on behalf of her and all of Israel, and let us say, Amen."

And on and on . . . speeches without end. The onlookers listen to her, wiping their eyes from time to time, and each one blesses her roundly.

When Esther-Khaye finishes her "saying," she straightens her back, takes the few groshn she is given, and a smile pours out over her lips, as if to say: "Pretty well done, don't you think?"

Lately Esther-Khaye the *zogerin* has also been busy "saying" during the year: either an American comes from across the sea to see his parents who are in the True World, and comes to Esther-Khaye, or she receives orders from America. Esther-Khaye does her work thoroughly; when she beseeches on behalf of an

American, she speaks quite differently. She displays her true talent. Then the wide sea separating Zabludove from America doesn't exist for her, it becomes all one city. And later in a letter, she sends her client greetings from his near and dear ones. She is faithfully paid for this.

And so year in, year out, every time with the same familiar pattern, which we all know so well and love.

Tall Libe

MOYSHE GOLDSHTAYN
Yizker-bukh; Otvotsk-Kartshev (Otwock-Karczew)

That's what everyone in Otvotsk called her, and she was known for the two ways she gained her livelihood: the first was delivering milk, and the second was making Jewish women *kosher*, as the attendant in the mikve in Otvotsk.

With the first light of every dawn, Libe could be seen carrying her two jugs of milk to all of the Jewish homes and boardinghouses.* Libe's tall figure was part of every street: Ludne, Gurne, Yoselevitshe, Statsishe, and the rest.

In the afternoon, Tall Libe attended to her second job: seeing to it that the Jewish women purified themselves in the mikve. Thus she was also called Libe the *tikerin* (mikve attendant).

Libe the *tikerin* kept a list of all the wives of Otvotsk in her head. She remembered each woman whose time to come to the mikve had arrived, and who hadn't done so. She knew all of the "backsliders," who didn't come at all or who stopped coming, even though they weren't pregnant. Sometimes she stopped such women in the street and said to them: "Listen here, you, I know what you're up to; you can't have it both ways. Either you're pregnant, or you've got to come to me."

Libe had written down a list of dozens of poor, sick people, either widows or people who were simply needy, who couldn't afford a glass of milk for themselves or for their sick child. Quietly, in secret, she brought to each of those homes a bit of milk, which she had managed to save in the course of a day. In winter, she knew in which homes people were freezing, because they didn't have the few pennies it would cost to buy fuel. She herself would bring them a little coal, some money, warm, cooked food or a piece of bread to keep body and soul together.

Until late at night we used to see Libe hurrying around town, going from one unfortunate to the next, bringing whatever help was needed.

*Otvotsk had a number of boardinghouses for vacationing Jews from large cities. Some were frequented by non-Jews also.

Long after nightfall Libe's toil would end, and she returned home to the single room that she shared with her already-sleeping family. She would fall onto her bed exhausted, in order to get up and start all over in a few hours, making her own living and helping the needy and suffering, which occupied her until late at night.

Reb Dvoyre Mash

A. KHROBOLOVSKY
Tshenstokhover (Czestochowa) Yidn

She bore the simple female name Dvoyre-Miriam, but out of great respect and honor, her husband, Yosl Shternberg, had titled her "Reb Dvoyre Mash." In financial and religious matters Dvoyre-Miriam fulfilled the male role, while her husband Yosl was the woman.

Dvoyre Mash and her husband Yosl lived on the edge of the forest, earning their livelihood in the city and in the villages.

Reb Dvoyre Mash arose early. She went about the hamlets and peasant houses, buying whatever was available: a chicken, a calf, a little milk, a quart of berries, a slab of butter or a cheese; later she would sell it to the summer people at their dachas, or to her regular customers in town. She had plenty to say to each one. She poured out her bitter heart at every stop, and mixing fire and water, she took care of every aspect of her business at once: buying, selling, bartering, and doing a little matchmaking on the side.

In the midst of all this she never failed, God forbid, to say her prayers. Whether in city or village, at home or on the road, she was sure to pray afternoon and evening. She might be sitting with a crowd of Jews or in a wagonful of gentiles; undeterred, she would stand up, rub her hands against the dry windowpanes, and pray. When she was finished, she resumed her business where she had left off, remonstrating endlessly.

At daybreak, when Reb Dvoyre Mash would set off with her packs and sacks, her husband Yosl, a Jew with a long, yellow beard, picked up his talis bag, kissed the mezuzah, and said "Good morning" to the goat who stood on the veranda. When he returned from the morning service, he ate breakfast and did the housework. Then he led the goat into the field to graze. And there, out in the open meadow, he sang Psalms by heart.

When General Haller's soldiers went on a spree, just after Poland regained statehood, and celebrated by beating Jews and tearing out beards, our Reb Yosl "the yidene" was one of their victims. The hooligans saw the goat in the pasture, along with Reb Yosl's waist-long beard. They set off in pursuit of Yosl. Yosl ran, and struggled to get free of the soldiers, but to no avail. He lost half of his beard to them.

When Reb Dvoyre Mash returned home in the evening and saw Yosl with only half a beard, she scolded him roundly for the first time ever, saying that he wasn't a man at all. If it had happened to her, she would have had their eyes out before she let them touch her beard.

That wasn't simply idle boasting. She could take care of herself in any situation. In addition to the strength it took to bear children, raise them, and provide for an entire household, Reb Dvoyre also managed to marry off her son Fishl, whose mind was disordered. Fishl's eyes were blue as cornflowers; he had a noble face and a sharp mind. The poor thing had become confused in his youth, from too much study. For years he had studied in various yeshivas, going from city to city and eating at the homes of strangers, until finally his brains addled.

Yet Fishl had a loyal mother named Reb Dvoyre Mash; she followed the advice of clever people, who said that the best cure for him would be to find him a wife. Reb Dvoyre didn't rest until she found Fishl's ordained mate, and one glorious evening the wedding was happily conducted.

Fishl was told that the "authorities" had ordered him to get married; Fishl was afraid of the "authorities." He sat at the table, breaking into laughter from time to time and sticking his tongue out at the guests. When the bride and groom were told to step on the glass under the wedding canopy, Fishl said that it was a shame to break glass, which is a useful thing. Nothing could convince him to step on the glass. Fishl stood under the canopy refusing to break the glass, until a strong Jew grabbed him by the collar and shouted, "Break it!" Fishl got scared, tapped his feet, broke the glass and the whole crowd shouted "*Mazel tov!*"

After Fishl's wedding Dvoyre went back to business even more enthusiastically. Now, in addition to supporting her husband and smaller children, she was responsible for her married son and his wife, and she hoped soon to see healthy grandchildren, who would live to be one hundred and twenty.

Crazy Sora

KHANE SHENTAL-RAVIV
Pinkas Bendin (Bedzin)

One saw an assortment of mentally ill people in the streets of Bendin. In general, they hurt no one, if no one bothered them. Children, however, did annoy them, shouting "*Meshugener!*" When they were harried thus undeservedly, they defended themselves by throwing stones and roundly cursing those who surrounded them. Of these unfortunate creatures, Crazy Sora stands fixed in my memory: she was well-known to everyone, because she spent her days running from one side of town to the other, dressed in colored rags, and laden with wood, tiny coals, and food which she had begged. She was always barefoot and in tatters, although people gave her clothing and shoes out of pity; she didn't wear them, but kept them hidden for her child, that is to say, her illness. It was said, although I don't know whether it was true or not, that she had had a daughter who had killed herself, or died a natural death. Since then she had been insane, and constantly spoke of a child; this and the curses that never left her lips combined to form a litany. She only interrupted this eternal monologue to beg alms, which people quickly gave in order to be rid of her. This was her "sermon":

"Give me a penny, but quickly, I have no time, if you won't give me a penny, give me a needle, spears should stab you in the world to come, give me a piece of coal, faster, Sora is cold, you are warm, your intestines should burn, your teeth should clatter, and you should go to Hell. Ha, you're trying to hide from me? Don't be afraid! I won't do anything to you. My child wants a drink, sha, sha, don't wake up my child. Quicker, give me alms, I have to run, they want to beat me! So help me, I stole nothing, let me warm myself a bit, Sora's hands and feet are frozen, give me a piece of bread for my child, quickly, quickly."

In 1928, when Poland suffered an especially severe winter, she was discovered frozen to death in the street.

When I came to Israel thirty years ago, and wanted to become a member of the Ohel Theater Company, I used Crazy Sora's monologue as an audition piece—and was accepted into the troupe.

Shloyme-Akive, the Town Fool

A. B. SHOSHANI
Govorove (Goworowo); sefer zikaron

There was no Jewish community in Poland without its town fool. Just as a town needed its barber-surgeon, its bathhouse attendant, night watchman, and midwife, there had to be a *meshugener*, who belonged to everyone in common and whose welfare was the responsibility of the entire community.

Generally, the town fools were of subnormal intelligence, depressive types, or wild creatures who harmed the inhabitants in various ways. Govorove was lucky. Its town fool was good-natured and smiling; he spoke in a singsong and made himself very useful by bringing water to people's homes and running errands. In short, he did whatever anyone asked him to.

Shloyme-Akive Beserman was a native of Govorove, born to a fine, established family. His father Reb Leybl, a respectable Jew with a long white beard and an excellent command of the holy texts, was a teacher in town. He also blew the shofar in the Great Synagogue on holy days. His brother Aviezer was the rabbi of Komarove. His second brother Tsodek considered himself a philosopher, read literature, and loved discussions.

As Shloyme-Akive himself related, he had had a bad fall out of an attic when he was a child, and his mind had never been right since. His father took him to every doctor in the region, but nothing could be done. Perhaps his story was correct, but it is also possible that he had been born with a defect. One thing is certain: his father did everything possible to help him. As a result, Shloyme-Akive was deeply devoted to his father. After his father's death, Shloyme-Akive went to the graveyard and started to dig him out of his grave. He wanted to carry him back home.

Shloyme-Akive was brought to the authorities when Govorove was still ruled by the Russians, before the First World War. The military suspected him of pretending to be insane, in order to avoid military service. However, he wasn't released, but sent to a military hospital for observation. After six months he was released, and he returned to town well-fed, relaxed, and absolutely delighted in general.

Shloyme-Akive had a phenomenal memory. He remembered stories from his early childhood, and recognized people whom he had seen only once many years previously. He "specialized" in recognizing *taleysim*. He could identify any individual talis out of a pile of dozens, and never made a mistake. Sometimes on Simkhes Toyre the taleysim got mixed together and their owners couldn't figure out which one belonged to whom. They would send for Shloyme-Akive, who handed everyone the correct talis without the slightest hesitation.

Shloyme-Akive was also a great "master" at eating. His belly held vast amounts of food; satiation was totally unknown to him. In general he was honest and never touched anyone else's property. But when it came to food, everything was his. Woe to the housewife who set the Sabbath fish on the windowsill to cool! Shloyme-Akive would steal it and consume an entire kilo of fish, or even two. Then he would stroll to the marketplace with his hands clasped behind his back, singing to himself: "Oh, were Yente's fish delicious!"

More than once the housewife would first discover the "disaster" after hearing Shloyme-Akive singing. But no one was angry with him. Everybody knew that if fish were left on the windowsill without being guarded, they automatically belonged to Shloyme-Akive.

In his free time, after he carried water to his clients, Shloyme-Akive used to stretch out by the stove in the study house, or in the *shtibl* of the Alexander Hasidim, to take a nap or to hum a tune. His memory also served him as a storehouse of melodies. He sang well, and remembered who had composed every tune that he heard. It was enough to ask him: "What melody did Yisroel-Leyb sing to?" He quickly answered by singing it. He often spoke to himself, carrying on endless debates.

He ate the Sabbath meal at the home of Reb Yeshaye Shmuel Nosns. Then he would go from house to house, eating a portion of cholent here, a slice of kugel there. He was happy if he only received a slice of challah.

Shloyme-Akive was ready to carry a package or do some other favor for anyone, even in the middle of the night. It wasn't, God forbid, for the sake of profit. The townspeople loved him. Once he grew sick, and everyone tried to help him; he was missed in town. Another time a brutal peasant from a nearby village threw him down a flight of stairs, and he lay unconscious. The whole town was in an uproar. People were ready to kill the peasant; the porters and butchers beat him to a pulp.

Shloyme-Akive was taken care of by Khaye-Zelde Klempner, the tinsmith's wife. This good woman was motivated solely by the desire to do a good deed. She fed him and washed his clothes, and treated him like her own child. Thus he was always clean and wore decent, warm clothes. He was very devoted to her as well.

Shloyme-Akive died during the war years.

Alter, the Village Peddler

YOSL SUKENIK
Sefer Kalushin (Kaluszyn); geheylikt der khorev gevorener kehile

My uncle Alter, or as he was called in Kalushin, Alter Shvartsbarts, finally became a village peddler after knocking himself out at all his other pursuits. Formerly Alter had worked in the forest, stripping bark from oak trees, which was used in treating hides by the tanners of Kalushin. But there was no living to be made from that work, and with no lack of troubles at home, Alter followed the advice of his father-in-law Elye Dovid Sosnovsky. The latter had been doing business for years in the villages of Skride and Olekshin, where he used to buy up parcels of woodland and cut the lumber for his shingle factory. Following his father-in-law's advice, Alter began selling notions in these villages.

The peddler Alter quickly began to sense hostility. Stones were thrown at him, dogs were set after him, and he suffered other anti-Semitic pranks. But having no other choice, he continued to travel around with his needles and shoelaces, combs and mirrors, beads and toys. For the children of all of his customers, he also brought candy and bagels. On his way back he always bought up various products, and thus loaded down with packages he used to trudge home every day. In general the peasants bought on credit, and Alter had to struggle to pay for all the merchandise he bought in town.

Every Thursday night Alter used to sleep over at the home of the wealthy peasant Galec in the village of Olekshin. There was always a room waiting for him at this honest and cheerful family's home. There he could say his afternoon and evening prayers and eat the bit of food he had brought along from home. Galec's two sons also behaved respectfully toward the Jew, their guest.

Likewise, Galec sometimes came to Alter's house in town. One Friday evening he arrived there with a wagonload of wood which he hadn't managed to sell and didn't want to bring back to his village. The peasant very nearly caused Alter to desecrate the Sabbath. Alter hurried to help unload the wood, and treated the peasant to shnaps, challah, and gefilte fish. Galec went away satisfied. Alter was even more satisfied, having managed to avoid sin, and quickly put on his Sabbath clothes.

Meanwhile Sabbaths and weeks passed, and the situation in the villages grew steadily worse. One Thursday night the mayor of Olekshin announced to Alter that the village elders had decided to open a store, where the peasants would be able to obtain everything cheaply. Indeed, the store soon opened. The priest himself stood with the sleeves of his robe rolled up, drawing herring from a barrel for the customers, and Alter feared for his livelihood. Anti-Semitic placards calling for a boycott against Jews hung on the municipal building. Alter reduced his trips to the village to twice weekly, and the roads became more and more dangerous.

Once, on a hot day when Alter sat down by the water to rest about two kilometers from Olekshin, the village blacksmith, who owed Alter fifty zlotys, came along and struck up a conversation with him: "Alter, I could kill you right here, you're rich, like all the Jews."

Alter quickly took out his wallet and showed him the twelve zlotys in it, saying: "Surely you are joking. You, too, are a father of children." The blacksmith thought for a while, and then said: "I've always known you were clever. You immediately saw that I was kidding."

From time to time peasants and their wives still came to Alter. He still managed to do some business with them at the market on Tuesdays, and they enjoyed unburdening their hearts to Alter and Alter's wife: one couple has a son who has left the path of righteousness, steals anything he can get his hands on, and spends his Sundays with the girls. They ask Alter to scold him if he runs into the youth at the marketplace. A second woman complains about her drunkard husband, and asks for advice; a third tells of fistfights over the inheritance of a field, with no end to the spilling of blood. Thus the peasant men and women partially maintained their relations with my uncle and aunt, remembering the village peddler who could be counted on for words of sound counsel and comfort.

One market day before Passover, when all the roads to town bore peasants with their wagons, the family Galec from Olekshin also came to town. They brought along their little six-year-old son Wacek for the first time. As was the custom among the peasants, the Galecs went off for a drink, leaving little Wacek behind on the wagon to guard its contents, and promising to bring back good things. Little Wacek stayed there alone; and when the hustle and bustle began in the marketplace, with housewives and servant girls inspecting the crates and sacks on all the wagons, including the one Wacek guarded, the little boy became terrified. He remembered that once when his cousin hadn't wanted to take him along to the market, the cousin had frightened him by saying that he wouldn't come back alive because Jews toss Christians children into their sacks and use their blood for matzo on Passover.

And indeed, Jews were coming with sacks . . . here comes a Jew with a sack, looking to see what might be bought from the little gentile on the wagon. But by coincidence, when Alter entered the marketplace to demand payment on debts owed to him by peasants from Skride and Olekshin, little Wacek saw him and ran to him, shouting: "Save me, dear Alter, take me home, the Jews want to make matzo out of me, there they are with their sacks!" My uncle tried to calm the little one, without success. He had to take the boy and the wagon to his house. At home neither food nor sweets helped. The child wouldn't let Alter walk a step away from him, until my aunt went to find Wacek's parents and told them what happened to their son.

When his parents arrived, Wacek broke out into fresh weeping, telling them of the danger he had been in. His parents calmed him and smiled, embarrassed.

When the Galec family returned to the market next week, they told my aunt and uncle about the troubles they'd had with their son for several days after the incident: he had been feverish, lying delirious and shouting repeatedly: "Alter, save me!" Then, when he got well, he had to suffer the taunts of his friends, who laughed at him as a coward who had to run to the Jews for protection. Wacek had answered that they were liars, and he would never believe them again. Galec and his wife swore that they had never believed such things, and they ordered brandy and sweets to make a toast. They clinked their glasses "To your health!," but my uncle was sunk in sorrowful Jewish thoughts.

The Kozhenitser Rebe

BINYOMIN ORENSHTAYN
Khurbn Otvotsk (Otwock), Falenits (Falenica), Kartshev (Karczew)

One of the remarkable rebes who resided in Otvotsk was the Kozhenitser, Reb Orele. His patriarchal outward appearance commanded the attention and respect of all, and his poise and comprehension were astounding. He made a good impression with his elegant dress. His noteworthy face, high forehead, heavy brows, and long, black beard carefully groomed and flecked with gray had a hypnotizing effect on his followers.

It wasn't easy to get close to him. His court was always packed full with Hasidim and one had no choice but to stand outside. One could hear fiddles playing various melodies, marches, and also modern dances.

Nonetheless, I decided to speak to the Rebe, and looked for a special opportunity to do so. It came in Purim of 1937. He was having a festive meal with his Hasidim in Warsaw at number 4 Franciszkanska Street, on the first floor, where there were large wedding halls.

The hall where the Rebe held court was packed with a varied audience: Hasidim in long coats, young men from yeshivas, and also a number of "modern Hasidim" wearing short jackets and fedoras on their heads.

I stood in an adjoining room and observed the celebration. When the Hasidim left the room for the ritual hand washing, I worked my way into the hall.

The press of Hasidim was unusually strong and it was impossible to stand; one couldn't move a step in either direction. Bit by bit, I battled my way to a place near the wall and perched myself on a bench. From this vantage point I could see everything: the Rebe in his full glory, his stewards, those accompanying him at the head table, and the massive press of Hasidim. The long tables were arranged like three sides of a rectangle. The Rebe sat in the middle with prominent Hasidim near him, their proximity befitting their rank. Among them were several wealthy fur dealers from Warsaw.

The tables were laden with appetizing dishes, but no one touched them until the Rebe made a blessing and distributed them. The ranking Hasidim were properly restrained during the distribution, because they were sure to get some in any case; but the standees went wild and grabbed much more food than they could possibly have consumed.

Every few minutes another Hasid donated a case of wine, and the neighboring wine dealer on Franciszkanska Street immediately brought it to the table. The Rebe and his Hasidim drank so much that it was amazing to see them maintain their equilibrium.

A choir stood on the table to the right. A yellow-bearded Hasid conducted. The choir sang the latest tunes, which I happened to hear somewhat later in the Ararat theater.

A young man sat not far from the Rebe on his left, wearing a short coat and a cap on his head, and holding a fiddle in his hand.

He was happy to satisfy the Rebe and played only what the Rebe requested. From time to time the Rebe took the fiddle from him and played it himself.

The Rebe was in a cheerful mood and observed everyone present with satisfaction, and thus he noticed me.

I seemed somewhat odd to the Rebe: I didn't press toward the table, I didn't grab any food, I just stood there on the bench. The Rebe beckoned to me with his finger. Not seeing any way to push myself through, I answered: "Rebe, I can't get through!" Before I finished uttering these words, I was taken in tow by two Hasidim, who shouted to the crowd to let us through, and thus brought me to the Rebe. The Rebe shook my hand and asked me a whole series of questions, which I proceeded to answer and follow with a question of my own.

"Rebe, is it proper to celebrate today, when the Polish parliament is considering a proposal to forbid kosher slaughter?"

The Rebe opened his eyes wide as he looked at me, and declared: "Don't you know that it's written explicitly, 'You shall celebrate and be joyous?' " And when I continued to talk about the political problems of the Jewish people, the Rebe told me not to leave, but to stay until he summoned me for a talk.

At the Rebe's "command" a Hasid brought me water so that I could wash my hands, and I received a slice of challah, fish, meat, half a bottle of wine, a package of dried figs, an orange, and the like.

I returned with all my victuals to my place on the bench near the wall. The Hasidim threw themselves at my plate and grabbed everything. Other Hasidim envied me for the great honor of having a talk with the Rebe.

The dinner lasted until two in the morning. Then the tables were pulled back to the walls and the dancing started. The Rebe stood in the middle of the circle, the fiddler played, the choir sang, and the rest of the Hasidim clapped their hands.

After the dancing, the Rebe took out a whip and began striking in a light, paternal way; a Hasid who pushed forward for a lashing received one that made him cry out in pain against his will, which satisfied him.

Finally, the Rebe entered another room and called me in. I asked him why the hasidic world wasn't unified in the face of the assault on Jewish rights.

"Don't you know that I don't get along with the B.G.?" asked the Rebe.

"I don't understand what the Rebe means," I replied.

The Rebe looked at me, astonished that I didn't know what "B.G." meant, and he explained that "B.G." meant the Rebes of Belz and Ger. The Rebe told me about the influence he had with President Ignacy Moscicki and about his approaching journey to France. The clock struck four; the Rebe was extremely tired and drowsy from the wine. He handed me a Havana cigar and we parted.

In the great hall the Hasidim awaited my return. They all came up to me, but I didn't let the cigar get away from me and I smoked it myself. The Hasidim looked at the burning cigar jealously, and every minute another Hasid asked me to sell him the cigar, or at least give him a drag.

Seeing that the Hasidim weren't going to let me out of the hall and were going to get the cigar anyway, I called over the conductor of the choir and gave it to him.

The director of the choir met me by chance in the ghetto of Otvotsk. I invited him several times to come visit me at 11 Shpitalna Street, where I lived in

Yekhiel Meyer Zolberg's villa. I asked him to sing, but he refused, because he was embittered and desperate owing to the tragic situation of the Jews and the social injustice in the ghetto. People grew swollen and starved to death while the upstart "king" Bernard Kronenberg, the commandant of the ghetto, fed his two dogs chocolate.

I listened with wonder to what he told me. How time had changed him! He was always absorbed in a world of melody and song, he had never been concerned with his surroundings; and now, beaten down by the tragic reality of the ghetto, he observed everything differently. I gladly accepted his invitation to visit the Rebe.

On Yom Kippur of 1941, I went to the new residence of the Rebe, which was next door to Kelner's villa. Watching the Rebe as he read the Torah, as he blew the shofar and led the services, I was amazed. He was unrecognizable. The carefree, cheerful look had disappeared from his face. Though he was quite a young man, his magnificent black beard had grown entirely gray; his strong body had shriveled entirely, and one saw such a lot of worry on his face that he seemed to have collapsed under the heavy burden of Jewish troubles and pain. It wasn't the right time to talk; one could see that he wanted to avoid all conversations in the face of the tragic reality for which he had no solution.

Shortly before the deportation, the Kozhenitser Rebe passed away; he died a natural death.

At that time it was considered a great honor and divine reward to pass into eternity in a natural manner and thus avoid the sadistic Nazi torturers.

Lifeways

Customs, Symbols, and Ceremonies

SH. ZABLUDOVITSH
Kehilat Vengerov (Wegrow); sefer zikaron

Engagements

Initial agreement: After the bride's and groom's families had agreed to a match, and finished discussing all of the conditions, a day was set for the outlines of the agreement to be written down. The bride's family prepared a meal on that day for relatives and close friends on both sides. At the meal the in-laws shook hands, drank a toast, wrote a document sealing the match, and set a date for the betrothal.

Betrothal. The betrothal was no less festive than the wedding. It took place at the home of the bride, where a generous feast was served. The guests were dressed in their holiday clothes. The parents of the couple filled in formulas on parchment in Hebrew and Aramaic: the names of the bride and groom and of their parents, the place, the dowry, and the gifts. The bride and groom signed the document, and then one of the invited guests read it in a loud voice. When the reading was finished, several plates were broken as a sign of luck, and everyone wished the couple and their parents "Mazel tov!" Then the feast began.

At the feast the parents gave the bride and groom valuable gifts, and there was always singing and sometimes even invited musicians.

Weddings and Sheva-Brokhes

In our town, Jewish weddings were celebrated with all of the traditional customs.

Several months before the wedding, material for the bride's and groom's wedding clothes were bought. Rich parents had the tailors come to their homes. Ten days before the wedding the cooking, baking, and frying began in the parents' house. Rich parents made a meal for the poor several days before the wedding, after which a substantial amount of money was distributed.

The bride and groom fasted on the day of the ceremony. The bride, dressed in white, sat on a podium. All of the guests wished the bride and then the in-laws "Mazel tov!" as they came in. Waiters gave baked pastries to everyone. Jewish musicians played festive tunes, and the girls danced.

The groom sat in front, surrounded by young boys, relatives, and friends. The tables were covered with white cloths, and many candles were lit.

Late at night the ceremony of veiling the bride began. The in-laws took the groom by the hand and led him to the bride's house. At the entrance, musicians played, while the groom approached the bride and covered her head with a white silk shawl. Then the groom was led back to where he waited. During this ceremony, the wedding jester began to sing rhymed couplets in Yiddish, and sometimes in Hebrew as well, accompanied by the fiddlers. The songs were taken from old Jewish folklore, and were often quite sentimental, making tears flow from the women's eyes.

Exactly one hour before midnight, the parents walked the groom arm-in-arm to the canopy. The musicians went first, playing festive music, and guests carried burning, multicolored candles; the groom was led to the synagogue, where the canopy had already been set up. When he was in place under the canopy, the whole crowd, including the town rabbi, stood near him, awaiting the bride's arrival.

The bride was accompanied by both of the mothers-in-law, and musicians played before her. Guests carried candles, while women danced near the bride with special challahs in their hands. These wedding challahs were braided and covered with many-colored poppy seeds. When the bride reached the canopy, the musicians ceased playing. The bride walked around the groom three times and stood at his left. The rabbi read the betrothal document and the wedding contract, both in Aramaic, blessed the wine, and gave it to the bride and groom to drink. Then the groom put the ring on the bride's finger and pronounced "Behold, I consecrate you to me." Then a glass was placed under the groom's foot, and he smashed it by stepping on it. The entire crowd shouted loudly, "Mazel tov! Mazel tov!" On the way back as well, the groom was led off first by himself, and the bride came after. Along the way the musicians played, as some relatives sang and others danced alongside with wedding challahs in their hands. Soon the bride and groom were conducted into a separate room for a few minutes of solitude. Then the groom was led to the men's table, and the bride went to the women's table. While everyone ate, the wedding jester sang to the bride and groom and the musicians played along.

After the meal, the wedding presents were announced; after a traditional wedding dance with the bride, everyone recited the grace after meals and the feast ended.

The next morning the hair of a pious bride was shorn and a wig was fitted on her head. At the same time she was given a black silk shawl and a fine bound prayer book.

The second day after the wedding, the *sheva-brokhes* began; evening meals were prepared for guests in the home of the bride. People sang, recited blessings, and sometimes danced as well. On the first Sabbath after the wedding, it was customary to send the bride a gift, such as a rich casserole, noodle or potato pudding, wine, beer, or fruit. That was the conclusion of a Jewish wedding.

Childbirth

When a Jewish woman bore a son, amulets containing the text of Psalm 121, "A Song of Ascents," were hung on the walls of the mother's room. These were supposed to protect the newborn child from "evil spirits." Every day boys came from kheyder, stood around the newborn child, and recited the prayers "Hear, O Israel" and "the angel who redeems me." All of the boys were given candy. This was repeated daily until the circumcision.

The circumcision was held in the home of the mother. The child was dressed in festive bunting, and the rabbi held the baby during the ceremony. The nearest female relative was the godmother. On the first Friday night after the birth of the child there was a special party where sweets, beer, and peppered chick-peas were served.

The First Day of Kheyder

When a boy began to attend kheyder, guests were invited to a feast, along with all the students in the kheyder. A feast was also given when the boy began studying the Five Books of Moses.

A special feast was given in the boy's honor when he reached age thirteen. His teacher taught him how to place phylacteries on his head and arm; on the day of his bar mitzvah, the child put on phylacteries and was counted as part of the minyan, the ritual quorum of ten men, for the first time. He was also called to bless a portion of the Torah reading. His father was called as well, and recited the verse, "Blessed be He who frees me of responsibility for his sins." At the feast at home afterward, the bar mitzvah boy presented a speech to the guests.

Our Community Also Shared the Troubles of the Individual

When someone grew seriously ill, the Psalm Society came and recited psalms day and night. Relatives and friends ran to pray at the gravestones of ancestors, and women who were friends or neighbors of the sick person prostrated themselves before the Ark of the Torah in the synagogue to ask God to show mercy. The sick person was given a pseudonym, and a prayer on his behalf was said in the synagogue.

When the time came for the sick person's death throes, the rabbi and the burial society came to recite the final confession with him, placed at his head the holy book *Me'ever Yabok*, which contains the laws of death, and stayed with him until his soul departed. Then they would say, "God gives and God takes, may the name of God be blessed."

The burial society decided where the burial plot would be, sewed a shroud out of white linen, and brought a board on which to lay the corpse for ritual washing. In addition the mirror was covered, the clock was stopped, and burning candles were placed at the head of the corpse. The Psalm Society said psalms until the funeral.

In front of every funeral went the sexton with a collection box, saying in a loud voice: "Charity saves from death." The corpse was carried to the synagogue. There the procession stopped, and the crowd begged the forgiveness of the corpse. The head of the Burial Society himself buried the corpse, placing two small pieces of wood in the corpse's hands and laying an earthenware shard on each eye. Boards were laid on top, earth was shoveled into the grave, and a board was placed in the ground at the head of the grave, bearing the name of the dead person, the date of birth and the date of death. Everyone said, "From dust you came and to dust you return, blessed be the true Judge." After the psalm, "He who sits concealed on high," the mourners said the prayer for the dead, and the head of the Burial Society tore the mourners' clothes. Prayer services were held at the home of the deceased for seven days. During the seven days of mourning the mourners sat on low benches in their stocking feet. After the services, the mourners stood up and everyone said to them upon leaving, "May you be comforted with all the mourners for Zion and Jerusalem."

After a death, all of the close neighbors poured out the water that they had in their houses. Neighbors who were *kohanim* had to stay out of their own houses until the corpse was removed from the house it had lived in. During the thirty-day period of mourning, the mourners were forbidden to have their hair cut; nor could they attend parties or hear music or song for an entire year. They were not allowed to renovate anything during that period and they had to say the mourner's prayer each day. For the entire year, they were forbidden to visit the grave of the deceased.

The Healer in Bilgoray

A. KRONENBURG
Khurbn Bilgoray (Bilgoraj)

Until the First World War, there was one doctor in Bilgoray, named Savitsky. Jews rarely used his services, because very few of them could afford a doctor. At that time, nearly everybody in town utilized a variety of folk medicines and cures.

Whenever anyone grew sick, the first thing to do was to extinguish coals: burning coals were tossed into a glass of hot water. If they sank, it was a sign that an evil eye had been cast on the invalid. A child would immediately be told the name of the sick person and the name of his or her mother, and sent to tell

Sholem Hershele's or Itshe-Meyer Melamed, who were considered specialists at exorcising the evil eye.

After the evil eye was removed, the sick person was watched to see whether he yawned. If he yawned, it was a sign that the person had indeed had an evil eye, and the the removal of the spell had helped.

If the invalid's state did not improve, there was a thorough interrogation of the child who had been sent to have the evil eye removed: perhaps he had forgotten or confused the name of the sick person, and that was why the cure hadn't worked.

In cases where someone became paralyzed, Sore Mordkhe-Yoysef's was sent for. She would pour wax over the person's head, and point out reasons why he had become frightened.

When anyone caught a *royz* (a case of erysipelas), Sore took a piece of flax, lit it, and passed it near the infected area, saying various spells and repeating constantly: "Black royz, into the field, into the field." Later she took a kerchief spread with honey and bound the royz with it.

When a really serious illness struck and none of these popular remedies helped, Shloyme the Healer was sent for.

Three brass plates hung by the healer's door, the symbol of his craft. Actually, he hadn't finished his degree: he had served as a medic in the Russian army, and when his tour of duty was over, he became the town healer. He wore a stiff, black top hat and a pointed little beard, and he was the only man in town who wore a short jacket. He used to wash with perfumed soap, and it was whispered among the women that the healer ate tomatoes, which were held to be non-kosher in Bilgoray at that time.

When he made a house call, he was received with great honor, and the family hung on his every word. He asked the invalid to describe his pain, checked his pulse, and took out various instruments from the little bag he carried with him. He checked the patient's throat, and then gave him aspirin (he either was unable or not permitted to write prescriptions). In addition, he applied cups and leeches, painted throats, and gave enemas. Anyone who had a toothache went to Shloyme Healer. Shloyme would sit him down on his chair, grab hold of the tooth—and before the patient could scream—Shloyme Healer handed the tooth back to him.

He was also the only barber in town.

When he became old, his son accompanied him, and later inherited the position of town healer.

The Town's New Torah Scroll

YAAKOV (BEN MOSHE) PLOT
Sefer ha-zikaron le-kehilat Kamin-Koshirski (Kamien Koszyrski) ve-ha-seviva

This took place before the First World War.

Milke the Bobe had neither studied in a gymnasium nor graduated from a midwife's school, yet nearly all of the women called on Milke to serve as their midwife when they went into labor, trusting her more than any of the others. Thus she had to work constantly, without getting a chance to rest even on the Sabbath or holidays.

Since she didn't have any children, when she had managed to save some money she decided to commission a Torah scroll, and to donate it to the small synagogue of the Stepiner Hasidim, where she went to pray on the High Holy Days.

She quickly made an agreement wth Reb Aba the Scribe, an extremely pious Jew. Every day, before working on the Torah, he went to the mikve for a ritual immersion. When Reb Aba had finished, she asked Reb Moyshe the cattle slaughterer, who also conducted the prayer service in the Stepiner synagogue, to proofread the Torah and make sure that there weren't, God forbid, any mistakes in the text.

A week before the celebration of the completion of the Torah Milke the Bobe began to prepare a feast for all the Jews of the town, and she hired a band of musicians to come from Ratne, just as though she were preparing for a wedding. She also had the sextons from the various study houses go from house to house inviting everyone to the celebration.

On the afternoon before the party, Reb Aba the Scribe brought the holy scroll to the house of Milke's relative, Reb Peysekh Hersh the teacher. There the Jews of the town assembled. Milke's relatives, friends, and prominent members of the community had the honor of inserting a letter in the final column of the Torah scroll. The mood was festive. The tables were covered with cloths, and bore platters of honey cake and bottles of brandy; the crowd drank a toast to Milke and wished her "Mazel tov!"

After sundown the assembled community, led by the rabbis, took the Torah out and carried it under a canopy. The *klezmorim* [folk musicians] played happy melodies and everyone paraded through the streets of the town with candles in their hands, dancing and singing, until they arrived at the Stepiner synagogue. There the new Torah was read for the first time, and the rabbis and community leaders were called up to bless portions of the reading.

After the reading was finished and the Torah scroll had been set into the Ark, everyone sat down at tables set with all manner of delicious food. They ate and drank while the musicians played. The cantor and the Hasidim sang, and everyone danced, joyful over the Torah scroll that Milke had donated to the Stepiner synagogue.

And the "mother-in-law," the Bobe Milke, went about glowing with pride and filled with joy at having lived to lead her own Torah scroll under the wedding canopy.

The Angry Dance

YOM-TOV LEVINSKY
Sefer Zembrove (Zambrow)

It was in Zembrove, in the year 1908. My grandmother, Rivke-Gitl, was angry with her old in-law Khaye Tukravitsh. She considered her youngest son Berl's match to Khaye's granddaughter Nekhama below his station. The fact that Nekhama was also *her* granddaughter didn't help. During Berl and Nekhama's wedding the two grandmothers had to apologize to each other, which they did by dancing an angry-dance* just before the bride's face was covered with the veil. My grandmother Rivke-Gitl, a portly lady, held herself proudly. My other grandmother, Khaye, was tall, thin, and had a light step. The crowd stands around in a circle. Rivke-Gitl stands off to a side, sulking, her head lowered. Khaye dances, glides toward her, with a smile on her lips. The guests sing along with the music:

> Why are you so angry, without a reason why?
> Stop sulking, smile at me, lift your head to the sky.

Rivke-Gitl doesn't raise her head, but moves a little further off, goes over to the other side. But Khaye chases after her, gliding like a butterfly toward Rivke-Gitl, with the little smile. The crowd keeps singing. Khaye stretches out her hands. Grandmother Rivke-Gitl withdraws her hands; she doesn't want to make up. Khaye dances around again, from the other side. Rivke-Gitl grows a bit softer, lays her hands on her heart, and dances along, opposite Khaye. Khaye stretches her hand out again, Grandmother Rivke-Gitl shakes her head "No," and dances backward. The crowd grows more cheerful, and sings to the accompaniment of the musicians:

> Let's make up, the world is like a dream
> Let's make up, let us be at peace.

---

*One of several ritual dances traditionally done at Eastern European Jewish weddings. The purpose of the dance is to underscore the conflict, thereby turning private resentment public and generating communal pressure to resolve the conflict.

Grandmother Rivke-Gitl keeps dancing, forward, toward Khaye, and Khaye toward her. Each stretches her hands out toward the other: the crowd sings, "Make up, make up," the musicians let loose, "Make up, make up," the two pairs of hands lock together, one embraces the other, and they kiss each other. The guests do not restrain themselves and sing forcefully, clapping their hands: "Let's make up, make up!" The fiddle of a musician from Tiktin blends in with a thin little sigh, "make up, make up," as Goldetshke's son with the bass fiddle joins in. Khayele's husband's fiddle squeaks and Shimen Poyker keeps the beat: "Make up, make up . . ." The two women enter a dance, hand on shoulder, until the rest of the wedding party arrives. The bridegroom covers the bride's face and Sonye Batkhn from Bialystok stands on a chair to serenade the bride, accompanied by the musicians.

A Disrupted Seder Night

YITSKHOK GURVITS
Pinkas Navaredok (Nowogrodek)

What I am about to relate happened not very long ago, about thirty-five years ago at most, in the days when Reb Yosl's yeshiva was filled with the finest young men from the yeshivas of Kovno and Slobodke, genuine Talmud scholars, many of whom were ordained to judge questions of law. Many were so diligent that their voices could be heard chanting the holy texts as they studied all night long in the large study house and in all the buildings that surrounded the synagogue courtyard. The people of Navaredok, especially the women, showed the greatest respect and friendliness to these youngsters. Not only did they provide them with the best food they could, but desiring to avoid humiliating the young men by forcing them to come to the women's houses to eat, they brought the dishes to the students' own quarters.

I remember one fellow by the name of Reb Yoysef, a young man from Galicia. He was tall, with a bright, round face, and a little black beard. He learned quickly and with deep insight. He was fully at home in an entire half of the Talmud; he was intellectually gifted and persistent. It was a pleasure to discuss scholarly matters with him, which I frequently had the opportunity to do, since he stayed at the home of my father-in-law. The residents of the neighborhood kept him well-fed. As I remember, my mother brought food on Sundays, my mother-in-law on Mondays, and Tsivye, Yisroel Vilner's wife, on Tuesdays. When Tsivye Yisroel's brought the pot of stew and put it into the oven so that it wouldn't, God forbid, grow cool before Reb Yoysef was ready to eat, the smell wafted through the entire room.

One Tuesday I came in to chat with Reb Yoysef, and saw that he was eating. "Hearty appetite!" I said. "How does it taste?"

"Very good, everything is as it should be."

"It's only as tasty as it is," I replied, "because it was cooked by a beautiful young woman."

The young man's expression changed; he was clearly angry. "I don't know her. I don't know who brings me the food."

"That's just it," I said. "If you knew who was bringing it, you'd like it even better." The young man's face grew dark, he gave me an angry look, but I could tell that he didn't dare lash out at me for teasing him, and he changed the subject of the conversation.

Every Sabbath Reb Yoysef ate at the home of the richest man in town, Reb Shimen-Hershl Israelit, may he rest in peace. When he came home Reb Yoysef would say: "He seems to be a very simple Jew, this Shimen-Hershl, and he's capable of showing such friendliness to people. I feel very comfortable there, and I don't deserve the honor he gives me." This Reb Yoysef had one fault: he was too pious. His extreme piety led to the most bizarre episodes, one of which I'd like to describe here.

It was a few weeks before Passover, and in those days, one could tell that Passover was coming to Navaredok several weeks in advance: vessels, chairs, tables, and stoves were scraped and scoured with water, women went around in a constant dither, and there was an endless amount of work to be done. In my father-in-law's house people walked on straw mats and loose straw for an entire week. The chairs and tables stood outside in the yard, and people took their meals in the yard as well. My father-in-law, may he rest in peace, walked around angrily muttering and complaining, "Where did you women discover all these rules and regulations?" But my mother-in-law was very pious—in fact, her name was Frume, "the pious one"—and regardless of my father-in-law's muttering, everything was scoured ten times. When the oven was being made kosher for Passover, Reb Yoysef suddenly showed up and asked to be allowed to make the chimney kosher as well; even my mother-in-law's piety didn't go quite that far, and she was very curious to find out how one made a chimney kosher. Reb Yoysef did it quite simply: he brought a large bundle of straw, stuffed it into the chimney, lit it, and nearly burned down the entire house; but there was no question about it, the chimney was now kosher. When my father-in-law found out about the whole story, he raised a scandal, complaining angrily to Reb Yoysef: "In what holy book did you learn to do this? You'll be a rabbi in some town someday, and everyone will be ruined on account of such idiotic strict interpretations and crazy customs." Reb Yoysef Porush didn't answer at all. He just smiled good-naturedly, as if to say, "I've done what I had to do."

From Purim until Passover Reb Shimen-Hershl's house saw constant work. Nobody knew anything about eight-hour days in those years. The girls worked until midnight all year round, and Sore-Esther, may she rest in peace, knew how to keep them to that schedule. But from Purim to Passover they simply worked all night long, without resting. Sore-Esther's job was twofold then: both to check up on the girls in the shop, to make sure they weren't catnapping, and to prepare for Passover in her kitchen and in the house. The non-Jewish serving girls worked extra hard as well, for in Shimen-Hershl's house, everything had to be just so for Passover.

When the day before Passover arrived, Reb Yoysef prepared himself ritually. He went to the bathhouse half-starving, because he had eaten neither leavened nor unleavened food that day, nor dish from any of the housewives, just as if everyone had completely forgotten about him. My father-in-law brought Reb Yoysef a plate of kashe and potatoes with cracklings, which he ate without interest. Deep in thought, he remarked to me, "You know, the day before Passover makes me very sad."

He held out until evening, and when he went to the synagogue his mood picked up. On his way from the synagogue to Reb Shimen-Hershl's house Reb Yoysef felt quite good. The huge table was magnificently set, with the large chandelier and candlesticks, with plump, fresh featherbeds, in short, with all due tradition and pomp. Everyone sat down and listened as the master of the house and Reb Yoysef Porush both said the blessings. The youngest son asked the four questions. Then, as everyone began to recite the haggadah, just after the phrase "We were slaves," Shimen-Hershl and Sore-Esther both dozed off. Reb Yoysef, who was deeply absorbed in the haggadah, didn't notice at first. But when he heard the first snores of these overworked folk who hadn't had a proper night's rest for weeks, he became upset and started to recite the haggadah in a loud voice, trying to awaken them from their sweet repose. But the louder Reb Yoysef said the haggadah, the more deeply they slept. One by one, the children dropped off as well. Reb Yoysef finished the haggadah and sat like a silent martyr.

What was he to do now?

Reb Yoysef began to pace back and forth across the room, thinking lonely thoughts. He thought of his home, of his wife and child, and tears welled up in his throat. He thought to himself, "This is the path you shall follow to the Torah." He put on his coat, left the warm house, shut the door from outside, and left—but where to?

His feet carried him to my father-in-law's house, where I had been invited to the first seder. We had just started to eat.

"What, Reb Yoysef? Finished already?"

He told us the entire story, and each word was full of deep sorrow. Wanting to cheer him up, I asked him: "Couldn't you have gotten dumplings from the servants?"

He answered my joke quite seriously: "The gentile woman was lying in the kitchen, with her rear in the air, you should pardon the expression, snoring like an ox; next to her on the sideboard lay the serving girl, stretched out like a pretzel with her hair loose. The harmony of their snoring reminded me of some sort of wild music. I barely made it out of the kitchen."

"Sit down at the table," said my father-in-law. "I forgive you for making the chimney kosher." Reb Yoysef threw off his coat, and left his white kitl (ritual gown) on. We sat down at the table and enjoyed ourselves, eating and drinking with a proper festive spirit. Reb Yoysef told stories about Galicia, and I told stories about Saratov, halfway through the night. We stayed up the entire night, in fact, and every two or three hours we checked to see that there hadn't been a robbery at Shimen-Hershl's house. When daylight came and we entered his house, this was the scene displayed before us: a small flame still burned in the large lamp; the long, beautifully set table with the candlesticks, with the cups full of wine, with the kharoyses and bitter herbs stood untouched; and Shimen-Hershl himself, wearing his kitl with a belt tightly tied around his waist, with his long, half-silvered beard and his yarmulke on his head, sat sleeping in his feather-erbed, looking like a High Priest. We found Sore-Esther sleeping as well, with her elbow on the table and her right hand supporting her chin.

When we woke them up, saying, "Gentlemen, it is time to recite the morning Shema," they were terribly embarrassed, asking our pardon and begging me to keep secret, and God forbid, not tell anyone. I promised not to tell, but I ask you, how long can one keep a secret?

I think thirty-five years is long enough.

A Purim in the Region of Sants

LEON ABLEZER
Sefer Sants (Nowy Sacz)

I still remember an event that took place in our shtetl when I was eight years old: there was a Jew named Reb Moyshe Shrayber, who lived on the Hungarian side, in Filkhov. Reb Moyshe Shrayber came to pray with us at Hanusove on Sabbaths and holidays. Naturally, he came to the reading of the *megile* on Purim as well. He was a noted Talmud scholar and quite wealthy, and he raised his four sons and three daughters to follow in his footsteps. His oldest son, Reb Tsvi Shrayber, became a rabbi in Australia as early as 1912, and his second son, Reb Simkhe Shrayber, became a well-known merchant and community leader in Kshanov (near Cracow). His third son left for Palestine in 1934, and died there in

1945 (his wife and children live in Haifa). His fourth son, who was handicapped, was an excellent violinist.

Here is the story: one Purim morning after the reading of the megile, my father-in-law, Reb Leyzer-Dovid Kornraykh, invited everyone to his home for a drink and a snack, and we all went there, young and old. The crowd started drinking glass after glass, and after eating a bit, everybody had one more glass. Then we got up from the table and began to dance. And when young Hasidim start dancing, they really dance! Almost the whole town joined in, including the local gentiles, who had also been treated to a drink.

In the middle of the celebration, Reb Moyshe Shrayber stood up on a chair and announced: "Listen, everybody! I demand that everyone, young and old, travel home to Filkhov with me, and join me in a feast fit for a king. If anybody dares to refuse, I promise to smash all of your windows." No sooner said than done. Tipsy as he already was, Reb Moyshe didn't even wait for a response, and immediately broke two of the windows in my father-in-law's house.

He was quickly pacified. We poured several more glasses of ninety-six-proof liquor into his mouth. Eventually he fell asleep and we stretched him out on the floor. Then my father-in-law (also tipsy) covered him with a white sheet, placed two large candles at his head and feet, and eulogized him, provoking general hilarity. But suddenly Reb Moyshe stood up and repeated his demand: It was either a party at his house, or broken windows. Seeing that we had no choice in the matter, Reb Khayim Hanusover gave an order to his gentile servant (an Italian who lived at Reb Khayim's from his youth until his death at the age of fifty, and who spoke Yiddish): "Yashke! Harness ten sleds with good horses. We're going to Reb Moyshe Shrayber's house in Filkhov."

What can I tell you? In less than half an hour, ten teams harnessed to sleds were standing ready (the snow was always deep around the time of Purim in our parts), with good coachmen in the front seats. All of us, children included, of course, piled in and sang loudly all the way to Filkhov.

Now another chapter begins. On the way to Filkhov, one passes through Podolik, where a well-known family of lumber merchants named Goldberg lived, namely: Reb Yankev Goldberg, his son Reb Sender Goldberg, children, and grandchildren. Reb Sender sat in the sled with us, and as we approached his house, he jumped off. He stopped the first sled, driven by a gentile coachman, saying, "I will not allow Jews to pass by my house without stopping for a drink!" Say what we would, we had no choice. The whole crowd descended from the sleds and went into the house, where there was also a tavern stocked with liquor. We sat down to fresh-set tables and stayed for four hours, eating, drinking, and dancing.

After the party at Reb Sender's, everyone climbed back into the sleds and traveled to Reb Moyshe Shrayber's. I even remember the song that we sang then:

Things are going badly, badly for the Jews.
They go to see the rebe, they go to see the rebe.
Jews, Jews, go back home, grain is sure to grow.
Jews, Jews, go back home, grain is sure to grow.

And thus singing, we arrived at Reb Moyshe's house. With our help, his sons brought up his largest barrel of wine from the cellar (it held about 200 liters), and we began drinking it like water. Even the coachmen were drunk. In addition, his son Dovid the fiddler played while he conducted. We danced, sang, and drank, until I understood for the first time the meaning of the verse, "Until you cannot differentiate between 'Cursed be Haman' and 'Blessed be Mordechai.'" You think that was the end of it? You're making a big mistake!

About three in the morning, Reb Moyshe Shrayber stood up once again and announced that we were going to ride again, this time to Reb Dovid Hokhhayzer's house in Granastov. He permitted no discussion. We had to get back into the sleds and ride to Granastov, some seven kilometers from Filkhov. On this ride I found out what a "shortcut" means. In fifteen minutes we arrived at Reb Dovid's house and woke up the entire household. The gentiles of the village also came running, wondering what all the singing and dancing was about.

There we spent the whole day of Shushan Purim, because Reb Dovid's wife Pesl picked out four turkeys and four geese and sent them off to Lublov the slaughterer (about ten kilometers away) so that no one would be hungry. There we really celebrated Purim until the following morning, and we didn't go home until the third night. That was a Purim; that's how Jews celebrated in those days. And Simkhes Torah was the same.

The Death of the Bukovsker Rebe, Dovid Shapiro

A. SHARVIT
Sefer zikaron le-kehilat Sanok ve-ha-seviva

One detail about the death of the Bukovsker Rebe, whose court was located in Sanok, was much discussed at the time. Reb Meyer Shapiro had already become the rabbi of Pyetrkov, and a deputy of the Agudas Yisroel party in the *Sejm*, the Polish parliament. On account of the two men's close friendship a dispatch bearing the news of the tragedy was immediately sent out, saying that the funeral would not be held until Reb Meyer Shapiro's arrival. It was a bitter day in midwinter. Snow and ice covered the roads and highways, and all traffic had stopped. Even the trains were unable to run on account of the frozen tracks.

Rabbi Shapiro, fearing that he would miss the funeral, demanded a special train from the government to take him to Sanok. This was one of his privileges as a Sejm deputy. The railroad authorities provided him with a special car with its own boiler, although they announced that they would take no responsibility for the train's getting through. The Railroad Ministry immediately announced to all of the stationmasters between Pyetrkov and Sanok that a special train bearing a V.I.P. would be passing through. They were all sure that one of the state leaders would be on board, and they were stunned to see a Jew with a fur hat on his head instead. Many Jews came to the stations to greet the rabbi when they found out, and some boarded the train and accompanied him to the funeral. Rabbi Shapiro arrived in Sanok as the funeral train was gathering up steam, because the procession couldn't wait any longer. He pressed through the huge crowd, approached the coffin and called out in a powerful voice: "Dovid, King of Israel, lives!" emphasizing the word "Dovid," which was the dead Rebe's name. It was a clear message about the continuation of Bukovsker Hasidism and the survival of his court, which passed to the children of the Bukovsker Rebe, who had been orphaned so young.

Concerning the Opponents of Hasidism in Lizhensk

VOLF RAYKHNTAL
Lizhensk (Lezajsk); sefer zikaron le-kedoshei Lizhensk she-nispu be-shoat ha-natsim

Certainly there are still former residents of Lizhensk living who remember my father and how he conducted himself. While still a boy he used to walk to see the old Rozvadover; he was a fervent Hasid of the Rozvadover dynasty. Later he became a *misnagid*, an opponent of Hasidism, who brought the Zionist vision from Vienna and inculcated it deeply in his dearest student Reb Mordkhe Rays, with whom he founded the Mizrachi circle in Lizhensk. This required nerve, entailing excommunication and unpleasantness. He did what he had to do, remaining true to his conviction without fearing the disruptive consequences. I will recount an event which I myself witnessed, to demonstrate just how determined he was.

On the anniversary of the death of Rebe Elimelekh of blessed memory, hundreds of Jews, along with rebes of various dynasties, used to come to our city. The Rozvadover Rebe was represented by the great Plantser Rebe of blessed memory. Spending a Sabbath in our city, he held his gatherings at the study house. Just at that time my father had been studying Midrash with a group for many years, and this Sabbath was no exception. The rebe had napped, and was well-rested; he used to stay with Reb Kalmen-Volf Kalbakh. Everything was arranged for him, and he began to make his way to the study house along with both local and recently arrived Hasidim, led by Anshl Vaynman. He was ready to begin the gathering, but my father sat at the table studying, and he wouldn't hear of giving up the table. He added that for the purpose of meeting to gobble food and swill liquor they could have rented a hotel room rather than entering a study house, where the Torah is at home. Unfortunately, my father's students were no great heroes: neither Meyer Shtrukh, nor Motl Karp, nor Volf Vaks, nor the others. Seeing that he had no one to lead into battle—although they were profoundly respectful of my father concerning study, they were frightened of the Rebe—he was at a loss for what to do, but being a wise Jew, he had an idea. He arose, closed the Midrash, and announced to his students: "Since I see that the Rebe's gluttony is more important to you than the Torah and my teaching, I will no longer learn Midrash with you."

It wasn't easy for my father to sacrifice the pleasure he had had from studying Midrash. Yet he had no other choice, knowing that the measure of a conviction is a man's willingness to suffer on account of it and show that it means more to him than his personal comfort, or cordial relations with others.

Thus were the misnagdim of Lizhensk. Torah was more important to them than coarse methods of winning influence.

There were misnagdim in Lizhensk, and the book of Lizhensk will be incomplete if they go unmentioned, especially since the Zionist movement arose from among the misnagdim, along with the state which has been a haven for Jews. May their memory be blessed.

A Strike in Kheyder

YOYSEF FRIDMAN
Loshits (Loice); le-zeykher an umgebrakhte kehile

My teacher, Tsalke Zabirer, had a vicious temper. His students were scared to death of him. Woe to the child that made the teacher angry. Tsalke let out all of his bitterness on the child's backside. And he knew how to beat children better than he knew how to teach them. I don't know what resources of strength our teacher drew on when he beat children; as a rule he was a real weakling, barely able to keep his soul in his body. He spent more time lying in bed than teaching us. We children were delighted when he had to stay in bed. As soon as the teacher lay down, we turned the kheyder topsy-turvy. The rebe would cough and curse like a fishwife from the other room.

Our kheyder was always jammed full of children. There was no lack of poor people in Loshits, and whoever didn't have enough money to pay tuition sent his children to Tsalke Zabirer, the teacher at the free talmud toyre. The children were of various ages. Most of them were slow, malnourished, and undisciplined.

It was hard for my parents to make up their minds to send me to that sort of kheyder. Yet for poor people who "don't want their child to grow up to be a non-Jew," Tsalke Zabirer would have to do. I was the youngest, the smallest, and the weakest of all the children in the kheyder. My terror of our teacher was boundless. I was very frightened of being struck. If the teacher had hit me the way he beat other children, I don't think I would have gotten out of his hands alive. Therefore I studied hard. On the second or third day of the week, I would already have memorized the week's Torah portion. Thus I became the best student in class. When Reb Yoysef used to examine us, I would always get a few kopeks and a pinch on the cheek.

The other children envied me bitterly. Precisely those children who were incapable of learning were the ones who were physically strong, and they made my life miserable.

I don't remember whether I or someone else first thought of having me creep under the table, whisper the Torah portion to the other children, and thereby save them from beatings. The rebe was satisfied, thinking that the children were learning well, and the children were even happier. The teacher didn't even think of looking under the table, until we came to the difficult portion *Mishpatim*. The rebe couldn't understand: here it was only Wednesday, and the children knew such a difficult text inside out? Tsalke sat at the table, sucking his beard, scratching his head and looking this way and that, while my insides churned as I sat underneath, whispering to my fellow students. I didn't notice that the rebe had already seen me and had stood up. He went over to the stove, picked up a poker, and fell on me so viciously that I thought I was about to die. In an instant I fled underneath the bed, but the poker reached me there as well, and shredded my sides.

Deeply hurt, I went outside, gathered all the boys together, and made a "speech"—the first speech of my life. With my child's vocabulary, I called on them to refuse to be beaten anymore, and to strike in protest. All the children agreed not to return to kheyder. We decided to walk to Mord. We actually set off down Shedlits Street, but just past the edge of town we were terrified by the bundles of grain in the fields, and we went back to town.

Yet we didn't return to kheyder until we were assured that the rebe would no longer beat us.

My "Days" in Slonim

Z. SHER
Pinkas Slonim; sefer gimel

My home town of Rozhinoy boasted a yeshiva which was famed in all of the surrounding towns and cities. When I was twelve years old, I was already a student of the head of the yeshiva, Reb Itsele. He was the greatest scholar in town after the rabbi, Reb Shabse Volakh, who was considered to be one of the most brilliant men of his generation. (He was the uncle of the famous Communist leader and Soviet Foreign Minister Maksim Litvinov, whose real name was Volakh.)

When I left the yeshiva, my father had to decide what to do with me. His heart wouldn't permit him to apprentice me to an artisan, because he dreamed of my becoming a rabbi. On the other hand, it was impossible for him to let me stay in the house doing nothing and eating for free. His meager weaver's wages didn't even suffice for the upkeep of his second wife, my stepmother, and the child they had had. He decided to send me to study at the famous Slonim yeshiva. My father had a cousin there with whom I could stay. Immediately after Sukkes, he packed a few shirts and several freshly washed pairs of leggings into a bundle (I never wore socks during my childhood), hired a carriage, and set off for Slonim with me.

My father's cousin lived in an alcove in the home of a certain Shmuel Stolyer, the cabinetmaker, on the artisans' street. Her husband was in America, and she had remained in Slonim with a two-year-old daughter. Shmuel Stolyer was a short, wizened little man, with many wrinkles in his face, and strict, angry eyes. He was always shouting at someone: either at his wife, or at his workers, or at neighbors in the street. In Slonim he was known by the nickname Shmuel Khemele's, or Khemele Crazyman. When he overheard someone referring to him as "Khemele," he used to grow bitterly angry.

My father was unaware that Khemele was Shmuel's nickname. Plodding through the deep mud of the artisans' street and holding me by the hand, he began asking people where Shmuel Khemele's lived. Who did he happen to ask, but Shmuel Khemele's himself! The latter shot him an angry look, and shouted, "Reb Jew, find out who you're looking for before you make your inquiries!" and he began to run away as though someone were shooting at him. After running a short way, however, he turned his face toward my father and shouted angrily: "Over there, that's his house."

My father's cousin inhabited a small, narrow alcove. One bed stood there, in which the cousin, a very fat woman, slept together with her young daughter. I would have to sleep head-to toe in the same bed.

My father left me with his cousin, depending on her to find "eating days" for me. When we parted, he gave me an entire "quarter" (twenty-five kopeks), kissed me, and told me to be a good boy and study with fervor.

Owing to the fact that my father had so innocently called my cousin's landlord "Khemele," I got nothing but trouble from him. He constantly drove me out of his yard, and I was confined to my cousin's alcove like a prisoner.

His furniture workshop was at his house. The beautifully turned knobs, and the carvings of various animals and birds, such as lions and eagles, on the furniture—on beds, chairs, cupboards, and sideboards—teased and enticed me, and the smell of fresh-planed wood shavings and the turpentine with which the furniture was polished wafted to my nostrils with such a sweetness that I would have given a lot just to spend a few minutes in the furniture workshop. But it was impossible for me, because Shmuel Khemele's wouldn't let me in.

His only worker, the apprentice Idl, was a short lad with black eyes and hair, and with an open, cheerful face. He sympathized with my wish to spend some time in the workshop, and once he whispered in my ear with utmost secrecy that Master Shmuel would be away that night. He had gone to a wedding with his wife. If I came into the workshop late at night, when it was dark there, I could like down to sleep next to him on the wood shavings.

With my heart pounding, I waited for evening, when it would grow dark in the workshop. Then with quiet steps I slipped into the workshop and lay down next to Idl on the mountain of freshly planed shavings. I felt exalted and happy, as though my greatest wish had been fulfilled. Yet I couldn't fall asleep, for fear that the boss would catch me. I lay next to Idl for a few hours, and then with soft, barefoot steps, in order not to wake him, I slipped back out of the furniture workshop and returned to my cousin's alcove.

My father had asked my cousin to arrange eating days for me. However, she couldn't find more than four "days" per week for me, and even these were with poor families. (She fed me herself the other three days.) One of the four days, the Sabbath meal, wasn't bad at all, but the other three I was hungry.

Mondays I would eat at a shoemaker's house. When I arrived the first time, he was beating his wife with a broad, leather shoemaker's strap. She wept and cried out, but he cut her like cabbage.

I stood embarrassed, with my eyes to the ground, and finally left the house hungry, never to return. I had lost my Mondays. From then on, I got by on Monday with the bit of thin soup distributed at the yeshiva.

Tuesdays I ate at the home of a poor widow with four children. Apparently she was very pious, and poor as she was, she had a yeshiva student one day a week in order to earn merit in the World to Come. But she was always bitter and depressed, and very dirty. The house was never clean, the beds never made. She went barefoot, her feet black from dirt, in a dirty petticoat and a jacket whose color was impossible to discern. Her hair was disheveled. She sighed constantly, and never said a friendly word to me. She used to set a plate of groats and a piece of bread on the dirty table with a sigh, and go off into another room.

My third day was at the home of a poor storekeeper. He had a small grocery in the front of his little house, and both man and wife were constantly busy in the store. I wasn't fed there; they took care of me by giving me three kopeks. I used to buy a portion of chick-peas from the woman who sold them at the yeshiva, and that would have to last me through the day.

However, my fourth day, the Sabbath, was good. On the Sabbath I went to a tinsmith. He was a tall, handsome, cheerful Jew with a blond beard. He wasn't very bright, though, and was henpecked by his young wife. She was very pious, and considered it a great mitsve to feed a yeshiva boy one day each week. Indeed, she took care of me: in the course of the three Sabbath meals, she stuffed as much food into me as I could hold. She would put another piece of fish, of meat, or of kugel onto my plate, and say with pious goodness: "Eat, eat, it will give you strength to learn."

The people of Slonim had a special dish called a *gutman*. (This is a sort of pudding of buckwheat meal, sauteed with fried onions and rose oil.) It became a strictly observed custom for my young hostess to bake me a small gutman every Sabbath. After services on Saturday morning, before serving the *cholent*, she used to bring out the nicely browned gutman she had made just for me. Her face shone as I sat eating it.

The tinsmith was extremely fond of gutman; as I sat eating mine, he used to look at me with greedy eyes, and saliva ran from his mouth. But he didn't dare touch it for fear of his wife. Just once, when we sat at the table humming a melody, he stole a glance at his wife, and thinking that she wasn't looking, he stretched his hand to my plate for a piece of gutman. She immediately noticed this, and struck his hand with the spoon she was holding, shouting:

"Where are you sticking your hand, you? My big scholar! Don't you know that the gutman is for the yeshiva boy? Do you sit studying like he does?"

And she glanced at me piously.

I felt sorry for the tinsmith. His eyes, greedy for a piece of the gutman, haunted me, and I didn't enjoy eating. Nevertheless, the Sabbath was my best day. Just that one day in the week, I ate my fill.

I studied at Slonim for two semesters. Then I was told that I was competent to study on my own, without attending the yeshiva. So I left Slonim, and returned to my hometown.

From American Universities to the Polish Yeshivas

KHAYIM SEMYATITSKY
Sefer Mir

In America one often hears about restless youth who wake up one morning and set off to wander in foreign places. Their daily routine at home bores them. Their fresh blood yearns for the wide world, for unknown landscapes. Where do they go? Many become sailors and travel the wide seas; others set off for the wilderness of South America, and so forth. Among them are many Jewish youngsters. Recently, however, many American Jewish youngsters can be found where one would least expect them: in the old Jewish *shtetlekh* of Poland and Lithuania, far away from big cities and railroad lines, where only one melody has sounded for many years, the melody of Talmud study.

There one can meet Jewish young men from New York and Cleveland, from Pennsylvania and Kansas, from every part of America. In the yeshivas of Mir, Slobodke, Volozhin, and Telz, dozens of boys with yarmulkes on their heads stand at wooden lecterns with open Talmuds in front of them. They have left their comfortable homes in America and crossed the Atlantic in order to study Torah in the far-flung shtetlekh of our grandfathers and great-grandfathers.

American yeshiva boys in Poland and Lithuania, young students in the old country, who have already graduated college—this is something new. The Jews who live in the towns shrug their shoulders without understanding: they've seen Americans coming for a visit to their relatives, and just as quickly going away again, but strapping young men of eighteen and twenty, without friends or relatives in town, coming four thousand miles to study for twelve or thirteen hours a day—this has never happened before.

The largest colony of American yeshiva boys is located in the small town of Mir. The town lies a mere twenty viorst from the Soviet border. In this out-of-the-way corner there are forty-eight boys from New York, Brooklyn, Illinois, Kansas, Texas, and even as far as Winnipeg in Canada.

If you think that studying in such a yeshiva is easy, you're mistaken. At seven o'clock in the morning one must be in the yeshiva, ready for the morning prayers, and study concludes only at ten o'clock in the evening. The only times for rest come at breakfast and lunch, and during a brief walk in the nearby woods in the evening. The rest of the time all the students are steeped in study. The *bokher* from Baranovitsh debates with the boy from New York, while the Hasid from Lublin sways next to the doctor from Harvard University, as they both lean over the dusty pages of the Talmud, which bears the marks of the many generations that have studied from it.

The Americans are mostly sons of wealthy parents, except for several children of American rabbis. None of them lacked the best of everything in America. Yet when they came to Mir—a place that isn't even on the map—they had to change their entire lives. The hot bath, the playing field, and the automobile, the neatly pressed suit, and the theater—Mir knows nothing of all this.

Indeed, it was difficult for them to accustom themselves to life there at first. They suffered most from the fact that there were no clean washrooms. A certain young man went so far as to write a letter to his mother—not from Mir, but from the Telzer yeshiva—that for the first three days he couldn't satisfy his natural functions because the habits there were so strange.

In Mir, however, it was recognized that the Americans couldn't live that way, and the yeshiva was the first to introduce plumbing. A wealthy Jew from Buffalo, who visited his sons in the yeshiva, found that the sanitary facilities were quite backward. He donated half of the sum necessary to install the plumbing. The second half was given by the "Joint" [American Jewish Joint Distribution Committee] and the yeshiva thus became the first modern building in town.

A Jew from Chicago introduced electric lighting into the yeshiva, which now has its own generator and seventy electric lights. As far as eating goes, however, no changes have been made, and the housewives of Mir give the "Amerikantses" the same food they give the Polish boys. Many American boys complain in letters to their parents that it's impossible to get any ice cream, that oranges are worth their weight in gold, and that figs aren't to be had for love or money. The good-hearted Jewish mothers take pity on their children, and send packages of oranges and figs for their sons to eat for breakfast.

However, one issue led to a minor dispute between the administration of the yeshiva and the American boys. This was the matter of playing football. The former student of Harvard University knows that one can study all his subjects and still find time to go outside in a sweater and toss a rubber ball back and forth between lectures. In Mir this is not approved of. One time, five or six Americans decided to get some exercise in the morning, and began playing football right in front of the yeshiva. Their Polish friends and the townspeople stood astounded. It was the first time they had seen scholars who were also ballplayers. The leaders of the yeshiva immediately let the group of Americans know that they had "gone too far," and after a quiet protest the players gave in.

An exception is made during the summer, when the students go off to cottages in the country to rest, and the Americans eagerly pick up the ball, just as they do in America.

The First Yiddish Library

DVOYRE KUTNIK

Yizkor kehilot Luninyets (Luniniec)/Kozhanhorodok

When my father moved from Kozhanhorodok to Luninyets after the great fire, he decided to open a popular library. He was undaunted by the great difficulties presented both by the tsarist regime, which did not give its permission, and by the religious Jews, who were afraid that "Avrom Hershl will be trafficking in forbidden books."

My father ordered from Warsaw and Vilna several shipments of books in Hebrew and Yiddish. The Hebrew books were mostly works of the Jewish Enlightenment by Kalman Shulman, [Avraham] Mapu, [Y. L.] Peretz, Sholem Aleichem, Mendele [Moykher-Sforim] and others. In Yiddish, there were Peretz, Sholem Aleichem, Mendele, [Yankev] Dinezon, and others.

At first, the Yiddish books were not very successful. Then my father, who understood the psychology of the small-town reader, ordered the novels of Shomer [Nokhem-Meyer Shaykevitsh], and [Oyzer] Bloshteyn. The townspeople read these eagerly, devouring the stories about counts and countesses. It must be said that through Shomer, people became used to reading books.

Bit by bit my father inculcated in people an appreciation of the Yiddish classics. Every Friday afternoon our house was visited by seamstresses, serving girls, salesgirls, and also working men, tailors and shoemakers, who remembered to stop off at Avrom Hershl Melamed's [the Teacher's] house on their way back from the bathhouse. The books were mostly hidden in the dresser, while revolutionary pamphlets were kept under the straw mattress on my mother's bed. More than once when a policeman appeared on our street, my mother grew pale with fear. One time she took all of the pamphlets out from under her bed and burned them.

The library had a powerful influence on the readers. The small-town inhabitants acquainted themselves with the wider world. Their eyes were opened, and they began to understand that there was a world full of problems beyond Luninyets, and even beyond Pinsk. Here in Detroit, I frequently meet a woman from my town, who tells me her memories about the books she used to borrow from us every Friday, down to the names of their heroes.

The library was destroyed in 1915, when we left Luninyets for Kozhanhorodok, fleeing the approaching Germans. The Cossacks who occupied our house burned all of the books, thereby putting an end to the first Yiddish library.

My Grandmother Sews
Her Own Burial Shroud

BLUME GOREN-MALOVANY
Sefer zikaron le-kehilat Kolno

The only one of my grandparents whom I knew was Sheyne-Rokhl Malovany, my father's mother. She was a widow. Her husband, my grandfather Meyer-Dovid, died tragically. He was a lumber merchant who used to transport lumber to Germany. A wagon filled with lumber in which he sat overturned, and my grandfather was killed. He was buried in Johannisburg, Germany.

After the accident my grandmother became depressed and lost interest in her own life. She devoted all of her energy to doing good deeds, such as cooking for sick, poor, or lonely people; sitting at their bedsides; and helping in any way she could. I remember well how she used to send me off to carry food to a needy person.

Grandmother Sheyne-Rokhl was the oldest female member of the town burial society. She was responsible for sewing burial shrouds and carrying out the most important services to the deceased. I didn't like going to my grandmother's house because she was constantly surrounded by sorrow. Her house was different from ours and from everybody else's. With my child's insight, I understood that a home shouldn't be gloomy. It should be lively, full of cheerfulness. Even my grandmother's wall clock terrified me as it mournfully tolled the hours.

My grandmother sewed shrouds for herself. She often requested that her older grandchildren help her out. One time when I was there she gave me the job of sewing ribbons for the shrouds. They were to be used for binding the feet of the dead woman. She gave me a large needle with strong white thread, unknotted, and said, "Sew!" I looked at the door in terror, thinking of running away, and wondering what poor woman's fate it would be to lie in these shrouds.

My grandmother continued to sew the shrouds for herself. Whenever a towns-woman died just before the Sabbath or a holiday, and there was no time to sew a shroud for her, my grandmother gave away her own shroud, and soon sat down to cut new linen and begin working all over again.

When one sews clothes, one must try them on. And my grandmother did just that. The entire family, including the elder children, saw our grandmother in her burial shroud. It was kept a secret from us smaller children, however.

Since my father Yisroel was my grandmother's oldest son, he attempted to keep my grandmother from feeling entirely alone, and always sent one of the older children to sleep at Grandmother's house. Later the task of sleeping at Grandmother's house every night fell to my brother Meyer-Dovid.

One night he saw my grandmother getting out of bed, washing her hands, putting on the shroud, putting two pair of glasses on her nose, taking a prayer book in one hand, and striking her heart with the other as she said a wailing last confession. My brother saw it quite clearly because a small lamp burned all night there. The first time he was badly frightened. Then he became used to it, because she did it every night. Thus she prepared herself to pass away into eternity.

When she had already grown very weak, two women from the burial society came to request the honor of being taught how to sew shrouds. She wouldn't hear of it. She wanted the great honor to pass by inheritance to her daughter Rashke Oler, who was then one of the younger members. Aunt Rashke was unable to take on the responsibility, however, because her children wouldn't let her. Grandmother had no choice but to give the honor and the responsibility to other women, and she taught them to sew shrouds.

When our grandmother passed away, she was honored as a saint. She was carried around the synagogue and the study house. In front of the wagon her grandchildren carried the Talmud that my father had donated to the study house.

Events

The Butchers of Zhirardov Commission a Torah Scroll

K. GRUSHKA

Pinkas Zhirardov (Zyrardow), Amshinov un Viskit

I'm going to describe the butchers' society, which I knew intimately from my childhood on. When I was only seven or eight years old, my father took me along every Sabbath to pray with the other butchers at Yisroel Shoykhet's ("Butcher's") house (on the highway, a few houses away from the steam mill). After the service everyone said a blessing, had a glass of wine, and chatted about events of the day. Once, I remember, Dovid Elving came to pray. He had just come back to Poland; he talked about Dr. Herzl and started a dispute. Everyone considered him to be an apostate, and nobody was impressed by his speech.

In time the butchers' society decided to have a Torah scroll written. It was agreed that the Torah should be one the likes of which had never been seen in Poland. It should be something to be proud of. But where were they to get so much money? It was decided that once a week (or once a month, I don't remember which) each butcher was to donate a calfskin, which would be treated and made into parchment.

A scribe with a fine hand was found, and work was begun. Everything went according to plan until an incident occurred that caused an interruption.

The incident took place in 1904 or 1905. There were four ritual slaughterers in Zhirardov: Binem Shoykhet, Binem-Mendl Khazn-Shoykhet, Zalmen Shoykhet, and one other whose name escapes me; I remember that he was the son-in-law of Binem, who had taught him the trade [this is correct—his name was Dovid Nayman—eds.]

Then Binem-Mendl decided to leave the town, and a search began for a new ritual slaughterer-cantor. A dispute arose between the rabbi and the butchers' society. The rabbi was to receive eight hundred rubles from the new appointee, and the butchers, who claimed that the cantor-ritual slaughterer made a living from them, demanded money as well. Since they needed money to have their Torah scroll completed, they insisted on being paid off. They announced that if they didn't get the money, they wouldn't let the new ritual slaughterer practice his trade.

One Sabbath two Hasidim announced that if the new slaughterer gave money to the butchers, the rabbi would declare any animal that he slaughtered un-kosher. The butchers responded by repeating their warning that they wouldn't let the slaughterer practice if he didn't give them any money.

When the new slaughterer saw that he had no choice, he began to negotiate with the butchers, and it was agreed that he would pay them four hundred rubles. When the rabbi was told of this, he announced that he would condemn the slaughterer's meat and have meat brought in from the neighboring towns of Viskit and Amshinov. The butchers threatened to soak with gas any meat brought in from outside.

Then the solidarity of the butchers broke down. Avrom Shoykhet, one of the strongest of the butchers, who was known for using oxen slaughtered in War-saw, brought an animal to be slaughtered. Khayim Shoykhet came along, made the ox unkosher while it was being slaughtered, and threatened to slaughter Avrom himself if he tried the same thing again.

When the rabbi heard about this, he was forced to apologize, and things quieted down.

The writing of the Torah scroll continued meanwhile, but the scribe died in the midst of his work. Work was stopped until a scribe with a similar handwrit-ing was found.

In the meantime my parents moved to Lodz. That was in the beginning of 1906. Things went very well for us from the first. Khayim Shoykhet came to us and asked my parents to return to Zhirardov. My father wanted to stay in Lodz, however, and our situation grew better and better.

Some time later, when I was thirteen years old and a tailor's apprentice, I came home to find my father not at home. My mother told me that Khayim Shoykhet had come to bring my father to Zhirardov for the celebration of the completion of the Torah scroll.

When my father came home, he couldn't stop talking about how wonderful the celebration had been. There was eating and drinking without end, and eight days of dancing in the streets.

The Righteousness of Revolutionaries

BORUKH SHTULMAN
Sefer Kalushin (Kaluszyn); geheylikt der khorev gevorener kehile

A memoir of the year 1905, dedicated to the
memory of my brother, the martyr Meyer Shtulman.

I was about seven years old at that time and the event, like all events of one's youth, is engraved in my memory forever.

My father of blessed memory, the head of the rabbinical court, was sitting with the other two judges, Noyekh Reb Mordkhele's and my brother-in-law Yekhiel Meyer, and the three of them were busy studying. There were no hearings or legal questions to be resolved that day because revolution was in the air and no one stepped out of their houses, except for the "strikers," as they were then called.

Suddenly the door opened, and three tall youngsters came in. The three were Avromtshe Gelibter, Yoysef Dobzhinsky, and Leyzer Bilke. The latter immediately shot off his revolver into the cupboard, and Reb Noyekh fainted. My brother-in-law Yekhiel-Meyer didn't know what to do. I and my brother Meyer—still a small child—simply looked on curiously. The only one who retained his self-control was my father.

"Jews, what is it you demand? Is shooting correct Jewish behavior?" my father asked. Then one of the three, Avromtshe Gelibter, stepped forward saying: "In the name of the revolutionary committee we have come to demand that you give us the money that the bourgeoisie entrusts to you when they come to settle disputes."

My father pulled the drawer of the table out as far as it would go, and said to them: "You see, dear Jews, there's lots of money here in this drawer."

Then he began taking out little bundles wrapped in red kerchiefs, showing them: "This bundle of one hundred rubles belongs to a poor orphan, her inheritance from her parents. And the other kerchief with two hundred rubles is a poor bride's dowry: her groom swore that he wouldn't marry her until the dowry was entrusted to the rabbi. All of the other bundles also belong to poor orphans, brides, and widows. As for the bourgeoisie, as you call them, they do indeed entrust great sums to me, but only in promissory notes."

To prove it, my father took out of the drawer notes for a thousand rubles, which Jewish lumber merchants had given him as collateral for various deals, and concluded: "So, if you wish, take the money that belongs to the poor brides, widows, and orphans. As far as the notes for large sums go, you can take them too, but they aren't of any value to you."

It grew quiet and remained that way for some minutes, until Avromtshe Gelibter stepped forward again: "Listen, Rebe, we won't take money from poor orphans and widows, although we're desperately in need of money." Then he took a look at the cupboard and said that they'd send one of their men the next day to fix the hole made by the revolver. Shortly afterward they left, shouting "Long live the revolution!"

After their departure my father said to the two judges: "You see? A Jewish soul cannot be fathomed. Even their path includes pity toward widows and orphans, and on account of that God will forgive them."

The Ruined Wedding

(ON ACCOUNT OF AN AGREEMENT BETWEEN THE RABBI OF KHMELNIK AND THE MUSICIANS)

MOYSHE-LEYZER MINTS
Pinkas Khmelnik (Chmielnik)

One day the rabbi of Khmelnik, Reb Avrom-Yitskhok Silman of blessed memory, summoned the Khmelnik town jester, the leader of the musicians, and addressed him thus:

"Yoysef-Leyb, I know that you are an honorable Jew, and I want you to promise me that you and your children and grandchildren, the musicians of Khmelnik, will never play at a wedding where boys and maidens dance together."

"I promise you that," responded Yoysef-Leyb Batkhn [Jester].

Virtually all of the musicians in Khmelnik at that time belonged to one large family. Yoysef-Leyb Batkhn played the bass, his son Sane played fiddle. His grandchildren, the children of his eldest daughter Khane (whose father, Velvele Klezmer, played several instruments himself, such as the fiddle, the trumpet, and the clarinet) were four: Notl, the eldest, was a good fiddler; Avremele played clarinet; and Yisroel banged the drum. The youngest, Elye, was still quite young, but later on he became a great musician. He graduated from the conservatory in Vienna and quickly became famous for the cello concerts he gave in the great cities of Poland, such as Kelts, Lodz, Warsaw, and Cracow. He married a girl from Kelts, but died quite young. His only son survived Hitler's hell, and now lives in America.

Word about the rabbi's conversation with Yoysef-Leyb Batkhn quickly carried across town. Many years passed, and everything was "right and proper," as we used to say.

Until Hershl Stelmakh's son, Yankl Rimazh, returned from military service, and before we knew it, he became engaged to Yakhne Libe, Elye Penzel's daughter. I remember it well, for I was present at the betrothal as well as at the wedding. My mother, may she rest in peace, was a blood cousin of Libe Elye Penzel's, and since I was the youngest in the family, I was taken along to nearly all of the celebrations to which my parents were invited. Precisely in which month the wedding took place, I don't remember, but I'm quite sure that the year was 1895. The wedding took place at the home of the groom's brother, Yisroel Stolyer. He had his workshop together with his apartment on the alley or yard, where Shiele Melamed had his schoolroom, in the passageway from Synagogue Street to the small marketplace.

Yisroel Stolyer emptied out his workshop and also removed the furniture from the other room, set up tables with long benches, and got everything ready for the wedding.

After the ceremony, as is customary in a Jewish wedding, the newlyweds were led into a private room, where a bite to eat had been prepared for them so that they could break the difficult fast of their wedding day. Bowls of golden chicken soup were waiting as well. Meanwhile the young men began dancing. Girls danced also, but separately. They danced folk dances and waltzes, in which boys dance with boys and girls dance with girls. Everything went fine until the young folk grew tired and settled down to rest a bit. Later the groom's younger brother, Shmuel Stelmakh (wheelwright), got up. Although he was a carpenter by trade, all of his father's children were called by their father's trade. Shmuel was already one of the "play-boys," as they were called in Khmelnik; he worked in the big city, where the pay was a lot better. He wanted to show his friends that he was a real sport, that he could afford to pay the musicians for a long dance all by himself. The dance was a kind known as a "Kutner" or a "Larsey," in which eight couples take part. He asked the musicians how much he had to pay for the Kutner, and they told him that it cost a whole ruble. He gave them a ruble, and the leader of the musicians, Yoysef-Leyb, threw the coin into the tin can that was tied to a leather belt and hung from the shoulders of the young musician who played the drum.

The tin can, it should be mentioned, was locked with a padlock, the key to which was always left at home. It was agreed among the musicians that none of them was to keep the key on his person. After the wedding ended, they all gathered at the home of the jester, opened the can, counted the money, and distributed proper shares to each one.

So, the couples began getting into position for the dance. The musicians began playing in rhythm. Since they were standing way up in the first room, they couldn't see what was happening in the much larger second room, especially as the youngsters who weren't dancing blocked off the view into the room. Thus no one would see that boys and girls were dancing together. But a mishap took place. The musicians began playing the second introduction to the Kutner dance before the dancers had finished the first steps. One of the young men who was conducting the dance shouted out to the musicians not to change the music. Since Sane, who was playing first fiddle, didn't understand what the young man wanted, he came closer to the entrance to the second room in order to ask him. He was rather tall, and could see over the heads of the people who were blocking the doorway. He looked over, and saw the boys dancing with the girls. With his eyes to the ground, Sane returned to the musicians and said something in the musicians' jargon, which no one else understood. The musicians immediately stopped playing. The dancers grew frightened and stopped dancing. The boys came out of the second room, demanding to know why the musicians weren't playing. Yoysef-Leyb explained why they had stopped and scolded them for their behavior, which had caused the musicians this embarrassment: "Everyone in Khmelnik knows about our agreement with the rabbi, which prohibits us from playing when boys and girls dance together."

"And what about my ruble? After all, I paid you to play!" stormed Shmuel.

"We've been playing, and we will play, on condition that you dance separately, not together with girls."

One thing led to another, until Shmuel tore Sane's fiddle out of his hands and broke it over his head. The fiddle collapsed in splinters. They also wanted to break the bass. Yoysef-Leyb blocked their way, guarding his bass with both arms. But he was unsuccessful, for he and his bass were both thrown to the ground, and soon there was a heap of musicians on the floor. Yoysef-Leyb and his bass were both stepped on. When I saw all this, I burst out crying and shouted: "They're killing my uncle!" All of the musicians were beaten except for one, the drummer, who carried the money can on his back. When he saw what was happening, he must have thought to himself: Better take off, Yisroel, and save our few pennies.

And that's how the playboys of Khmelnik got back at the musicians for trying to keep their agreement with the rabbi.

When Libe Elye Penzel's, the bride's mother, saw what had happened, she wrung her hands, ran to Yoysef-Leyb, and begged with tears in her eyes: "Yoysef-Leyb, you mustn't leave my child's celebration. To me, you're not Yoysef-Leyb Batkhn [the Jester], but Yoysef-Leyb my blood cousin, my dear guest at our daughter's wedding."

My uncle Yoysef-Leyb was moved by her speech, but it was hard for him to say anything to her; he took out his handkerchief and wiped the tears from his eyes. He wished her joy from her children, said good night, and went outside, where Sane and the grandsons were waiting for him.

When Yoysef-Leyb left the wedding, Libe broke out crying: who would be the Master of Ceremonies when the wedding presents were given?

The next day Libe Elye Penzel's went to Yoysef-Leyb's house to bring him his fee. But Yoysef-Leyb refused to take the money. The tin can stood on the table, however, and Libe put the money into it, saying, "I know that you suffered a deep humiliation, yet you'll need to fix the fiddles and the bass. The money will come in handy."

People talked about the town's ruined wedding for a long, long time.

The First Suicide in Town

MENDL NISNBOYM
Apt (Opatow); sefer zikaron le-ir va-em be-Yisrael

The old hasidic world is filled with fantastic superstitions. Among us yeshiva students, it was said that for looking too much at a woman—God preserve us!—one was hung by the eyebrows in Hell. All of us took this quite seriously, and we were extremely strict with ourselves.

There was only one of us who dared to rebel, didn't believe in "old wives' tales," and received his punishment in this world. He wasn't, God forbid, hung by his eyebrows: his sentence was even more cruel and bizarre.

Listen to this: it happened to Shloyme, Lame Berl's son. Between lessons one day, he happened to look out the window of the study house, and his eyes met those of a beautiful girl from a well-to-do family.

And, as it is written, "he looked, and he was harmed." From that day on he knew no rest, and as it soon became apparent, the mutual glances had hit their mark in both hearts. After a number of secret meetings, a passionate attraction developed between the two, just as it's written in all of the romances: "They swore true love, never more to part."

As it turned out, however, Shloyme was drafted. There was no money for a bribe to have him rejected; where was a poor teacher with small children such as Lame Berl, who barely managed to make enough to keep going from day to day, to find money for a bribe? And, when even "injuring" himself did no good, and the doctor slapped Shloyme on the back after examining him—he went off to the army and became a soldier.

Before he left, the couple said goodbye, renewing their oath to remain true and to wait patiently for each other under any circumstances until they could be together.

Sorele's parents didn't know anything about the affair, and if they had, it probably wouldn't have helped her; after all, how long can a Jewish girl wait to get married?

And there was really nothing she could do, when one morning her parents announced to her that she had become a bride. True, she didn't know the groom yet, but there was nothing to worry about, she would, God willing, know her spouse tomorrow right after the ceremony, like all respectable Jewish girls.

That is just what happened. Despite all of her weeping and pining, Sorele married against her will the man whom her parents had chosen.

The day came when Shloyme went on furlough, and naturally, he immediately ran home to be with his beloved. The news that his Sorele had long ago been married to another hit him like a blizzard out of a clear blue sky.

Our Shloyme was overcome by the news. He clutched his head, and ran off helter-skelter to the river Shluze. Everyone who witnessed his terrible disappointment ran after him, but to no avail: Shloyme jumped off the bridge, right into the water.

I was one of the many witnesses who stood for several hours and waited until Shloyme's body was dragged out of the Shluze.

It was fated that this year Shloyme was to be the Shluze's annual sacrifice, and the whole affair confirmed the fact that Satan dances when one first glances at a woman.

A Hasidic Demonstration

AVROM LITMAN

Tshenstokhov (Czestochowa); nayer tsugob-material tsum bukh *Tshenstokhover Yidn*

The following events took place after the outbreak of the First World War, in 1914. The German army had occupied Tshenstokhov, and began to introduce "order" into the city. Announcements bearing one order after another began to appear: this is permitted, this is forbidden. There were a lot more "forbiddens" than "permitteds."

The Germans knew that they were on enemy territory. They had taken the entire territory of Poland into their iron paws and set a military dictatorship over it, which kept the Polish population in constant fear.

The Germans were able to take Poland with little loss of blood, because the commander of Tsar Nikolai's army, Nikolai Nikolayevitsh, had ordered the Russian forces to withdraw "deep into the interior." The Russians ran, and the Germans chased close behind them.

The goal of the German General Staff was to take the Ukraine, the rich breadbasket which would keep their "beloved Fatherland" free from hunger.

But what were they to do until they reached the Ukraine; who knew when they would finally arrive there?

An order came soon from the German General Staff: "Take the rich harvest of Poland's fields, the grain, the cattle, the poultry, the butter and cheese: the Fatherland must be sated. . . . There must be no hunger in Germany."

Tshenstokhov immediately felt the taste of Kaiser Wilhelm's policies: the food stores became empty, and there was less and less to eat. People slowly began to starve. Malnutrition brought about all sorts of diseases: stomach typhus, spotted typhus, swollen bellies, jaundice, and other troubles. The mortality rate rose so high that the Germans feared for the health of their army, which kept on pouring into Poland.

"How can we prevent the Kaiser's army from falling victim to the epidemics?" worried the General Staff. The suffering of the local Polish population hardly troubled them.

The first measure taken by the German commander in Tshenstokhov was in the area of hygiene, ordering the city and its people to be scrubbed and disinfected. Every day a different part of the city was surrounded, and the people were led to the bathhouse. People's heads were shaved, and large and small were disinfected. For the Jews it was nothing new to go to the mikve in preparation for the Sabbath or a holiday, but being dragged to the mikve on a plain weekday— Tshenstokhov had never seen such a thing since the city had found its way onto the map of Russian Poland.

The Germans knew quite well that cleaning and scrubbing the population would do little to stop the epidemics. In addition to hygienic means, it was also necessary to see to it that the population didn't starve, that there was something for people to eat, even just bread and potatoes.

The leaders of the German Ministry of Economics searched for a solution: how could they avoid the catastrophe which would follow if the German soldiers became infected with the typhus bacillus? The entire army might, God forbid, wind up in the hospital instead of marching to St. Petersburg! How were they to combat the epidemics?

The people of occupied Poland had no food. "That stands to reason, you know, because the Fatherland has simply taken all of Poland's food." So the big shots in Berlin decided that the Polish population was to receive just enough bread and potatoes to stay alive.

No one had to worry much about the wealthy classes in Poland. They took care of themselves on the black market, where they obtained not only bread and potatoes, but also geese, butter, and cheese. Although the shortages were immense, everything could be gotten for money. But the workers, the paupers— what was to be done about them?

The population was divided into districts, where bread and potatoes were sold at reasonable prices. True, the bread was black as coal or yellow as lime, because the flour was mixed with corn and other cheap grains, but the lines of people waiting for their rations spread across all of Tshenstokhov. Wherever one looked, it was nothing but lines, lines, lines.

The city fathers of Tshenstokhov instituted a system by which each resident of a district had to stand in line on one particular day of the week in order to buy his rations. If that person failed to come on the appointed day, he had to wait until the next week and meanwhile he would go without.

That was the setting for the following incident: while Reb Avigderl's Hasidim stood wrapped in their prayer shawls, reciting the *Shmone esre* prayers for the Sabbath, a Jewish woman ran in and announced in a loud, tear-choked voice:

"There is a tragedy in our city. . . . Jews are desecrating the Sabbath in public. . . . How can you pray, when Jews are standing in line to buy potatoes on the Sabbath? Rebe, why are you silent?"

A tumult erupted in the synagogue. The Rebe, who hadn't yet finished praying, waved his hands this way and that. One Jew with a black beard and huge hands ran up to the pulpit, banged his hand on a Bible, and declared:

"Jews, this must be stopped! It's sacrilege! What good are our prayers when Jews are desecrating the Sabbath in public?"

Suddenly we heard a shout: "Let's go in our prayer shawls to Rabbi Nokhem Ash in his synagogue, and convince him to arrange things with the commander so Jews won't have to desecrate the Sabbath. It's the end of the world, Rebe!"

The Rebe finished the *Shmone esre* prayers. The tumult continued, as the Hasidim ran from one bench to another, unable to sit still. In the midst of the tumult I heard the Rebe asking my father: "Meyer-Yoyne, what do you think we should do? Perhaps we should indeed go to the rabbi."

My father cited the old principle that "the law of the state is law," that laws made by the secular rulers also apply to Jews. It was a matter of life and death, he said; Jews were starving, and therefore had no choice but to buy on the Sabbath. If it was possible to convince the commandant to change the law, that would be fine. But who knew whether it could be done?

At this point the Hasidim interrupted my father. They went up to the rebe, took him by the arms and led him out into the street. The crowd set off after the rebe and began to march in their prayer shawls to the Old Synagogue—to the town rabbi, Reb Nokhem Ash.

I went along. My father held my hand. He constantly admonished the crowd: "It's not the rabbi's fault. . . . It's a decree from the Germans, there's nothing to be done. . . . Lives are at stake . . ."

When the demonstrators arrived at the synagogue, they forced their way inside and ran up to the pulpit. Here the tumult was even greater than before. People shouted and clamored, waved their arms and turned to the rabbi, demanding a response.

Reb Avigderl climbed the steps to the Ark of the Torah, leading with tears in his eyes.

The rabbi stood there, pale, stroking his long white beard and consulting with the rebe. The rebe calmed his Hasidim. It became as silent as before Kol Nidre. The rabbi raised his hands, smoothed his beard, and murmured in a trembling voice: "It is a decree of the state. . . . I'll do everything I can to have the decree changed. It is wartime, remember that. May God help me to convince the commandant. . . . I'll . . . Gentlemen . . ."

The rebe began to leave the synagogue. Crestfallen, his Hasidim followed.

That was the first time that I, a thirteen-year-old boy, had participated in a demonstration against the State.

The Dispute Over the Succession to the Rabbinate

MORDKHE FRIDNZON
Pinkas Khmelnik (Chmielnik)

It was Erev Yom Kippur in the year 1920. A heavy rain fell incessantly on the town, deepening the mood of the Day of Judgment. Jews carrying *taleysim*, worried and enveloped in thoughts of repentance, hurried to their hasidic prayer rooms or synagogues to pray for a better year, a year of health and good fortune.

But the Hasid didn't reach his prayer room, and the artisan didn't reach his synagogue. Everyone's steps led to Telts Street, to the rabbi's home. The sad news had spread rapidly that Rabbi Avrom-Yitskhok Silman, of blessed memory, had passed away. Telegrams informed the leading scholars of the cities and towns that they should come to pay their last respects to the learned and honest Jew. The Jews of Khmelnik were concerned about burying the rabbi before Kol Nidre.

The bitter dispute began that day. When the burial society came to conduct the funeral, the rabbi's son Tevye, who was the official rabbinical judge in town, came out and demanded a signed statement to the effect that he was to be his father's successor. But he met determined opposition.

Under pressure from Tevye, the rabbis who had come to the funeral held a meeting and requested that the Jewish community accede to Tevye's candidacy as rabbi of Khmelnik. The community held a meeting chaired by the community chairman, Dovid-Yoysef Zilberberg, who opposed Tevye's candidacy. After lengthy debates they proposed Tevye's elder brother Leyzerl, who was the rabbi of Zaleshits, as town rabbi, with Tevye to remain as judge. When the proposal was rejected by Tevye, and the possibility that the corpse would be desecrated by remaining unburied throughout Yom Kippur grew greater and greater, the community promised Tevye that he would be the rabbi for the time being.

Jews and Christians, women and children accompanied the rabbi to his eternal rest. All of the stores were closed. Wherever the coffin was carried, even Christian merchants closed their shops in solidarity with the mourners. The coffin waited near the synagogue, while the crowd listened to the eulogies of several rabbis.

It was quite late when the rabbi was buried. His three sons—the rabbis Yenkele, Leyzerl, and Tevye—said *kaddish*, accompanied by the bitter wailing of those in attendance. As though they had lost all energy, the townspeople set off for home, thinking of their guide, the rabbi, who used to stand on the podium in the synagogue delivering sermons which taught them to be upright Jews in the spirit of the Torah. Everyone was depressed after that sad Sunday of Erev Yom Kippur.

Not until the middle days of Sukkes did the town begin to gossip about who would be the new rabbi.

When he received his weekly pay, Tevye realized that his efforts had been fruitless. He continued to receive a judge's wages, not a rabbi's. An argument began. Many of the Hasidim, among them the chairman of the community council, believed that a city like Khmelnik needed a greater scholar than Tevye as its rabbi. They proposed the rabbi of Rakov, who had the same right to the rabbinical seat as did Tevye. A grandfather of the Rakover's had been the rabbi of Khmelnik before Tevye's father, but for various reasons he had had to resign. After Tevye's father died, many people claimed that the rabbi from Rakov had an equal claim to inherit the post.

The dispute began to take on serious proportions. The meetings of the community were full of arguments and scandal. It was difficult to reach an agreement. Meanwhile, Tevye didn't remain silent. A council of advisors formed around him, sharpening the dispute by bringing more people in to take sides. The city divided into two camps—the artisans on Tevye's side and most of the Hasidim on the Rakover Rabbi's side.

Not far from Khmelnik there is a town called Shidlov. Jews from Khmelnik used to go to the rabbi of that town to ask for advice. Women used to pour out their bitter hearts to him. People used to give him requests written on slips of paper, together with a few zlotys. For this they would receive a blessing, and they were confident that these blessings were effective.

The Shidlover Rebe had followers in Khmelnik. He called two of his committed Hasidim, Aron-Shloyme Fridnzon and Binyomin Zonshayn, and proposed to them a solution to the dispute in Khmelnik. The Shidlover Rabbi thought that Tevye was not an appropriate candidate for the rabbinate in Khmelnik. Therefore he was ready to give Tevye twenty thousand zlotys, the amount that a capitalist needed to emigrate to the land of Israel, if Tevye would do so. In addition, the Shidlover Rebe offered to see to all of the administrative tasks and to repair the bath and the mikve, which were in an unsanitary condition, if Tevye would agree to the candidacy of that rebe's son-in-law, the Shidlover rabbi, who was also a brother of the famous Radomsker Rebe, as rabbi in Khmelnik. Fridnzon and Zonshayn immediately went to Moyshe Melman, Tevye's main advisor and a community representative, describing the proposal to him and offering him one-tenth as much money as Tevye would receive. Melman agreed, promising to do what he could to carry through the plan, and stating his opinion that it was the only way to resolve the dispute.

Several days later Melman told the two representatives of the Shidlover Rebe that he had spoken to Tevye, telling him that a delegation from the Rebe would like to speak with him. Melman had arranged a time and place for the meeting, but he hadn't told Tevye what the meeting was to be about. Tevye received the Shidlover Hasidim at his home. Various topics were discussed, but when it came to the question of the rabbinical seat the delegates went away disappointed, convinced that no further discussions would be possible. After Tevye refused the proposal of the Shidlover Rebe, the rabbi of Rakov obtained the support of the Shidlover and Radomsker Hasidim. Then the two community representatives, Moyshe Melman and Nosn Shur, went over to the Rakover's camp. This realignment gave the chairman of the community council a chance to put the Rakover Rabbi's candidacy to a vote, and this time his candidacy was approved by a majority.

The decision required the approval of the Polish authorities. Mutual recriminations went on until the matter reached the Polish courts. Prior to the first hearing attempts were made to settle the issue before it fell into gentile hands. The two sides were offered rabbinical arbitration on condition that both give their written agreement to abide by the arbitrator's decision. Tevye, however, argued that the rabbis had already made a ruling at the grave of his father. A race to bribe Polish officials began. Money was raised for this purpose from the supporters of either side. Tevye and his mother also spent the money they received from the community on legal expenses, while the other side matched their expenditures with their own. The hearings drew on without results, and were eventually postponed until further witnesses could be called.

Meanwhile the followers of the Rakover Rabbi made the acquaintance of a certain grain merchant by the name of Avrom Tsimron, from the town of Stopnits, who frequently bought grain from noblemen. A daughter of one of these noblemen worked in the Interior Ministry. A bracelet studded with diamonds was purchased, which the merchant gave as a present to this woman, asking her to intervene on behalf of the Rakover. She promised to settle the matter once and for all, and that is what happened. A directive was sent from the Interior Ministry to the Polish mayor endorsing the candidacy of the Rakover rabbi, Rabbi Elyezer-Yoshua Epshtayn, as the rabbi of the Jewish community of Khmelnik.

Ignoring the continuing arguments and disputes, the Rakover moved with his family to Khmelnik, where his supporters, led by the community representatives, awaited him. The automobile bearing their possessions drove to the apartment that had been rented for them right in the center of town—on the marketplace square. The community representatives delegated to the rabbi authority over religious matters.

Yosl the town *shames* now had much work to do. He constantly went around town calling Hasidim to come to meetings, maintaining contacts between the rabbi and the community council and other leading personalities in the town, as well as accompanying the rabbi to weddings, circumcisions, and the like.

The rabbi's home was filled with Hasidim until late at night. When the Hasidim went home and Yosl Shames put out the heavy candles that winked through the windows out onto the marketplace, it was a sign that it was very late, and strolling young people began to go home as well.

The desire for revenge on the part of Tevye and his supporters grew stronger and stronger, and in every street where the Rakover Rabbi walked there were those who insulted him. Tevye also announced in the prayer house that he was forbidding people from eating meat that the Rakover Rabbi had declared kosher. Whoever ate meat slaughtered by slaughterers whom the Rakover supervised might as well have eaten nonkosher meat, he argued, because according to the rabbis who had been at his father's funeral, the Rakover wasn't legally the rabbi of Khmelnik and therefore had no authority to pronounce anything kosher. Some days later the Rakover replied in kind, declaring meat slaughtered under Tevye's supervision *treyf* [ritually unclean]. For a pious Jew, there was no choice but to give up eating meat. It was the same with marriages: whoever was married by one of the rabbis was considered according to the ruling of the other rabbi as living illegally with his wife. On Passover, one rabbi pronounced an oven contaminated with leaven that the other had declared kosher for Passover. The dispute didn't stop at words but carried over into physical violence. One time when the Rakover Rabbi left the prayer house after a sermon together with Dovid-Yoysef Zilberberg, a group of artisans was waiting outside, and one of them struck Zilberberg in the head with a bottle. The enmity and ongoing intrigue between Tevye and the Rakover were unbearable. In addition, a large segment of the populace mixed in, compounding the situation. Each side had its "enforcers," who were purchased for the price of a drink of brandy, and who prevented the opponents' rabbi from walking through the streets.

Even among the police there was a Rakovite and a Tevyite. Boltshikovsky, the tall policeman with heavy, coarse boots and baggy golf pants, with a face pitted like a piece of round matzo, frequented the Rakovites. He took a little bit from each of the storekeepers, such as food, shoes, and clothing. Mayde, the policeman with the upturned nose who threw his support to Tevye's side, was better acquainted with Jewish affairs. He also worked with the secret police, and more than one Jewish youngster was sent to prison by him for illegal political activities. Mayde could often be found getting drunk at the tavern of Tevye's cousin Leybl Silman. As payment for the liquor, he helped Tevye set the Rakover up as a political criminal. One Sabbath morning police arrived with an order to arrest the Rakover on charges of being a Communist. The rabbi was led through the town in chains, followed by a horse and wagon. At the edge of town the rabbi was put into the wagon and taken to the prison in Pintshev accompanied by police. After great efforts, the rabbi was eventually freed on bail.

Thus the dispute drew on until the beginning of the Second World War. On September 5, 1939, when the Nazis entered Khmelnik, Tevye and the Rakover hid in different cities. After a time they both returned to Khmelnik and were reconciled with each other. Both later shared the fate of the Jewish community of Khmelnik.

An Escape from Certain Death

KHAYIM RAYTSHIK
Sefer zikaron le-kehilat Rozhan (Rozan)

In the year 1920 the Bolsheviks marched through Rozhan on their way to Warsaw. They didn't hold out there very long because General Haller mounted a resistance and they were forced to retreat. The "Polish Democratic Army" retook the regions which the Russians had captured, and Rozhan became a

Polish town. Although the Russians weren't in Rozhan for more than two weeks, they brought about great changes in Jewish life.

Religious and spiritual life stopped. Jews suddenly were perceived as counter-revolutionaries and had to hide their feelings, attitudes, and ideas. Furthermore, a "reclassification" took place. Workers who for generations had allowed the burghers and "magnates" of Rozhan to have the last word suddenly received authority and themselves became the masters of the town. They ruled quite strictly. The powers-that-be dealt only with the workers, and this had a terrible effect. Suddenly an employer was no longer the boss, and had to consult the worker. The entire Jewish community trembled.

Understandably, the reborn Polish regime was much more welcome. Along with it came a restabilization of the Jewish community. Jews were able to breathe freely. But for me the moment of the Polish return was a moment when my life was in danger, and I will never forget the episode which I am about to relate.

During the two weeks the Bolsheviks ruled, they decided to rid Rozhan of the "reactionary, nationalist, destructive elements." They arrested fourteen Polish burghers, the landlords of the city, sent them away to the forests near Bialystok, and there put an end to them.

Among the Polish notables such as Zavodsky, Banislavsky, Myedzinovsky and others, was Pan Gos. He was a personal friend of my father, may he rest in peace. What do I mean by "a friend"? He used to come to my father's inn each day, eat and drink as much as he wanted, and not pay. Jews were afraid of him because he had power in court, and my father decided that it would be wiser not to demand payment from him and maintain the appearance of friendship.

His wife, Gasova, claimed that it was my father's duty as a friend to go to the Bolsheviks and try to get him freed. If my father had done so, he would have paid dearly for the intervention. His pleading would have meant he was a reactionary, and he would have immediately been suspected of anti-Bolshevism. So he decided not to risk his life for the sake of the Polish drunkard. Thus Pan Gos ended his life with the rest of the fourteen Poles.

When the Poles returned, four armed Polish military policemen came into our house and arrested me. I was led off to the military commandant. Afterward, it turned out that the widow Gos had, for her own reasons, not accused my father, but had chosen me as her victim instead.

When the commandant saw me, his face fell. He had expected that a giant would be brought in, a dangerous criminal, but what a disappointment! A youth of small stature stood before him, trembling, with two hanging sidelocks. My appearance didn't fit the picture that she [Mrs. Gos] had drawn. The accusation was absurd, but he had to do his duty.

He removed from the writing table a long sheet of paper with a long complaint from Mrs. Gos. He asked whether I was Khayim Raytshik; whether I had been in the Communist political police; and whether I had taken part in the arrest and murder of the fourteen honorable Polish citizens in the Bialystok woods.

According to the complaint signed by the widow Gos, I had also made Bolshevik propaganda speeches, and the like. I was warned to tell the truth and the whole truth to the commandant, because it would go worse for me if I didn't. He didn't even wait for my answer; he knew who he was dealing with. All the same, I was frightened to death.

While this was going on, the door to the next room opened and in came a tall, stocky peasant who was armed to the teeth. My heart, which had been ticking like a cheap alarm clock throughout the interrogation, suddenly stopped. I thought to myself, "Here comes the judge, jury, and hangman, and it will be the end of my young life." The peasant saw my fear. He looked at me with a smile and, turning to the commandant, said, "I know this youth very well. During the years I've been chief of police here, I've known his parents as well. They are a fine, loyal family of good Polish patriots. Look at the child: Do you really believe he could be capable of such deeds?"

I finally recognized him. He was a regular guest in our tavern. Apparently he had his own accounts, either with my father or with Gos. One way or the other, Police Chief Falinsky's intervention saved the day. If not for him, who knows what my fate might have been?

Such things happened in our Rozhaner history, and may I be permitted to recount my personal episode and thereby illustrate the life of Jews in Rozhan and in all of Poland. This is what Jewish life was like; this was the worth of Jewish life when it lay in gentile hands.

A Murder in the Forest

YEHOSHUA AYBESHITS
Vyerushov (Wieruszow); sefer yizkor

The month of August 1929 was terribly hot, and the mood among the Jews of our town was dejected, as a result of the tragic news from Israel about the Arab pogroms.

One such morning an elderly peasant woman came to Getsl Partek. The woman crossed herself and burst into hysterical weeping. At first, Reb Getsl paid no attention to her weeping, thinking that she had had one drink too many on an empty stomach. When she calmed down, she related a gruesome story. While she was looking for mushrooms in the Partshits Forest, she had come across a murdered Jew lying in a pool of blood, wrapped in talis and tefillin.

The news spread around town like lightning, and a terrible panic broke out, because many of the Jews of Vyerushov made their living as village peddlers. Frightful rumors spread; there was speculation about mass murder, since no one knew what had actually happened.

The Jewish alderman, Reb Motye Behagn, ran off to the police commander Urbaniak as soon as he heard the news, demanding that he take immediate steps. The police chief wasn't eager to act; he dismissed the story as the invention of a drunken peasant woman. Yet eventually Urbaniak was convinced that not only had a terrible murder taken place, but that the murderer himself had fallen into his hands.

This is what happened. That same day (it was a Tuesday), a young gentile from Partshits entered the haberdashery of Yosl Koyen (Reb Hillel Koyen's son) and Ruven Aleksandrovitsh, asking to see an outfit. Ruven Aleksandrovitsh served him, while Yosl observed him from the side. Yosl suspected something fishy. First of all, why would a peasant be shopping on a Tuesday (which wasn't a market day), and second, it was unheard of for a gentile not to argue about the price before anything else. Yosl signaled to Ruven, telling him to keep a sharp eye on the gentile. Ruven immediately understood Yosl's suspicion, and in order to gain time, asked the gentile to pull down his pants (pardon the expression) in order to fit the outfit more accurately. The gentile, not very eager to do so, nevertheless obeyed, but quickly—as though he had just remembered something—pulled his pants back up. He left them down long enough, however, for Ruven to notice flecks of blood on his underwear. It was clear to Yosl and Ruven that the murderer was standing in front of them. Apparently the gentile also noticed them looking at him with suspicion because he left in a hurry: the outfit "wasn't his style." Yosl sent one of his assistants after the gentile, while Ruven went to the police. Urbaniak immediately sent a policeman to find the murderer. The suspect, aware that he was being followed, tried to lose his trackers. He might have managed to disappear, but a couple of strong Jewish boys grabbed him and handed him over to the police. With great "ceremony" he was led off to the police station.

As soon as he was brought in, Urbaniak greeted the murderer with two fiery slaps. "Either way," said Urbaniak. "If he's the murderer, he deserves it. If not, big deal, he'll hold it on account."

To everyone's astonishment, the murderer immediately broke down and admitted everything, smiling cynically the whole time. This is what he related:

"Yesterday morning, on my way to Tshastar, I passed through the forest. Suddenly I saw a *Zhid* praying. The Zhid was standing there wrapped up in a white cloth, standing stock-still, as though he were sleeping." (The Jew had probably been reciting the *Shmone esre* prayers.) "Without thinking about it much, I took out my axe and gave him a solid blow right on his head. The Jew fell down, covered with blood, but he still showed signs of life. I struck him a few more times, until I was quite sure he was dead. I took the cloth off of him, and I found 780 zlotys in his pocket. Then I went over to the stream nearby, washed the blood off myself, and continued to Tshastar, to enjoy myself at the tavern."

The panic in town grew from minute to minute. We still didn't know who the murdered man was. Several young people announced that they would volunteer to search for the body, but it was unnecessary. The criminal himself—under police guard—led everyone to the scene of the crime in the Partshits Forest, where the victim lay in a pool of congealed blood. Looking at the horrible scene, everyone present, including the Christians, broke out in bitter wailing. The murderer was unimpressed by this, and even dared to smile. Several Jewish youths attacked him, and if it weren't for the intervention of the police standing by, the matter would have been solved then and there.

The murdered man was Yankev-Kopl Rotbard from Kshepits, the son-in-law by marriage of Yisroel-Dovid Shterns. He was a quiet man, who wouldn't harm a flea. In Kshepits he had been a grain dealer, but in Vyerushov he had become a village peddler, for lack of a better way of making a living. He never complained, accepting everything with love.

The police refused to allow him to be buried until a medical investigation was completed, so a number of young men remained at the site saying Psalms until the next morning.

The next day, Wednesday, almost the whole town of Vyerushov was present, despite the fact that it was market day, as the doctor from Povyatov conducted the autopsy. No one had the patience to remain in town.

The whole town attended the funeral. The cries and wailing reached up to Heaven. The rabbi and others who delivered eulogies wept and sobbed like small children.

The murderer was sentenced to eight years in prison all together. He argued that the victim had annoyed him—even though he had earlier admitted to the police that he had attacked the Jew while the latter was praying.

A few months later the wife of the murdered man bore a son, who received his father's name; Yankev-Kopl Rotbard.

The Pogrom in 1936

MORDKHE ZLOTNITSKI-ZAHAVI
Yizker-bukh Suvalk (Suwalki)

I remember the year 1936 very well. It was the year of the pogroms in Pshitik and Brisk, the year Goering visited Minister Bek "for a hunting trip."

The air of Suvalk was suffused with Nazi poison. In the streets Americans photographed graffiti reading "Down with the Jews!" After a soccer match between the Maccabi club and a Polish team the Jewish athletes left the field under a hail of stones.

But the local anti-Semitic hooligans were itching for somthing bigger; they wanted to arrange a proper pogrom. It happened on a glorious day in May. Together with several friends, I was sitting in the clubhouse of a Jewish organization on Kosciuszko Street. Suddenly the siren began to sound. We thought it was a fire, but when we went out onto the balcony this is what we saw:

A large gang of young Poles were going around with sticks, breaking the windows of all of the Jewish stores. They cruelly chased Jewish passersby and when they saw us on the balcony, they set off toward us. We quickly locked the door. We were three boys—Yankev Vilensky, Moyshe Nignibutsky, and myself—and three girls. All we had at hand to use as weapons were billiard cues. We readied ourselves. However, the hooligans set off in a different direction, and the worst we suffered were the stones they hurled through the window.

Awhile later we were joined by several comrades with proper weapons. They reported that several people had already been wounded and said that we had to go out into the street and protect the Jews.

Kosciuszko Street was dead. Broken doors, pieces of glass, and assorted merchandise were scattered on the ground. There wasn't a single policeman to be seen. We left the girls inside the club, together with a couple of the boys.

Suddenly Polish policemen ran up, shouting "Go home on the double!" We turned into Yatkeve Street, but three Polish youngsters appeared out of nowhere and attacked us. At first we took some solid blows, but when we realized that they were alone, we showed them what we were made of.

Moyshe Nignibutsky gave one of the hooligans such a beating that all he could do was moan "Oh, Jesus Mary!" Yankev and I took on the other two, who were dressed in gymnasium uniforms. They were strong fellows, but I gave one of them such a shot with my hand in the nose, that red began to flow and he ran away. The third one was really in trouble. Vilensky was a carpenter with a pair of hands made of iron (he later died in Russia), and he simply wanted to strangle his opponent. We barely managed to prevent him from doing so.

The only people on the street that evening were Polish policemen. Jewish comrades gathered at Sanubsky's tavern, at the Maccabi club, at Betar, or at Hashomer Hatzair.

The next day the Jewish women were afraid to go out into the street. Although things were quiet, the Jewish youth were ready for any situation. The Polish gentiles were ready too. Then something strange took place, something I will always remember: When evening came, the hooligans went out "for a walk" with wooden sticks and iron bars in their hands. Later the Jews approached from another side—butchers with chopping knives under their coats, coachmen, shoemakers and others, all solidly built young fellows. They flooded the main street. The Poles gradually retreated, and within an hour they had disappeared entirely. The Jews controlled the street. It was a great victory, a sign that "they" were afraid.

A Communist Assembly Elects a Zionist as Representative

YAAKOV (BEN MOSHE) PLOT

Sefer ha-zikaron le-kehilat Kamin-Koshirski (Kamien Koszyrski) ve-ha-seviva

While I was working in the printing room of the newspaper *Leninski-Szliachom*, a representative of the Central Committee of the labor unions in White Russia (a Jew from Minsk named Gurevitsh) came to Kamin to sign up the workers and organize a union in town. Like all important Communist activists, he often came into the editorial and print rooms, and became friendly with me. When all the workers had been signed up, a general assembly was called to elect a committee. I decided not to attend the meeting because I was afraid I would be proposed as a candidate, and I was hardly looking forward to that honor. I "became ill" and stayed home.

The proofreader at the newspaper was a Polish Jew who had spent long years in prison for being a Communist and who now occupied a ranking position in the regional Soviet. When he was told that I would be unable to attend the meeting because I was ill, he came to see me at home. He told me that a good friend of mine had told him that I had to attend the meeting; otherwise, I would be accused of being an enemy of the Soviet regime. I quickly decided to go along with him, and tried to think up a way to avoid having myself nominated.

The meeting was held in the large new movie theater that the Polish government had built in the middle of the marketplace. The hall was jammed full of workers, both Jewish and Christian. The chairman of the regional Soviet (a Russian Jew), the secretary of the Communist party, the chairman of the NKVD, and the editor of the newspaper all sat on the dais. The chairman of the meeting, a Jewish Communist from Poland, opened the meeting. The union representative and the regional secretary both made speeches. They explained that the candidates should be workers who came from proletarian backgrounds— neither former merchants nor those who once belonged to Zionist or Bundist organizations since these were enemies of the working class.

I consulted with my editorial colleagues, and a resolution was introduced to the effect that each section should propose one worker as a candidate for the committee. The proposal was accepted. I immediately announced a candidate from our section to fit all of their qualifications.

I was satisfied to have successfully avoided being a candidate. Candidates were proposed for the other sections, many of whom were rejected when it was pointed out that they had once belonged to Zionist youth organizations.

My name was put forth for the supervisory board. I immediately announced that I couldn't accept the appointment, but I was told that not I as an individual, but the meeting as a whole, would decide. But then my "friend" from the presidium took the floor and announced that I wasn't qualified because I was an enemy of the working class. He read out a long list of my Zionist sins, adding: If other candidates had been rejected on the grounds of their having previously been Zionists, I was guilty of being their teacher. I saw through his provocation, and kept my mouth shut. Then the chairman of the meeting took the floor and explained that he knew me to be an honorable man. When he had worked in the Kamin region twelve years previously in the Communist movement, I had been the founder of the town's labor union. I had defended the workers' interests and struggled to improve their working conditions without making any distinctions between them on the basis of party affiliations. Finally, I had belonged to Poalei Tsion, the Labor Zionists, not to the right-wing Zionists. I was the appropriate candidate for the supervisory board.

After him, the union representative spoke again, and said, among other things, that while he had been here he had gotten to know me, and he too had nothing personal against me. Nevertheless, as a Zionist, I was forbidden to be a candidate. To explain why belonging to Poalei Tsion was no virtue, he told the following parable: there are Jews who say that only the right side of a pig is forbidden as food, while the left side is kosher. But Jews who are truly pious say that both sides of the pig are forbidden. The same with the Zionists: both the right-wing and the left-wing Labor Zionists are forbidden. He hoped that the assembled workers would reject my candidacy.

But then I experienced a moral triumph that I will never forget. Young working Communists took the floor, several of whom had once been in Zionist youth organizations. With youthful enthusiasm and pathos, forgetting about the consequences, they began to defend my candidacy and my activities among the workers in the previous years. They, too, concluded that I was the most appropriate candidate for the supervisory board.

Several members of the presidium continued to speak against Zionism as a "counterrevolutionary" movement, as the enemy of the working class, and I was called upon to recount my biography in public. I replied that I had nothing to add since so many of the comrades had already spoken about me.

My candidacy was put to a vote, and the presidium was astonished; all the workers, Jews and Christians, Communists and unaffiliated, voted for me. Opposed? Not a single one.

Jewish Fighters on the Battlefields of Spain

GINA MEDEM
Tshenstokhover (Czestochowa) Yidn

In December 1937, Jewish workers and artisans of Polish towns and cities, as well as emigrants in Paris, Brussels, and Antwerp, from Holland and Czechoslovakia, from Austria and the land of Israel organized a Jewish unit, while the Polish Thirteenth Brigade was fighting at the front in Aragon. This was in accordance with a decision of the staff of the Forty-ninth Division, under the command of the Polish General Walter—now the hero of the battles for Warsaw and Silesia in the Soviet-established and Soviet-armed Kosciuszko Division, which accompanied the Red Army in its victorious march across Poland toward Berlin. The Jewish company in the Palafox Battalion was named after the Jewish worker Naftali Botwin, who was shot in Lemberg in 1929.

In memory of that martyred hero who shot the Polish spy and traiter Cechnowski, the first, historic Jewish battle unit was organized by the light of a small candle in the trenches of Aragon, Spain, some thirty feet away from the enemy. The unit had its own commandant and a monthly journal which appeared in Yiddish, called *Botwin*.

For the first time in five hundred years Jewish type was sent from Paris to print a Yiddish newspaper, *The Freedom Fighter*, in the town of Albacete, not far from the old university town of Murcia, where anti-Jewish laws were once printed by the Spanish monarchs. On the front page stood the motto of the Polish Brigade: "For your freedom and ours."

Hundreds of young and middle-aged fighters passed before my eyes and into my heart. My entry into Madrid, as a member of the anti-Fascist Writers' Congress in June 1937, contained an unforgettable moment which no director of a modern film could ever have invented.

Riding down the Avenida del Prado, Madrid's greatest thoroughfare, the motorcade containing the members of the congress (we had driven from Barcelona and Valencia to Madrid in eighty-four automobiles) stopped briefly to meet with the representatives of General Miaja, the commander of Madrid. A young, excited blond soldier ran past the motorcade carrying a copy of the *Naye Presse*, a Yiddish newspaper from Paris. He waved the newspaper like a flag, waiting for a member of the congress to declare himself a Jew. I did just that, and the young man's joy was indescribable. Knowing that the congress was to begin that evening, he had obtained leave from the front—a twenty-minute tramway ride from the center of the city—and set off to find a Jewish writer. When I asked him his name and told him mine, his face grew even redder, more flushed. "Gina

Medem! My comrades at Puente Francesa won't believe me, when I tell them I saw you." So I playfully wrote my name and the date on his newspaper.

We agreed that he would come with several of his friends from the battalion to the official greeting of the Writers' Congress. He had time to tell me his name—Feldman—and then the autos started up again and he was gone, running as he had come, and waving the newspaper. I didn't see him again because that evening the Fascists set off an explosion under a house where they had dug a tunnel to our lines, and he was wounded together with a group of Spaniards.

The next day several Polish-Jewish fighters from the front came to greet us: Sevek, Yuzek Mazel, and Binyomin Lifshitz, known by the name of Barcelo Larento, a member of the Bundist youth organization *Tsukunft* in Warsaw and one of the few Bundist workers who came to fight in Spain.

Yuzek Mazel (Sulinsky), born in Russia and raised in Warsaw, later one of the editors of the Polish brigade weekly, *Dombrowczak*, was the inspiring and tireless archivist who helped me publish my book in Madrid, *Jews–Freedom Fighters*. He gave me countless interesting details and dates concerning the Thirteenth Brigade, where the Naftali Botwin Company was later organized. He told me proudly that under Gershon Shur and Captain Elboym, the first commandants of the Brigade, Spaniards, Greeks, and Jews from many countries all fought together, including Matyas Katz, from Hungary, Yoyne Brodsky from Palestine, Efroyim Vuzek, Shloymele Feldman, Rotenburg, and many, many others.

Every city in Poland left sons under an olive tree or in a vineyard in Spain, both Pole and Jew. These names became legends, for they were names of pioneers in the battle against Hitlerism. These names will be sanctified as long as one progressive person remains in the world, for they were our first teachers on the battlefield and they didn't separate word from deed, slogan from action. They inspired the "brothers of the forest," the heroic Jewish and non-Jewish partisans who fought four years later, between 1941 and 1944, on the roads to Kelts, Lublin, Tshenstokhov, Warsaw, Torne, Lemberg, and Lodz against the very same Hitler and Franco who hadn't been able to take Madrid.

Legends and Folklore

The Ancestors' Merit and the Blessings of Laughter

YISROEL ASHENDORF
Yizker-bukh Khelm (Chelm)

There is one Khelm which was the world of the ancestors, which is now the Khelm of the dead. That Khelm pulsed year in, year out with powerful currents of Jewish social life, with political parties and cultural institutions, and with a rich reserve of cultural activists. There were enough of them not only for Khelm itself, but to enrich other Jewish settlements as well, as distant as my shtetl, near the Russian-Romanian border, which was fortunate in having a Hebrew teacher from Khelm (Moyshe-Leyzer). He taught me the Bible and modern Hebrew literature, and encouraged me in my first poetic efforts.

I'm also aware of the multifaceted activities of the various societies of emigrants from Khelm around the world, but here I am concerned with a different Khelm, the Khelm of laughter, the Khelm of the spirit.

Once upon a time, every Jew loved hearing a joke. Others enjoyed telling jokes, but there were also quite a few who created jokes as well. Virtually every shtetl had its wit or jester. Yet most of them didn't go beyond the borders of their shtetl. Only a few such as Hershele Ostropolyer and Efrayim Graydinger traveled further, carrying along with them the names of their towns. The towns themselves, however, didn't play any particular role in their stories. The heroes remained Hershele and Efrayim as individuals. The only city that has made its mark on the history of Jewish folk humor is Khelm: Khelm itself is the hero, not as an individual, but as a collective.

Many tales and anecdotes grew up over the years. Did they really take place in Khelm rather than in other Jewish towns? That isn't really so important. What's important is that they existed here. Do some of them have roots in the humor of other peoples? What's important is that they are made Jewish through Khelm. The fact that these rather than other stories are told about Khelm is in itself sufficiently distinctive and interesting.

The foolishness of the people of Khelm isn't the kind of foolishness that is associated with ill will but rather the sort that accompanies well-meaning naiveté. The people of Khelm aren't in the habit of deceiving others; they always fall victim to their own inventions. In that sense they are similar to Don Quixote, who was always so eager to help others that he earned himself heavy blows from man and from fate.

Usually Jewish jokes bite, they stab, they burn with pepper and salt. The humor of Khelm is naive and mild, not the jokes of deceivers and swindlers but those of the deceived and swindled. And most important: those who tell jokes about Khelm aren't satisfied with the bare bones but add the flesh and blood that make a story.

For instance: The first snow of the winter fell in Khelm, covering over the mud of autumn and the filthy roofs of the houses. It dazzled the eyes! But when the *shames* (sexton) went to wake the Jews up to pray, he would tread on the pure white snow and make it dirty. The people of Khelm worked hard, thinking of ways to avoid this. The upshot—the decision to carry the shames around on a table supported by four men—is unimportant. That is merely anecdotal. The important thing is the striving of the people of Khelm toward purity and beauty.

Another: the town shames had grown old and weak. The townspeople tried to find a way to avoid his having to trudge all over over town each morning, banging on shutters.

Finally, they decided to bring the shutters to the synagogue. The shames could bang them there, and avoid the effort of walking around town. What characteristic of the people of Khelm does this reveal? Mercy.

Third story: a man from Khelm bought a sack of feathers at a fair and carried it across the fields toward Khelm. On the way he suddenly realized: "The wind is blowing in the direction of Khelm—why should I carry this load on my back? I'll let the wind carry them to my house." Here we see that the Jew of Khelm is ready to entrust his possessions even to the wind; the Jew of Khelm has faith.

I will also mention the famous tale in which the people of Khelm set off across the world seeking justice.

These few stories reveal to us the soul of Khelm: a soul which yearns for beauty, which is full of mercy, which possesses faith, which seeks justice. Such a noble character has the Jew of Khelm!

True, he seldoms reaches his goal. He suffers constant reverses, but has that not been the fate of the honest and the righteous since the world was created?

Various Yiddish writers have attempted to set the stories of Khelm in a literary form, each in his own style. Wasn't Khelm a model for Sholem Aleichem, when he painted his portrait of Kasrilivke? Didn't he have the people of Khelm in mind when he sketched the little people with grand ideas?

Hundreds of Jewish cities and towns in Poland have been destroyed, but the Khelm of the spirit remains unvanquished. Khelm was created by the Jewish people, and it will live on with the Jewish people. In our exodus from Poland we took along so much pain and tragedy that we certainly need a bit of joy as well. Let us, therefore, tell and retell our tales of the cheerful and naive Jews of Khelm.

Three Parables of the Dubner Magid

LEYZER SHTAYNMAN
Dubno; sefer zikaron

The Seeing and the Blind

It is told:

The Dubner Magid was once asked why a rich man would rather give alms to a poor man who was blind, lame, or hunchbacked, than to a poor man who was a Talmud scholar.

The Dubner answered short and sharp:

"That's because the rich man isn't sure that he himself will never go blind or become crippled. But one thing he's sure of: he'll never be a Talmud scholar!"

A Lawsuit With a Horse

Once a freethinker proposed to the Dubner: "Let's have a debate, and we'll see which of us is right."

The Dubner looked at the audacious youngster and said, according to his custom: "Young man, I'm going to tell you a story.

"Once upon a time a rabbi took a coach to Vilna, and the horse had to drag the wagon up a sandy path. The coachman jumped down from his seat in order to lighten his horse's load. The rabbi immediately jumped out as well. The coachman said to the rabbi, 'You can sit—after all, you're a passenger, and you've paid to ride.' "

"The rabbi answered, 'But the horse might complain that the hill is too high; he might bring a suit against me in a religious court. It's true, I might win, but I just don't want to get involved in a dispute with a horse!' "

A Peasant in a Frock Coat

One day a peasant came into town to do some shopping. It was a cold winter day. The peasant was wearing a warm fur; underneath he had on various tattered garments, and on top of everything kerchiefs and rags to keep warm. He looked in the window of a shop that had beautiful, expensive clothes, and said to himself: "If I put that frock on, I'd look like a real gentleman, just like the nobleman Yanesku."

He went into the store and asked to see a fine, black frock coat, like the fancy people wore.

The experienced salesman quickly decided what the peasant's size was, brought him a coat, and showed him into the dressing room.

The salesman waited a little while, and then another little while, but the peasant didn't come back into the shop. He went into the dressing room, and saw his customer desperately struggling to get the coat on, without success. The peasant shouted at him: "What kind of frock coat did you give me? It isn't my size! Are you trying to make fun of me?"

The salesman replied: "I'm not making fun of you—you're making yourself ridiculous. The frock is exactly your size. But before you try on a coat like this, you have to first take off the fur and all the rags you're wearing."

That's the parable. And what is the moral?

One moral is very simple and direct: One must rid oneself of coarse ways before trying to become respectable.

But the Dubner made the moral more profound, extending its meaning to the entire Jewish people, chanting in his characteristic, heartfelt melody:

"The moral comes to tell us: the holy Torah and the commandments which the Holy Blessed One gave us were exactly suited to our nature and to our needs. But we clothe ourselves in all sorts of rags, all sorts of evil habits and sins. Then we complain that the Torah isn't appropriate for us, that it is hard to observe the commandments. Let us first throw away our rags, and then we'll see that the Torah fits us perfectly!"

The Slaughtering Knife and the Saw

VELVL GREYNIMAN
Disna (Dzisna); sefer zikaron le-kehila

One beautiful morning Zalmen Shoykhet [ritual slaughterer] sat outside his house, sharpening and polishing his knife, and humming the rebe's favorite melody. In came his wife Sore-Batye, telling Zalmen that she was preparing pickles and needed several boards.

Sore-Batye's word was sacred law to Zalmen. He put his knife down on the table, went off to his neighbor, Yisroel Stolyer [carpenter] to borrow a saw, came home and made the boards. When he was finished, he put down the saw and carried the boards off to Sore-Batye.

When the slaughtering knife saw all this, he couldn't understand what was going on: "Zalmen, with his noble hands that hold only me, how could he have held that saw, that lowlife?" He turned angrily toward the saw and said:

"Look at that thing standing over there. It can't even count to two. And such a face! It grinds and gnaws its way through with that row of teeth. I, on the other hand, am smooth, beautiful, and shiny. When Reb Zalmen picks me up, he focuses all his attention and winks to the Creator to let him know that he's doing His will. But you, good-for-nothing?"

Replied the saw:

"Listen to him singing! We know all about your sharp little tongue. I saw, and I know my place, together with the artisan, who's always the black sheep of the family. But you, slaughtering knife! You have all the luck. You cut throats, and people say a blessing!"

Khayim-Yisroel Melamed and the Kozhenitser Magid

DOVID BEN ZELIG GERSHT
Vurke (Warka); sefer zikaron

Khayim-Yisroel was different from most of the teachers in Vurke. He was loved by the entire Jewish population, both by the fathers and the students. Not only was Khayim-Yisroel a good teacher but he was known for his purity and cleanliness. His schoolroom fairly glittered with spotlessness. He lived on the market square, one flight up, and in order to get to school, one had to climb a dark stairway. His hearing was very sharp, and he could discern the footsteps of a child or a grown man from afar. Even during a class, he would suddenly grab the lamp which he always kept lit and run to light the way into the room for his guest. His wife, Sore-Gitl, was also popular in town on account of her goodness and propriety. Khayim-Yisroel honored his wife greatly, and when a guest entered his apartment, the first thing he would do was to introduce his wife, something which was not done by Jews of the older generation. Khayim-Yisroel was fascinated by antiques. In his room stood a large cabinet filled with valuable metal items: large brass candlesticks and various Hanukkah lamps, spice boxes for Havdalah, and other Jewish antiques. For each guest he would open the case and display these things which he had inherited from earlier generations. On each item a card was hung showing the year it was made.

When I studied with Khayim-Yisroel, there were about thirty of us in the class. Khayim-Yisroel knew each child as an individual. He knew what the child's home situation was like, and tried to help any child who needed help.

He arranged for his students to come to him every Sabbath afternoon, in the summer to study *Pirkey oves* [*Ethics of the Fathers*] and in the winter, the psalm *Borkhe nafshi*. Both parents and children came gladly, because to be under Khayim-Yisroel's supervision was a pleasure and not a hardship, as it was with other teachers.

When a festival was approaching, one sensed its approach in Khayim-Yisroel's schoolroom weeks and even months in advance. Thus, at Hanukkah he would already be preparing for Passover: Hanukkah was the time to render goose fat for

Passover. Our teacher used to help his wife cut the fat into small pieces and throw them into the pots. When the fat began to melt, the smell wafted all through the house. When the fat was all rendered, he set a plate of hot, fragrant cracklings on the table and said, "Eat, children, enjoy. If you eat the cracklings, you'll know that you should treat your teacher with due respect, and not give him any trouble until after Passover." Our affection for him was so great that more than once we forgot that it was time to go home already.

Besides our studies (with Khayim-Yisroel we already studied the Five Books of Moses with Rashi's commentary, as well as a bit of Talmud), from time to time he would tell us stories about Vurke in previous years. He was a good storyteller, and as soon as he said that he was going to tell us a story "that happened here in Vurke many years ago," we all opened our mouths and ears in order to catch every word. But Khayim-Yisroel didn't tell stories on the spur of the moment; he always chose the right day for the story which he had decided to tell.

Out of all of Khayim-Yisroel's stories I will tell just one as an example. The holiday of Tu-Beshvat was approaching. That year Tu-Beshvat fell on a Wednesday. On Sunday, Khayim-Yisroel was already warming us up for the story.

Wednesday came. We students had been eager since morning to hear the story which, as our teacher had told us, was connected to the town of Vurke. We sat around the table impatiently waiting for him to begin. Khayim-Yisroel stroked his beard several times and said, "Today is the fifteenth of Shevat, the New Year of Trees. In honor of the holiday I will tell you a story which my grandfather told me when I was your age. What I'm going to tell you took place here in Vurke when the Kozhenitser Magid [the Preacher], may the memory of his righteousness bless us, was still alive.

"My grandfather lived in the village of Grobev, which is situated on the other side of the Pilitse River. Like every Jew, he prepared for the Sabbath all week, in order to celebrate it with good, tasty Sabbath dishes. Every Friday morning he walked a few kilometers to Vurke to buy braided challahs which only the bakers of Vurke knew how to make. As usual, he took up his pack that Friday morning, went off to Vurke, filled his pack with challahs, and prepared to return to the village.

"Upon arriving at the market square in Vurke, he saw a wagon with two horses. In the wagon sat a Jew with an imposing face, dressed in a silken overcoat, with a broad fur hat on his head. He held in his hand a large text, in which he was thoroughly absorbed. My grandfather also noticed that with his left hand the man was making quick gestures, as though asking himself questions and responding to them.

"Grandfather, dressed in simple village clothes, approached the wagon, throwing the heavy pack of challahs from one shoulder to the other as he did so. When he was near the wagon, he heard a voice saying, 'Good Sabbath, Honorable

Jew.' When grandfather came even closer, the coachman hollered out, snapped the reins, and stopped the horses. Grandfather took the heavy pack off his shoulder and leaned against the wagon. As he stood there, the pious Jew raised his eyes from the book and repeated, 'Good Sabbath, Honorable Jew.'

" 'How can you be sure I'm a Jew?' asked Grandfather. 'My clothes say that I'm a peasant.' The coachman answered:

" 'Jewish challahs can be smelled a long way off, especially on Friday.'

"Grandfather, remembering that he hadn't given the Jew a proper greeting, said, 'Sholem aleykhem, Sir! I am Nakhmen Grobever.'

" 'And I am the Kozhenitser Magid [preacher],' answered the Jew sitting in the back of the wagon.

"A shudder of joy ran through my grandfather. This was really something, quite an honor, to see the famous sage face to face. He didn't think long before asking, 'Rebe, how can I help you?' I have no money, for I've spent it all on these challahs for the Sabbath; if it would please the Rebe, I could give him a fresh challah from Vurke.' The magid smiled and said:

" 'One doesn't buy merit with money, but with good deeds.' He raised his hand toward the east and added, 'I must arrive in Kozhenits before nightfall so as not, God forbid, to desecrate the Sabbath. You, sir, have to go to Grobev, which is on the way to Kozhenits. Be so kind as to put your sack in the wagon and climb up yourself; we'll travel together a piece.'

"Grandfather sprang into the wagon without hesitation; the coachman snapped the reins once again, and they set off. The Magid buried himself in his text again. Grandfather felt a bit disappointed, because he had wanted to hear a few words from the holy man. The wagon rolled along the sandy path, and the horses seemed tired; the preacher closed his book and reached out his hand to the trunk for another text. Grandfather took the opportunity to say, 'Rebe, it is still a long way to the Pilitse; the horses are tired; who knows whether we will find a ferry to take us across the river? Perhaps the Rebe will agree to spend the Sabbath at my home in the village? We have a synagogue with a full *minyan* and for the village Jews it would be a great honor to have the Rebe spend the Sabbath with us. Sunday morning the horses will be rested, and the Rebe can return to Kozhenits.'

"The Magid placed his hand on my grandfather's shoulder and said, 'Reb Nakhmen, you should not worry; I'm not worried either. He who lives forever will not permit me to desecrate the Sabbath.' He took out a second book and buried himself in it.

"All at once the coachman turned around and said to grandfather, 'Reb Nakhmen, you're from around here; be so kind as to point out someplace close where we can cross the Pilitse.' Grandfather showed him the right way, and the river appeared in view quite soon. Grandfather looked closely in the direction of the river; perhaps there was someone there who could tell him where to find a gentile with a ferry to carry the wagon and horses across. Suddenly he saw a cowherd leading a herd of cattle. When the cowherd came closer, he called him over and asked him whether he knew a ferryman. The cowherd showed him a hut not far from the river where a German named Fetsch lived. He had several ferries which he rented out. The coachman whipped the horses and they soon arrived at the German's house.

"They stopped by the gate. The preacher jumped down from the wagon to stretch out, and Grandfather and the coachman went up to the gate. Two large dogs greeted them with loud barking. The gentile who sat on a chair in the yard got up immediately, quieted the dogs, and came to the gate. Seeing the preacher with his imposing face and fur hat, he understood that he was in the presence of a great 'rabbin.' He immediately put his hat on and asked how he could help the 'rabbin.' The preacher replied briefly that he had to cross the river in order to reach Kozhenits before nightfall. The German went right off to his stall, pulled out two large oars, dragged them over to the shore, lashed together a large raft, and called out: 'Everything's ready.' Together with the coachman, he led the horses and the wagon onto the raft, invited the preacher to come aboard, and after him, Grandfather and the coachman. He thrust the oars and the raft began to glide over the water. In a few minutes they were across. The German opened up the railing of the ferry, led out the horses and wagon, and the three of them were soon ready to set off again. The preacher climbed onto the wagon, then grandfather and the coachman did likewise, and the wagon sped away.

"The German stood on the bank, astounded. The 'rabbin' hadn't even thanked him for the good deed he had done. He watched the wagon draw away for a long while, went aboard the ferry, and prepared to return. As he was about to leave, he noticed that the wagon had turned around.

"The preacher told the coachman to drive back to the riverbank. The coachman did the preacher's bidding without question. Speaking to himself, the preacher repeated several times: 'We made a big mistake.' Seeing that the 'rabbin' was coming back, the German left the ferry and approached the wagon. When he reached it, he stretched out his hand and grasped the sideboard, and the preacher called out immediately: 'We were in such a hurry that we forgot to thank you for the great favor you've done us.' He reached out his hand to the German and blessed him: 'May God see that you live well for 120 years.' The German was struck dumb with deep emotion. The preacher winked to the coachman, and they set off once again. The horses set off at a terrific pace and before Grandfather knew it, they had arrived at the village of Grobev. Grandfather jumped down from the wagon with his sack of challah, thanked the preacher, and didn't catch what the preacher said because the wagon had taken off. He watched the wagon for a short while before it disappeared from view."

When our teacher Khayim-Yisroel had finished the story, one of the students asked, "And did Fetsch, the German, really live 120 years?"

The teacher answered, "I don't know whether he lived 120 years or less than that, but every Jew in Vurke knows that the German had a long life, and his children and grandchildren still tell the wonderful story about the Kozhenitser Magid. The German's house is still standing, and the ferry was put in a special place, where it is guarded as a relic."

In Khorostkov During the First World War

S. ANSKY
Sefer Khorostkov (Chorostkow)

From Gzhimalov I traveled to Khorostkov, a sizable town of over 350 families. Some of them left when the Russians occupied the town, but they were replaced by over 1,000 homeless refugees, mostly from Husiatyn.

I rode to the home of one of the members of the committee, and stayed there along with the rest of the committee. We reviewed the needs of those requiring assistance. The greatest lack was in clothing, especially shoes; entire families couldn't go outside because they had no warm clothes. A tragic situation: the committee had received a few dozen pairs of shoes, but it was holding them until it received more. Why? If these few pairs of shoes were distributed, those who didn't receive any would have spoken ill of the committee.

There was an epidemic of stomach typhus and scarlet fever in the town, but no medicine with which to combat these diseases.

During the committee's meeting, an elderly woman burst into the room, approached me, and without formalities began to speak rapidly and boldly:

"I'm a grandchild of Reb Zusye Anipoler and a great-grandchild of Reb Levi-Yitskhok Berditshever; on my mother's side I'm descended from the Baal Shem. There are seventeen hasidic rebes in our family, and I'm a distant cousin of the great Brodsky."

Having poured forth her entire pedigree, she gave me a sharp look, wanting to determine just how much I was impressed.

"What is it you want?"

What did she want? What sort of question was that to ask? Obviously, someone descended from so many great men has a right to expect special consideration! When I explained to her that pedigree had no bearing on our decisions, she looked at me in astonishment, raised her shoulders in great protest, and went out.

In the evening, after we had finished our work and were sitting together over a glass of tea, an old man came in. He was the town cantor—tall and thin, with soft, young, sparkling eyes. He had come to ask for help. His request was so modest that I immediately promised it to him. During our conversation I mentioned hasidic stories. The cantor responded warmly, and enthusiastically began telling story after story. He told them in rich detail, like a true poet. Every story that he told was a work of art. I deeply regretted not being able to record them word-for-word. Typically, almost all of them had to do with the Messiah. I later ascertained that older Jews all over Galicia were deeply interested in the idea of the Messiah. Only one of his stories has remained in my memory.

"When Reb Yisroel Rizhiner was in prison, his circle of intimates and all of his Hasidim spared no effort in their attempt to have him released. And when he was freed, their joy was beyond measure. Only one of his Hasidim, a certain Reb Motele, who had always been dedicated to the Rebe body and soul, neither danced nor sang. He sat as if in mourning, and wouldn't speak with anyone. When he was asked why he was still sorrowing, he burst into tears and replied: 'I had hoped that the Rebe was the Messiah. When he was arrested, I was over-joyed, and I thought that the Messiah's trials were beginning. I complained to myself, 'May the boil burst already!' But the boil didn't burst; the Rebe was freed, and everything is as it was before. So how can I be happy?"

As he sat telling stories, I suddenly heard the soft, mournful tones of a fiddle behind me, playing an old melody. As I looked around, I saw a ragged, half-starved, and embittered Jew about fifty years old. He played an old, cheap fiddle, and both of them wept. Silent tears poured from the musician's eyes, and a quiet, heartrending weeping poured from the fiddle's strings. Both wordlessly asked for help. The musician was from Podvolotshisk; he had lost everything he owned, and gone into exile with his fiddle, his only comfort. But that had been stolen from him as well. Having returned from Penze, there was nothing for him to do here. There were no weddings or celebrations where a musician might find work. But when he found out that "an officer of the committee" had come, he managed to obtain a fiddle, and came to greet me. He stood in the doorway and began to relate to me his poverty, his loneliness, and sorrow.

I noticed that the folk songs and folktales deal very often with mourning and weeping. "Everyone began to weep and lament," "weeping and wailing," and so forth. Russian folk songs also repeatedly use the phrases, "bathed in tears," "covered with tears," and the like. I had always assumed these to be mere poetic expressions. Now, in Galicia, I realized that they were realistic descriptions. I saw people "covering themselves with tears." Apparently, there are moments when tears pour from the eyes unbidden and unnoticed, and take the place of words. That happens when words have utterly lost their power, when there is no one left to speak to.

When the musician stopped playing and I asked him to sit with us, the old cantor was reminded of a legend about a melody.

"A Jew came to the Rizhiner Rebe to ask his opinion about a certain matter. The Rebe sang the song *Eliyohu Hanovi* to him, with a gentile melody, and told him to memorize the tune. Although the Jew didn't understand the Rebe's reason, he obeyed and memorized the melody. Fifteen years later, the Jew happened to be traveling through a demon-inhabited forest at night. As he proceeded, he saw a short gentile with a pipe walking next to him. He was badly frightened. The gentile asked him where he was going. 'Into town,' he replied.

"The gentile said, 'I'm also going into town.' Then the gentile grasped his hand and said, 'Sing something to me.' The Jew grew even more terrified. But then he remembered the version of *Eliyohu Hanovi* which the Rizhiner had taught him, and he began to sing. He continued to sing it until they arrived in town, and the gentile disappeared."

In Khorostkov I met Rabbi Frankl of Husiatyn and Reb Lipe Shvager. They ran a sizable book dealership together, mostly consisting of old Jewish religious texts, rare books, and manuscripts. They were the leading Jewish antiquarians in Galicia. Their whole collection was demolished in the pogroms and the fire. They had managed to save only a few of the manuscripts and rare books, some of which I took along when I left and gave to the museum in Petrograd for safekeeping.

Reb Lipe Shvager, a close relative of the Kopitshinetser Rebe, told me a wonderful story that has rich symbolic and mystical overtones. (Incidentally, the story is included in my cycle of hasidic tales.)

When the war broke out, the Kopitshinetser Rebe was at a health spa in Hamburg. His whole family was with him there, along with Lipe Shvager. When the Russians began to occupy Galicia, the Rebe summoned Shvager and said to him:

"You should know that I possess two letters in the hand of the holy Baal Shem himself. They might, God forbid, be lost in the course of the war. Therefore, travel immediately to Kopitshinets and save the letters. If you are unable to return, hide them in a safe place. You should also know that many dangers await you on the way: You could be killed by a bullet, or you may be the victim of a frameup, heaven forfend! But the dangers must not stop you from carrying out your holy mission and saving the letters."

Shvager immediately agreed and asked the Rebe, "And what about all of your possessions, about the gold and silver and other valuables at your courts?"

It was said that there were a few million kroner worth of precious items at the court.

"All that is dispensable," the Rebe replied quietly, "but the Baal Shem's letters must be saved."

Shvager departed. He arrived in Kopitshinets several hours before the Russians entered the town. There was no chance of going back. But he had time to rescue and bury the letters. He placed them in a tin box and buried them two meters deep in a cellar wall at the Rebe's court. He buried some of the Rebe's gold and silver in the same cellar. He was unable to go to the cellar for three or four months afterwards. During the period he came close to death on several occasions; he was arrested and accused of espionage. Finally, when he went to the cellar, he found none of the precious items which he had buried. Everything had been dug up and robbed. The wall in which the box containing the letters had been hidden had also been dug into, and the box had disappeared.

It's not hard to imagine the impression this made on Shvager. He nearly died of sorrow. But a few days later, when he searched the wall again, he found the box, intact and undisturbed. But when he opened it, he found to his astonishment that on the letter written in the Baal Shem's own hand (the second letter was only signed by him), all of the writing had disappeared and only a blank sheet of paper remained.

To tell the truth, I didn't entirely believe the story. I put it down as one of those legends which are easily credited in such times of turmoil. Therefore, I asked Shvager to show me the letters. The letters were hidden in the innermost room in Kopitshinets, and Shvager didn't want to show them to me. But when I met him in Kopitshinets a couple of weeks later and insisted, he rather unwillingly agreed. He brought them into the synagogue, wrapped in paper. He unwrapped them with the utmost care, avoiding touching them. I saw two old, folded sheets of paper. One was covered on both sides in a thin, crowded hand, which Shvager told me was Reb Gershon Kitever's (the letter has already been printed). On the very edge of the second side, in long, sharp, separate letters, the signature was barely noticeable: "Yisroel Baal Shem." The second, disintegrated (both letters were written in 1753) and with pale marks from dampness or tears, was completely blank, without the least trace of writing. Shvager looked at the letters with intense, mystical concentration, and said quietly:

"It's said that the writing disappeared because of moisture, and that it could be restored with chemicals. But we Hasidim think differently . . . quite differently."

Dear God!
(THE STORY OF A JEWISH MILLER)

DOVID KAHAN
Pinkas Navaredok (Nowogrodek)

To the memory of my brother Yitskhok-Ayzik, his wife Beylke,
and their children, Shoshana, Tsvi, and Arye,
who were tortured and killed by the Nazis.

It happened in those near and distant times even prior to the First World War. The small village of Slobodke, nearby the Jewish town of Navaredok, consisted of one small street bordered by wooden houses with thatched roofs. On top of the hill the small church with its weathered cross looked out between haggard trees over the cemetery where generations of peasants lay buried. Below flowed currents of water that powered the mill belonging to a Polish noble spinster, who had leased it to a wise Jewish miller, for as long as people could remember. In the miller's house, whose wooden walls trembled day and night because they were joined to the water mill, there was a great celebration one day. The miller's elder daughter, who had married a talmudic scholar awaiting his first rabbinical position, gave birth to her first son and on this day was his circumcision.

From the town came the religious officials, led by the rabbi and *mohel*, and from near and far came Jewish millers; all sat down to a feast fit for a king. On the second day, when the new mother was up and about, a celebration was held for the peasants from the surrounding villages who brought their grain to be ground at the mill, and together with the peasants came the Orthodox priest. He was a broad-shouldered man, with a face fleshy as though it were made of buttermilk; a broad, beet-red nose; watery eyes; and long flaxen hair falling like ribbons from his head and beard. The priest, who had imbibed a fair amount of whiskey and nibbled on herring and white rolls, demanded to see the child. He drunkenly pounded his chest with his fist and complained to the old miller, the grandfather:

"What? Have we no stake in your daughter? Did she not grow up among our children? Why may we not look upon her first son?"

The miller had no choice but to bring out his daughter, who held her new-born son on a white pillow. The priest, whose heavy silver cross dangled over his protruding stomach, opened his eyes wide with astonishment, looked at the boy and suddenly, drunkenly fell with his face to the ground, crossed himself, and cried:

"Dear God! He resembles our Savior!"

The peasants all heard this, kneeled, crossed themselves, and murmured:

"Dear God, our Savior!"

And in this manner the peasants in the region related that a grandson of the miller had been born who was a little Jesus. All this only added to the miller's prosperity.

When the child grew up, he was inundated with love by the peasants. The miller sought to find a rabbinical post for his son-in-law, the child's father, so as to remove the child from the village, where the youth was aware and took pride in the fact that the peasants spoke of his resemblance to Jesus. The child together with his parents left the village and moved far away to a small town somewhere in the Ukraine.

The child, who grew by leaps and bounds, was drawn to his birthplace and to the peasants, even though he was a student in the yeshiva. He would drop in on his grandfather on holidays, and spend time with the peasants, who were delighted and pampered him. The lusty peasant girls received him with particular affection, pressed him to their ample breasts, and kissed him. The boy grew up, left the yeshiva after receiving his rabbinical ordination, and joined a Russian revolutionary group, being spared from prison on account of his face. When his grandfather, the miller, died he returned to the village and took over the mill. The old noblewoman was dearly fond of him, but above all, the simple peasants loved him, and he them. At Eastertime he would distribute white flour to the peasants and go to their houses to partake of the traditional thirteen cereals.

The First World War erupted. The Germans occupied the area, and requisitioned all mills, but not the mill of "Jesus." A few requisition officers were stationed at the mill and if they did not quite believe that this *Jude*, the miller, was Jesus, they certainly believed in his gifts: white flour, well-churned butter cooled in the waters of the mill, rich egg-cheese balls, and a nice piece of pork as well. These packages were sent to Germany on a weekly basis, and the old soldiers protected the miller from harm.

With the advent of the Russian revolution came peace between Germany and Russia. The Germans left the area, and the Bolsheviks took over the towns and villages. One day an agitator came to the village, a man with a sharp, fiery tongue. He assembled the peasants in the center of the village and delivered an indoctrination speech:

"Tell me, comrade peasants: the land of the noblewoman, which you peasants work, to whom should it belong?"

And they all cried out, "The land must belong to the state!"

"And the factories in the cities, where the workers toil, to whom should they belong?"

"To the state!"

The young agitator, a Jewish lad, now fired up, asked, "And to whom should the village water mill belong?"

And the peasants tossed their hats in the air, and shouted: "The mill belongs to our Jesus! The mill will always belong to our Jesus!"

"What Jesus? Who is he, where is he?" blazed the young agitator.

The peasants responded, "Jesus is our Itske."

The mill was requisitioned after all, but Jesus remained there as the miller.

When the Poles came with their aristocratic pretensions and anti-Jewish agitation, Jews from both towns and villages set off for the land of Israel. The miller too felt a pull toward the Holy Land, but he was too attached to the peasants who smiled through their mustaches and said:

"If *we* were to go to Palestine, then Itske would come too." But the older children of the miller went to Israel, along with other youths, intending to settle. The miller and his wife, together with their younger children, remained in the village, and maintained their friendship with the peasants.

The Second World War broke out, and the Nazi beast ravaged the cities and villages of Poland. When they began slaughtering people, the Germans demanded that the peasants destroy their Jews, but the peasants from the village protected their miller. They, along with the miller, believed that they would persevere and survive those bloody and frightful days.

But one day the village was encircled by German soliders who descended upon the mill and led away the Jewish miller, his wife, and two children. A third child hid among the sacks of flour and they did not find him. The whole village stood watching. Along with the peasants stood a young priest, a native of a nearby village. When the peasants saw the miller, who was covered with white flour, his noble face and golden beard truly resembling the image of the tortured Jesus, they all knelt and crossed themselves, and the young priest murmured softly:

"The cursed Antichrists are tormenting our miller. Let God's wrath fall upon them."

The German soldiers drove the miller and his family to the Jewish cemetery. The peasants hoped that the hidden child, who was tucked among the sacks of flour, would be saved. But the Germans had a list of the miller's children, and they set watch around the mill. The peasants hoped that when night fell, they would be able to spirit the child away and hide him. When it grew dark, and the child believed that the Germans had gone, he peeked outside and was captured by the soldiers. In vain the peasants pleaded that the Germans might leave the child with them in the village; the Germans took him to his grave.

In the stillness of the night the waters of the mill joined the peasants in mourning their miller and his family. The young priest crossed himself and whispered:

"May God's wrath be poured out upon the Germans and upon their children, for all eternity."

Holocaust

A Final Moral Lesson

PESAKH MARKUS
Lite; band eyns

Reb Nokhem, the son of the poor water carrier in Yanishke and student of the Musar leader, Reb Note Hersh, the "Old Man" of Slobodke, became the leader of the Musar movement after his Rebe's death. In his talks he extended his mentor's concept of the spiritual elevation of man. He also mentioned that Slobodke was the new Nehardea, and passed along moral sayings of Rav and of Reb Tanhuma. But Reb Nokhem didn't have the latter's sermon in Nehardea on martyrdom in mind. He saw no need for it, and might have lived his entire life that way. He was only interested in the living person. He continuously speculated about how man might reach a high enough level to be truly worthy of being called Man.

When his students in Slobodke brought the news about the great cruelty of the Germans, he was overwrought at first; he went around asking himself: "Is this Man, God's greatest creation? My rebe, Reb Note Hersh, spoke about spiritual elevation his whole life long. How can it be?" Reb Nokhem fell into despair, and even stopped giving his moral sermons. But suddenly it was as if he had awakened, and he began to say encouraging things, not only in the evening, but also after morning prayers, and on into the day. He begged his students to improve their ways, to examine them constantly, to test them violently and make them fine and noble; to constantly break their own wills without giving in as much as a hair, to labor to deserve to be called by the elevated title of Man.

Reb Nokhem Yanishker spoke about spiritual elevation in Slobodke and meanwhile the Hitlerites awakened maliciousness. All of the evildoers had already allied themselves with them, and their cruelties had reached to the heavens. And as once the students at Nehardea had asked Reb Tanhuma, those at the Slobodke yeshiva now asked Reb Nokhem:

"Please explain to us! Don't you see now, Rebe, that man is lower than the animals? And you, Reb Nokhem Yanishker, still speak about the elevated nature of man. The German cutthroats rob and slaughter Jews without remorse, and we, your students, who wouldn't dare touch the belongings of another, you preach morality to us? You still demand that we bear ourselves ever more purely because we still haven't reached the level of humanity. It's almost an insult to be called a man now. So raise your voice and ask Heaven why we are being punished so bitterly."

Reb Nokhem Yanishker didn't think it proper to mention the Germans by their unholy name in a place of sanctity, and as though he were speaking about a matter concerning only himself, he said to his students:

"If the world conducted itself as it should, perhaps we here in Slobodke could allow ourselves to pardon a bad habit, and rest from constantly wrestling with our stubborn wills. But now that evil is so widespread, who shall uphold the world, if not Slobodke? And I, Nokhem Yanishker, am in no way as quiet and meek as you suppose. I had already gathered myself to interrogate the Creator, and ask him: 'Why? Why do you punish your Jews so terribly?' And there were other such 'whys' I wanted to ask him. But I realized that I myself could be asked: 'Nokhem, why have you been silent and not asked, Why are you silent about us, the sinners?' Man has to have both 'whys.' We can only make requests of the Holy Name. But what can accomplish as much as our own good deeds? The more you increase holiness here, the less room there will be for evil."

With his own quiet speech, Reb Nokhem had aroused himself. The evils that Jews were suffering made him grow older. He grew entirely gray, and when he prayed, tears flowed from his eyes. He had to hide his face with his hands, so that the students wouldn't see that their Rebe was crying. And sometimes a hoarse, stubborn moan tore out of him, which scratched and scratched on the windows like a buzzing fly and wouldn't go away.

His students knew that he was full of sorrow and that his strength was failing; he was barely able to stand and was forced to deliver his talks from a chair. So they sought all possible methods to hold back the bad news from him. He knew that.

As the Germans tore into Lithuania with storm and bloodshed, there was nothing left to hide from him. The windows of the yeshiva were already trembling from the bellowing of German artillery. The students noted to their great astonishment that he, their Rebe, had grown quite calm. He went away to purify himself with a ritual immersion, dressed in his Sabbath clothes, checked the mezuzes on the doors, and the fringes of his *arbe kanfes* [ritual undergarment]. But they quickly noticed that underneath his collars burial shrouds were to be seen; and with everything ready, he set himself by his prayer stand and gathered the strength to stand up. But suddenly, the wrinkles of his brow began to move up and down. The students understood that a difficult question in morals was troubling their Rebe. He was trying to find a commentary on a matter that was giving him problems. And then his eyes lit up and he waved with his hand, his way of showing that he had something to say. His students quickly gathered around in a circle and he began talking, at first softly, and then louder and louder:

"I, Nokhem Yanishker, have thought on my own account: everyone knows that a Jew must prepare himself to undergo martyrdom. But what is the true nature of this greatest of all holy deeds? And we must know this quite exactly. For all deeds can be redone, but martyrdom is the final deed. I, Nokhem Yanishker, thought to myself that the risk in carrying it out is great. Even if one suffers the worst agonies one can still commit the worst transgression—desecration of the Name [of God]. The distinction between sanctification of the Name and desecration of the Name is a very small one. In a material transaction, the richer the customer, the cheaper the relative price of the merchandise. Here it is precisely the opposite. The poorer a man is in learning and good deeds, the less he has to pay for sanctification of the Name. For such a person, the agonies themselves suffice, even if he regrets not belonging to the evil nation. But a man must pay dearly for the purchase of sanctification of the Name. One small mistake, a foolish thought, or even asking for the mercy of the evildoers, and the sanctification is replaced by desecration. And for nothing has such a person allowed his body to be destroyed. I, Nokhem Yanishker, have never searched for a bargain in my entire life. I have toiled with myself, sought with my effort, to earn the world to come, like my father, the water carrier of Yanishke, sought to earn his bread through his own effort. And I would be most happy if Heaven would now demand from me a dear price for sanctification of the Name."

Reb Nokhem stopped to catch his breath and continued his last conversation with his students:

"Most of all, man must take care not to let the evildoers soil his soul. But that does not mean that he should abandon his body and despair of his life. No, it is now that your body must be privileged. You must spare it more than you did before. But increase your love of your soul as well. And thus, as your love of your body and your soul grows, you may reach the highest level. But if you do not love the body, how great can your love for your soul be?"

Reb Nokhem Yanishker, the profound master of morals, wanted to make his concept of sanctification of the Name still clearer, but someone opened the door of the yeshiva and cried in terror:

"The Germans are coming!"

Reb Nokhem Yanishker drew himself up to his full height, and in an earnest voice, said to his students:

"With the power that the law gives me as your Rebe and with all my authority, I order you to leave me here and to run to save yourselves. Guard your bodies and guard your souls. Don't put your lives in danger on account of external appearances, but don't hesitate for a minute to sacrifice yourselves because of internal reasons. Also, I beg you and command you to always remember people who will die at the murderers' hands. It is not for man to decide who is a martyr and who is not. For them, all who die must be considered as martyrs, remember this, my beloved students in Kovner Slobodke, the Nehardea of Lithuania. And if peace will return to the world, you should continuously tell of the greatness and wisdom in Torah and morals of Lithuania, what a fine and honorable life the Jews led here. But don't dissolve into tears and mourning. Tell it peacefully and calmly, as our Holy Tanaim did in their midrash *Eykho Rabosi*, about the destruction of the Holy Temple. And like them, the holy wise men, you should also recreate your speech in letters. That will be the greatest revenge you can take on the evil ones. In spite of them, the souls of your brothers and sisters will live on, the martyrs whom they sought to destroy. For no one can annihilate letters. They have wings, and they fly around in the heights . . . into eternity."

The Typhus Epidemic and a Wedding at the Cemetery

MOYSHE BORUKHOVITSH
Yizker-bukh fun der Zhelekhover (Zelechow) yidisher kehile

The typhus outbreak in the Nazi ghetto of Zhelekhov took on serious proportions in the following months; there were many deaths. At that critical time the Judenrat removed from the ghetto Dr. Shkap, who was very popular on account of his dedication to the sick. The Judenrat had the German authorities in Garvolin send Dr. Shkap to Sabin. The reason for this was that the doctor stood at the head of "Jewish Social Self-Help," against which Finkelshteyn and his people* fought bitterly. This reprehensible act angered the entire population, which was too weak to oppose the Judenrat's blackmail. Instead of Dr. Shkap, the Judenrat brought Dr. Zhilkevitsh from Warsaw, and Shloyme Hoyker was given full control of the hospital. To avoid a disinfection and four weeks' quarantine, one had to bribe Shloyme Hoyker.

My sister Faygl traveled to Warsaw and contracted typhus there. The news was sent to us from Warsaw. My youngest sister Sorele set off; the trip wasn't the easiest, taking two days. Sorele found our sister dangerously ill. Our entire family sought all possible forms of medical aid for her. There were many Jewish doctors in Warsaw, who had been sent to Poland by the Nazis; with their help, our sister managed to remain alive. With the help of our friends and relatives in Warsaw, an ambulance was obtained from the First Aid squad for an appropriate sum of money when she recovered, and we brought her to Zhelekhov.

After my sister's illness, everyone at home, including myself, came down with typhus. We all tried to avoid the Judenrat hospital and the disinfection. Shloyme Hoyker's inspectors found out about my illness and came to take me to the hospital. I hid in an attic, and contracted a bad lung inflammation. It took quite a bit of effort for the doctors to save me. Shloyme Hoyker still wanted to profit from my disease, however, and threatened that he would find me, put me in the hospital, carry out the disinfection, and seal everything. We saw that we couldn't get out of his clutches, so we decided to pay Shloyme Hoyker two hundred zlotys, and his assistants, twelve hundred.

*The Judenrat.

While the epidemic claimed its victims from among the Jewish population, the German policemen struck and terrorized Jews; and with the help of Jewish informers, they carried out inspections, seized merchandise, and carried the owners off to the police station, where they were beaten and fined. My sisters were expecting a wagonload of two barrels of oil, which the Pole Yazhembek was supposed to bring. As soon as he arrived, the Germans threw him off the wagon and arrested him. They also inspected our house, confiscated goods, and murderously beat my brother-in-law, Khayim-Meyer Vaynberg. The same thing happened to my neighbor Note Yom-tov, from whom they took two tin boxes of manufactured items which he had hidden under the floor. Note Yom-tov was led off to the police station, along with the merchandise. There the policeman Buchholz placed a tin typewriter cover on his head and beat him with a piece of iron until he lost consciousness. After pouring water over him they stood him up again and beat him until they grew tired. Then he was ordered to pay one thousand marks for the beating. The same was done with many Jews; and to our humiliation, the goods were then sold by the Jewish informers.

The typhus outbreak kept up, and became ever more deadly; rarely did anyone recover. It turned into a full-scale epidemic. Among others, those who died were Hershl Hefner and his son Yisroel Meyer, Peysekh Lukavyetzky and his brother Nakhmen, Noyekh Myadavnik, Velvl Dramlevitsh, Moyshe Shpringer, Moyshe Gutman, one of Yisroel Shidlavitsh's boys, and a great number of the homeless who lived in Zhelekhov. The mortality rate among them was very high on account of their poor living conditions. On account of all this, a meeting was called at the home of the rabbi, may the memory of his righteousness bless us, attended by the two experts in rabbinic law Reb Yekhiel and Reb Zaynvl, and many homeowners as well as the Judenrat. It was decided to attempt all the remedies which were known to those present at the meeting. Money was to be gathered for "the redemption of souls"; everyone had to give money for each person in his house. The amount depended upon whether one was poor, middle class, or wealthy; the money was to be used to buy shoes and clothing for the needy. A committee was named, consisting of Avremele the rabbi's son, Note Yom-tov, Yisroel Shildkroyt, Moyshe Fas, and myself.

The campaign was very successful. A great sum was collected. The tanners—Yekl Dangat, his brother-in-law Noyekh Fel, Yankl Goldfarb, and Dudshe's son-in-law—gave a large amount of leather for the uppers. The wealthier tanners, relatives of Judenrat members, who were exempt from all taxes, also failed to participate in this campaign. Wooden soles were ordered from the carpenter Yaske Siver, and simple country shoes were made. Since there wasn't enough for all the needy, the committee decided to give only one pair to each family, so that at least one person in each family would be able to go out and bring something home to eat. And that's how it was. In many poor homes the entire family sat sorrowing at home, while one put on the shoes and went into the street to find a piece of bread, a bit of wood, and some turf for the fire, and a few potatoes. When he came home and took off the shoes, another one squeezed into them. Walking in the wooden shoes on the ice in cold weather was a unique form of hell; pedestrians could be heard several blocks off. The poor man had to have a lot of luck and a contact in the committee to receive two pairs of shoes for his household.

At the meeting it was also decided to arrange a wedding at the cemetery. This would be in accordance with an old custom whenever there was an epidemic (may we be preserved!). At the same time, there was to be a ritual burial of the worn-out scraps of holy books in the attic of the study house, so that the wedding would become a funeral as well.

An appropriate couple was sought. It wasn't easy to find volunteers. After much searching, a groom was found—Motele, a son of Moyshe Beyger. The bride was Khavele, the daughter of Sore and Velvl Yudkes, a spinster over fifty, who lived in the street between White Khayim's house and Velvl Vishnyer's house. "In a propitious hour" the couple agreed to the wedding and to its location at the cemetery next to the grave on condition that the community clothe them. Two pairs of wooden shoes were immediately gotten for the bride and groom, and the community bought some scraps to make them clothes.

On the day of the wedding the groom's father protested, declaring that he wouldn't let his son be married until he, too, received a pair of wooden shoes. The community fulfilled his demand, and led the couple to the wedding canopy which was to be set up at the new cemetery. The procession was followed by several wagons bearing old books and accompanied by the rabbi, his children, the rabbinical experts, and almost all of the residents of the Zhelekhov ghetto. The musicians played along, and the mood was very bitter.

At the cemetery, the texts were buried first, and then the wedding was conducted with all of the proper details. The rabbi performed the ceremony. Various prayers intended to ward off the epidemic were said, followed by cries of "Mazel tov!" The couple was led back to the wedding hall in the Judenrat's quarters. At the command of the Judenrat, the Jewish police kept order. A marvelous feast was served; the crowd enjoyed itself and also pleased the bride and groom. Wedding contributions were called for, bringing in a substantial sum which was then given to the couple. F. Likhtensheyn, who gave himself the title "the editor from Lodz," had composed several verses appropriate to the occasion, which the crowd sang. Thus was celebrated the graveyard wedding which was to save the Jews from typhus.

How I Read Yiddish Literature
to an S.S. Captain

BERL MANPERL
Mezritsh (Miedzyrzec); zamlbukh

This happened in 1943 in Mezritsh, when the German murderers terrorized their defenseless Jewish victims with all the dark force of their fiendish power. They tortured, beat murderously, ridiculed, degraded, and outraged our deepest and most intimate human sensibilities. Whoever was "blessed" with a bullet and redeemed from agony was considered lucky. Our only friend was Death; we ate from the same plate as Death; the only one whom we had ceased to fear was Death.

We were utterly abandoned, given up to the brutal hands of the brown Hitlerite beast, and to the worst element from among our Christian neighbors—Poles, Ukrainians, Lithuanians and others—who stood ready to serve the "master race," ready to murder and rob.

Four terrible, bloody slaughters had already been carried out in our city of Mezritsh, after which only some four thousand of the original Jewish population of eighteen thousand remained. The rest had been eliminated in various ways; most of them were shot in the city—men, women, and children. The elderly were led off in closed freight cars to Treblinka, where they were killed with poison gas, and later burned in the ovens.

In the bit of ghetto within which the last few Jews were confined, life continued under indescribably awful conditions. By eights and by tens, suffering, stepped-on, hungry, lice-ridden, we crowded into the small rooms that the brown beast had designated as the only cage in which we were permitted to suffocate, and even to cannibalize each other.

There were also hours when we would abandon our cramped, lice-ridden nests, and gather in little groups outside to breathe a bit of fresh air and wait for a miracle, a sudden redemption. . . . But the heavens were closed to us, and all help was far away. No miracle took place, and there was no hope of being redeemed from our agony. All these dark forces had one goal: to eliminate us from the face of the earth, to eradicate us so thoroughly that not even the least remnant would remain.

And as we whispered in the silence, Gestapo hangmen would appear out of thin air, in order to carry out a "small" slaughter against us, to satisfy themselves with a few more victims to add to those who died in the major *aktsyes* [actions].*

It was mere sport to them, a way of quenching their thirst for blood. Sensing

*Roundup of Jews for deportation accompanied by brutal beating and killings to terrorize the remaining Jews into compliance.

the approach of the two-footed beasts, we used to escape with our last ounce of strength, each to his own hiding place—to the bunkers, the holes, the hidden attics—in order to conceal our tortured bodies and souls. . . . In an instant the ghetto became as dead as a graveyard, without the least sign of life. Each of us, lying in his "burrow," felt the black wings of Death spread above us. Strange— the more we were terrorized, the stronger grew the urge to live. "Stay alive"; "survive"; "even like this"; "just live . . ."

Pain, resentment and longing consumed our hearts and poisoned our blood. The mixture of feelings was maddening; on one hand a heartrending longing for our lost nearest and dearest; and on the other hand, bitter resentment of fate for having left us alive to suffer.

Yet among us, the surviving remnant no longer afraid of Death, a constant wager with Death was played out:

Who will survive whom? . . . Who will overcome whom?

Saturday, May 1, 1943. Today we returned early from work, because May 1 is a "holiday" for the brown-shirt Hitlerite hordes as well. We are a group of slaves harnessed in hard labor outside the ghetto at the Mezritsh local command post, where several hundred Jews survive by performing various tasks for the German garrison.

A group of twenty of us sit in the home of Berl Vakhtfoygl, lonely and saddened.

I sat on my straw sack, from beneath which I had just pulled out the few books which I had managed to rescue from my library and hidden here from the wild eyes of our torturers. A bad end awaited anyone caught carrying anything printed, especially in Yiddish; for such a crime the sentence was a bullet in the head.

The only possessions I still had were the following books: *The Psalm Jew* [by Sholem Asch]; *In Polish Woods* by Joseph Opatashu; a volume of Ansky's *Collected Works;* and the *Parables* of E. Shtaynberg.

Looking into these books allowed me to forget my troubles for a while and remember a not too distant past.

This time I didn't read. Rather I attempted to strike up a conversation with my comrades in tragedy about the first of May, attempting to comfort them by discussing the losses the Germans were suffering at the front, and their reversal at Stalingrad. The "second front"—the dream of all the murdered Jews, who believed that it would save them from death—had finally opened. True, our little band of survivors had no prospects of living through the whole war. Yet we would die encouraged, knowing that their end was approaching, that the Jewish communities of Israel, of America, and of other lands that the "master race" hadn't reached would survive intact.

Suddenly there was a banging on the front door, and before we had time to think about who it might be, the local commander, S.S. Captain Klauck, entered the room.

I sat frozen with my book open; I hadn't had time to shove it under my mattress. He ran up to me, grabbed the book, and said in a grating voice: "What are you reading, Jew?" Pale as death I stammered: "Yiddish literature, Commander."

"Is there such a thing?"

"Yes, Commander."

"Read some of it," he ordered me. A deadly silence reigned in the room, no one dared move a muscle, and everyone, including myself, thought that my life was over and Death had won this bet. But if I had no choice but to read for him, I wanted to choose something that would remind him of our situation. I wanted to show him that "they" were accomplishing nothing by exterminating us, that others before them had already tried the same thing—true, with less success. And I, confused, covered with cold sweat from fear of Death, read him Ansky's legend about Moses Montefiore. The latter, meeting the Russian Tsar Nikolai in London, purchased all the Jews in Russia from him for three rubles each. When the tsar arrived home and told his advisors about the good deal he had made, which would also serve to rid him of the *Zhides*, his advisors told him that each of the *Zhides* brought at least ten rubles into his coffers each year. Later, when Moses Montefiore came to Russia in his famous carriage in order to take delivery of the Jews, he spent the Sabbath at the home of a great Russian prince. Suddenly a messenger came from the tsar, bringing a sealed packet for him.

Moses Montefiore would under no circumstances open the packet, since breaking the seal was forbidden on Sabbath. The prince opened the packet himself, and was killed on the spot: it was a letter bomb. Shortly afterward the queen of England declared war against Russia.

The S.S. captain contained himself a bit more, and in a calmer tone asked me to read one of Shtaynberg's *Parables*.

I began to read more loudly and with more expression the parable, "The Needle and the Bayonet." The content, more or less, is this: a soldier returned from the war, and placed his rifle, with bayonet attached, against a dresser. A needle was stuck into the cloth on top of the dresser. The needle was terrified by the rifle and the bayonet, and trembling, asked the bayonet what it pierced. When the reply came back, "I pierce people, people," the needle broke out in a fit of helpless laughter and shouted:

"I pierce bolts of linen, I make shirts, I make things. But you pierce people from now until Doomsday, what can you make out of them?"

When I finished reading, the captain flung the book onto the floor and hissed through his teeth: "Shit . . . pacifism!" With a sharp bang he slammed the door and went out.

On the same night, the morning of May 2, we were driven out of the house half-naked by the Jew-killers, and the fifth *aktsye* in Mezritsh began.

What I've described is merely a drop from the great goblet full of pain and agony, which I drank to the dregs during the time when the Hitlerite beast ruled, sowing murder and destruction among our people.

And now, years after the liberation, living in our own land, on our own earth, my soul is constantly full with the dark days of death and destruction in our Jewish city of Mezritsh, a town and a mother in Israel.

Terror in Vishnevits

BY ONE WHO WAS SAVED
Vishnevits (Wisniowiec Nowy), sefer zikaron le-kedoshei Wisniowiec
she-nispu be-shoat ha-Natsim

July 23, 1941: This morning Ukrainians were seen running around on a rampage. They seized everyone they saw out on the streets of the Jewish quarter, and dragged them off amidst bloodthirsty shouts of joy. At one place they brought together sixty-five Jews and led them away. We don't know exactly where that took place, but we do know that none of the captives returned. For many days we investigated where they had gone and where their grave might be, but our investigations were fruitless.

After that a week passed without any unusual events. Apparently, the Ukrainians themselves and their Nazi overseers were a bit frightened by what they had done, and they restrained themselves.

July 30, 1941: The Ukrainians' deed of last week was repeated today, but on a larger scale. This time they developed a better technique for killing Jews. They gathered four hundred Jews together on one of the "boulevards" in the center of town. Then they forced them to lie down one by one with their faces to the ground, and walked on the Jews with their hobnailed boots and with heavy sticks in their hands. If anyone so much as raised his head to see whether they had finished their business, a Ukrainian immediately jumped on his back and began beating him with his stick. Thus Jews remained for hours on the ground, beaten, wounded, and bloodied. They lay waiting either for worse things to happen, or for the Ukrainians to sate their sadistic desires with the moaning and blood of the Jews, and release their captives.

When they had assembled the number of Jews that the Germans had demanded of them (including the town rabbi Reb Yoysef Erlich, my brother, and others), they led their prisoners out of town on foot, and to this day we don't know where their remains are. The Ukrainians kept their mouths sealed, and didn't say a word about their heroic deeds. They didn't give out a hint as to where the graves were.

After every such deed, there were widows, orphans, and lone parents, whose world was empty and whose lives consisted of a single, burning thirst to have some news of the dear ones who had been torn away to an unknown place.

Then the Ukrainian women appeared. They went directly to the unfortunates, speaking woman to woman with heartfelt sympathy, with sorrow and understanding. They explained that their own Ukrainian husbands or sons were guarding the Jews at the place where they were being detailed. They transmitted a "message" from their men, saying that the victims' families shouldn't worry, that the victims were alive and in need of food and clothing.

The sorrowing relatives were gratified. Their hearts wanted the news to be true, and so they believed it. With tears of joy in their eyes, they wholeheartedly thanked the news bearers. They happily gave the kind Ukrainian women everything that they had requested, thinking that they would thereby warm the bodies and refresh the souls of their loved ones.

The Ukrainian women came every day, saying that the prisoners lived and were in need of things. The sufferers took everything they had and sent it away. They took off their last pieces of clothing, all for their faraway loved ones.

After a short time, the mothers did not have anything to feed their children; the children's bellies grew swollen, and they died of hunger. Dozens died every day; the streets were full of bodies of children who had fallen victims to the vile Ukrainian women. There is nothing more horrible than to see a child who is thin and dehydrated suddenly swell to twice its normal size and then, just as suddenly, die.

The tragedy of men who were the "heads" of their families, men who were supposedly dictators in their households, began earlier, when the Russians occupied the town. Suddenly the proud bread givers became superfluous; those who had supported their families by hard work became unnecessary beings, with no worth or reason to exist. Under the Russian regime, even before the Nazi tragedy, their patterns of life fell apart. The supports of the social order were removed. Without any effort on the part of the Russians, a shock went through the Vishnevits Jewish community, which was founded on family unity.

What happened to the men during the brief Nazi occupation followed the same pattern, although it was more intensive. Men were transformed into shadows; helpless, fathers ceased being the center of the family and everyone knew that they weren't the same men they had once been.

People stopped spending time together. Everyone had lost hope, and in this case the "shared troubles" only deepened the humiliation and agony, the sense of a void and the helplessness. The streets of Vishnevits became desolate. On top of the physical terror which possessed those condemned to death, there was the moral torture to which the once-proud men condemned themselves.

As the days passed, something changed. Here and there, figures appeared in the street. One raised one's eyes, ashamed, and silently said "good morning" with a look and a heavy sigh. The sigh drew out a matching sigh from one's fellow, and a prayer from his eyes: perhaps. Meanwhile things had calmed down somewhat. We didn't hear anything about new special *aktsyes*. The Jews began to conceal the shock of the catastrophe. The only signs of coming evil were the bread rations, which grew smaller from day to day, and the increased difficulty of obtaining food.

Remarkably, the Jews believed that everyone who had been taken away from town was still alive. "It stands to reason," they explained to themselves, "that if they had wanted to kill them, they would have done it right here. Who would have stopped them? They were taken someplace else because they were needed for work. Furthermore, if they were killed someplace else, it's a sign that the Nazis were afraid to kill them here, because somebody's keeping an eye on the Nazis. And in that case, we're safe." And they ended with a joke: "Look at them: they're the rulers, but they're afraid and always carry guns. We're the minority, but we're not afraid and don't carry any weapons. We only have to hang in there. Whoever can hang on in any situation and in any circumstances will survive them. Holding on, not falling apart: that's the main thing."

The Families in the Bunkers

MORDKHE HERSHKOVITSH AND ARON MATUSHINSKY
Sefer yizkor Myekhov (Miechow)

On February 24, 1938, I was serving in the Polish army, stationed at Cracow. I was in the artillery. When the war broke out, I fell prisoner to the Germans. I returned to Kshoynzh in 1940, when the Germans had already begun persecuting Jews and imposing forced labor on them. They took my father Volf Hershkovits, may he rest in peace, from our house with his hands raised, and he was forced to march through the streets shouting that the Jews were themselves responsible for the war.

At that time I was the only support of my family. I risked my life traveling from village to village, and thus eked out a living.

In 1942, when the Germans began sending Jews to the work camp at Plashuv, I didn't go to the transport. The Germans, assisted by the Polish police, led me to the middle of the marketplace, beat me thoroughly, and locked me up in the local prison. Thus they forced me to work. On the way to work, however, I jumped off the truck, ran away, and hid in the villages.

When the town was evacuated, my father was taken away with all of the town's homeowners. However, I, my mother Hinde, my brothers Yitskhok and Aren-Noyekh, sisters Dvoyre-Brayndl and Gutshe, and my brother-in-law Aren Matushinsky, went to the nearest village, Gebeltov, and hid on the estate of the nobleman Drzanat in the root cellar. My father had been the nobleman's tavern keeper for many years. At night we used to steal outside, looking for something to eat. We lived there for eight months like animals, subsisting on raw beets and whatever else we chanced across.

In the same village the following people were hidden by the family of the Christian Josef Konieczny: Meyer Matushinsky and his wife Rivke (the daughter of Yisroel Leyzerkes) with their four children Khanele, Yosele, Malkele, and Volf; Meyer's brother Yekl Matushinsky; Yekhiel and Henekh Leyzarek and their youngest sister Tobe: may they all rest in peace. As it happened, Yekl and Henekh chanced upon our bunker while they were out looking for food. It was a miracle sent from Heaven.

Until then we had known nothing of each other's whereabouts. When they saw our situation, they included us in their bunker at the Christian Josef Konieczny's house.

Our life there was difficult, but we were all together, and we lived on whatever we could. The Christian family was very kind to us, and helped us in every way possible.

Our fear increased and our situation grew worse from day to day. The Germans used all sorts of methods, attempting to find all the Jews who had hidden in the villages and forests. They didn't lack for helpers.

The situation became unbearable in 1943. It was impossible for all of us to remain in one place. My brother-in-law Aren and his wife Gutshe decided to go to the family of a Christian they knew named Wladek Kukuryk in the village of Shvyentshitse, where they remained until they were liberated on January 15, 1945.

They helped out the Kukuryks, doing whatever they could in the house and farm. No money was demanded of them. When Kukuryk's wife fed the cattle every morning, she also took care of them.

Aren and Gutshe survived until the end of the war, sheltered by this family of righteous gentiles. They remain grateful to the Kukuryk family for their humane behavior.

The rest of us who remained with the Konieczny family had a very hard time. Meyer Matushinsky, who had left money and valuables with the Christian Marjan Zelickewicz for safekeeping before the evacuation, risked his life to go to Kshoynzh to ask Zelickewicz for food and some of the money, which he badly needed just then. The Christian drove him away, adding that he shouldn't dare come again. If he did, said Zelickewicz, he would turn him over to the Germans; this time he was letting him get away alive.

Broken, hopeless, and fearful, he returned to the bunker and suffered along with his family, believing that they might somehow manage to survive the war.

But fate had it otherwise. On May 5, 1944, A.K. [*Armia Krajowa*]* groups

*The "Home Army" of the Polish resistance.

came into the village of Gebeltov. Obviously, they had received reports from their collaborators that Jews were hiding there. The Polish partisans did indeed fight against the Germans, but they also fought against Jews. Since they were incapable of joining the Germans in equal combat, they poured out all of their enmity and anger on the few surviving Jews.

A squadron of fifty men with horses and machine guns arrived, surrounded Konieczny's house, and demanded that we come along with them, bringing all our possessions. They had brought along horses and wagons for that purpose. We got in and rode far away from the village. There the following terrible scene took place.

In the Adama forest they ordered us to descend from the wagons, and tortured us in an attempt to make us reveal the hiding places of other Jews. Of course, we gave them no information; we understood the situation. We were all to be shot; and indeed, Meyer and Rivke Matushinsky and their four children; Hinde Hershkovitz and her children Yitskhok, Aren-Noyekh, and Dvoyre-Branyndl; and Tobe Leyzarek were all killed that day.

As they were about to start shooting, Yisroel [sic] Leyzarek's daughter Tobe asked to be the first one shot. We took advantage of the moment to begin running. Yenkl Matushinsky, Yitskhok Hershkovits, Yekhiel Leyzarek, Henekh Leyzarek, and I, Mordkhe Hershkovits, ran aimlessly, thinking only of staying alive. I found a ditch, which I entered. The A.K. men, chasing after me on horses, overlooked me.

Henekh Leyzarek met a peasant plowing his field. He took one of the plow handles, and thus saved his own life. The peasant later sheltered him for several days. He survived.

Yekhiel Leyzarek ran to the village of Kshesivka. He had many acquaintances there and thought he would be able to survive. However, the gentiles handed him over to the Germans; some even say that they carried out the sentence themselves. My brother Yitzkhok Hershkovits was fat, and it was hard for him to run, so he took off his boots, thinking that would make it easier. But the A.K. caught him and shot him.

Yenkl Matushinsky survived the war. Later, when he went to the village of Matsyeyuv to ask the Christian Kania Jendryk for the money he had left with him, the latter not only refused to return the money but murdered Yenkl with his own hands.

The rest of the family who were shot were buried in the Adama forest.

Virtually all of the Christians who hid Jews were murdered by the A.K. The Konieczny family, who had hidden Jews from Kshoynzh, came to a bitter end.

Konieczny's house was set on fire. His wife and daughter were shot. The father and son, however, were in the field at that moment. Hearing what had happened, they didn't return to the village; they wandered lost and homeless in the fields, lacking the means for survival.

Frontispiece from the yizker book, *Tshenstokhover Yidn*.

Upper right: The dedication of a new synagogue in Lenin. (Courtesy of H. Drogin) *Lower right:* An orphanage in Lenin. (Courtesy of H. Drogin) *Below:* Market day in Slonim.

Below: The market in Warsaw's old city. (YIVO) *Upper right:* Civilian transportation during the First World War. (YIVO) *Lower right:* Women pose with embroidery in Lenin. (Courtesy of H. Drogin)

Upper left: A sports club outing in Chmielnik. (*Pinkas Chmielnik*) *Upper right:* Jewish sports club of Bialystok. (YIVO) *Lower right:* The organ grinder's parrot draws lucky tickets. (*Bialystok Photo Album*) *Lower left:* A village couple. (YIVO)

Above: A village peddler. (*Sefer Yizkor-Rozvodov*) *Upper right:* Talmud study in Orla. (YIVO) *Lower right:* Carrying *cholent*, the Sabbath meal, to the baker's oven on Friday afternoon in Bialystok. (YIVO)

Upper left: Two little girls from Galicia. (Courtesy of G. Fetterman) *Kheyder* students. (YIVO) *Lower left:* A purim play at the Tarbut School in Torne. (YIVO) *Lower right:* A Simkhes Toyre celebration in Warsaw. (YIVO) *Upper right:* A family orchestra in Bialystok. (*Bialystok Photo Album*)

Lower right: A Poale Zion May Day Parade in Warsaw. (YIVO) *Above:* Jewish musicians perform at a Christian wedding. (YIVO) *Upper right:* A characteristic moving scene. (YIVO)

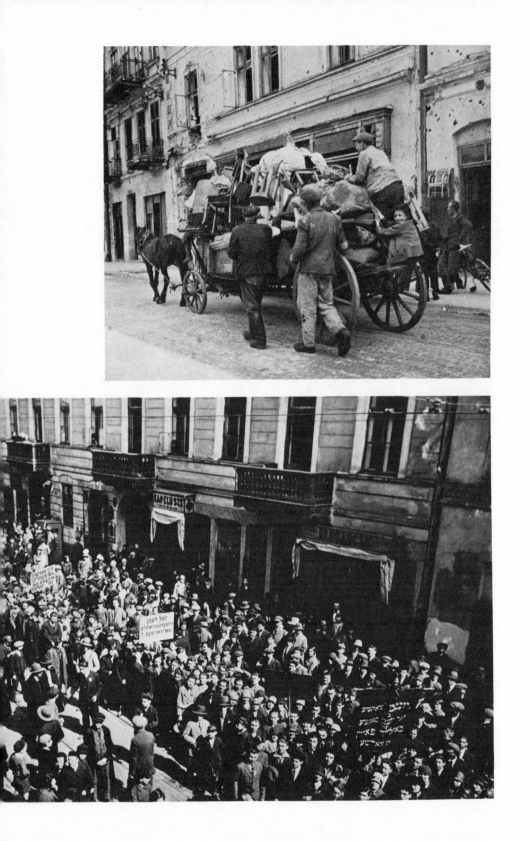

Above: At the soup kitchen in the ghetto. (YIVO) *Upper right:* A survivor returns to Chmielnik after the Holocaust. *Lower right:* Building a monument on the site of a mass grave. (YIVO)

Above: A memorial service of survivors. (*Sefer zikaron lekehilat Tomaszow-Mazowieck*) *Below:* The first Passover seder after liberation in Radom. (YIVO)

How I Hid Twelve Jews

STANISLAW SOBCZAK
Sefer Frampol

The author of the following lines, Stanislaw Sobczak, a Pole from Frampol, maintained his humanity during the terrible years of the occupation, and risked his own life and those of his family to hide twelve Jews from Goray and Frampol. He maintains correspondence to this day with many émigrés from Frampol in Israel. When he heard about the planned Frampol *yizker-bukh*, he sent his brief memoirs of that era by way of our fellow Frampoler, Shmuel Mahler of Haifa.

On November 1, 1942, the Germans befell defenseless people of Jewish origin. Twelve Jews from Frampol and Goray hid with me. Several days before the shooting, all of the Jews in Goray had been driven to Frampol, and some of them hid with me during the shooting. Placing my own life and the lives of my family in danger, I took these people in—not for the sake of profit, but because my conscience wouldn't permit me to leave the unfortunates in the murderers' hands. These were the names of those who were under my roof; from Goray: Moyshe Zalts and his sister; from Frampol: Avrom Shtaynberg and his family of four; Moyshe Tsimerman, Nakhmen Kestnboym, Lina Hof, Shmuel Honigman and his wife, and Shmuel Mahler. Honigman's wife died a natural death while they were with me.

I put all these people in a special hiding place in the yard, which was constructed with a double floor. It was very difficult for me to feed and care for them. I couldn't go to them by day, because I had to watch out for my neighbor; we didn't get along, and he constantly spied on me. Once, when my neighbor happened to come into my yard and noticed that there was a Jew there who wanted me to hide him, my neighbor denounced me to the Germans, who were in town just then. I was arrested and tortured for several days. I was helped then by a certain woman, a refugee from Silesia, who knew German, and who testified that the accusation was false.

In order to avoid arousing suspicion, I had to tend to the hidden Jews at night. I took away their potties and gave them food. While they were with me, I knew no rest; I lived in constant worry and fear that I would be discovered, and the affair would end in catastrophe for me. I couldn't make up my mind to tell the unfortunates to leave and search for another place. My conscience wouldn't let me. Once the marshal came to tell me that Germans were going to quarter in my barn. He didn't know how long they'd be staying. I accepted the news quite casually: fine, let them stay in my barn! And before I knew it, they had arrived. I was overcome with fear. I felt hot and cold flashes. The Germans were in the barn, and there was no way of getting to the people under the floor. Finally, however, I figured out another way to get to the hiding place; exactly how I did it is difficult to describe.

Another time, the marshal came to me, accompanied by Germans, just when I had let two people out of the hiding place into the room. My daughter noticed the marshal and the Germans and distracted them, at the same time calling loudly to me: "Papa, the marshal is calling you!"

The refugees used that moment to jump into the cellar. At the same time the marshal stuck his head into the yard, and it was a miracle that the incident passed without trouble.

Once there was some unpleasantness among the refugees: one man said that hiding someone was worth millions. He had noticed that Shmuel Mahler had money, and he wanted the money for himself. He threw himself at Mahler, attempting to choke him and steal the money (incidentally, I wrote to the man, but he didn't even answer me).

When the front neared us and the Germans began burning everything, I was afraid that those hiding in the cellar would be destroyed. Therefore, I told them to leave the hiding place. They wanted to give me everything they had, but I didn't want to take anything from them because I knew they would be needing it. I told them to go through my field in one direction, but they chose another route instead. There they encountered Polish partisans, who killed some of them and robbed them of everything they had. Some twenty A.K. partisans later came to me and announced that I was to be punished for the crime of hiding Jews. They ordered me to lie down and gave me such a beating that I was confined to my bed for two weeks, unable to move so much as an arm or a leg. The daughter of the local dentist witnessed them. The partisans took my horse and wagon, my pigs, and everything they could carry.

Wanderings of a Child

YEHUDIS PSHENITSE
Pinkas Novy-Dvor (Nowy Dwor)

When the war broke out in 1939 I was a child of merely eight years, but I was forced to mature quickly. At nine I was responsible not only for my own upkeep, but for that of my entire family.

I don't remember Novy-Dvor as it was in prewar times, with Jewish youth and Jewish life, as the older townspeople relate. I remember only a Novy-Dvor of tears, bombs, and deadly fear.

I remember: the wagon sits in front of our house, and a gentile is taking our belongings out. My parents, with faces full of worry, help him load the wagon, while my grandmother Yokheved sits outside, seeing that nothing is stolen. I casually ask, "Mama, where are we going?"

"To a new apartment in Warsaw," she replies. I was pleased with the idea of moving to the great city of Warsaw, of taking part in big-city life.

My happiness didn't last long. The tragedy soon began, and my family was separated. My sister and brother, my parents, my grandmother Vite, and I left Warsaw after a short time and moved to Rembertov. My grandfather Srulke and his family remained on Stavky Street in Warsaw.

Conditions grew steadily worse; my father lay sick in bed and my mother was swollen from hunger. That was when I became the breadwinner for the family.

Bearing a sack and a letter from my father to Arnold Bolden, asking him to help us out with some food, I set off along various paths for Novy-Dvor. Arnold Bolden, an ethnic German, was a good friend of my father. I gave him the letter, and he responded with sincere concern. He filled my sack with food, and I started back to my parents, who awaited me impatiently.

Unfortunately, my route back was impeded. The German guards detained me, took my sack of food, gave me a few heavy blows, and sent me back to Novy-Dvor. Once again I went to Arnold Bolden; once again he gave me food, and this time he accompanied me back to Rembertov. He sorrowed deeply for my father, and with that the friendship ended.

Then I began to set off across the peasant villages, begging for bread. Outside the ghetto I used to gather pieces of stale bread, a few potatoes, and bring it all into the house to keep my parents alive. More than once the guards detained me, took everything in my bag, and beat me. I returned weeping to my parents, who were waiting for a bit of bread. I continued in this way, day and night, for several long months.

One day my grandmother Vite said to me, "Go back to Novy-Dvor with me. That is where I want to die." I parted with my sick parents, and went with my grandmother. The way was difficult, but we made it. As soon as we arrived, however, everyone was evacuated to Pomyekhovek.

I neither knew nor understood that it was to be the final march for everyone there. Perhaps the adults didn't understand that yet, either. By coincidence, I happened to meet Arnold Bolden there; he was one of the ranking Germans. He said to me, "Leave your grandmother here. She is old already, but you are still a small child. I want to get you out of here." At first I didn't want to follow him, preferring to stay with my grandmother, but eventually he convinced me and led me away. Suddenly before my eyes I saw ditches being dug, and people being thrown in alive. When I saw my grandmother being pushed, I burst out weeping and tried to run to her, but Bolden dragged me away by force. I don't even remember how I made it back to Novy-Dvor.

I went to see the priest, who had known me as a small child, when I used to go into the church with our Christian maid. I wept and begged the priest to save me. I told him what had happened to my parents. He calmed me and promised me that he would give me as much help as he could. He hid me in his cellar. Every day I went to church with him, and I became one of the best singers in the church choir. After a time he gave me false papers, with my name listed as Kristina Pavlovna. I began to feel like a genuine, born Christian.

That didn't last long, however. One day, when I was walking to church, a Christian stopped me on the street and said, "What are you doing here?" I ran away in terror. When I told the priest, he calmed me, telling me to go back into the cellar and be as quiet as possible.

That same day two Germans went to the priest, demanding that he surrender the Jewish girl whom he had hidden. He denied that there was anyone in his house. They threatened to shoot him, but he continued to insist that he was hiding no one.

The Germans tortured him in various ways, but he continued to refuse to give me up until he fell to the ground covered with blood. His body was pierced in several places, and his face was unrecognizable. Then the Germans left him as he was and went away. Before he died, the priest asked his housekeeper to take me out of my hiding place and bring me to him because he wanted to bless me.

When she led me to him, all I saw was a pool of blood and the priest's body, torn into pieces. I fainted. When I came to, he raised his crushed and broken hand and caressed me. Finally he told his housekeeper to give me over to trustworthy people, to behave toward me like a mother so that no one would suspect I was Jewish. Thus, leaning against him, I felt his body grow cold.

Once again he asked that I be hidden in a safe place, and then he died. I can't remember the priest's name. He was a parish priest in Novy-Dvor.

The housekeeper led me away from the priest and cleansed me of his blood. She changed my clothes, and at five in the morning she led me to Modlin. She left me there and disappeared.

Suddenly an express train came. I entered a car that was occupied by drunken Germans. I walked through the car unnoticed, and sat down next to two civilians. As I began to drift to sleep, a Christian approached me and asked who my parents were. I told him that my father had small children, that we were very poor, and that I had to find work. He didn't know I was a Jewish girl. I wore a crucifix on a chain around my neck. The Christian took me to a village called Farlin, near the town of Tshervinsk. There he introduced me to a peasant named Stanislav Kanya, for whom I worked until I was liberated.

One time the peasant's wife sent me to fetch wool from her sister in Tshervinsk. I hid there for a while, taking the opportunity to rest a bit from the heavy farm work. When I went out in the street to return to Farlin, it was already seven in the evening, and I encountered a German patrol.

The patrol wanted to detain me, and in terror of their command, "Halt," I began to run. The Germans chased me, shooting their rifles. I ran to the

Christian cemetery and jumped into a large grave with deep walls. I remember everything that happened there as if it were a dream because I was delirious through it all.

I felt dead bodies under my feet, which had been thrown in during the war; I felt worms and animals there. I saw the Germans wandering around with portable lamps, looking for me. I pressed my body against the side of the grave and waited. The Germans left, but I was still afraid to show myself. I stayed in the pit for one more day, and at one o' clock in the morning, I left the grave.

I can't remember exactly how I managed to get out of the grave. I only remember that it was very difficult for someone of my height to climb the steep walls. I climbed over the cemetery's high fence, set off in the direction of a nearby village, and knocked on the window of a house at nightfall. A Christian woman opened the door, and I asked her to let me stay the night. She immediately brought water so that I could wash; the smell of the dead was on me, and I was covered with worms.

I lay down on a bundle of straw, covered myself with rags and fell asleep. I slept so soundly for two days straight that the peasants thought I was dead and almost buried me alive. When they saw me waking up, they brought a doctor, who confirmed the fact that I was still alive. At his order, they took me to a hospital where, as I regained full consciousness, I realized that my hand had been wounded. Whether the wound was the result of a bullet or a blow, I don't know. I didn't remember what had happened to me since I had jumped into the grave. The Christians explained to me what had happened, once I was able to comprehend it.

At the hospital, I was asked who I was and where I had come from. I gave them Stanislaw Kanya's name.

A piece of wood was removed from my wounded hand at the hospital. Mrs. Kanya came to visit me, and I returned home with her.

I stayed with her until the day of the liberation. She found out that I was Jewish just one day before that, when the village marshal approached me and said, "Do you know that you're Jewish?" I crossed myself, and told the marshal that he had gone mad.

The day after the liberation, when I went to milk the cows, I gathered my things and escaped.

My Escape from the Ditches of Slaughter

MORDKHE VAYSMAN
Sefer Vladimirets (Wlodzimierzec)

It was a brightly lit night in the middle of the month of Elul, in the year 1942. We all stayed locked up in our houses, sensing that the police watch had been strengthened. From behind the house as well, we heard the footsteps of the patrols in the garden, which would peer into the closed stores from time to time. Locked in our house, we spoke only of death; each of us reviewed his sins and good deeds. Many recited Psalms in a weeping voice. At dawn the next day, we prayed with a *minyan* at Burak's place; he had a Torah scroll in his house, and services were held there regularly. Among the congregation was a Jew who had a reputation as a holy man, as one of the thirty-six hidden just men who sustain the world. There were some in town who believed everything he said, which is only understandable in view of the terrible trials that we were undergoing. Since there was no way to avoid these troubles, people sought whatever support and comfort that they could find in supernaturalism. This man was one of the refugees who had come to Vladimirets during the war.

Many of the neighbors gathered together at Burak's, both men and women. All of them were depressed and discouraged, and fear of death was visible on their faces. Suddenly the "holy man" stood up and said in a commanding, hopeful voice:

"Women, go home and prepare for the Sabbath! I tell you, a miracle is going to take place."

His words made such an impression that even on that terrible Friday which stood in the shadow of annihilation, they awoke a certain hidden hope: "He probably knows what he's talking about, he can't be speaking in vain."

Not far from Burak's house lived a Ukrainian Christian woman by the name of Zosya. When she saw me that morning, she gave me a forlorn look and offered these words of "comfort."

"Oh," she said, "it's not bad for you Jews, you will certainly be buried in the ditches that they've dug, but us, who knows what will happen to us?"

Her intentions were good, but who could have found her words comforting?

When the Ukrainian police came to our house and began driving everyone out with curses and shouts, it was already late; we were among the last to be driven to the assembly point. We had already heard shooting and seen people running everywhere in search of hiding places. I had always been one eager to act. But now I felt utterly helpless, without any desire to escape. It didn't even cross my mind to leave my wife and my two dear daughters, one two and one six years old. I knew that the thread of our fates had been cut. We had been caught in the trap, and the powerful urge that had always led me to act in the past had disappeared.

As we left the house, all we took was food for the children. Each one of us put on the best clothes he or she possessed. Many people brought along their talis and tefillin, and I did likewise. I also put a box of matches into my pocket, thinking that I might be able to set something on fire, although I couldn't imagine anything that I could take revenge on with the aid of a match's small fire.

When we arrived at the assembly point, we were ordered to sit. Before we had arrived there had been shooting. Jews had run away, and many of them had been shot. From time to time more Jews who had been found in their houses were brought in. I sat with my wife, my daughters, and my mother-in-law. My father didn't sit with us. The Germans, desiring to confuse us and mask their intentions, divided the assembled Jews into groups, one of which consisted of the members of the *Judenrat* and their families. My younger brother, who worked as a servant of the Germans, was among them. Because of my brother, my father was included in the group as well. In addition, there was a group of artisans, whose skills the Germans were supposedly interested in.

Suddenly a Ukrainian policeman stepped forward and said: "Whoever has hidden gold, silver, or other valuables can come with us and remove them from their hiding places. Those who do so will be allowed to remain alive."

I do not remember whether anyone was taken in by that, but the existence of a supposedly protected group of craftsmen induced several of us to try to figure out a way to be included among them.

My family and I found ourselves among the group considered worthless, those who were destined for annihilation. Not far from us among the craftsmen sat Burak's family, with whom we were very close. We said to our six-year-old Dvoyrele:

"Run, Dvoyrele, and go sit with Burak's children. Perhaps you'll stay alive that way."

Dvoyrele obeyed us and quickly went over to Burak's family; but she couldn't stand it for very long. She wanted to be with her mother and father, and soon afterward ran back to us.

I sat broken and depressed. I thought of my wife and daughters, for whom I could do nothing. I looked all around me, and saw the Jews of Vladimirets, who were all condemned to death. Family upon family sat there, grandfathers and grandchildren, generations of Jewish love and hope. I saw them bound to one another with the last ounce of love of the condemned. Many of the old men were wrapped in their taleysim saying penitential prayers and Psalms. Not far from us sat Reb Zelig Tsherniak with his family, one of the most popular and respected families in town. The town itself was surrounded by the Ukrainian police, but at the assembly point itself there were several Germans and only a few Ukrainians. I had always known that our cause was lost and never had been aroused by false hope; now I felt more hopeless than ever.

"We have nothing to lose," I said to a few young men who were sitting next to me. One of them was a refugee from Warsaw who had finally found himself in the Vladimirets ghetto. "Perhaps it would be worthwhile to attack these Germans and take their weapons. With a few rifles we'd be able to accomplish something before we die. We should do something!"

It's quite possible that these were just empty words. The urge to act, which had abandoned me when we were leaving our house, had revived in me. I was restless, and knowing that we had nothing to lose and no way out, I was prompted to say what I did.

Time drew slowly on, until four in the afternoon. Sitting bent over on the ground, overwhelmed by despair, prayers, and tears, we saw a row of Germans and Ukrainians approaching the assembly point, and all at once an order was shrieked at us: Stand up and march out!

Now it became clear that the promises made to the two selected groups, the artisans and the families of the Judenrat, had simply been made to turn our heads and confuse us. Quite the contrary: the families of the Judenrat went to their deaths first. Children held fast to their parents; whole families took their last steps together. The Jews were herded in the direction of the village of Zhulkin. As we walked, I saw murdered Jews lying here and there on the field. Probably they were among those who had run away from the assembly point in the morning. Near the road I saw a murdered young girl. I didn't know her; her dress was red with blood and her eyes stared out.

We walked in the middle of the road, with guards on both sides of us—Ukrainians on one side and Germans on the other.

I remember clearly that a young man suddenly ran away from one of the first rows in the direction of the fields, but he was shot. The young man paused and soon fell.

Several of the Ukrainian policemen who were accompanying us began saying quietly:

"You're all lost, you have no hope. We just came from Sarne—all the Jews here have already been 'asleep' for a long time. Perhaps one of you has a watch—it would be a shame for it to go to waste. If any of you has something valuable, give it to us, it would be a shame to lose it."

Thus the Ukrainian police spoke to me and to other Jews, but no one answered them. Now and then we heard the same refrain, attempting to arouse in us sentiments of responsibility for the precious items that might, "God forbid," go to waste.

On one arm I held my two-year-old Khayele, and my other hand held that of my six-year-old Dvoyrele. My entire being was focused on my little family. The tragedy had awakened the essence of my love for them. There was only one prayer in my heart: that the moment would come soon for us to release our souls, bound one to another.

We reached the ditches, and more Germans with machine guns came up. They ordered the men to separate from the women, but the families clung together. With iron rods and whips they began beating us, ripping apart the knotted families. My wife shouted to me: "Mordkhe, give me the children, you can see that your resistance is useless."

The Germans left the women and children by the first ditches. They ordered us to walk further, near the ditches that had been assigned to us. They ordered the men to strip completely naked and fold our clothes into a neat pile. Then we were ordered to step away from our clothes and assemble in rows of five. I stood together with my younger brother Yenkele and my father. We were certain that they would kill us immediately after we stripped, but their procedure was quite different.

Five in a row, we stood several meters away from the ditch that was soon to be our grave. My row was one of those near the grave. I remember that Yankev Ayznberg was standing a few rows in front of us.

"Jews, we should do something, we're lost in any case," someone shouted.

Suddenly from among the rows the son of the Trisker ritual slaughterer called out:

"Jews, don't worry, we'll arrive just before the Sabbath! Jews, don't worry!"

Various cries and weeping were heard, mixed with voices loudly proclaiming *"Shema Yisroel!"* As a response to the cries of our martyrs, the Germans and Ukrainians began to bellow and curse.

The first row was ordered to jump into the ditch. The ditch was deep and wide, and a German with a machine gun stood at one end. Those who jumped in stretched out next to one another and were slaughtered with one salvo. Meanwhile the next row already stood at the edge of the ditch. The moment came for my row to enter the ditch.

I was horrified by what I had seen. I didn't want to live, I just wanted Death to come quickly. I wanted to see him face to face and not have to wait. I wanted him to come quickly, so that I wouldn't have to wait in a row for him to arrive on command. Was it possible for me to realize my desire?

There I stood at the edge of the ditch, ready to jump in. I saw the German standing next to me, with his sleeves rolled up and his blood-drunk eyes. I saw his fingers stretched out toward me, pointing downward, as if to say: Jump!

A moment before, vague thoughts of dying differently than they wanted me to die had flickered in my mind; I had tried to think of something, but couldn't think of anything effective. But just at the moment when the German motioned to me to jump into the ditch, a bizarre, illogical, instinctive thought hit me like a fiery rod, and showed me what to do: to run past the rows of guards and be killed right there, to be killed as a resister, an escapee, rather than following their order—to tear through and be killed running away from the ditches rather than inside them.

And that's what happened. Instead of jumping into the ditch, I ran, as though possessed, with all my strength off to the right. I made it through the short distance between one policeman and the next, and ran in the direction of the brush bordering the forest, not far from the ditches. I heard the report of shots behind me and the whistle of bullets around me. I ran as if without breath. One thought filled me: I was running after I was already dead, I had certainly been killed, and nevertheless I was still running.

Thus I ran, not a great distance, and I found myself among the trees in the forest. Deeper and deeper into the forest I ran. When I stopped for a moment, I realized to my astonishment that I wasn't dead. I hadn't even been wounded.

A flicker of life and hope lit inside me, a desire to live and fulfill a great mission. I had to remain alive in order to relate what my eyes had seen. This desire quickly began to be realized as I thought of plans to defend myself.

Those moments when I had been driven by hidden instincts had passed, and now I consciously decided to walk deeper into the forest. Naked as the day I was born, I walked among the trees. In the distance I clearly heard the shots coming from the ditches of death.

Passover: Under the Rule of Hitlerite Tyranny

BINYOMIN ORENSHTAYN
Khurbn Otvotsk, Falenits, Kartshev (Otwock, Falenica, Karczew)

During the winter of 1943, the Soviet army made great gains on all fronts. The Germans armies withdrew from every battlefield in great panic.

A ray of hope finds its way into the hearts of the enslaved Jews that perhaps, unexpectedly, one glorious day the tyrannical Hitler's power might fall and the long-awaited liberation might come.

Cold logic says clearly that the Nazi murderers will manage to annihilate the captive Jews, who are exploited until the very last moment. But the hope still glows in our hearts that on account of an unexpected event, and maybe even a miracle, the Germans won't succeed in carrying out their fiendish plans and some of the Jews will be saved from a sure death.

Deep, deep in everyone's heart lies hidden the hope that he will be among those for whom the miracle will happen. Yes! All those who had once considered themselves rationalists, logical and practical thinkers, set aside all of their knowledge and theories, and in the face of the approaching danger, began to believe in miracles.

In this sort of exalted mood, I made a vow to myself to celebrate the seder on Passover of 1943, under any circumstances, if the miracle will happen to me and I will be left alive. Among the Jewish people of Europe, on whom the curse of slavery and destruction has fallen, a curse without equal in the entire history of humanity, no change in this exalted awaiting of liberation takes place. Rivers of innocent blood still flow. In the defenseless, condemned sons of the Jewish people, who have until now expressed their struggle in a passive form, a will to struggle actively and positively arises, though it be unequal and desperate, in order to protect the honor of the people.

At that time, I was in the camp of Kartshev, 4 kilometers past Otvotsk and 32 kilometers outside of Warsaw. A series of events took place then which exemplified the heroism of Jewish resistance.

On January 4, 1943, two bold, courageous Jewish youths, Izio Fayner and Mendl Fishelevitsh of Tshenstokhov, took weapons in their hands and threw themselves at the two S.S. men and Jew-murderers, Roan and Soppart. In Bialystok, young Malmer attacked three S.S. men with a jar of sulfuric acid. Three youths escaped into the woods from the camp at Kartshev, and on the way they took revenge on the persecutors of the Jews, attacking and killing the German guards. They took the Germans' guns and clothes in order to continue the armed struggle and to disguise themselves in German uniforms. Similar events took place in Vilna, Mezritsh, and other regions. On a larger scale, the first resistance in Warsaw broke out on January 17, 1943. Organized community groups located in entire apartment houses on Zamenhof and Muranowska streets led a successful fight against the bloody murderers of the Jewish people. The same happened in many ghettos and camps.

Along with these events came an armed raid in Kartshev. The Germans ascertained, on the basis of their interrogations of Polish witnesses, that Gypsies had taken part in the attack. The role of the Jews was also evident because footprints in the snow led from the place of the attack to the Jewish camp.

German policemen in Panzer helmets, led by the bloody Lipschitz, chief of police in the Warsaw region, came to liquidate the Gypsy colony. To everyone's amazement, it turned out that the Gypsies had at their disposal an entire arsenal, including machine guns and grenades. A bitter struggle ensued and there were casualties on both sides. The police received reinforcements and the battle grew unequal; the Gypsies fell heroically. A number escaped; they were arrested a few days later by the Polish police in the service of the Nazis, and shot next to the Kartshev mill near the camp.

The Polish police demanded ten Jewish inmates to bury the murdered Gypsies near the mill. As it happened, I was one of those sent. I observed two Gypsy youths, fifteen or sixteen years old, whose lives had been cut short. Blood had flowed from their heads over their black, silken hair. The black eyes and mouths were open; one felt as though they wanted to speak and look at their killers, but their senses had been snuffed out.

The Polish policeman pushed me away and cold-bloodedly approached the two, looked in their mouths to see whether they had any gold teeth, and removed their boots and fur coats.

After the burial the Polish policeman went away with his loot, satisfied. I returned to our camp with the other Jews, embittered by the tragic and bestial reality.

A few days later Velvl Kolokovitsh called all the inmates together in the guardroom and said to them:

"Brothers, the situation is tragic; whoever gets the chance should escape. No good can be expected here. I myself am leaving. I would be totally lacking in national consciousness if I didn't make you aware of this and left you to fate."

Those rumors were accurate which said that when the police were finished with their barbaric slaughter in Warsaw they would come to exterminate all the Jews in the camp at Kartshev. Minute by minute the camp emptied out, and whoever had the slightest chance ran away. I was among those who escaped.

By the time the police came for the shooting, everyone in the camp had escaped. That was on May 7, 1943.

After the escape from Kartshev, I was in Warsaw, and several days before Purim I arrived in the small Tshenstokhov ghetto, where I worked for the Hasag Fur Company.

A miracle had happened to me; I had saved myself from a sure death, and I didn't forget my vow to celebrate the seder in 1943. But as coincidence had it, the German boss, Willy Nitsiolek, scheduled me to work nights during the week of Passover.

Against the choice of not going to work hung threats of being cruelly beaten, thrown into prison, and having one's name added to a blacklist—that is, becoming a candidate for death in the first selection.

I decided to fulfill my oath and not go to work. My request to Yozhek Lisek, the foreman, to sign me in was useless. He argued that the word of the German boss was law.

The day before Passover, I went into the infirmary of the ghetto hospital, pretending to be sick, and asked to be excused from work for the two seder nights. Dr. Bresler examined me and found no reason to excuse me. I appealed to his conscience and told him about my vow and about the liquidation of the Kartshev ghetto. Dr. Bresler declared, "You have found and touched my deepest feelings, and I couldn't refuse you, even if I wanted to. But I beg you, please don't go out during the next two days; the risk would fall on both of us.

Furthermore, I won't put your name on the sicklist, because Denenhardt looks it over, and sometimes he inspects the sick himself."

At that time, Dr. Bresler's deed entailed the risk of his security and his life.

Celebrating the seder became an *idée-fixe* in my mind. It seemed to me that observing the holiday would bring the liberation of the Jews from Nazi tyranny and slavery. The urge to observe the generations-long tradition was also great; it became a symbol of the existence of the Jewish people for me. The seder nights also had a special magic because I had always spent them with my family. It seemed to me that the souls of my nearest and dearest would come to me, the souls of those who had been torn away from me and killed in such a terrible way. I wanted to speak with them, to tell them of my pain. I wanted to ask their pardon for clinging so tightly to life when they were no longer with me, for forgetting them in moments of my own physical pain and torture.

In the evening the men and women of the day shift returned to the small ghetto. Yisroel-Yoysef Kutner, the cantor, arranged a minyan and we said the evening prayers. When the prayers were finished, the assembly went to their homes to celebrate the seder.

When I arrived home, the table was set for Passover; on it were set matzo, wine, kharoyses, and a haggadah. Thus my neighbors had attempted to ameliorate our tragic life in the ghetto in a small way.

We sat down at the table. I blessed the wine and began to recite the haggadah. My voice broke; it was impossible to forget the gruesome reality. It was the first seder since the *aktsyes*, the deportations, and selections of 1942.

The troubles had already begun by Passover of 1940. The seders of 1941 and 1942 had been celebrated in the ghetto, but the Jews had not lost hope and most important, everyone was together. Now everyone was orphaned, solitary, and embittered.

The phrase "season of our redemption" sounded like mockery. Was it possible for us to be made happy by the erstwhile redemption when our contemporary reality was even more bitter and horrible? Could we believe in redemption when death waited for us at every step? Reality slipped away from me.

It seemed I was sitting in the circle of my family, which appeared before me in the glory of pure affection and devotion to one another.

Here sits my father in his white holiday gown, like a proper king; my mother like the symbol of all that is dear and holy; my brothers, sisters, and our invited guests. The mood is festive, the children are dressed up in new clothes and happiness shimmers on everyone's face. The traditional holiday of Passover is celebrated, and everyone remembers the most important events in the people's history and the miracles that came to pass. Three generations are sitting at the table, mother and father, sons and daughters, and grandchildren. Family harmony prevails, the love of each for each other and for the entire people, who yearned for freedom and were redeemed from slavery.

All at once this lovely image of the past disappeared. Instead the terrible images of reality appeared before me, despair and loneliness engulfed me, and unbidden tears flowed from my eyes. No word of comfort, no hope, no future, no way out.

Everyone sitting at the table felt the same and stopped reciting the haggadah. Instead of the desired liberation came ever sharper repression.

The sadistic Nazi murderers continued their victorious war against the defenseless Jews, who had been transformed into unpaid slaves. The smokestacks of the crematoria did not cease smoking for a minute. The world's conscience was moved neither by the frightful pain of the defenseless victims nor by the legendary heroism of the Jewish fighters, who died in unequal combat with the enemy.

A year later: Passover of 1944. I no longer have a name. I am called Number 54, and I am even more embittered and solitary. I still live, solely on account of a coincidence, a miracle. Nearly all of my intimate circle, my friends and acquaintances have long since been killed. Of the Jewish population of Tshenstokhov, which had numbered sixty thousand, some six thousand remained, who were slave laborers in the Hasag factories. I am in the camp of the closed Hasag Fur factories, which is surrounded by barbed wire and guarded by murderous degenerates of all sorts—ethnic Germans, White Russians, and Ukrainians.

I am in the barrack that bears the number seven. The night of the seder I spend lying in a bunk, on a paper sack stuffed with straw, embittered and hopeless.

I can no longer read the prayer "redeem us from slavery unto freedom," which is totally contradictory to reality. We have been forgotten by man and by God, and no one is troubled by our fate. No hope, no comfort. Yet there are those in the camp in whose hearts rays of faith and hope still glow.

The cantor, Yisroel-Yoysef Kutner, asks me to come to his bunk. He has scratched together a few pieces of matzo and performs a sort of seder. He pushes a piece of matzo into my hand and says to me, "Say *shekhiyanu* —bless the Lord who has preserved us until this time."

A year later: Passover of 1945. There is no limit to human troubles and pain. Each time is worse. I have already survived the concentration camp at Buchenwald, that hell, where that terrible specter of death—the crematorium—burns day and night. Now I find myself in another concentration camp, Dora.

I work in a deep tunnel beneath high mountains that proudly rise thousands of meters into the sky. Who is interested in the magic of nature, which for us is a disappointment and a curse? The sun shines, but it doesn't reach us. We are deep in the tunnel, like living men in their graves. Our tortured and shrunken bodies freeze in the cold; the constant hunger and hard work lead us toward a slow death. Every day tortured comrades fall, and their bodies are burned in the crematorium.

I feel my strength ebbing as well. I sense that this situation cannot long prevail, and if the Allied armies won't free us from this hell, death will redeem us from this frightful torture.

My mind grows ever weaker. Moments of resignation come, moments of total indifference to the thought of death, which would put an end to this terrible pain and slavery.

These thoughts are driven out with fantastic thoughts about a real liberation. The Allied armies are so close, perhaps there will be a miracle. A double miracle—our liberation and the downfall of the Nazi murderers. In one moment we could be free, equal to everyone else in the world, and as for later . . . what will come, will come.

Dreams, fantastic dreams of hungry, naked, frozen, humiliated slaves, trodden like dust. The dreams press deeper and deeper into my soul and enchant me with their glory and magic.

Various rumors spread. Secrets are passed on, about a quick liberation, about a beautiful, free world, where we will be equal citizens, proud and free. At such moments one forgets the hunger, the cold, and the physical pain; the thought of surviving these troubles reigns, the thought of fighting against death with one's last strength, against the death awaiting our tortured bodies.

Once again I lie on a straw-filled paper sack on a bunk during the seder night of 1945, enveloped in a world of dreams, fantasies, and associations. My neighbor, a fellow Tshenstokhover by the name of Shimen Gostinsky, looks at me with pleading eyes and asks me a concentration camp question for Passover:

"Tell me, will this hell last much longer? I beg you, say at least a few comforting words. I can't stand this any longer."

Yisroel-Yoysef Kutner, the cantor, the deeply religious Jew who has survived all these troubles together with me and withstood various religious temptations without allowing his spirit to be broken for a minute, comes to my bunk. But this time, he is unable to break off even a small bit of matzo for me, as he did the previous year.

He hungers, like everyone else, and has just the meager bit of risen bread that he receives in the concentration camp. He brings me a different gift, in the form of comfort and hope, saying to me: "Don't lose hope. It is expressly written that one is a slave for six years and in the seventh year one is set free. We have been under Hitler's tyranny and enslavement for six Passovers now. Soon we will be redeemed, and next Passover we will celebrate properly the season of our redemption."

Tragic and bitter days came, accompanied by hunger, pain, loneliness, blows, heavy labor, mass deaths, and evacuation.

In our new location in the concentration camp at Bergen-Belsen, Yisroel-Yoysef Kutner's prophecy came true; the liberation came on the fifteenth of April, 1945. It brought with it glorious, exalted moments of pure joy, new hopes, encouragement, and strengthened will.

The appearance of the first English tanks, the joyful sound of the radio speakers announcing the Allied victory, and the friendliness of the victorious soldiers all seemed a kingdom of dreams and fantasies.

With the fall of the Nazis, Passover is indeed the festival of liberation for me. Through a miracle, I have been rescued from Nazi bondage. Yet I feel like a solitary twig from a ruined garden.

I Was a German "Soldier"

NEKHEMYE VURMAN
Yizker-bukh Koriv (Kurow)

I will never forget the last days of my life in Koriv.

It was the end of August 1939, shortly before the outbreak of the Second World War. For a boy of thirteen it was difficult to understand exactly what war was. My father, of blessed memory, often reminisced about the First World War. And now I began to see with my own eyes and feel with my own skin what war was. Here I would like to very briefly convey my experiences from September 1, 1939, until January 18, 1945. The suffering lasted sixty-four months and eighteen days. The road was long.

It was Friday morning, September 1. My father wakes me from sleep and says to me: "Get up, it is war; the Germans have invaded Poland." I didn't believe him. But my father said: "Come to the radio, you'll hear it." I hear the Polish marshal speaking on the radio, saying:

"We won't permit it!"

I turn the radio dial further and hear Hitler, may his name be blotted out, saying that he won't spare the bombs. As it turned out later, he kept his word. Just eight days later, on Friday morning, September 8, people began to flee the city, as if they knew what would happen a few days hence.

Each Child Receives His Packet of Money

Beneath our apartment was a walled cellar. During the week we brought merchandise down from the store bit by bit in order to save at least some of it from an eventual fire. Every member of the household received from our mother, may she rest in peace, a sewn-up little linen bag filled with money, so that whatever happened, none of us would find himself penniless. Each of us also received a backpack with underwear and the most necessary articles of clothing, which had been prepared earlier. At precisely twelve o'clock on the same day, when we finished bricking up the doorway to the cellar, there was a

huge explosion and the whole house shook. A second and third explosion soon
followed. I ran out to see what had happened. I walked up to the co-op. I saw
Itshe Hanisman running with a wounded arm, and nearby the police station
was burning. The three bombs had fallen there. There were dead and
wounded. I quickly returned home and told what I had seen. My father locked
the store, each of us took our backpacks, and we went off in the direction of
the New Market. We stood there a few minutes next to the windmill. My
father ran back into town to see what was happening, ran into the house, and
got out a few cotton quilts. While he was locking the door on his way out, the
key broke in the lock. As he was telling us about the key, we saw from the hill
that our house was burning. It was 5 P.M. We left the hill without a word, and
set off in the direction of Krupe.

The Rebe of Modzhits: "Today You Don't Have to Light Candles!"

We arrived in Krupe. My father went to a Christian he knew and asked him to
let us stay in his barn. My father entered the barn and put down our things, but
I couldn't rest. I was curious to hear, to know, to see everything. I ran out to the
highway leading to Myekhov. I saw masses of Jews running in the direction of
Myekhov; among them rode the Modzhitser Rebe and his secretaries in a coach.
The coach stood still. The coachman gave the horse water, women wept, children wept, and women fainted and ran to the Rebe for his blessing. One woman
asked:

"Rebe, what shall I do, I have no candles for the Sabbath."

Answered the Rebe: "You don't need to light candles today; if you look
around you'll see that your candles are already burning."

A second woman asked: "What shall I do, I can't stay here, I have to go to
Myekhov to my children."

The Rebe answered her: "Protection of life supersedes the Sabbath!" And he
got back into his coach and rode away.

We couldn't eat then; nothing would go down. Several more of our acquaintances came into the barn. We made pallets of straw on the dirt floor and lay
down. No one even thought of sleeping. Late at night my cousin Moyshe
Shmuel-Yitshkok's came. He told us that all four corners of town were burning,
except for a few houses around the New Market. One Jewish house was among
them; it belonged to my cousin Yankl Faynshmit. The house was filled with
Jews, including my uncle Shmuel-Yitskhok and his family.

Lying on the straw, various fantasies went through my mind. I, the youngest,
didn't dare say a word, but there were frequent sighs: "Father in heaven, twenty
years of work up in smoke, now comes that damned Hitler, what will be with
us, with all Jews?"

The Ethnic German with the Secret Transmitter; Wandering; Typhus

We spent the night in the barn. At daybreak we went into the bushes, because
the Germans were dropping bombs over our heads again. We had to lie with our
heads down hidden in the bushes an entire day because the gentiles used to say
that the bombs were aimed only at Jews. The bombing was frightful. All day we
didn't dare move, but when it grew dark, we stretched out and went into the
barn. My father went out to get something for us to eat. The next day, Sunday,
my father decided to go into town to see what was up. We went back into the
bushes and stayed there another full day. We didn't see our father come back,
and wondered what had happened to him. It began to grow dark; my father
returned with a loaf of bread and other foodstuffs. We sat silent as my father told
us what he'd been through that day: when he came to town, he'd sought out the
wojt (sheriff) Sheleznyak, the police chief, and other Christians in town and
consulted with them. They decided to go question the ethnic German Urlich,
who had a mill on Warsaw Road. As it turned out, the German had a secret
radio transmitter, from which he told the Germans exactly where to bomb. He
and his son were arrested and turned over to the Polish military staff. It was also
decided that important documents would be destroyed to keep them from falling
into German hands. The same day a bomb fell next to the Jewish house at New
Market, and my cousin Hersh-Dovid, Shmuel-Yitskhok Naymark's son, died of
fear. The next day we went to the village of Klode, where things were a bit
calmer. The chairman of the farmers' co-op gave us a room. We stayed there a
short time, until the German army marched into our town. My eldest brother,
Khayim-Elyezer, lived with his wife in Uzhendov, near Kroshnik. He came
running when he heard that Koriv had burned, and found out that we were in
the village. Then we decided that I, my brother Moyshe, and my sister Kha-
vetshe would ride to Uzhendov with my brother, while my father and mother
and my sister Khanetshe would go to Lublin. When we arrived in Uzhendov,
the Germans were already playing the boss to the hilt; "contributions" were
demanded of Jews. Every day Jews were grabbed for work, so that we began to
sense the coming German slaughter. I wasn't there long. My uncle from Ostrovtse found out about the tragedy that had befallen us and sent a messenger to
say that we should come to him, but we didn't want to go without our parents'
approval. My father rode to Uzhendov and it was decided that I would go to my
uncle. At my uncle's in Ostrovtse I learned the furrier's craft. Six months later
my father came as well, because the ethnic German Urlich from Koriv was
trying to find and kill him. A bit later my sister Khanetshe came. From time to
time my father came to have a look at the family and went right back, and thus
time passed, until the typhus epidemic broke out in 1941. The Jews of the town
were already confined to a ghetto then, and they were forbidden to leave their
homes. For just two hours a day they were allowed to go out and get the bread

they received with their ration cards. Whoever broke the curfew was shot. Everyone who had contracted typhus was to be brought into the ghetto hospital, in the bes-medresh. It was common knowledge that no one ever returned from the hospital. Hundreds died. I contracted typhus then too, and lay secretly at home. An old healer cured me, procuring medicine outside the ghetto through various means. Thanks to the attention of my father and the healer, I got well again.

In 1942, when the first bitter reports came of evacuations of Jews from various cities in Poland, we found out that Ostrovtse was to be among them. Jews ran to the work bureaus to get working cards, thinking this would help. I got work in the big ironworks. My father and sister got work cards for other factories.

Shops, the Bunker. My Sister-in-Law Shot with Her Child. I Become a German Soldier.

When Jews sensed that the black cloud was hanging over the city, we decided that my father and sister should hide in a bunker which had been prepared earlier by my uncle in the tannery outside the ghetto. At midnight on October 9, 1942, my father and sister stole out of the ghetto and hid there. I remained sleeping at home.

At six o'clock the next morning the Gestapo was stationed all around the ghetto, and an order went out for everyone to be out of their homes in ten minutes. Anyone who didn't come right into the marketplace would be shot. Everyone who had a work card from the ironworks was to go to a special area near the work bureau. I ran to the work bureau with my card; while running, I stepped on Jewish corpses. The shooting went on endlessly.

When I came to the workplace a Gestapo man was standing at the entrance with a stick in his hand. The entry was through a little door, and whoever went in received vicious blows. I couldn't avoid them myself. Some five hundred of the roughly sixteen thousand Jews in Ostrovtse were there, all men. We stood for an entire day. During the evening a troop of Ukrainians came and took us into the factory. Once in the factory, I made contact with my father through a Christian, and also sent a messenger to Uzhendov to find out how my mother, sister, and brothers were doing. Uzhendov had been liquidated one month before. I received bitter news: my sister Tsivye and her child, who had been hiding at the home of a Christian, had been shot. Another Christian had betrayed them. My mother and sister lay in hiding among Christians. My brothers Moyshe and Khayim-Elyezer were in the forest. I did everything possible to remain in contact. When we had been in the factory for eight days, all of the Jewish workers were ordered to assemble with our possessions, that is, the packs on our backs. We didn't know what would happen. We thought we were to be shot or deported. We were led to an open place behind the factory. The Gestapo soon came and ordered us to surrender everything we owned, including money, gold, and even the underwear in our packs. Anyone found to possess something that he hadn't surrendered would be shot. Three youngsters were shot then and there. We surrendered everything, and stood naked and barefoot. Then we were led back into the factory.

After the whole townful of Jews had been evacuated, a smaller ghetto of one and a half blocks formed, and we were taken there. Every morning we were taken to work under heavy guard. While in the ghetto I heard from my father that he and my sister could no longer stay in the bunker, because their food had run out. Furthermore, the Christian janitor at the tannery wouldn't let them stay any longer. Seeing no other choice, I told them to sneak into the ghetto. They arrived safely in the early morning. They received working cards with the help of my cousin and went to work with everyone else each day. People continually entered the ghetto this way. On January 10, 1943, the Gestapo conducted another deportation, but my father and sister managed to remain in the ghetto. The ghetto grew ever smaller. I continued to work in the iron foundry, while my father and sister were employed in a brickworks.

Three months later, in April 1943, the ghetto was liquidated entirely. All the Jews were taken to a work camp outside of town, called *Judenarbeiterlager des Eisenwerker Ostrowiec.* It was surrounded by barbed wire, and we lived in horse barns. My father and I were in the same barrack; my sister was in a women's barrack. Guard posts manned by Ukrainian police surrounded the camp. Every day we were led to work under heavy guard. The camp was directed internally by a Jewish council and Jewish camp police.

On November 10, 1943, came the great tragedy: I lost my father. A murderous Jewish hand was responsible: the Jewish police chief removed thirty Jews from the camp, including my father, and sent them off to be shot in Radom. I decided to leave the camp and seek revenge outside. While in the camp, I had remained in contact with my family. They were then in the camp at Budzhin, near Kroshnik, except for my oldest brother, Khayim-Elyezer; he had joined a partisan detail in the woods near Garbov. I kept in touch with him through a special messenger. In 1944 I managed to escape from the camp as had my sister Khanetshe. I didn't know that she had escaped, nor did she know that I had escaped. It was as though we had the same idea, without speaking to each other. On my way from the camp I had to go through the factory where I had previously worked. I hid there for four days without food or water. It was difficut to leave the factory, guarded as it was by the Ukrainians, but on the fourth day I felt all my strength gone, and decided to leave at all costs. Returning to the camp would have meant suicide. I had to try my last bit of luck. It was Friday night; with my last ounce of strength I managed to climb the ten-meter-high walls and run outside of town. I went into the fields and lay down among the grain.

The next morning I went into town looking for food. None of the Poles would give me a bit of bread. I made it to a bakery, got on line with the Poles, and managed to buy one kilo of bread with the money I still had. I felt a bit stronger. I went to the Christian who was the messenger between me and my family. Several days later he directed me to a partisan detail in the forests outside of Ostrovtse. Among the partisans I sensed strong anti-Semitism, even though the group included several Jews along with Poles and Russians. The Jews were given the most dangerous assignments, and had no choice but to carry them out. Despite everything, we were glad for the chance to take revenge.

I didn't remain among the partisans long. As fate had it, a powerful German army surrounded the forest with tanks and airplanes and burned it four weeks after my arrival. After several days of fighting, we had to leave the forest. We were short on food and ammunition. The expected reinforcements never came. Instead, an order came from the commandant: each of us was to escape on his own and try to save himself. Retreat was impossible, and the nearest partisan group was in the woods near Logiv.

In the partisan group I became friendly with a Pole from the town of Apt. We were constant companions, and together we escaped from the forest to Apt. I stayed with him awhile, until a neighbor of his betrayed me and handed me over to the German gendarmes. Upon arrival at the gendarmerie, I naturally received a royal welcome. It began with blows. I insisted, however, that I was a Christian, that my blood and bones were Polish. I crossed myself, saying that I didn't understand a word of German. Since it was already evening, the gendarmes decided to hold me in a cellar in the yard until the next morning, when a doctor would be brought to determine whether I was a Jew or a Pole. If the doctor found me to be a Jew, I would be shot that day. Luck played into my hands again, and I managed to escape from the cellar before daybreak. After my escape, I contacted the Pole from Apt again, but he said he was afraid to hide me any longer. I had no choice but to set off into the wide world to seek my fate.

The Russian army was already on the banks of the Vistula, and I set off in that direction. Perhaps I would be able to cross over to the Russian side. But this was impossible. I was already near the German lines, but there was no way of crossing them. Being so near to the German positions, I thought of going to a German field kitchen and asking in German whether I could work there. I hadn't eaten for several days, and figured: first of all, I wanted something to eat; and second, I was near the front; perhaps I could manage to get across. The German cook immediately agreed to take me on. I ate and slept alongside the German soldiers. After several days I was well acquainted with the cook and also with the *Oberleutnant* who oversaw the staff. After a week, the kitchen was moved to the village of Volkovonovke, near Ozhorov. My officer and I were quartered in the same room. My name was Marian Schmidt.

Without warning, the officer called me into his office and asked me who I was and where I came from. I told him I was an ethnic German from a town on the other side of the Vistula, that the Russians had bombed our town, and that my parents had died during the bombardment. I tried to sound convincing. Then he asked me if I wanted to volunteer for the German army and serve as his private adjutant. Seeing no way out, I agreed. He gave me various papers to sign. Two days later he called me back into his office and told me happily that he had already received his captain's approval to enlist me as a German soldier. He gave me a receipt so that I could get my uniform from the army warehouse.

A few minutes later I wore the uniform of a German soldier. All of the soldiers in the company congratulated and welcomed me. Soon our cook went away on leave, and I was left to run the kitchen. Twice a week I did guard duty in the village, together with another soldier. While on guard, I carried arms. The worst thing for me was raising my hand and saying "Heil Hitler." After a while it became easier. I also served as the company translator: I went with a group of soldiers, and whenever anything had to be asked in Polish, I was given the job. During a roundup, I came across a Jew who was being hidden by a gentile. I miraculously managed to save the Jew, using the excuse that he was sick.

Contact with Partisans Again. I Spy.

One of the commanders of my former partisan group was being held prisoner. It was a little harder for me to get him out, but I promised to free him the next day. Through him, I renewed my contact with the partisans. I saw him every other night. He advised me not to leave the German army. Instead, he assigned me to obtain passwords and military information.

In December 1944, a gentile Pole from Ostrovtse recognized me and told a German officer that I was a Jew. I quickly found out by happenstance. The report was passed along to my officer, but he pretended to ignore it. On December 31—St. Sylvester's Day—at night, my officer called me in and told me that he had a report that I was a Jew. He was supposed to determine whether it was true. Then, to my amazement, the officer declared that he didn't care whether I was a Jew or not. He assured me that as long as I was in his hands nothing would happen to me—but I should be very careful.

On January 12, 1945, came the order to withdraw from the Vistula toward Germany. I accompanied the withdrawal, surviving terrible Russian bombardments. There were less and less Germans all the time.

I Escape to the Russians. They Take Me for a German. I Find My Sister. My Brother the Partisan Falls.

On January 15, 1945, I happened to be present at a conversation at the general staff, headed by the German General Mueller. I heard that the Russian army was ten kilometers away, and that the Germans were surrounded. I decided to go along no further. In the evening I went to a Christian Pole to get civilian clothes. He didn't want to give me anything, but I threatened him with my revolver.

At night I stole over to another village, which was already free of Germans. I encountered a Russian patrol on the way. They held me, and noticed that I had a German uniform on under my civilian clothes. They wanted to shoot me, but I managed to convince them that I wasn't a German. They took me to Konsk, where the Russians were encamped. I was taken to the commander and interrogated. I showed them I was a Jew and a partisan. They immediately put me in contact with my partisan commandant, who supported my claim. I was turned over to an officer and taken to Ostrovtse.

On January 18, 1945, I was freed. Remarkably, as I climbed down from the auto, I saw my sister Khanetshe, walking sorrowfully. She saw me and cried out in joy; our happiness was indescribable.

I immediately decided to go to Lublin in order to find out what had happened to my family, including my brother Khayim-Elyezer, with whom we had lost contact just six months previously. I passed through Kroshnik, where I found out about the tragic death of the partisan commander, Khayim-Elyezer Vurman—the Almighty shall avenge his death—who fell in battle against the Germans three hours before the liberation.

I rode on to Lublin, meeting other Jewish survivors from Koriv. I went to Koriv to have a last look at my hometown.

I came into town, and stood for a few minutes near the market well. I didn't recognize the town. It looked like an abandoned cemetery. I was overcome with terror. I stayed for a day, and then went back to Ostrovtse to be with my sister.

The Capture of Girls

TALA MASKAL-SHULTS
Sefer Kolo

Autumn, 1941. A magnificent, golden Polish autumn. The days are bright and clear, but there is darkness in the soul. Every Jewish heart trembles at a glance from the S.S. beasts. More and more often they appear in the streets, like wild dogs hunting new sacrifices to the god Moloch. The war machine demands countless workers in order to destroy ever faster the fruit of generations of human effort. They are not disturbed by the weeping of children, by the cries of the parents who remain, and by women left alone. New restrictions are constantly issued.

The city's quiet is a portent of the coming storm. Signs of worry and fear are on the pale faces of dear ones. What will the approaching High Holy Days bring? There isn't a trace of a holiday spirit; on the contrary, depression and sadness constantly increase. Someone is already missing from every home, and no one knows where they have been carried off to.

The melodies that the wind used to carry from the synagogue are no longer heard. Battered walls, the last remnants of that beautiful building, stretch out from the earth like hands reaching toward Heaven, demanding the punishment of the Nazi vandals who burned it down. Panic stalks Jewish homes. Children in cradles, listless, look at their parents' pale, twitching faces and know that something is wrong. In the homes where, miraculously, men remain, prayers are murmured: Lord, lessen our suffering!

The day before Yom Kippur. My younger sister and I walk to our Grandmother Esther, wish her a prosperous year, and receive her blessing. Grandmother had barely managed to press us close to her when my Uncle Danyel ran in frightened. He shouted out:

"Run, children, quickly! Hide yourselves! They say Jews will be seized today!"

My eyes fell on my grandmother's pale face and saw her own eyes wet with tears. She looked at us helplessly. She held us even tighter and whispered:

"May God preserve you from the enemy's hands!"

Alerted by the warning, we stopped in at our Aunt Golde's on the way home and told her the terrible news. As soon as she understood what we told her, she made her decision: the two of us, together with her daughter Mina, were to hide in the basement.

All night we lay restless and cramped, fearing that any minute the Nazi bloodhounds would be on our trail. At daybreak, I said that I wanted to go out for a while and scout out the situation. The others agreed.

I closed the door behind me. Several Gestapo men appeared out of nowhere and ordered me to go with them. My little sister, hearing the shouts, forgot the danger she was in and came out of the cellar. She fell at my neck, and broke out into fearful weeping, trying to tear me away from my captors' hands.

The Gestapo men decided to take my sister along as well. I forgot my own troubles and began to plead with them: "Let her be! She's barely twelve years old!" They let her go free.

A push against my shoulder separated us. I was led to the study house, the collection point for every transport.

There were several girls from our town already at the study house. What awaited all of these blossoming young lives? Where would they be sent and annihilated? I sank in tortured thoughts, not observing what went on around me.

After I had calmed down a bit and gotten used to my surroundings, I saw girl prisoners standing nearby. In addition to them, separated by a barricade, stood parents of children. They had been brought here because they wouldn't confess where their daughters lay in hiding. I looked at them: their faces were lifeless, gray as ashes.

The Gestapo tortured these parents, trying to squeeze information out of them. In order to mask their desperate cries, they forced the sufferers to sing. The whips flew up and down, and the faint and battered were doused with a bucket of filthy water. Among the tortured was my Aunt Tobe.

When she attempted to fix her disheveled hair (the hair on her head was always combed, like a crown), a Gestapo scoundrel ran up to her and dragged her by her hair until she lay in excrement and a bundle of her hair lay in the degenerate's hand. I was so upset about my own excrement that I bit my fingers until they bled. These vicious pranks and our helplessness sorrowed my heart until I thought it would burst.

The news that parents were being tortured in an attempt to find out their daughters' hiding places quickly spread around town. Young girls came into the study house on their own in order not to cause their parents any agony.

The hours drew on endlessly. I sank back into all sorts of reveries. A woman's soft weeping brought me out of my reflections: it was the voice of my beloved Grandmother Esther. She had stolen up to the open window, wanting to have a look at me. In a voice saturated with tears she said: "My child, dear one, my heart somehow tells me that I will not see you again." She took my outstretched hand and tenderly caressed it, as if to ease my pains. A Gestapo soldier noticed this, and drove her away from the window with an animal bark.

Exhausted from all these experiences, I fell asleep on a bench. When I awoke, everything was buzzing around me as in a beehive. Near me stood Tseshya Vaynboym, Toybe Shmerlovska, Freydl Frayman, Genye Fogel, Adela Brand, and others. I found out from them that we were to be sent to Germany.

My Uncle Danyel came to the window and called me over. He was wearing an armband of the Jewish militia; he whispered to me that he was making a great effort to have me freed at the railroad station. My sister Gutke came with him. Her face was strange, yellow as wax. She stood stiffly. Suddenly she ran to me, crying: "I want to go with you, whatever happens to you will happen to me!" I absolutely refused to agree and explained to her that as things stood, it was meant for her to stay with our grandmother. (My father had been sent to the Gostinin Ghetto, and our mother had died young.)

After I was separated from her, I stood confused and depressed; I didn't hear the command, "March!" A hard push from the S.S. man reminded me where I was. I got in position, and the line of girls began to move. We walked in the direction of the station. After us came those parents who had been unwilling to confess their daughters' hiding places, despite the torture. We were guarded by Gestapo men who carried loaded rifles, as if they were guarding criminals.

The line of girls was accompanied all down the highway by the remaining sorrowing parents and family members. Their weeping could have moved a stone, but not the hearts of the Nazi murderers. With wild cruelty they pushed the semiconscious young girls and murderously used their rifle butts against the parents who stretched their hands out to their beloved daughters.

It seemed to me that I was part of my own funeral procession. I said goodbye to every house, to every street of my birthplace, where I had spent the best years of my childhood.

At the station, the parents were placed off to the side, while the girls were pushed into the railroad cars. Suddenly my Uncle Danyel ran up. Before he could say a word to me, he was thrown out of the car. He shouted back to me: "Be well, dear one. I could not rescue you from the devil's hands!"

When the train started up, our cries drowned out the sound of the chugging locomotive and the hurrying wheels, which clacked out in rhythm: Forever! Forever! Forever! Hometown of Kolo!

In the Hall of Death

The beginning of winter, 1943, Birkenau concentration camp. Several girls from Kolo, including myself, were led to Block 19, which was called the "hall of death."

My place on the wooden bunk was next to Tseshya Vaynboym, Avrom's daughter. She was full of life. In the worst moments, she found a way to free herself, not to give in, not to stop believing in the sunrise.

Despite the difference in age between us, we understood each other well. We shared our bits of bread, often our last bits, and helped each other in difficult times. We became so close that we would communicate with our eyes if necessary.

One day Tseshya met her younger sister, Leyeke. I am unable to describe the joy of these two sisters, who found each other after a separation of two years. I will always remember their meeting: they wept and laughed for joy, hugged and kissed each other, and I along with them.

Since Leyeke lived in the next block, we met her only at night, or in the fields at work.

The situation in the women's camp continued to grow more terrible and harder to bear. The light clothing we wore on cold autumn days left its mark. We felt the cold particularly during the long roll calls. Various diseases attacked the weak ones, the worst of which was typhus. People died like flies at the end of summer. Thus, standing in line for the roll call, the knees of someone standing next to you would collapse, she would fall, and her blank eyes looked at you as if begging for help. After a short while, they closed forever. We, the living, dared not extend a hand toward the fallen, because one earned vicious blows on the head from the S.S. for the least motion during roll call. Happy were the fallen, who did not struggle with death, who lay just a short time in its throes and quickly gave up their souls.

We girls of Kolo held together, coming together on our plank bunk every evening. Each of us looked closely at her comrades, for none of us was sure of tomorrow: would we meet again after work? Who would be missing, who would remain? Every day there were changes, surprises and sacrifices.

Together with us in the camp at that time were Khaytshe Podritse, Lyusha Blum, Dasha Shtaynberg, Sore Volovitsh, Hanka Gotsman, and Dita Lantsman. Dita was the first to die, the first sacrifice from among the girls of Kolo. One cold morning, as I left the barracks, I saw her lying on a heap of the dead; she lay with her eyes half-open. My heart froze, tears poured from my eyes and my fists clenched, ready to attack the murderers with their last strength.

Many questions demanded answers, many of them remained total mysteries: would there be no end to the barrack and block elders, the partners of the Angel of Death? Thinking this way, bizarre cries suddenly interrupted my thoughts, and I saw a frightful picture before my eyes: girls were running from place to place, seeking somewhere to hide. Their faces were creased with terror, their eyes were wide open and full of fear. They all ran, ran, ran . . . A nightmare. A tragedy approached us. Petrified, I continued looking: sick and half-dead women were being thrown out of the block, and suddenly my ear caught the dreaded camp-word: "*selektsye!*"*

Fast as an arrow from a bow, I ran to Tseshya Vaynboym. I knew that she was sick with typhus and running a high fever. Like bolts of lightning, painful thoughts struck me: How can she go to the roll call? Won't she collapse on line?

At all costs, she had to be gotten out of the block: that was what I decided. It was less dangerous to stand on line than to remain in the block. I ran toward her, and saw her running to meet me; I took her hand, and together we got in line for the roll call. Her face was as yellow as wax, her eyes clouded. Pressing herself close to me, she asked:

"Tala, how do I look?"

"Fine, Tseshya! Hold strong, and God will help!"

"But I can't stand up!" she complained.

"Stand!" I shouted at her, not knowing myself from whence such a tone had come to me.

I had my own troubles: I was swollen from hunger, and even more exhausted than before.

The selection began: girls were dragged out of line and the S.S. wrote down their numbers, laughing. Sister was torn away from sister, mother from daughter. Some wanted to accompany those selected in order to end their lives together with their dear ones. Even that the beasts would not permit.

The quiet was broken by the heartrending cries of the newly selected victims. Tseshya whispered in my ear: "Tala, we are lost!" At the same moment, the

---

*A lineup for the purpose of selecting inmates to be killed.

murderers were at our row. My heart banged like a hammer, my feet shook. Every moment contained my fate—life or death. I didn't want death; with all of our terrible experiences, the spark of hope had not been extinguished. My mind urged: Let them pass by! And at that moment my beloved friend Tseshya was torn away from me. I tried to hold onto her with my hand. But the command fell: "Right!" Tseshya was leaving me, saying: I had a premonition . . . better this way, I have no more strength.

The "lucky" ones were led into Block 8, and the victims were led into Block 19, Tseshya among them. They were driven into the "hall of death."

Those kept in Block 8 weren't let out until nightfall. I felt drawn to see my comrades, to whom I was closely bound. In the evening I was told that the unfortunates hadn't been led away yet; they were still being allowed to suffer in the crowding and the dirt, to fool themselves with the hope that they might yet remain alive.

I didn't go to them empty-handed, but what I brought was a poor gift: a cup of coffee—what else did we have?

Coming into the block, the blood froze in my veins. Who could paint the hellish picture that revealed itself to my eyes? At the threshold lay a heap of corpses; they had passed away during the day. It was no more cheerful inside: shadows of people moved on the bunks. Some were resigned, others apathetic; several drew away as I entered, from fear and perhaps from hope for a miracle to save them?

The first one I saw was Tseshya, and I handed her the cup of coffee. With yearning hands, she brought the warm drink to her dry lips. She took a long sip, and stopped. She was burning with fever. When she was a bit stronger, she said to me:

"Tala, I am not sorry to be leaving this ugly world. I'm going to my death as if it were a dance at Yazhvinsky's dance hall. Finally, finally, I will be rid of these unbearable pains. But I grieve for the fate of my sister Leyeke, she will remain alone. Look out for her, Tala, help her in any way you can!"

After a short pause, she added:

"When I am led to the crematorium and you see the smoke rise from the chimney, know that the deaf heavens, which have not heard our cries for help, have taken me."

My eyes wept, and my mouth could bring forth no words. I had not the strength to comfort her, thinking about my own unknown fate: who knew whether the same might not happen to me tomorrow?

It was hard to go away. Suddenly I heard Dasha Shtaynberg's voice in the distance: "Tala, give me a drink, I'm burning up!" I fulfilled her request with the little bit of coffee that remained. The voice of Sore Volkovitsh reached me. She said to me naively: "I don't know whether they'll be able to gas me—I have such a strong heart!"

I could stay no longer: I would have gone insane. How could I stand it? Such young lives cut down so early, staring the Angel of Death in the face—waiting for death is worse than death.

I said goodbye to each of them and barely got out alive. At the door I stood a moment, looking around. Their glances accompanied me but I no longer saw them.

Their last walk before going to the crematorium was their march to Block 25.

At lunchtime the next day, I saw them through my little block window, being led to the ovens. They were sent to the gas chambers in a closed truck. Echoes of "*Hatikvah*" and "*Shema Yisroel*" carried through the void, and then all became silent again.

Thus departed young lives. It is hard to comprehend how those who remained bore the agony of separation. There is no question that it was the sense of revenge that gave us the strength to go on living, to hold out until the end.

Awhile later, I passed by the block again. It was empty; our dear young girls of Kolo were not there. They disappeared in smoke, and the wind spread their ashes all across this false and cruel world, which silently allowed their doom. In my ears ring until this day their protests and cries of distress, which no one heard.

Kol Nidre in Auschwitz

YOYSEF VAYNBERG
Sefer Strizhuv (Stryzow) ve-ha-seviva

The dismal days of autumn bring a terrible epidemic: one *selektsye* after another. As soon as people are brought into the camp, their fate descends on them. Of the "older" numbers, few are left. A mad lust for blood possesses the Germans. The worse the news from the front, the madder and more bloodthirsty they become, as if they wanted to take revenge for their losses at the front on the unfortunates in the camp. Every few days we are ordered to run naked, and the weaker ones are sent to the ovens. Resigned, the designated victims runs into the barracks from where they are led to be burned. Apathetic and without faith, the others drag themselves off to work: tomorrow the same fate would meet them! Every day new people are brought into camp; they are brought here from all over Europe to be tragically murdered. We are already used to the terrible stench of burning bones. The stench is already considered part of the nature surrounding us, like the beautiful mountains which circle the camp like a crown; like the dew which covers the grounds each dawn; like the river, whose waters murmur secrets from the wide world in the still nights; like the stars in Heaven and like the trembling leaves on the trees; like the grain in the nearby fields, which waves in time with the wind, and like the bright clouds which mix together with the smoke rising from the crematoria smokestacks.

I sense all this glorious nature as a pain inside: all that is on the other side of the wires, but we are on this side, where all is death. Resentfully I watch the fantastically beautiful sunset. The magnificence of nature mocks our fate.

Thus each day passes, more terrible than the day before. But somewhere in my heart hope still clings: still, perhaps? I hold to life's last thread. The fear of the next day has not yet disappeared altogether.

For a few days, the secret about the women's camp has been whispered around. The women are no longer led out to work. They are locked inside the wires. It is said that many women have become infected by scabies, and there has been a major selection. At night wild wailing is heard, as if thousands of people were being slaughtered at once. The German kapos, who know everything, say that four thousand women have been chosen for the ovens, and they are all cramped together into one barrack. They have been lying there for four days already, heaped on one another, without food or drink; they have torn the roof away with their bodies; the S.S. are shooting them like rabbits.

At night no one can fall asleep. Tomorrow is the day before Yom Kippur. These High Holy Days are tragic.

In the morning we discover that an order has been sent from Berlin not to burn the women but to cure their infestation. A bit of hope steals its way into my heart: still, perhaps?

After the evening roll call, we go to Kol Nidre.

For a long time already we have been promising each other to observe the Kol Nidre service this year. A Jewish block elder has allowed us to pray in his block. Someone has brought a talis from the clothing warehouse. The seriousness of the moment is felt in camp. It seems that the entire world is preparing for Kol Nidre.

In the morning the entire sky was clouded over. At midday the cloud rose, and it rained. The sun hid somewhere behind the clouds. Heaven wept for an entire afternoon. Now, before Kol Nidre, it calmed itself a bit: the rain stopped. The world around lies desolate. The sun feels guilty and doesn't dare show its face.

From every block, people assemble at the barrack of the Jewish block elder. People stretch out on the pallets, stand pressed next to one another. Everyone who feels a Jewish heart beating inside has come, even the block elders and kapos. They are always the grand aristocrats. Now they stand among the ordinary "prisoners." They are possessed by dread. Even the German block elders and kapos, those terrible murderers, are silent. They avoid the barrack, moving in a large semicircle around it. Today, they have somehow grown afraid of the Jews.

The rabbi prays.

He was only recently brought into camp. Those who knew him helped and supported him in any way they could. So many rabbis have died already; not one other is left. This one at least must remain alive.

Wrapped in the talis, he says the Prayer of Purification. Everyone hears his voice clearly. Everything is frozen "as if our bodies are placed on top of the altar to be willingly accepted by the Almighty, as a sacrifice dedicated completely to God." Through the boards of the barrack I look at the crematorium, from which smoke reaches into the gray heavens.

And I hear the voice of the rabbi, as though it no longer came from his heart, but as if his heart itself had opened and wept:

"And a portion of our fat and our blood."

He wraps himself more tightly, and repeats the words; but now his heart bleeds, and he omits "and a portion": "our fat and our blood." The congregation repeats: "our fat and our blood." As if under a spell, everyone stops at these two words. The rabbi cannot go on. Louder and louder the congregation repeats: "our fat and our blood."

Someone shouts: "The blood and fat of our parents, children, and relatives."

Tears pour from everyone's eyes. The weeping flows together, like a river. Hearts of stone have given way.

I do not weep. I cannot tear my eyes away from the clear smoke of the crematorium. I feel a terrible weariness in my bones. It is unbearably hot in the barrack.

When the rabbi says, "With the consent of the Almighty," I am transported as if to another world. It seems to me that I am sitting somewhere in a catacomb in Spain. I see the bonfires and the grim Torquemada, the unfortunate Jews who burn for the Sanctification of the Name. The smoke of the burned is carried straight into Heaven. I hear the *Shema Yisroel* carried by the smoke and, later, people wrapped in black, who come into the catacombs with their faces covered.

"We pray together with the sinners!" cry the figures in black. A terrible cry ascends from the images. I hear the rabbi saying: "From this Yom Kippur until the next."

And suddenly everything is silent. A dead stillness prevails in the barrack: no one prays, no one weeps on. It is as if everyone's tongues were bound.

Only from outside do we hear the terrible wailing. On the road by the wires the women are being led to the ovens. The sound of the trucks' motors are drowned out by the naked women's cries. There are many in the barrack whose dear ones are being led away. Everyone is still, as if trying to discern the voice of a loved one among the screams. Through the open gates, we see the victims lift up their hands toward the sky and plead for mercy. The women see the men in the barrack. Their shouts grow louder. Everyone inside is petrified.

The rabbi is the first to arouse himself. He interrupts Kol Nidre and begins the morning service: "Let us gather our strength for the holiness of this day."

In the silence of the barracks his voice is heard, as if responding to the women's cries. His voice resounds, and when he comes to the words, "And who by fire"—a lament tears out from every throat: "And who by fire!"

The phrase, "who by fire," comes as if from the other world.

The rabbi continues, but his voice is drowned out by the tragic cries, "who by fire," as if the Jews wanted to quench the terrible fire with their words.

But the motors don't stop rumbling. More and more victims are led off to be burned.

"Who by fire!" the congregation does not stop shouting. The voices of the condemned mix with the men's prayer. As if hypnotized, everyone shouts: "Who by fire!" as if praying to be burned in the fire as well.

In the midst of the prayer, the voice of the shofar interrupts:

Tekiah, shevarim, teruah.

Tekiah gedolah.

The shofar awakens the men as if from a dream. At first it is quiet in the barrack. I hear my heart bang. Soon the whole crowd weeps. The voices of the naked women reach Heaven. The crowd weeps softly.

In the block where we prayed, next to the oven which has been turned into a podium, the rabbi lies wrapped in a talis. The shepherd's soul has departed.

Fires burn in the woods by the crematorium all night; the ovens are not big enough.

The Transport from Auschwitz

ELIAHU SHIMON HIFKA
Sefer ha-zikaron le-kedoshei Bezoyn (Biezun)

In the middle of the night of April 17 or 18, 1945,* a sudden alarm! The entire camp was aroused. Something was going to happen, but what, no one knew.

The S.S. men and the entire camp administration ran back and forth around the camp. People said that the whole camp had been mined, and that it would soon be blown up because the Russians were already near. Finally an S.S. man came in and said that the whole camp was to be evacuated. The evacuation began immediately. At the gate each prisoner was given a loaf of bread and half a package of margarine, and we were driven on by the S.S. men like sheep. We marched in columns of four hundred men as far as Glayvits, where we were to remain for several days and then proceed further. But the Soviet army continued to approach until it arrived at the outskirts of Glayvits. Then we were driven to

*The chronology is incorrect since the author indicates that he was in Sachsenhausen from January to April 1945. Auschwitz was liberated in October 1944.

the railroad station and into coal cars, 150 men to a car, and the trains started off. Two S.S. men carrying machine guns were assigned to each car. They were warmly dressed in furs and felt boots, although we wore only our camp uniforms and one blanket each. We rode by day and by night.

Where were we being transported to? We didn't know, and when someone died in our car, we threw him out in order to have a little more room. Dozens were thrown out each day in this fashion. There was nothing to eat. We ate the snow that covered us. When we stopped at a station in Germany, everyone came to see the Jews in the train. During this exhibition we were pelted with snow and stones.

The transport was led by the well-known murderer of the Birkenau crematorium. Whenever he felt like it, he ordered the camp commandant to shunt the train onto a side track, and then he displayed his bestiality. He ordered all of us to get out of the train, run one hundred meters, and remain standing until we heard another order. Then he ordered: "Everyone back onto the train!" After three days of hunger, it wasn't easy to climb back into the cars.

Then he came up with this trick: he arranged with the engineer to have the train pull out after one blast of the whistle. In a flash the train gave such a jerk that everyone who was in the process of clambering on fell off; several fell under the wheels and were cut in two. He did this a second time three days later, when we had been on the way for six days. During this time we had gotten a bit of bread: three loaves had been thrown into each car full of 150 men. The second time he pulled his trick, almost half of the prisoners remained sitting in the snow. Their feet were so stiff that they were completely unable to walk. Then Germans in civilian clothes came along and began to shoot prisoners in the back of the head with revolvers. Not one of us even shuddered; apparently people were satisfied that their sufferings were at an end. I myself envied them a few days later. We waited for the recurrence of Molier's cruelty. But, as if to spite us, he didn't repeat the trick.

Thus we arrived at Mauthausen in Austria. But the camp was overflowing, and we were not accepted. We still hadn't gotten out of the cars. In any case, the murderer didn't want to interrupt his game. We traveled back from Austria into the Sudetenland, and from there to Czechoslovakia, where we arrived early one morning, before dawn.

We stopped at the main railroad station in Prague. For those of us who were still alive, this was a lucky thing. As soon as the people of the city found out that a train full of prisoners was there, they ran to us from all sides, showering us with bread, hot potatoes, and flasks of hot tea. The S.S. didn't want to permit this, and set a heavy guard. But the Czechs were not scared off and continued to throw food to us. Fortunately for us, there was a bridge suspended above the tracks we were on. From this bridge souls descended to half-dead people. While we were in Prague the rail lines were completely blocked, and we remained there for twenty-four hours. Thus we had food to eat until the end of our tragic journey.

In Prague a delegation of the Red Cross requested that they be allowed to remove the sick, but Molier categorically refused to let them do it. In his transport, he said, no one was sick. In order to convince the delegation, he went from car to car, asking if anyone was sick. Since we knew that he wouldn't let the sick out anyway, none of us responded. Next to me lay a man who was almost dead, and we announced to the delegation that one person was sick. Then Molier ordered him to be handed over. But when he saw the man, he said that it wasn't worthwhile, because the man was already three-quarters dead. The delegation wanted to take the man, but Molier refused.

As a signal that there were sick men in the transport, we began to throw out the dead as soon as the train moved. Their number was very large: there were five or six in each car, and there were forty-five cars in the transport. We also threw out letters. The whole route through Czechoslovakia was lined with Czech policemen. After fourteen days we arrived in Sachsenhausen, where we were taken off the train. This is how we were removed:

Boards were set out from the doors of the wagons to the ground, and we were ordered to run out quickly, one by one. If someone was unable to run, he was led off to the side. As I found out later, these were doomed to a different sort of death: there were no gas chambers here, but there were showers. The unfortunates were brought to the shower-block and given a shower. Thus ended the lives of those who could not run.

At the Germans' command, about one hundred prisoners from the transport entered the camp. The rest were transported further, and some were killed in the showers. We were led into a hall bearing the number 008. We remained there for eight days, after which we were given work details. We were set to building Heinkel 126 airplanes. I remained there from January until April 19th.

The bombardment was heavy. Finally the long-awaited day came when the factory was demolished.

One beautiful morning American airplanes flew overhead and destroyed the entire plant. In doing so, they killed two thousand of us. That didn't upset us, because the pain and hunger were so great that each of us desired to die.

Then we survivors were driven into one central square in the camp, and it was announced that we were being evacuated from the camp.

On the morning of April 19, 1945, the S.S. began to drive us out of the camp, five hundred men in a group, under heavy guard. We marched night and day, and whoever was too weak to walk, and fell, was immediately shot. Behind each column followed a platoon of S.S. men, who made sure that none lived who were left behind. Even when someone fell dead, they shot him just to be sure. There was nothing to eat. Every two hours we rested for twenty minutes. We rested in the woods, and when we left a resting place, not a blade of grass or a shred of tree bark remained. We ate whatever our teeth could chew.

We stayed in one forest for six days, because it was impossible to go further. We had absolutely no strength left. Horrible, unbelievable scenes took place in that forest. I myself, who took part in and observed these scenes, can't believe that they were true.

We were watched by a tight ring of S.S. men. We barely moved. Every minute we heard a scream, but it was impossible for us to run and see what was happening. The screams repeated themselves in different locations. Then we found out the reasons for the screams. They were the screams of people being attacked by half-starved wild men, who bit at each other's living limbs. When someone was thus attacked, and was too weak to defend himself, dozens fell upon him and tore him to pieces. The S.S. men were delighted to see men made wild by hunger. They neither sensed nor believed that the end to their sadistic pleasure was soon to come.

On the seventh day we marched further, but our number was half of what it had been in the forest. The other half remained under S.S. watch. I am certain everyone was shot there.

I had a bit of luck on the way. An S.S. man gave me his pack to carry, and although it was too heavy for me, I didn't dare refuse. With my last ounce of strength I carried it, and the S.S. man marched at my side. Then God performed a miracle. Two airplanes came and we were forced to run into a ditch or into the forest. I fell with the sack under a tree, and remained lying there. When the airplanes left, we stood up and continued marching, but I didn't see the owner of the pack.

I continued to carry the pack until nightfall, when I decided to find out what was inside it. The most important thing I found was bread and sugar. When I found this, I stopped looking. I covered myself in my blanket like everyone else, and celebrated. When I was full, I searched further in the pack. I found good clean clothes which I quickly put on. But what pleased me most of all was the revolver that I found there. I knew the S.S. man would shoot me when he found me, so I decided that when that happened I would first shoot him, then myself.

Fortunately, I didn't see him until the first of May. I touched the cold metal of the revolver by my breast. But my fear disappeared when I realized that he wasn't even thinking about me. I walked past the Angel of Death as though we'd never met. I threw away the rest of the things, sharing the food with my comrades. I felt like the greatest hero among the thirty thousand prisoners because I had the revolver.

Then came bad news. A young Russian who had been a servant of the S.S. officer came into the forest and told us that he overheard two S.S. men saying that everyone in the forest, regardless of nationality, was going to be shot that day. Everyone's bones grew cold: we felt that this was the last day of the Hitlerites' rule, and we already knew that the "Fuehrer" was dead. The news that we were to be shot spread through the entire forest. The Russians among us immediately began to organize self-defense, accepting anyone who was able to stand on his feet. Ten members of the self-defense organization were assigned to each S.S. man. Every five meters stood an S.S. man with a rifle, and every twenty meters stood one with a machine gun. We took our orders, not knowing from whom. Every minute another order came.

The last order was this: When we saw that the S.S. were retreating from one side of the ring, we were to understand that they were about to open fire from the other side. Then we were to throw ourselves at the S.S. men, without waiting for any more orders.

I kept my revolver in my hand the whole time. I chose a German with a machine gun. We gradually crept closer until we were barely a meter away from them, instead of the usual five. With one leap we could be upon them.

Thus we were on watch for twenty-four hours. The entire night of the first and second of May we didn't close our eyes. No one felt hunger anymore. New columns of prisoners kept coming into the forest all night, another sign that we were to be destroyed. But our hearts grew lighter when the new arrivals brought the news that they had met soldiers on the way who had thrown away their guns, put on civilian clothing, and marched with the columns.

When daylight came, we found that there were some among us who weren't prisoners because they had hair on their heads. We also found out that some of us had hand grenades which they had found as they walked. Thus both our hopes and our courage began to grow. We began to believe in our strength, and along with it came daring. Turning to each one who had hair, we removed his pack of food and frisked him to see if he was carrying weapons. We knew that they were German soldiers, but they were suddenly so weak that we could do whatever we wanted with them.

And still the S.S. men didn't move from one side to the other. They stood in place, but it was obvious that they had nowhere to go. They trembled like little fish, and their terror stilled our hunger.

About two o' clock in the afternoon two tanks suddenly appeared, with stars on their sides. They were American. An officer came out of one of the tanks and explained to us in German that we were about to be freed, that American military personnel bringing food and medicine were on their way, and that we shouldn't move.

We didn't believe him. We thought it was a German ploy; the two tanks didn't make much of an impression on us. Furthermore, we were still surrounded by S.S. men, and it was hard to understand what was happening. Finally it became clear. Some of the S.S. men dropped their weapons and disappeared. Red Cross trucks full of food and everything we needed drove up immediately. We didn't understand that one mustn't eat a great deal after such a long fast, and several of us died from overeating.

While we were eating, we suddenly heard shots. It was hard to discern from where the fire was coming. It lasted for a few minutes and then stopped. Meanwhile we remembered that we, too, had weapons, and we answered the fire. We realized that the fire had come from the remaining S.S. men, who with one salvo had murdered three hundred of our comrades. That was in a woods near Schwerin [East Germany]. We didn't leave the forest that night, but kept watch with various sorts of weapons. In the morning we began to go our separate ways.

The dead were assembled by the U.S. Army, and brought into the town of Schwerin. The Germans were forced to wash the dead and dress them in white. Then the Americans assembled the entire population and announced through a megaphone: these were victims of Hitlerism, who were to be buried in the middle of the town square as a sign that such things should never happen again.

Crosses were set at the graves of members of other nationalities, and Stars of David at the graves of Jews. The city of Schwerin is now occupied by the Russians.

I began writing this account "The Transport from Auschwitz," on January 24, 1945, on scraps of paper which I kept until the liberation.

Return

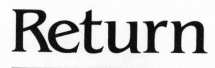

Searching for the Life That Was

NOKHEM KRUMERKOP
Sefer Tarnogrod

Finding myself in Lublin when the war ended, I began to think about ways in which I, as a Jew, could travel to Tarnogrod, which entailed great dangers. At that time the Kelts pogrom also took place, costing the lives of forty Jews, and the anti-Semitic bands terrified every surviving Jew. Jews were warned not to ride trains until the hooliganism stopped.

But my heart was pained, and would not let me rest. Seeing the great catastrophe that had befallen the Jewish people, my desire to live was lost; but at the same time the Jew felt within himself the mission of continuing the lives of his slaughtered parents and relatives. Despite the most gruesome nightmares, he knew that he must continue living. To ride from Lublin to Tarnogrod with a beard like mine meant risking my life.

After considering all of the risks involved, I went to a barber and wept over my beard as it was cut off. I left long mustaches like those of a Polish peasant, put on peasant boots and a peasant cap, and set off for Tarnogrod at the end of May 1945.

I took the train as far as Zamoshtsh, where I met a few surviving Jews, slept at the home of a Jew, and set off on the train in the morning to Zvyezhinyets. From there I took the local train to Bilgoray.

It was hard for me to tell whether there was another Jew on the train. Perhaps he was disguised as a gentile, as I was. But all of the passengers were positive that there wasn't a single Jew on the train. It was hard to believe that a Jew would dare to travel on that line in those times.

When I arrived at Bilgoray, Polish coachmen stood in front of the station. They fell upon me, asking where I was headed; each one wanted to take me. I stood mute for a while, searching with my eyes: perhaps Mendl Roshe's would appear, or Mendl Avel, or another of the Jewish coachmen of Tarnogrod, who used to drive to Bilgoray and back each day.

But my search was fruitless. None of them was left. Gentile wagons had taken their place. Having no other choice, I approached one of the Polish coachmen, and we settled on a fare to Tarnogrod. For a short while we both sat silently. He was the first to speak; I tried to answer as little as possible, so that he wouldn't realize I was a Jew. Then he pointed in front of himself with his whip and said:

"See, on both sides of the road are buried Jews whom the Germans shot. Jews from Tarnogrod, Bilgoray, and the surrounding villages lie there. The Germans knew what they were doing when they shot all the Jews. It was a good thing they did, and we should be grateful to them for it."

The gentile sat talking with his back to me, and I sat as if petrified. As I looked around I saw that the entire road from Bilgoray to Tarnogrod was the same as before. Nothing had changed: the same houses, the same gentiles, the same women drawing water from their wells, just as before. Only the coachman wasn't the same. I no longer heard the rich Yiddish tongue and the Yiddish *"Vyo, ferdelekh!* Giddyap!"* I no longer heard the melody of the prayer, "Let us give strength to the holiness of this day," which Yoysef Magid used to sing as he rode with his passengers to Bilgoray. Depressed, I thought to myself: Where am I going, and to whom? Is there really no one left? Is it possible that an entire city of Jews was slaughtered?

Frozen in these tragic thoughts I arrived in Tarnogrod. I didn't want to ride straight into town, and asked the coachman to let me off near the factory at the Bilgoray gate.

There I met Sore Magram. She stood on the porch of her house, and looked at me without recognizing me. Seeing her, a Jewish woman of Tarnogrod, joy flooded through me for a moment. I approached her, told her who I was, and saw how she, too, was filled with the same joy.

Belkhatov Without Jews

YOYSEF RAYKH
Belkhatov (Belchatow) yizker-bukh

I feel oddly alien today in the town where I was born and raised, where I know each corner, each stone, where every house, every store reminds me of familiar people who lived, worked, and dealt here, scrimped and saved penny after penny, built a house for themselves, for children, for children's children. None of them foresaw the bitter fate of those for whom they struggled and built houses.

Here I stand in the marketplace and consider the house which is located right at the corner of Pobyanets Street. Here, a few steps up, was Hershl Plavner's store. I walk closer and am greeted with a bitter sight: now they sell holy pictures and crucifixes there.

I walk through the market and look at the stores of Yoysef-Leybish Grushke, Henekh Adler, Goldshteyn, and others. All of these shops have been taken by the new merchants.

I walk across to the other side of the marketplace and read the new signs on the stores. At one I read, "Village Cooperative," but underneath this inscription is still legible, insistent and accusing, an older inscription: "Tuvye Varshavsky."

Today is Monday, market day in Belkhatov. Once the market was jammed with people. Today, one can walk through quietly. The booths of the new merchants take up only a small part of the marketplace. Today, Belkhatov is like a large village. Of all the textile factories which were built by Jews, Orzhekhovski's is the only one still in operation; the others are idle and empty.

I look at Fraytog's factory. Various objects made of iron remain, the remains of the looms and other machines. I remember how my father used to talk about Perets Fraytog, how he had worked hard in his youth, carrying calves from the villages on his back, until he acquired money and built the factory.

A Pole complains to me that everything in town died along with the Jews, and there's no way to earn a living anymore. The Jews, he says, were resourceful and had initiative, and everything was busy around them.

The walls of the synagogue stand intact, but the windows are gone. Probably they were needed by the neighbors. The interior is utterly empty: the podium is gone, as are the Ark of the Torah, the lecterns, the benches. All that remains are the walls, empty, torn, and dirty. Everywhere there are broken, discarded boxes and dirt. In one place I saw a hole which has been dug, and next to it an iron pot. A Pole explains to me with a burst of jealousy that other Poles had dug up a treasure there, which had been buried in the pot under the floor.

The location of the cemetery was hard to find. I only managed to do so because the grain harvest was long past and the stalks no longer hid the bits of broken graves which lay like signs saying: Here lie the bones of generations of Jews, of our parents, brothers and sisters, and dear ones. Among the shards I recognized two pieces of my father's stone. When I returned a year ago, I saw another piece, which is now gone. Someone took it for sharpening scythes and axes.

On my way back from the graveyard, my eyes downcast, I found out where the gravestones had gone. The road to the Catholic cemetery from Startsev Street is planted with trees. There is a bridge just before the path, which was constructed out of gravestones. The path itself is also paved with Jewish gravestones.

In the meadow between Pobyanets Street and the woods flows a brook. In my days there were stepping-stones which we used to get across, while peasant wagons forded the stream.

Today there's a solid little bridge with massive supports, paved for a few dozen meters with Jewish gravestones. They have also been used to pave the sidewalks in various parts of town. They lie as if disgraced with their inscriptions in the Holy Tongue, with their engraved Psalms, menorahs, Jewish lions, and Stars of David. As they engraved these stones, the dust that flew from the stones consumed the lungs of my father and brother. How much effort and creativity they poured forth in order to find the right ornaments and inscriptions for each stone: for a young man, a broken tree; for a young woman, a broken candle; for a scholar, a bookcase and two deer; for a *Kohen*, two hands raised in reciting the priestly blessing, and so forth.

Now these stones—torn out of their graves—stolen from the dead, with the holy inscriptions "Here lies" and "May the soul of this holy man be in paradise forever" are trodden by strangers' feet, and desecrated.

An article was printed in the central organ of the Polish Socialist party, *Rabotnik*, which concluded by stating that from being a dirty, isolated town before the war, Belkhatov had grown into a town that was both clean and cultured.

We would like to say to these "cultured people": you live in our homes, you sleep in our beds and you use our bedding, you wear our clothes—at least *do not obliterate our holy places!*

My Tragic Night in Zhelekhov

KHANKE ASHLAK
Yizker-bukh fun der Zhelekhover (Zelechow) yidisher kehile

I do not have the strength to describe all of my experiences during the war. I do, however, want to retell one experience which is engraved in my memory, because it took place not during the war, but after the liberation, when the world had already begun to breathe fresh air, when our terror of the German murderers had passed. When the world had already returned to its normal order of life, I survived a terrible night—more terrible than the nights in Majdanek and Auschwitz, where I spent almost two years.

On May 17, 1945, I was liberated by the Red Army in the town of Bulivada, in the Czech Sudeten. Together with me was my comrade in suffering, with whom I had endured every camp, and we remained together in freedom.

After spending a month in a village in Czechoslovakia, we traveled to Poland to find out whether anyone in our families was still alive. We rode to Lodz and then to Warsaw, and to our great sorrow, found none of our relatives or close friends. We decided to travel to Zhelekhov, where I had had relatives before the war; my mother was from Zhelekhov. I had heard a lot about this remarkable town and thought: perhaps someone from my family had survived there. My girlfriend didn't want to part with me even for one day, although she had no one in Zhelekhov.

One evening when it was already dark (I don't remember the date), we arrived in Zhelekhov. I went to the address of a Polish acquaintance, Valdortshik. Before the war he had been the treasurer of the court in Zhelekhov and commander of the firemen. He didn't recognize me. When I explained to him who I was, he remembered my family. I asked about my family and received the answer that none of them was alive. After a brief conversation, the Pole took us to two Jews who lived with the Polish family Gugala.

We really didn't have anything left to do in Zhelekhov. We decided to spend the night and return to Warsaw the next day. But fate had it otherwise. We prepared places to sleep. Two other Jewish women came; there were six of us Jews, four women and two men.

As soon as we dropped off to sleep, we were awakened by a commotion at the door and window. We jumped up in terror. I managed to put on my slippers and throw on a coat over my nightshirt. The others were also half-naked, and we were driven out into the street by the men who entered. I don't remember how many there were. I only remember that everywhere I looked, the barrels of pistols and rifles were pointed toward us.

We four women were led out in front of the house and ordered to sit down on a bench. Then the men were led out naked and shot. A boy of twenty fell some three meters away from us. His name was Shloyme Hefner; he was from Zhelekhov. He had survived the war in the Soviet Union, returned to his hometown after the war, and fell at the hands of the bandits. The second Jew escaped. The bandits shot at him, but fortunately they missed.

Seeing this, we began to ask the murderers for mercy—not so much asking as simply begging for our lives. One of us, a pregnant woman, knelt and kissed the bandits' feet. She was answered with shots. The woman fell dead not far from us; they also shot at the second woman, Perl Faygnzukht. I was third on the bench, and then my girlfriend. She suddenly jumped out, ran off into the Pole's house and hid under the bed. I ran after her instinctively, and received a bullet in the fleshy part of my left leg. Fortunately, the bullet only grazed me, and I was able to keep running. When I ran into the house, my friend was under the bed. I turned to her:

"Saba, where are you? Turn toward me, I want to hide next to you, I'm wounded."

"There's no room here, there are suitcases under the bed, hide somewhere else," answered Saba.

I went into another room, hid under a sewing table in a corner, and covered myself with pieces of cloth.

The murderers came into the room and turned to the Polish family: "Where are the two *Jewesses* who ran away?"

No one replied. They searched under the bed with an electric flashlight and found my poor girlfriend. They wanted to pull her out from under the bed, and she pleaded with them in moving words which I will never forget:

"Sirs, don't kill me, I've lived through such a terrible war, I've lost everything and everyone, give me life, I want to live . . ."

A few shots resounded, and my comrade was silenced forever. Her name was Saba Edelman, and she came from Warsaw.

Immediately after they killed her, the bandits began searching for me. They came into the room where I had hidden. They searched every corner, under the bed, in the cabinets. They didn't look in the pile of cloth where I was hidden.

Thus ended the one night I spent in Zhelekhov after the liberation. Out of the six Jews in the house, only three remained alive. One woman received a bullet, was slighty wounded, and feigned death. When the bandits chased after us, the wounded woman got up and ran away. One person ran away at the beginning, and the third was myself.

My beloved girlfriend, who lived through Hitler's hell with me and was murdered at the threshold of a new life, was buried together with other victims of that night in Zhelekhov, the town where she had never been before, and of which she had never heard.

A Visit to My Town of Bilgoray

M. RAPOPORT
Khurbn Bilgoray (Bilgoraj)

I can never forget my town of Bilgoray and its beloved Jews. It is with deep respect that we should mention them; many of them had warm Jewish hearts. They were ready to sacrifice themselves for Jews and Judaism.

It is worth mentioning a Jew such as Levi Shtern, may he rest in peace, who was loved and honored by everyone. He was no rich man, but a baker. He was hale and hearty and worked very hard. Whenever he had time, he studied, or sought to help the poor and the sick. He was a trustee of the Rudniker Synagogue and of the burial society, secretary of the community council, and chairman of the society for visiting the sick; he was famous for his hospitality to strangers, gave much to charity, and also saw to it that others gave.

During the war, after Bilgoray was burned, he lived in Tarnogrod. He put his life in danger to bake bread in secret and help the poor and starving.

In the month of Elul 1942, he was led away together with his family and hundreds more Jews from Tarnogrod and Bilgoray to Belzhets, where they died in the gas chambers.

His son Yisroelke, who was a great scholar, was shot by the Germans in Pushtshe on the way to Belzhets when he left the carriage to relieve himself.

When the Jews were led through Bilgoray, Levi shouted from the carriage in a mournful voice, "Jews, where are we being taken?"

It is worth mentioning a Jew such as my uncle Avrom Harman; he gave generously to charity, gave shelter to strangers, and kept a special account book for loans that he made free of charge. Whenever someone needed to make a wedding, or was in any kind of trouble, he could turn to my uncle and was never refused. He had the merit to die in Tarnogrod shortly before the massacre. In accordance with his will, he was buried at the cemetery in Bilgoray.

It is also worth mentioning such shining scholarly figures, warmhearted Jews, such as Note Kronenberg, my uncle Yosele and my uncle Shmuel-Elye Rapaport, Hersh Vaysman, Henekh Hokhman, Yisroelke Shtern, Hersh-Yekhezkl Harman, Avremele Hokhman, Shmueltshe Shrayber, Motl Harman, and others. It is hard to recall all the dear persons of Bilgoray who were killed by the Nazi murderers.

Before Rosh Hashanah in 1944, immediately after the liberation, I arrived with the Polish army in Lublin. A day before Rosh Hashanah I walked to Bilgoray, for no trains were running yet.

Coming into the city, I was filled with despair. I was born in Bilgoray and lived there until the war, and now, walking around in broad daylight, I barely recognized the city: Lubelski Street, where the synagogue had been located, the great study house, the little study house, the bath house, the slaughterhouse, the Zikhron Yankev Kheyder, the old graveyard, the old rabbi's house, the new house of the Belzer Rebe's son, Reb Mordkhe of blessed memory, the meeting-houses of the Trisker and Rudniker Hasidim—everything was a void, and in midday there was no living soul to be seen.

The streets were paved with gravestones bearing Jewish inscriptions; this was itself terrifying and made everything seem like a vast graveyard.

I entered a store to buy some butter. It was handed to me wrapped in sheets of the Vilna edition of the Talmud. I stood as if petrified, remembering how hard it had been for a Jew to purchase a Vilna Talmud for his scholarly son-in-law. It seemed to me that I heard the melody of "Thus said Abaye and Raba." On my way out, I threw the butter away and hid the holy scraps of text.

This was my town of Bilgoray after the great catastrophe. With tears in my eyes I departed. Always in my ears I hear the echo of the mourner's prayer: *yisgadal veyiskadash . . .*

Appendix I: Bibliography of Eastern European Memorial Books

compiled by Zachary M. Baker

Introduction

This is a revised and expanded version of the "Bibliography of Eastern European Memorial Books" that originally appeared in the Fall 1979–Winter 1980 issue of *Toledot; the Journal of Jewish Genealogy* (compiled by Zachary M. Baker). That bibliography, in turn, was substantially based on the "Bibliographical List of Memorial Books Published in the Years 1943–1972," compiled by David Bass (*Yad Vashem Studies* 9, 1973).

Memorial books are listed here in one alphabetical sequence, and are entered under their official place names (as of 1938 in the case of Polish towns; as of 1913 for other localities). Included are memorial books for Jewish communities in pre–World War II Poland, Czechoslovakia, Greece, Hungary, Romania, the Soviet Union, and the Baltic States. Memorial books for German-Jewish communities are excluded from the scope of this bibliography, since by and large they take the form of historical monographs, not collective compilations of memoirs and eyewitness accounts. Readers interested in the German-Jewish memorial literature are referred to the published catalogue of the Leo Baeck Institute Library [*Leo Baeck Institut, New York, Bibliothek und Archiv. Katalog*, v. 1 (Tubingen: 1970)] and to the annual bibliography on German Jewry which appears in the LBI *Yearbook*.

Key to Symbols

1. Place names are given, with an indication in parentheses of the countries to which the towns belonged between the end of World War I and the outbreak of World War II. The following abbreviations are used: (B) Belorussian S.S.R., (C) Czechoslovakia, (G) Greece, (H) Hungary, (L) Lithuania, (LV) Latvia, (P) Poland, (R) Romania, (U) Ukrainian S.S.R., (Y) Yugoslavia.

2. Book titles are given in transliteration from the Hebrew or Yiddish originals. English titles are supplied in parentheses after the Hebrew or Yiddish titles. An asterisk (*) after an English title indicates that the translated title was supplied in the work itself. Otherwise the titles have been translated by the compiler.

3. The following cross-references are used:

a) A "see" reference sends the reader from an alternate spelling of a place name to the official form.

b) A "see under" reference sends the reader from the name of a town discussed in a special chapter of a book on another town to the full citation for the latter book.

c) A "see also" reference sends the reader to other books that include chapters on a town.

Note on Transliteration of Proper Names

Most proper names appearing within the narrative portion of this book are phonetically transliterated from the Yiddish original, according to rules established by the YIVO

Institute for Jewish Research. *Place names* are indexed so as to reflect these transliterated forms.

In the geographical index, wherever the official forms of place names diverge from the spellings used in the text they are included in parentheses next to the index entries. However, in the "Bibliography of Eastern European Memorial Books," official spellings of place names are used as entry headings. This is done for reference purposes, since official spellings are the forms that will be found in standard maps, gazetteers, and encyclopedias. The citations that appear in the bibliography of memorial books are transliterated according to the language employed on their pages, i.e., Yiddish or Hebrew. Place names *within* these citations appear in their official (usually Polish) forms, except where the title page forms vary widely from the official forms.

Aleksandria (P). *Pinkas ha-kehila Aleksandria (Wolyn); sefer yizkor* [Memorial book of the community of Aleksandria (Wolyn)]. Comp.: Shmuel Yizreeli; ed.: Natan Livneh. Tel Aviv, Aleksandria Society, 1972. 314 p., illus. (Hebrew)

Aleksandrow (P). *Aleksander* [Aleksandrow—near Lodz]. Ed.: N. Blumenthal. Tel Aviv, Association of Former Residents of Aleksandrow in Israel, 1968. 391 p., ports., facsims. (Hebrew, Yiddish)

Alt Lesle (P) see Wloclawek

Amdur (P) see Indura

Amshinov (Mszczonow) (P) see under Zyrardow

Andrychow (P) see under Wadowice

Annopol (P). *Rachov-Annopol; pirkei edut ve-zikaron* [Rachov-Annopol; testimony and remembrance*]. Ed.: Shmuel Nitzan. Israel, Rachov/Annopol and Surrounding Region Society, 1978. 80, 544 p., illus. (Hebrew, Yiddish, English)

Antopol (P). *Antopol (Antepolie); sefer yizkor* [Antopol (Antepolie) yizkor book*]. Ed.: Benzion H. Ayalon. Tel Aviv, Antopol Societies in Israel and America, 1972. 11, 754, 170 p., illus. (Hebrew, Yiddish, English)

Antopol (P). *Antopol (5400–5702); mi-toldoteha shel kehila ahat be-Polesie.* [Antopol, 1648–1942; from the history of one Jewish community in Polesie]. Ed.: Yosef. Tel Aviv, 5727 [1966/67]. 164 p., illus. (Hebrew)

Apt (P) see Opatow

Augustow (P). *Sefer yizkor le-kehilat Augustow ve-ha-seviva* [Memorial book of the community of Augustow and vicinity]. Ed.: J. Alexandroni. Tel Aviv, Association of Former Residents of Augustow and Vicinity, 1966. 549 p., ports. (Hebrew, Yiddish)

Auschwitz (P) see Oswiecim

Baia Mare (R) see Nagybanya

Baklerove (Bakalarzewo) (P) see under Suwalki

Balin (U) see under Kamenets-Podolskiy

Balmazujvaros (H) see under Debrecen

Baranovka (U) see Novograd-Volynskiy

Baranow (P). *Sefer yizkor Baranow* [A memorial to the Jewish community of Baranow*]. Ed.: N. Blumenthal. Jerusalem, Yad Vashem, 1964. xvi, 236 p., ports., tabs., facsims. (Hebrew, Yiddish, English)

Baranowicze (P). *Baranovitz; sefer zikaron* [Baranovitz, memorial book]. Tel Aviv, Association of Former Residents of Baranovitz in Israel, 1953. vi, 668 p., ports., map, facsims. (Hebrew, Yiddish)

Barylow (P) see under Radziechow

Baytsh (P) see Biecz

Beclean (Betlen) (R) see under Des

Bedzin (P). *Pinkas Bendin* [Pinkas Bendin; a memorial to the Jewish community of Bendin*]. Ed.: A. Sh. Stein. Tel Aviv, Association of Former Residents of Bedzin in Israel, 1959. 431 p., ports. (Hebrew, Yiddish)

Bedzin (P) see also under Piotrkow Trybunalski

Belchatow (P). *Belchatow yizker-bukh* [Belchatow memorial book]. Buenos Aires, Association of Polish Jews in Argentine, 1951. 511 p., ports., map (Yiddish)

Beligrod (P) see under Lesko

Belz (P). *Belz; sefer zikaron* [Belz memorial book]. Ed.: Yosef Rubin. Tel Aviv, Belz Societies in Israel and America, 1974. 559 p., illus. (Hebrew, Yiddish)

Bendery (R). *Kehilat Bendery; sefer zikaron* [Yizkor book of our birthplace Bendery*]. Ed.: M. Tamari. Tel Aviv, Bendery Societies in Israel and the United States, 1975. 446, 42 p., illus. (Hebrew, Yiddish, English)

Bendin (P) see Bedzin

Beresteczko (R). *Hayta ayara . . . sefer zikaron le-kehilat Beresteczko . . . ve-ha-seviva* [There was a town . . . memorial book of Beresteczko . . . and vicinity]. Ed.: M. Singer. Haifa, Association of Former Residents of Beresteczko in Israel, 1961. 555 p., ports., map, facsims. (Hebrew, Yiddish)

Bereza-Kartuska (P) see under Pruzana

Berezno (P). *Mayn shtetele Berezne* [My town Berezne]. [By] G. Bigil. Tel Aviv, Berezner Society in Israel, 1954. 182 p., ports., map (Hebrew, Yiddish)

Berezo (C) see under Postyen

Bershad (U). *Be-tsel ayara* [Bershad*]. [By] Nahman Huberman. Jerusalem, Encyclopedia of the Jewish Diaspora, 1956. 247 p., port. (Hebrew)

Berzhan (P) see Brzezany

Bessarabia (R). *Al admat Bessarabia; divrei mehkar, zikhronot, reshimot, teudot ve-divrei safrut le-kviat ha-dmut shel yahaduta* [Upon the land of Bessarabia; studies, memoirs, articles, documents and essays depicting its image]. Ed.: K. A. Bertini. Tel Aviv, United Assoc. of Former Residents of Bessarabia, 1959. 2 vols.: 266, 213 p., ports. (Hebrew)

Bessarabia (R). *Bessarabia ha-yehudit be-ma'aroteha; ben shtei milhamot ha-olam 1914–1940* [The Jews in Bessarabia; between the world wars 1914–1940*]. [By] David Vinitzky. Jerusalem–Tel Aviv, The Zionist Library, Gvilei Bessarabia, 1973. 2 vols.: 719 p., illus. (Hebrew)

Bessarabia (R). *Pirkei Bessarabia; measef le-avara shel yahadut Bessarabia* [Chapters from the history of Bessarabian Jewry]. Eds.: L. Kupferstein and Y. Koren. Tel Aviv, "Netiv," 1952. 140 p., ports. (Hebrew)

Bessarabia (R). *Yahadut Bessarabia* [The Jewry of Bessarabia]. Eds.: K. A. Bertini et al. Jerusalem, The Encyclopaedia of the Jewish Diaspora, 1971. 986 columns, ports., maps (Hebrew)

Betlen (R) see under Des

Biala Podlaska (P). *Sefer Biala Podlaska* [Book of Biala Podlaska]. Ed.: M.J. Feigenbaum. Tel Aviv, Kupat Gmilut Hesed of the Community of Biala Podlaska, 1961. 501 p., ports., facsims. (Hebrew, Yiddish)

Biala Rawska (P). *Sefer yizkor le-kedoshei Biala Rawska.* [Memorial book to the martyrs of Biala Rawska]. Eds.: Eliyahu Freudenreich and Arye Yaakobovits. Tel Aviv, Biala Rawska Societies in Israel and the Diaspora, 1972. 255 p., illus. (Hebrew, Yiddish)

Bialystok (P). *Bialystok; bilder album . . .* [Bialystok; photo album . . . *]. Ed.: D. Sohn. New York, Bialystoker Album Committee, 1951. 386 p. (Yiddish, English)

Bialystok (P). *Der Bialystoker yizker-bukh* [The Bialystoker memorial book*]. Ed.: I. Shmulewitz. New York, Bialystoker Center, 1982. xi, 396, 205, x p., ports., illus. (Yiddish, English)

Bialystok (P). *Pinkas Bialystok; grunt-materialn tsu der geshikhte fun di yidn in Bialystok biz nokh der ershter velt-milkhome* [Pinkos Bialystok (the chronicle of Bialystok); basic material for the history of the Jews in Bialystok until the period after the First World War*]. Ed.: Yudl Mark. New York, Bialystok Jewish Historical Association, 1949–50. 2 vols. (Yiddish)

Biecz (P). *Sefer zikaron le-kedoshei ayaratenu Biecz* [Memorial book of the martyrs of Biecz]. Ed.: P. Wagshal. Ramat Gan, Association of Former Residents of Biecz and Vicinity in Israel, 1960. 243 p., ports. (Hebrew, Yiddish)

Bielica (P). *Pinkas Bielica* [Book of Belitzah-Bielica*]. Ed.: L. Losh. Tel Aviv, Former Residents of Bielica in Israel and the USA, 1968. 511 p., ports. map, facsims. (Hebrew, Yiddish, English)

Bielsko-Biala (P). *Bielitz-Biala (Bielsko-Biala); pirkei avar* [chapters from the past]. [By] Elijahu Miron. Israel, 1973. 182 p., illus. (Hebrew, German)

Bielsk-Podlaski (P). *Bielsk-Podlaski; sefer yizkor* . . . [Bielsk-Podliask; book in the holy memory of the Bielsk-Podliask Jews*]. Ed.: H. Rabin. Tel Aviv, Bielsk Societies in Israel and the United States, 1975. 554, 44 p., illus. (Hebrew, Yiddish, English)

Biezun (P). *Sefer ha-zikaron le-kedoshei Biezun* [Memorial book of the martyrs of Biezun]. Tel Aviv, Former Residents of Biezun, 1956. 186 p., ports. (Hebrew, Yiddish)

Bikovsk (Bukowsko) (P) see under Sanok

Bilgoraj (P). *Bilgoraj yizkor-bukh* [Bilgoraj memorial book]. [By] Moshe Teitlboym. Jerusalem, 1955. 243 p., illus. (Yiddish)

Bilgoraj (P). *Khurbn Bilgoraj* [Destruction of Bigoraj]. Ed.: A. Kronenberg. Tel Aviv, 1956. x, 365 p., ports. (Yiddish)

Bisk (P) see Busk

Bitolj (Y) see Monastir

Bitshutsh (P) see Buczacz

Bivolari (R). *Ayaratenu Bivolari* [Our town Bivolari]. Eds.: Moscu Abramovici et al. Haifa, Bivolari Immigrants Organization in Israel, 1981. 160, 37 p., illus. (Hebrew, Romanian, English)

Bledow (P) see under Mogielnica

Bobrka (P). *Le-zekher kehilat Bobrka u-benoteha* [Boiberke memorial book*]. Ed.: Sh. Kallay. Jerusalem, Association of Former Residents of Bobrka and Vicinity, 1964. 218, 38 p., ports., facsims. (Hebrew, Yiddish, English)

Bobruisk (B). *Bobruisk; sefer zikaron le-kehilat Bobruisk u-benoteha* [Memorial book of the community of Bobruisk and its surroundings]. Ed.: Y. Slutski. Tel Aviv, Former Residents of Bobruisk in Israel and the USA, 1967. 2 vols.: 871 p., ports., map, facsims. (Hebrew, Yiddish)

Boiberik (P) see Bobrka

Bolechow (P). *Sefer ha-zikaron le-kedoshei Bolechow* [Memorial book of the martyrs of Bolechow]. Ed.: Y. Eshel. Association of Former Residents of Bolechow in Israel, 1957. 352 p., ports. (Hebrew, Yiddish)

Bolimow (P) see under Lowicz

Boremel (P) see under Beresteczko

Borszczow (P). *Sefer Borszczow* [The book of Borstchoff*]. Ed.: N. Blumenthal. Tel Aviv, Association of Former Residents of Borszczow in Israel, 1960. 341 p., ports, facsims. (Hebrew, Yiddish)

Boryslaw (P) see under Drohobycz

Bransk (P) *Bransk; sefer ha-zikaron*. [Brainsk; book of memories*]. [By] A. Trus and J. Cohen. New York, Brainsker Relief Committee of New York, 1948. 440 p., ports., facsims. (Yiddish)

Bratislava (Pozsony) (C) see under Various (Miscellany) *Arim ve-imahot be-yisrael*, v. 7

Brest Litovsk (P) see Brzesc nad Bugiem

Brezova nad Bradlom (Berezo) (C) see under Postyen

Briceni (R) see Brichany

Brichany (R). *Brichan; Bricheni ha-yehudit be-mahatsit ha-mea ha-aharona* [Brichany; its Jewry in the first half of our century]. Eds.: Y. Amizur et al. Tel Aviv, Former Residents of Brichany, 1964. 296 p., ports., map (Hebrew)

Brichevo (R). *Pinkas Brichevo* [Memorial book of Brichevo]. Ed.: K. A. Bertini. Tel Aviv, Former Residents of Brichevo (Bessarabia) in Israel, 1970. 531 p., ports., map, facsims. (Hebrew, Yiddish)

Briegel (P) see Brzesko

Brisk (P) see Brzesc nad Bugiem

Brisk Kuyavsk (Brzesc Kujawski) (P) see under Wloclawek

Brody (P) see under Various (Miscellany) *Arim ve-imahot be-yisrael*, v. 6

Broszniow (P) see under Rozniatow

Brzesc Kujawski (P) see under Wloclawek

Brzesc nad Bugiem (P). *Brisk de-Lita* [Brest Lit[ovsk] volume*]. Ed.: E. Steinman. Jerusalem, The Encyclopaedia of the Jewish Diaspora, 1954. 647 p., ports., map (Hebrew)

Brzesko (P). *Sefer yizkor shel kehilat Briegel-Brzesko ve-ha-seviva* [Memorial book of Briegel-Brzesko and vicinity]. Eds.: Hayim Teller, Liber Brenner (Yiddish). Ramat-Gan, 1980. 267 p., illus. (Hebrew, Yiddish)

Brzezany (P). *Brzezany, Narajow ve-ha-seviva; toldot kehilot she-nehrevu* [Brzezany memorial book*]. Ed.: Menachem Katz. Haifa, Brzezany-Narajow Societies in Israel and the United States, 1978. 28, 473 p., illus. (Hebrew, Yiddish, English)

Brzeziny (P). *Bzhezhin yizker-bukh.* [Brzeziny memorial book*]. Eds.: A. Alperin and N. Summer. New York, Brzeziner Book Committee, 1961. 288 p., ports. (Yiddish)

Brzeznica (P) see under Radomsko

Buchach (P) see Buczacz

Buczacz (P). *Sefer Buczacz; matsevet zikaron le-kehila kedosha* [Book of Buczacz; in memory of a martyred community]. Ed.: I. Kahan. Tel Aviv, Am Oved, 1956. 302 p., ports., facsims. (Hebrew)

Budapest (H) see under *Arim ve-imahot be-yisrael, v. 1*

Budzanow (P). *Sefer Budzanow* [Book of Budzanow*]. Ed.: J. Siegelman. Haifa, Former Residents of Budzanow in Israel, 1968. 319 p., ports., maps, facsims. (Hebrew, Yiddish, English)

Bukaczowce (P) see under Rohatyn

Bukowsko (P) see under Sanok

Bulgaria. *Yahadut Bulgaria* [The Jewry of Bulgaria]. Eds.: A. Romano et al. Jerusalem, The Encyclopaedia of the Jewish Diaspora, 1967. 1018 columns, ports., maps, facsims. (Hebrew)

Bursztyn (P). *Sefer Bursztyn* [Book of Bursztyn]. Ed.: S. Kanc. Jerusalem, The Encyclopaedia of the Jewish Diaspora, 1960. 426 p., ports., facsims. (Hebrew, Yiddish)

Busk (P). *Sefer Busk; le-zekher ha-kehila she-harva* [Busk; in memory of our community*]. Ed.: A. Shayari. Haifa, Busker Organization in Israel, 1965. 293 p., ports., facsims. (Hebrew, Yiddish, English, Polish)

Bychawa (P). *Bychawa; sefer zikaron* [Bychawa; a memorial to the Jewish community of Bychawa Lubelska*]. Ed.: J. Adini. Bychawa Organization in Israel, 1968. 636 p., ports., map, facsims. (Hebrew, Yiddish)

Byten (P). *Pinkas Byten* [Book of Byten]. Ed.: D. Abramowich and M. W. Bernstein. Buenos Aires, Former Residents of Byten in Argentina, 1954. 605 p., map, facsims. (Yiddish)

Cakovec (Y). *Megilat ha-shoa shel kehilat kodesh Cakovec* [Holocaust scroll of the holy community of Cakovec]. [By] Moshe Etz-Hayyim (Tibor Grunwald). Tel Aviv, 1977. 182, 12 p., illus. (Hebrew, Serbo-Croatian)

Calarasi (R) see Kalarash

Capresti (R) see Kapreshty

Carpatho-Ruthenia (C) see Karpatalja

Cernauti (Czernowitz) (R) see under Various (Miscellany) *Arim ve-imahot be-yisrael*, v. 4.

Charsznica (P) see under Miechow

Chelm (P). *Sefer ha-zikaron le-kehilat Chelm; 40 shana le-hurbana* [Yizkor book in memory of Chelem*]. Ed.: Sh. Kanc. Tel Aviv, Chelm Society in Israel and the U.S., [1980/81]. 828 columns, illus. (Hebrew, Yiddish)

Chelm (P). *Yizker-bukh Chelm* [Commemoration book Chelm*]. Ed.: M. Bakalczuk-Felin. Johannesburg, Former Residents of Chelm, 1954. 731 p., ports., facsims. (Yiddish)

Chernovtsy (Czernowitz) (R) see under Various (Miscellany) *Arim ve-imahot be-yisrael*, v. 4

Chervonoarmeisk (P) see Radziwillow

Chmielnik (P) *Pinkas Chmielnik* [Memorial book of Chmielnik]. Tel Aviv, Former Residents of Chmielnik in Israel, 1960. 1299 columns, ports., facsims. (Hebrew, Yiddish)

Chodecz (P) see under Wloclawek

Cholojow (P) see under Radziechow

Chorostkow (P). *Sefer Chorostkow* [Chorostkow book*]. Ed.: D. Shtokfish. Tel Aviv, Committee of Former Residents of Chorostkow in Israel, 1968. 418 p., ports., facsims. (Hebrew, Yiddish)

Chorzele (P). *Sefer zikaron le-kehilat Chorzel* [Memorial book of the community of Chorzel]. Ed.: L. Losh. Tel Aviv, Association of Former Residents of Chorzele in Israel, 1967. 272 p., ports., facsims. (Hebrew, Yiddish)

Chrzanow (P). *Sefer Chrzanow.* [The book of Chrzanow]. [By] Mordecai Bakhner. Regensburg, 1948. xiii, 377 p. (Yiddish)

Ciechanow (P). *Yizker-bukh fun der Tshekhanover yidisher kehile; Sefer yizkor le-kehilat Ciechanow* [Memorial book of the community of Ciechanow]. Ed.: A. W. Yassni. Tel Aviv, Former Residents of Ciechanow in Israel and in the Diaspora, 1962. 535 p., ports. (Hebrew, Yiddish)

Ciechanowiec (P). *Ciechanowiec; mehoz Bialystok, sefer edut ve-zikaron* [Ciechanoviec-Bialystok district; memorial and records*]. Ed.: E. Leoni. Tel Aviv, The Ciechanovitzer Immigrant Assoc. in Israel and the USA, 1964. 936, 78 p., ports., facsims. (Hebrew, Yiddish, English)

Ciechocinek (P) see under Wloclawek

Cieszanow (P). *Sefer zikaron le-kehila kedosha Cieszanow* [Memorial book of the martyred community Cieszanow]. Ed.: D. Ravid. Tel Aviv, Former Residents of Cieszanow in Israel, 1970. 331 p., ports. (Hebrew, Yiddish)

Cluj (R) see Kolozsvar

Cmielow (P) see under Ostrowiec

Cracow (P) see Krakow

Csaktornya (Y) see Cakovec

Csenger (H). *Sefer yizkor le-kedoshei Csenger, Porcsalma ve-ha-seviva* [Memorial book of the martyrs of Csenger, Porcsalma and vicinity]. [By] Sh. Friedmann. Tel Aviv, 1966. 108, 60 p., ports., facsims. (Hebrew, Hungarian)

Czarny Dunajec (P) see under Nowy Targ

Czerbin (P) see under Ostroleka

Czernowitz (R) see under Various (Miscellany) *Arim ve-imahot be-yisrael*, v. 4

Czestochowa (P). *Sefer Tshenstochov* [Memorial book of Czestochow]. Ed.: M. Shuzman. Jerusalem, The Encyclopaedia of the Jewish Diaspora, 1967–68. 2 vols., ports., (Hebrew, Yiddish)

Czestochowa (P). *Tshenstokhover landsmanshaft in Montreal* [Czenstochover landsmanschaft in Montreal*]. Ed.: B. Orenstein. Montreal, The Czenstochover Society in Montreal, 1966. 349, [28] p., ports. (Yiddish)

Czestochowa (P). *Tshenstokhov; nayer tsugob-material tsum bukh "Tshenstokhover yidn"* [Czenstochow; a new supplement to the book "Czenstochover Yidn"*]. Ed.: S. D. Singer. New York, United Relief Committee in New York, 1958. 336, iv p., ports. (Yiddish)

Czestochowa (P). *Tshenstokhover yidn* [The Jews of Czestochowa]. Ed.: R. Mahler. New York, United Czestochower Relief Committee and Ladies Auxiliary, 1947. cxliv, 404 p., ports., fascims. (Yiddish)

Czortkow (P). *Sefer yizkor le-hantsahat kedoshei kehilat Czortkow* [Memorial book of Czortkow*]. Ed.: Y. Austri-Dunn. Tel Aviv, Haifa, Former Residents of Czortkow in Israel, 1967. 435, 36 p., ports., map, facsims. (Hebrew, Yiddish, English)

Czyzewo (P). *Sefer zikaron Czyzewo* [Memorial book Tshijewo*]. Ed.: Sh. Kanc. Tel Aviv, Former Residents of Tshizhevo in Israel and the USA, 1961. 1,206 columns, ports., facsims. (Hebrew, Yiddish)

Dabrowa Gornicza (P). *Sefer kehilat yehudei Dabrowa Gornicza ve-hurbana* [Memorial book of Dombrawa Gornitza]. Eds.: N. Gelbart et al. Tel Aviv, Former Residents of Dombrowa Gornitza, 1971. 696 p., ports., facsims. (Hebrew, Yiddish)

Dabrowica (P). *Sefer Dombrovitsa* [Book of Dabrowica]. Ed.: L. Losh. Tel Aviv, Association of Former Residents of Dabrowica in Israel, 1964. 928 p., ports., maps, facsims. (Hebrew, Yiddish)

Daugavpils (LV). *Le-zekher kehilat Dvinsk* [In memory of the community of Dvinsk]. Haifa, [1975]. 63 p., illus. (Hebrew)

Daugieliszki (P) see under Swieciany

David Horodok (P) see Dawidgrodek

Dawidgrodek (P). *Sefer zikaron Dawidgrodek* [Memorial book of Dawidgrodek]. Eds.: Y. Idan et al. Tel Aviv, Former Residents of Dawidgrodek in Israel, [195-]. 487 p., ports. (Hebrew, Yiddish)

Debica (P). *Sefer Dembits* [Book of Debica]. Ed.: D. Leibl. Tel Aviv, Association of Former Residents of Debica, 1960. 204 p., ports. (Hebrew, Yiddish)

Deblin (P). *Sefer Deblin-Modrzyc* [Demblin-Modrzyc book*]. Ed.: D. Shtokfish. Tel Aviv, Association of Former Residents of Demblin-Modrzyc, 1969. 694 p., ports., facsims. (Hebrew, Yiddish)

Debrecen (H) *Mea shana le-yehudei Debrecen; le-zekher kedoshei ha-kehila ve-yishuvei ha-seviva* [Hundred years of Debrecen Jewry; in memory of the martyrs of Debrecen and vicinity]. [By] M. E. Gonda. Tel Aviv, Committee for Commemoration of the Debrecen Jewry, 1970. 264, 409 p., ports., facsims. (Hebrew, Hungarian)

Dej (R) see Des

Delatycze (P) see under Lubcza

Dembits (P) see Debica

Demblin (P) see Deblin

Derecske (H) see under Debrecen

Dereczyn (P). *Sefer Dereczyn* [Deretchin memorial book*]. Tel Aviv, Deretchiners Societies in Israel and U.S.A., [196-]. 494 p., ports., facsims. (Hebrew, Yiddish)

Derewno (P) see under Rubiezewicze; Stolpce

Des (R). *Des* . . . , *Bethlen, Magyarlapos, Retteg, Nagyilonda es kornyeke* [. . . and vicinity]. Ed.:
Z. Singer. Tel Aviv, Former Residents of Des. 2 vols.: 683 p., ports., facsims. (Hungarian)

Dibetsk (Dubiecko) (P) see under Dynow (*Khurbn Dynow*)

Dieveniskes (P) see Dziewieniszki

Disna (P) see Dzisna

Divenishok (P) see Dziewieniszki

Dmytrow (P) see under Radziechow

Dnepropetrovsk (U) see Yekaterinoslav

Dobromil (P). *Sefer zikaron le-zekher Dobromil* [Memorial book Dobromil*]. Ed.: M. Gelbart. Tel Aviv, The Dobromiler Society in New York and the Dobromiler Organization in Israel, 1964. 389, 138 p., ports., facsims. (Hebrew, Yiddish, English)

Dobryn (P) see under Wloclawek

Dobrzyn (P). *Ayarati; sefer zikaron le-ayarot Dobrzyn-Golub* [My town; in memory of the communities Dobrzyn-Gollob*]. Ed.: M. Harpaz. [Tel Aviv], Association of Former Residents of
Dobrzyn-Golub, 1969. 459, 29 p., ports., facsims. (Hebrew, Yiddish, English)

Dobrzyn (P). *Yizker bletlekh* [Our village*]. [By] Shmuel Russak. Tel Aviv, 1972. 6, 90 p.,
illus. (Yiddish, English)

Dokszyce (P). *Sefer yizkor Dokszyce-Parafianow* [*Dokszyc-Parafianow book**]. Ed.: D. Shtokfish.
Tel Aviv, Assoc. of Former Residents of Dokszyce-Parafianow in Israel, 1970. 350 p.,
ports., facsims. (Hebrew, Yiddish)

Dombrava Gornitsha (P) see Dabrowa Gornicza

Dombrovitsa (P) see Dabrowica

Drodzyn (P) see under Stolin

Drohiczyn nad Bugiem (P). *Sefer Drohiczyn* [Drohiczyn book]. Ed.: David Shtokfish. Tel
Aviv, 1969. 576, 67 p., illus. (Hebrew, Yiddish, English)

Drohiczyn Poleski (P). *Drohiczyn; finf hundert yor yidish lebn* [Memorial book Drohichyn*].
Ed.: D. B. Warshawsky. Chicago, Book-Committee Drohichyn, 1958. viii, 424 p.,
ports., map, facsims. (Yiddish)

Drohobycz (P). *Sefer zikaron le-Drohobycz, Boryslaw ve-ha-seviva* [Memorial to the Jews of
Drohobycz, Boryslaw and surroundings*]. Ed.: N. M. Gelber. Tel Aviv, Assoc. of
Former Residents of Drohobycz, Boryslaw and Surroundings, 1959. 224 p., ports.
(Hebrew, Yiddish)

Droshkopol (P) see Druzkopol

Druja (P). *Sefer Druja ve-kehilot Miory, Drujsk, ve-Leonpol* [The book of Druya and the
communities of Miory, Druysk and Leonpol*]. Ed.: Mordekhai Neishtat. Tel Aviv,
Druja and Surrounding Region Society, 1973. 225 p., illus. (Hebrew, Yiddish)

Druja (P) see also under Glebokie

Drujsk (P) see under Druja (*Sefer Druja*)

Druzkopol (P). *Ayaratenu Druzkopol* [Our town Droshkopol]. Eds.: Y. Shiloni et al.
[Haifa], Former Residents of Droshkopol in Israel, 1957. Ports. (Hebrew), mimeo.

Druzkopol (P). *Ayaratenu Druzkopol* [Our town Droshkopol]. [Haifa], [1956]. 108 p., ports.
(Hebrew), mimeo.

Druzkopol (P). *Di geshikhte fun mayn shtetele Druzkopol* [The story of my "stetele
Droshkopol"*]. [By] A. Boxer (Ben-Arjeh). Ed.: S. Eisenberg. Haifa, 1962. 108 p., ports.
(Yiddish), mimeo.

Dubiecko (P) see under Dynow (*Khurbn Dynow*)

Dubno (P). *Dubno; sefer zikaron* [Dubno; a memorial to the Jewish community of Dubno,
Wolyn*]. Ed.: Y. Adini. Tel Aviv, Dubno Organization in Israel, 1956. 752 columns,
ports., maps, facsims. (Hebrew, Yiddish)

Dubossary (R). *Dubossary; sefer zikaron* [Dubossary memorial book]. Ed.: Y. Rubin. Tel

Aviv, Association of Former Residents of Dubossary in America, Argentina and Israel, 1965. 377 p., ports., maps, music (Hebrew, Yiddish)

Dubrovitsa (P) see Dabrowica

Dukszty (P) see under Swieciany

Dumbraveny (R). *Sefer Dombroven; ner-zikaron le-moshava ha-haklait ha-yehudit ha-rishonah be-Bessarabia* [Dombroven book; memorial to the first Jewish agricultural colony in Bessarabia]. Ed.: Haim Toren. Jerusalem, Dombroven Societies in Israel and The Diaspora, 1974. 8, 252 p., illus. (Hebrew, Yiddish)

Dunajska Streda (C) see Dunaszerdahely

Dunaszerdahely (C). *Sefer zikaron le-kehilat Dunaszerdahely* [A memorial to the Jewish community of Dunaszerdahely (Dunajska Streda)*]. [By] Abraham (Alfred) Engel. Israel, Committee of Dunaszerdahely Emigrants, 1975. 429, 157 p., illus. (Hebrew, Hungarian)

Dunilowicze (P) see under Glebokie

Dvart (P) see Warta

Dvinsk (LV) see Daugavpils

Dynow (P). *Khurbn Dynow, Sonik, Dibetsk* [The destruction of Dynow, Sanok, Dubiecko]. [By] David Moritz. New York, [1949/50]. 156 p., illus. (Yiddish)

Dynow (P). *Sefer Dynow; sefer zikaron le-kedoshei kehilat Dynow she-nispu ba-shoa ha-natzit* [The memorial book of Jewish Dinov*]. Eds.: Yitzhak Kose, Moshe Rinat. Tel Aviv, Dynow Society, 1979. 324 p., illus., map (Hebrew, Yiddish)

Dzerzhinsk (B) see Koidanovo

Dzialoszyce (P). *Sefer yizkor shel kehilat Dzialoszyce ve-ha-seviva* [Yizkor book of the Jewish community in Dzialoszyce and surroundings*]. Tel Aviv, Hamenora, 1973. 44, 423 p., illus. (Hebrew, Yiddish, English)

Dziewieniszki (P). *Sefer Divenishok; yad vashem le-ayara yehudit* [Devenishki book; memorial book*]. Ed.: David Shtokfish. Israel, Divenishok Societies in Israel and the United States, 1977. 536 p., illus. (Hebrew, Yiddish)

Dzikow (P) see Tarnobrzeg

Dzisna (P). *Disna; sefer zikaron le-kehila* [Disna; memorial book of the community]. Eds.: A. Beilin et al. Tel Aviv, Former Residents of Disna in Israel and the USA, 1969. 227 p., ports., facsims. (Hebrew, Yiddish)

Edineti (R) see Yedintsy

Eger (H). *Yehudei Erlau* [The Jews of Eger]. Eds.: Arthur Abraham Ehrenfeld-Elkay, Tibor Meir Klein-Z'ira. Jerusalem, Eger Commemorative Committee, 1975. 64, 36, 100 p., illus. (Hebrew, Hungarian)

Ejszyszki (P) *Eishyshok, koroteha ve-hurbana* [Ejszyszki, its history and destruction]. Ed.: Sh. Barkeli. Jerusalem, Committee of the Survivors of Ejszyszki in Israel, 1960. 136 p., ports. (Hebrew, Yiddish)

Ekaterinoslav (U) see Yekaterinoslav

Erlau (H) see Eger

Falenica (P) see also under Otwock

Falenica (P). *Sefer Falenica* [Falenica book*]. Ed.: D. Shtokfish. Tel Aviv, Former Residents of Falenica in Israel, 1967. 478 p., ports., facsims. (Hebrew, Yiddish)

Fehergyarmat (H). *Ayaratenu le-she-avar Fehergyarmat* [Our former city Fehergyarmat]. [By] J. Blasz. Bnei Brak, 1965. 44, 52 p., ports., music, facsims. (Hebrew, Hungarian)

Felshtin (U). *Felshtin; zamlbukh lekoved tsum ondenk fun di Felshtiner kdoyshim* [Felshtin; collection in memory of the martyrs of Felshtin]. New York, First Felshtiner Progressive Benevolent Association, 1937. 670 p., illus. (Yiddish, English)

Filipow (P) see under Suwalki

Frampol (Lublin) (P). *Sefer Frampol* [Frampol book*]. Ed.: D. Shtokfish. Tel Aviv, [Book Committee], 1966. 414 p., ports. (Hebrew, Yiddish)

Frampol (Podolia) (U) see under Kamenets-Podolskiy

Gabin (P). *Gombin; dos lebn un umkum fun a yidish shtetl in Poyln* [Gombin; the life and destruction of a Jewish town in Poland*]. Eds.: Jack Zicklin et al. New York, Gombin Society in America, 1969. 228, 162 p., illus. (Yiddish, English)

Galicia (P). *Gedenkbukh Galicia* [Memorial book of Galicia]. Ed.: N. Zucker. Buenos Aires, "Zychronot" Publ., 1964. 334 p., ports., facsims. (Yiddish)

Galicia (P). *Pinkes Galicia* [Memorial book of Galicia]. Ed.: N. Zucker. Buenos Aires, Former Residents of Galicia in Argentina, 1945. 638 p., ports., (Yiddish)

Gargzdai (L). *Sefer Gorzd (Lita); ayara be-hayeha u-be-hilayona* [Gorzd book; a memorial to the Jewish community of Gorzd*]. Ed.: Yitzhak Alperovitz. Tel Aviv, The Gorzd Society, 1980. 79, 417 p., illus. (Hebrew, Yiddish, English)

Garwolin (P). *Garwolin yizker-bukh* [Garwolin memorial book]. Eds.: Moshe Zaltsman, Baruch Shein. Tel Aviv, New York, Garwolin Societies, 1972. 304 p., illus. (Hebrew, Yiddish)

Ger (P) see Gora Kalwaria

Gherla (R) see Szamosujvar

Glebokie (P). *Khurbn Glublok . . . Koziany* [The destruction of Glebokie . . . Koziany]. [By] M. and Z. Rajak. Buenos Aires, Former Residents' Association in Argentina, 1956. 426 p., ports. (Yiddish)

Glina (P) see Gliniany

Gliniany (P). *Kehilat Glina 1473–1943; toldoteha ve-hurbana* [The community of Glina 1473–1943; its history and destruction]. [By] Asher Korech. Jerusalem, 1950. 138 p., illus. (Hebrew)

Gliniany (P). *Khurbn Gliniane* [The tragic end of our Gliniany*]. New York, Emergency Relief Committee for Gliniany and Vicinity, 1946. [52] p. (Yiddish, English)

Gliniany (P). *Megiles Gline* [The book of Gline*]. Ed.: H. Halpern. New York, Former Residents of Gline, 1950. 307 p. (Yiddish)

Glinojeck (P). *Mayn shtetele Glinovyetsk; un di vayterdike vandlungen Plock-Wierzbnik, zikhroynes* [My town Glinojeck . . .]. [By] Shlomo Moshkovich. Paris, 1976. 335 p., illus. (Yiddish)

Glubok (P) see Glebokie

Glusk (B) see under Bobruisk, Slutsk

Gniewaszow (P). *Sefer Gniewaszow* [Memorial book Gniewashow*]. Ed.: D. Shtokfish. Tel Aviv, Association of Gniewashow in Israel and the Diaspora, 1971. 533, 19 p., ports. (Hebrew, Yiddish, English)

Golub (P) see under Dobrzyn (*Ayarati.*)

Gombin (P) see Gabin

Gomel (B) see under *Arim ve-imahot be-yisrael*, v. 2

Goniadz (P). *Sefer yizkor Goniadz* [Our hometown Goniondz*]. Eds.: J. Ben-Meir (Treshansky) and A. L. Fayans. Tel Aviv, The Committee of Goniondz Association in the USA and in Israel, 1960. 808, xix p., ports., maps (Hebrew, Yiddish, English)

Gora Kalwaria (P). *Megiles Ger*. Ed.: Gregorio Sapoznikow. Buenos Aires, Ger Societies in Argentina, Israel and the United States, 1975. 512 p., illus. (Yiddish)

Gorlice (P). *Sefer Gorlice; ha-kehila be-vinyana u-be-hurbana* [Gorlice book; the community at rise and fall*]. Ed.: M. Y. Bar-On. [Association of Former Residents of Gorlice and Vicinity in Israel], 1962. 338 p., ports., map, facsims. (Hebrew, Yiddish)

Gorodnitsa (U) see under Novograd-Volynskiy

Gorzd (L) see Gargzdai

Gostynin (P). *Pinkes Gostynin; yizkor bukh* [Pinkas Gostynin; book of Gostynin*]. Ed.: J. M.

Biderman. New York, Gostynin Memorial Book Committees, 1960. 358 p., ports. (Yiddish)

Goworowo (P). *Goworowo; sefer zikaron* [Govorowo memorial book*]. Eds.: A. Burstin and D. Kossovsky. Tel Aviv, The Govorover Societies in Israel, the USA and Canada, 1966. 496, xvi p., ports., facsims. (Hebrew, Yiddish, English)

Grabowiec (P). *Sefer zikaron le-kehilat Grabowiec* [Memorial book Grabowitz*]. Ed.: Shimon Kanc. Tel Aviv, Grabowiec Society, 1975. 432, 5, 26 p., illus. (Hebrew, Yiddish, English)

Grajewo (P). *Grayeve yizker-bukh* [Grajewo memorial book]. Ed.: Dr. G. Gorin. New York, United Grayever Relief Committee, 1950. 51, [38], 311 p., illus. (Yiddish, English)

Greece. *In Memoriam; hommage aux victimes juives des Nazis en Grèce*. 2nd. ed. Ed.: Michael Molho. Thessalonique, Communauté Israélite de Thessalonique, 1973. 469 p., illus. (French)

Greiding (P) see Grodek Jagiellonski

Gritsa (P) see Grojec

Grodek (near Bialystok) (P). *Sefer zikaron le-kehilat Horodok* [Horodok; in memory of the Jewish community*]. Ed.: M. Simon (Shemen). Tel Aviv. Associations of Former Residents of Grodek in Israel and Argentina, 1963. 142 p., ports., facsims. (Hebrew, Yiddish)

Grodek Jagiellonski (P). *Sefer Greiding* [Greiding book]. Ed.: Yehuda Margel. Tel Aviv, 1981 (Hebrew)

Grodno (P). *Grodno*. Ed.: Dov Rabin. Jerusalem, Grodno Society; The Encyclopaedia of the Jewish Diaspora, 1973. 744 p., illus. (Hebrew, Yiddish)

Grojec (P). *Megilat Gritse* [Megilat Gritze*]. Ed.: I. B. Alterman. Tel Aviv, Gritzer Association in Israel, 1955. iv, 408 p., ports. (Hebrew, Yiddish)

Gross Magendorf (Nagymagyar) (C) see under Dunaszerdahely

Grozovo (B) see under Slutsk

Gusiatyn (U) see Husiatyn (U)

Hajdunanas (H) see under Debrecen

Hajdusamson (H) see under Debrecen

Halmi (R). *Zikhron netsah li-kehilot ha-kedoshot Halmin-Turcz ve-ha-seviva asher nehrevu ba-shoa* [In memory of the communities of Halmin-Turcz and vicinity]. Ed.: Yehuda Shvartz. Tel Aviv, Halmin-Turcz and Vicinity Society, [1968]. 138 p., illus. (Hebrew)

Haydutsishok (Hoduciszki) (P) see under Swieciany

Hivniv (P) see Uhnow

Hlusk (Glusk) (B) see under Slutsk

Hoduciszki (P) see under Swieciany

Holojow (Cholojów) (P) see under Radziechow

Holszany (P). *Lebn un umkum fun Olshan* [The life and destruction of Olshan]. Tel Aviv, Former Residents of Olshan in Israel, 1965. 431, 136 p., ports., facsims. (Hebrew, Yiddish)

Holynka (P) see under Dereczyn

Homel (Gomel) (B) see under Various (Miscellany) *Arim ve-imahot be-yisrael*, v. 2

Horochow (P). *Sefer Horochow* [Horchiv memorial book*]. Ed.: Y. Kariv. Tel Aviv, Horchiv Committee in Israel, 1966. 357, 79 p., ports., map, facsims. (Hebrew, Yiddish, English)

Horodec (P). *Horodec; a geshikhte fun a shtetl, 1142–1942* [Horodec; history of a town, 1142–1942]. Ed.: A. Ben-Ezra. New York, "Horodetz" Book Committee, 1949. 238 p., ports., map, facsims. (Yiddish)

Horodenka (P). *Sefer Horodenka* [The book of Horodenka]. Ed.: Sh. Meltzer. Tel Aviv, Former Residents of Horodenka and Vicinity in Israel and the USA, 1963. 425, vii p., ports., maps, facsims. (Hebrew, Yiddish)

Horodlo (P). *Di kehile fun Horodlo; yizker-bukh* . . . [The community of Horodlo; memorial book . . .]. Ed.: Y. Ch. Zawidowitch. Tel Aviv, Former Residents of Horodlo in Israel, 1962. 324 p., ports., facsims. (Yiddish)

Horodlo (P). *Kehilat Horodlo; sefer zikaron le-kedoshei Horodlo (Polin) ve-li-kedoshei ha-kefarin ha-semukhim* [The community of Horodlo; memorial book . . .]. Ed.: Y. Ch. Zawidowitch. Tel Aviv, Former Residents of Horodlo in Israel, 1959. 260 p., ports., facsims. (Hebrew)

Horodno (P) see under Stolin

Horodok (P) see Grodek (near Bialystok)

Horyngrod (P) see under Tuczyn

Hoszcza (P). *Hoshch; sefer zikaron* [Hoshtch-Wolyn; in memory of the Jewish community*]. Eds.: B. H. Ayalon-Baranicka and A. Yaron-Kritzmar. Tel Aviv, Former Residents of Hoshtch in Israel, 1957. 269 p., ports., facsims. (Hebrew)

Hoszcza (P). *Sefer Hoshtch; yizker-bukh* [The book of Hosht—in memoriam*]. Ed.: R. Fink. New York and Tel Aviv, Society of Hosht, 1957. xvi, 294 p., ports., facsims. (Yiddish)

Hotin (R) see Khotin

Hrubieszow (P). *Pinkas Hrubieszow* [Memorial book of Hrubieshov*]. Ed.: B. Kaplinsky. Tel Aviv, Hrubieshov Associations in Israel and the USA, 1962. 811, xviii columns, ports. (Hebrew, Yiddish, English, Polish)

Husiatyn (U). *Husiatyn; Podoler Gubernye* [Husiatyn; Podolia-Ukraine*]. Ed.: B. Diamond. New York, Former Residents of Husiatyn in America, 1968. 146, [40], 123 p., ports. (Yiddish, English)

Husiatyn (P). *Kehilatiyim: Husiatyn ve-Kopyczynce* [Two communities: Husiatyn and Kopyczynce*]. [By] Abraham Backer. Tel Aviv, Husiatyn Society, 1977. 286 p., illus. (Hebrew, Yiddish)

Husiatyn (P). *Mibet aba; pirkei zikhronot mi-yemei yaldut be-ayarat moladeti Husiatyn* [From my parents' home; memorial chapter . . .] [By] A.Y. Avitov (Birnbojm). Tel Aviv, The Author, 1965, 155 p., ports. (Hebrew)

Husiatyn (P). *Sefer zikaron Husiatyn ve-ha-seviva* [Memorial book of Husiatyn and the surrounding region]. Ed.: Avraham Beker. Tel Aviv, Husiatyn-Galicia Society, 1976. 499 p., illus. (Hebrew, Yiddish)

Iklad (R) see under Szamosujvar

Ileanda (Nagyilonda) (R) see under Des

Ilja (P). *Kehilat Ilja; pirkei hayim ve-hashmada* [The community of Ilja; chapters of life and destruction]. Ed.: A. Kopilevitz. [Tel Aviv], Association of Former Residents of Ilja in Israel, 1962. 466 p., ports., facsims. (Hebrew, Yiddish)

Indura (P). *Amdur, mayn geboyrn-shtetl* [Amdur, my hometown]. [By] Iedidio Efron. Buenos Aires, 1973. 252, 33 p., illus. (Yiddish, Spanish)

Istrik (Ustrzyki Dolne) (P) see under Lesko

Ivano-Frankovsk (Stanislawow) (P) see under Various (Miscellany) *Arim ve-imahot be-yisrael*, v. 5

Iwacewicze (P) see under Byten

Iwie (P). *Sefer zikaron le-kehilat Iwie* [Ivie; in memory of the Jewish community*]. Ed.: M. Kaganovich. Tel Aviv, Association of Former Residents of Ivie in Israel and "United Ivier Relief" in America, 1968. 738 p., ports., map (Hebrew, Yiddish)

Iwieniec (P). *Sefer Iwieniec, Kamien ve-ha-seviva; sefer zikaron* [The memorial book of Iwieniec, Kamien, and the surrounding region]. Tel Aviv, Iwieniec Societies in Israel and the Diaspora, 1973. 484 p., illus. (Hebrew, Yiddish)

Jablonka (P) see under Nowy Targ

Jadow (P). *Sefer Jadow* [The book of Jadow*]. Ed.: A. W. Jassni. Jerusalem, The Encyclopaedia of the Jewish Diaspora, 1966. 472, xxiii p., ports. (Hebrew, Yiddish, English)

Janova (L) see Jonava

Janow (near Pinsk) (P). *Janow al yad Pinsk; sefer zikaron* [Janow near Pinsk; memorial book*]. Ed.: M. Nadav (Katzikowski). Jerusalem, Assoc. of Former Residents of Janow near Pinsk in Israel, 1969. 420 p., ports. (Hebrew, Yiddish)

Janow (near Trembowla) (P) see under Budzanow, Trembowla

Jaroslaw (P). *Sefer Jaroslaw* [Jaroslav book*]. Ed.: Yitzhak Alperowitz. Tel Aviv, Jarosaw Society, 1978. 371, 28 p., illus. (Hebrew, Yiddish, English)

Jaslo (P). *Toldot yehudei Jaslo; me-reshit hityashvutam be-tokh ha-ir ad yemei ha-hurban al yedei ha-natzim* . . . [History of the Jews of Jaslo . . .]. [By] Moshe Natan Even-Hayim. Tel Aviv, Jaslo Society, 1953. 360 p., map, ports., illus. (Hebrew)

Jaworow (P). *"Judenstadt Jaworow;" der umkum fun Jaworower idn* [Swastika over Jaworow*]. [By] S. Druck. New York, First Jaworower Indep. Ass'n, 1950. 69, iv, 35 p., ports. (Yiddish, English)

Jaworow (P). *Matsevet zikaron le-kehilat Jaworow ve-ha-seviva* [Monument to the community of Jaworow and the surrounding region]. Ed.: Michael Bar-Lev. Haifa, Jaworow Societies in Israel and the United States, 1979. 252 p., illus. (Hebrew, Yiddish)

Jedrzejow (P). *Sefer ha-zikaron le-yehudei Jedrzejow* [Memorial book of the Jews of Jedrzejow]. Ed.: Sh. D. Yerushalmi. Tel Aviv, Former Residents of Jedrzejow in Israel, 1965. 490 p., ports., facsims. (Hebrew, Yiddish)

Jedwabne (P). *Sefer Jedwabne; historiya ve-zikaron* [Yedwabne; history and memorial book*]. Eds.: Julius L. Baker and Jacob L. Baker; assisted by Moshe Tzinovitz. Jerusalem–New York, The Yedwabner Societies in Israel and in the United States of America, 1980. 121, 110 p., illus. (Hebrew, Yiddish, English)

Jeremicze (P) see under Turzec

Jezierna (P). *Sefer Jezierna* [Memorial book of Jezierna*]. Ed.: J. Sigelman. Haifa, Committee of Former Residents of Jezierna in Israel, 1971. 354 p., ports. (Hebrew, Yiddish)

Jezierzany (P). *Sefer Ozieran ve-ha-seviva* [Memorial book; Jezierzany and surroundings*]. Ed.: M. A. Tenenblatt. Jerusalem, The Encyclopaedia of the Jewish Diaspora. 498 columns, ports. (Hebrew, Yiddish)

Jeznas (L). *Le-zikhram shel kedoshei kehilat Jezna she-nispu bi-shnat 1941* [Memorial book of the martyrs of Jeznas who perished in 1941]. Ed.: D. Aloni. Jerusalem, Former Residents of Jeznas in Israel, 1967. 105 p., ports., maps, facsims. (Hebrew), mimeo.

Jonava (L). *Yanove oyf di breges fun Vilye; tsum ondenk fun di khorev-gevorene yidishe kehile in Yanove* [Yizkor book in memory of the Jewish community of Yanova*]. Ed.: Shimeon Noy. Tel Aviv, Jonava Society, 1972. 35, 429 p., illus. (Yiddish, English)

Jordanow (P) see under Nowy Targ

Jozefow (P). *Sefer zikaron le-kehilat Jozefow ve-le-kedosheha* [Memorial book to the community of Jozefow and its martyrs]. Ed.: Azriel Omer-Lemer. Tel Aviv, Jozefow Societies in Israel and the U.S.A., 1975. 462 p., illus. (Hebrew, Yiddish)

Kadzidlo (P) see under Ostroleka

Kalarash (R). *Sefer Kalarash; le-hantsahat zikhram shel yehudei ha-ayara she-nehreva bi-yemei ha-shoa* [The book of Kalarash; in memory of the town's Jews, which was destroyed in the Holocaust]. Eds.: N. Tamir et al. Tel Aviv, 1966. 533 p., ports., facsims. (Hebrew, Yiddish)

Kalisz (P). *The Kalish book*. Ed.: I. M. Lask. Tel Aviv, The Societies of Former Residents of Kalish and the Vicinity in Israel and the USA, 1968. 327 p. (English)

Kalisz (P). *Sefer Kalish* [The Kalish book*]. Tel Aviv, The Israel-American Book Committee, 1964. Vol. 1.: 624 p., ports., facsims. Vol. II, 1968. 598 p. (Hebrew, Yiddish)

Kalusz (P). *Kalusz; hayeha ve-hurbana shel ha-kehila* [Kalusz; the life and destruction of the community]. Eds.: Shabtai Unger, Moshe Ettinger. Tel Aviv, Kalusz Society, 1980. 325, 330, 15 p., illus. (Hebrew, Yiddish, English)

Kaluszyn (P). *Sefer Kaluszyn; geheylikt der khorev gevorener kehile* [Memorial book of Kaluszyn]. Eds.: A. Shamri and Sh. Soroka. Tel Aviv, Former Residents of Kaluszyn in Israel, 1961. 545, [15] p., ports., facsims. (Yiddish)

Kalwaria (P) see under Wadowice

Kamenets-Litovsk (P) see Kamieniec Litewski

Kamenets-Podolskiy (U). *Kamenets-Podolsk u-sevivata* [Kamenets-Podolsk and its surroundings]. Eds.: A. Rosen, Ch. Sharig, Y. Bernstein. Tel Aviv, Association of Former Residents of Kamenets-Podolsk and Its Surroundings in Israel, 1965. 263 p., ports., facsims. (Hebrew)

Kamien (P) see under Iwieniec

Kamien Koszyrski (P). *Sefer ha-zikaron le-kehilat Kamien Koszyrski ve-ha-seviva . . .* [Kamin Koshirsky book; in memory of the Jewish community*]. Eds.: A. A. Stein et al. Tel Aviv, Former Residents of Kamin Koshirsky and Surroundings in Israel, 1965. 974 columns, ports. (Hebrew, Yiddish)

Kamieniec Litewski (P). *Sefer yizkor le-kehilot Kamenits de-Lita, Zastavye ve-ha-koloniyot* [Kamenetz Litovsk, Zastavye, and colonies memorial book*]. Eds.: Shmuel Eisenstadt and Mordechai Gelbart. Tel Aviv, Kamieniec and Zastavye Committees in Israel and the United States, 1970. 626, 185 p., illus., map (Hebrew, Yiddish, English)

Kamiensk (P) see under Radomsko

Kammeny Brod (U) see under Novograd-Volynskiy

Kapreshty (R). *Kapresht ayaratenu-undzer shtetele Kapresht; sefer zikaron le-kehila yehudit be-Bessarabia* [Kapresht, our village; memorial book for the Jewish community of Kapresht, Bessarabia*]. Eds.: M. Rishpy, Av. B. Yanowitz. Haifa, Kapresht Society in Israel, 1980. 496 p., map, illus. (Hebrew, Yiddish)

Kapulye (Kopyl) (B) see under Slutsk

Karcag (H). *Toldot kehilat Karcag ve-kehilot mehoz Nagykunsag* [History of the community of Karcag and the communities of the district of Nagykunsag]. [By] Moshe Hershko. Jerusalem, Karcag Society, 1977. 53, 219 p., illus. (Hebrew, Hungarian)

Karczew (P) see under Otwock

Karpatalja (region C). *Karpatorus* [Karpatorus*]. Ed.: Y. Erez. Jerusalem, The Encyclopaedia of the Jewish Diaspora, 1959. 582 columns, ports., facsims. (Hebrew)

Karpatalja (C). *Sefer zikhron kedoshim le-yehudei Karpatorus-Marmarosh* [Memorial book of the martyrs of Karpatorus-Marmarosh]. [By] Sh. Rosman. Rehovot, 1969. 643 p., ports. (Yiddish)

Kartuz-Bereze (Bereza Kartuska) (P) see under Pruzana

Kazimierz (P). *Pinkas Kuzmir* [Kazimierz—memorial book*]. Ed.: D. Shtokfish. Tel Aviv, Former Residents of Kazimierz in Israel and the Diaspora, 1970. 655 p., ports., facsims. (Hebrew, Yiddish)

Kedainiai (L). *Keydan; sefer zikaron* [Keidan memorial book*]. Ed.: Josef Chrust. Tel Aviv, Keidan Societies in Israel, South America, and the United States, 1977. 39, 313 p., illus. (Hebrew, Yiddish, English)

Kelts (P) see Kielce

Keydan (L) see Kedainiai

Khmelnitskii (U) see Proskurov

Kholm (P) see Chelm

Khotin (R). *Sefer kehilat Khotin (Bessarabia)* [The book of the community of Khotin (Bessarabia)]. Ed.: Shlomo Shitnovitzer. Tel Aviv, Khotin (Bessarabia) Society, 1974. 333 p., illus. (Yiddish)

Khozhel (P) see Chorzele

Kielce (P). *Sefer Kielce; toldot kehilat Kielce* [The history of the community of Kielce]. [By] P. Zitron. Tel Aviv, Former Residents of Kielce in Israel, 1957. 328 p., ports. (Hebrew, Yiddish)

Kiemieliszki (P) see under Swieciany

Kiernozia (P) see under Lowicz

Kisvarda (H). *Sefer yizkor le-kehilat Kleinwardein ve-ha-seviva* [Memorial book of Kleinwardein and vicinity]. Tel Aviv, Kleinwardein Society, 1980. 79, 190 p., illus. (Hebrew, Hungarian, English)

Kitai-Gorod (U) see under Kamenets-Podolskiy

Kitev (P) see Kuty

Klausenburg (R) see Kolozsvar

Kleck (P). *Pinkas Kleck* [Pinkas Klezk; a memorial to the Jewish community of Klezk-Poland*]. Ed.: E. S. Stein. Tel Aviv, Former Residents of Klezk in Israel, 1959. 385 p., ports., map, facsims. (Hebrew, Yiddish)

Kleinwardein (H) see Kisvarda

Klobucko (P). *Sefer Klobutsk; mazkeret kavod le-kehila ha-kedosha she-hushmeda* [The book of Klobucko; in memory of a martyred community which was destroyed]. Tel Aviv, Former Residents of Klobucko in Israel, 1960. 439 p., ports., facsims. (Yiddish)

Klosowa (P). *Sefer Klosowa; kibutz hotzvei avanim a(l) sh(em) Yosef Trumpeldor be-Klosowa u-flugotav, measef* [The story of Kibbutz Klosova*]. Ed.: Haim Dan. Beit Lohamei Hagetaot, Ghetto Fighters House, 1978. 405 p., illus. (Hebrew)

Knenitsh (Knihynicze) (P) see under Rohatyn

Knihynicze (P) see under Rohatyn

Kobryn (P). *Kobryn; zamlbukh (an iberblik ibern yidishn Kobryn)* [Kobryn; collection (an overview of Jewish Kobryn)]. Ed.: Melech Glotzer. Buenos Aires, Kobryn Book Committee, 1951. 310 p., illus. (Yiddish)

Kobryn (P). *Sefer Kobryn; megilat hayim ve-hurban* [Book of Kobryn; the scroll of life and destruction]. Eds.: B. Schwartz and Y. H. Bilizky. Tel Aviv, 1951. 347 p., ports. (Hebrew)

Kobylnik (P). *Sefer Kobylnik* [Memorial book of Kobilnik*]. Ed.: I. Siegelman. Haifa, Committee of Former Residents of Kobilnik in Israel, 1967. 292 p., ports., map (Hebrew, Yiddish)

Kock (P). *Sefer Kotsk* [Memorial book of Kotsk]. Ed.: E. Porat. Tel Aviv, Former Residents of Kotsk in Israel . . . , 1961. 424 p., ports., map, facsims. (Hebrew, Yiddish)

Koidanovo (B). *Koydenov; zamlbukh tsum ondenk fun di Koydenover kedoyshim* [Koidanov; memorial volume of the martyrs of Koidanov]. Ed.: A. Raisen. New York, United Koidanover Assn., 1955. 216, [41], 207 p., ports., facsims. (Yiddish)

Kolbuszowa (P). *Pinkas Kolbishov (Kolbasov)* [Kolbuszowa memorial book*]. Ed.: I. M. Biderman. New York, United Kolbushover, 1971. 793, 88 p., ports. (Hebrew, Yiddish, English)

Kolno (P). *Sefer zikaron le-kehilat Kolno* [Kolno memorial book*]. Eds.: A. Remba and B. Halevy. Tel Aviv, The Kolner Organization and Sifriat Poalim, 1971. 680, 70 p., ports., facsims. (Hebrew, Yiddish, English)

Kolo (P). *Sefer Kolo* [Memorial book of Kolo]. Ed.: M. Helter. Tel Aviv, Former Residents of Kolo in Israel and the USA, 1958. 408 p., ports. (Hebrew, Yiddish)

Kolomyja (P). *Pinkes Kolomey* [Memorial book of Kolomey]. Ed.: Sh. Bickel. New York, 1957. 448 p., ports. (Yiddish)

Kolomyja (P). *Sefer zikaron le-kehilat Kolomey ve-ha-seviva* [Kolomeyer memorial book*]. Eds.: D. Noy and M. Schutzman. [Tel Aviv], Former Residents of Kolomey and Surroundings in Israel, [1972]. 395 p., ports., facsims. (Hebrew)

Kolonia Synajska (P) see under Dereczyn

Kolozsvar (R). *Sefer zikaron le-yahadut Kluzh-Kolozsvar* [Memorial volume of the Jews of Cluj-Kolozsvar*]. Ed.: M. Carmilly-Weinberger. New York, 1970. 156, 313 p., ports., facsims. (Hebrew, English, Hungarian)

Kolozsvar (R). *Zikaron netsah le-kehila ha-kedosha Kolozhvar-Klauzenburg asher nehreva ba-shoa* [Everlasting memorial of the martyred community Kolozsvar-Klausenburg which perished in the Holocaust]. [Eds.]: Sh. Zimroni, Y. Schwartz. Tel Aviv, Former Residents of Kolozsvar in Israel, 1968. 118 p. (Hebrew, Hungarian), mimeo.

Koltyniany (P) see under Swieciany

Konin (P). *Kehilat Konin be-frihata u-ve-hurbana* [Memorial book Konin*]. Ed.: M. Gelbart. Tel Aviv, Assoc. of Konin Jews in Israel, 1968. 772, 24 p., map, facsims. (Hebrew, Yiddish, English)

Konyar (H) see under Debrecen

Kopin (U) see under Kamenets-Podolskiy

Koprzywnica (P). *Sefer Pokshivnitsa* [Memorial book of Koprzywnica]. Ed.: E. Erlich. Tel Aviv, Former Residents of Koprzywnica in Israel, 1971. 351 p., ports., facsims. (Hebrew, Yiddish)

Kopyczynce (P) see under Husiatyn (*Kehilatiyim*)

Kopyl (B) see under Slutsk

Korczyna (P). *Korczyna; sefer zikaron* [Korczyna memorial book*]. New York, Committee of the Korczyna Memorial Book, 1967. 495 p., ports. (Hebrew, Yiddish)

Korelicze (P). *Korelitz; hayeha ve-hurbana shel kehila yehudit* [Korelitz; the life and destruction of a Jewish community*]. Ed.: Michael Walzer-Fass. Tel Aviv, Korelicze Societies in Israel and the U.S.A., 1973. 61, 357 p., illus. (Hebrew, Yiddish, English)

Korelicze (P) see also under Nowogrodek

Korets (P) see Korzec

Koriv (P) see Kurow

Korzec (P). *Korets (Wolyn); sefer zikaron le-kehilatenu she-ala aleha ha-koret* [The Korets book; in memory of our community that is no more*]. Ed.: E. Leoni. Tel Aviv, Former Residents of Korets in Israel, 1959. 791 p., ports., facsims. (Hebrew, Yiddish)

Kosow (East Galicia) (P). *Sefer Kosow–Galicia ha-mizrahit* [Memorial book of Kosow— Kosow Huculski]. Ed.: E. Kresel. Tel Aviv, Former Residents of Kosow and Vicinity in Israel, 1964. 430 p., ports., facsims. (Hebrew, Yiddish)

Kosow (P). *Megiles Kosow* [The scroll of Kosow]. [By] Yehoshua Gertner. Tel Aviv, Amkho, 1981. 156 p. (Yiddish)

Kosow (P). *Pinkas kehilat Kosow Poleski* [Memorial book of Kosow Poleski]. Jerusalem, Relief Org. of Former Residents of Kosow Poleski in Israel, 1956. 81 p., ports. (Hebrew)

Kostopol (P). *Sefer Kostopol; hayeha u-mota shel kehila* [Kostopol; the life and death of a community*]. Ed.: A. Lerner. Tel Aviv, Former Residents of Kostopol in Israel, 1967. 386 p., ports. (Hebrew)

Kotsk (P) see Kock

Kowal (P) see under Wloclawek

Kowel (P). *Kowel; sefer edut ve-zikaron le-kehilatenu she-ala aleha ha-koret* [Kowel; testimony and memorial book of our destroyed community]. Ed.: E. Leoni-Zopperfin. Tel Aviv, Former Residents of Kowel in Israel, 1959. 539 p., ports. (Hebrew, Yiddish)

Kowel (P). *Pinkes Kowel* [Memorial book of Kowel]. Ed.: B. Baler. Buenos Aires, Former Residents of Kowel and Surroundings in Argentina, 1951. 511 p., ports., facsims. (Yiddish)

Kozangrodek (P) see under Luniniec

Koziany (P) see under Glebokie; Swieciany

Kozieniec (P). *Sefer zikaron le-kehilat Kozieniec* [Memorial book of the community of Kozieniec]. Ed.: B. Kaplinski. Tel Aviv, Former Residents of Kozieniec in Israel . . . , 1969. 516 p., ports., map, music, facsims. (Hebrew, Yiddish)

Krakow (P) see also under *Arim ve-imahot be-yisrael*, v. 2

Krakow (P). *Sefer Kroke, ir va-em be-yisrael* [Memorial book of Krakow, mother and town in Israel]. Eds.: A. Bauminger et al. Jerusalem, The Rav Kuk Inst. and Former Residents of Krakow in Israel, 1959. 429 p., ports., facsims. (Hebrew)

Krakowiec (P) see under Jaworow (*Matsevet zikaron le-kehilat Jaworow* . . .)

Krasnik (P). *Sefer Krasnik*. Ed.: David Shtokfish. Tel Aviv, Kraśnik Societies in Israel and the Diaspora, 1973. 673 p., illus. (Hebrew, Yiddish)

Krasnobrod (P). *Krasnobrod; sefer zikaron* [Krasnobrod; a memorial to the Jewish community*]. Ed.: M. Kushnir. Tel Aviv, Former Residents of Krasnobród in Israel, 1956. 526 p., ports., facsims. (Hebrew, Yiddish)

Krasnystaw (P). *Yizker tsum ondenk fun kedoyshey Krasnystaw* [Memorial book of the martyrs of Krasnystaw]. Ed.: A. Stunzeiger. Munich, Publ. "Bafrayung"—Poale Zion, 1948. 150 p., ports. (Yiddish)

Kremenits (P) see Krzemieniec

Kripa (Horyngrod) (P) see under Tuczyn

Krivitsh (P) see Krzywicze

Kroscienko (P) see under Nowy Targ

Krosniewiec (P) see under Kutno

Krynki (P). *Pinkas Krynki* [Memorial book of Krynki]. Ed.: D. Rabin. Tel Aviv, Former Residents of Krynki in Israel and in the Diaspora, 1970. 373 p., ports., map, facsims. (Hebrew, Yiddish)

Krzemienica (P) see under Wolkowysk (*Volkovisker yizker bukh*)

Krzemieniec (P). *Kremenits, Vishgorodek un Pitshayev; yizker-bukh* [Memorial book of Krzemieniec]. Ed.: P. Lerner. Buenos Aires, Former Residents of Kremenits and Vicinity in Argentina, 1965. 468 p., ports., facsims (Yiddish)

Krzemieniec (P). *Pinkas Kremenits; sefer zikaron* [Memorial book of Krzemieniec]. Ed.: A. S. Stein. Tel Aviv, Former Residents of Krzemieniec in Israel, 1954. 450 p., ports., facsims. (Hebrew, Yiddish)

Krzywicze (P). *Ner tamid; yizkor le-Krivitsh* [Kryvitsh yizkor book*]. Ed.: Matityahu Bar-Ratzon. Tel Aviv, Krivitsh Societies in Israel and the Diaspora, 1977. 724 p., illus. (Hebrew, Yiddish)

Kshoynzh (Ksiaz Wielki) (P) see under Miechow

Ksiaz Wielki (P) see under Miechow

Kunow (P) see under Ostrowiec

Kurow (P). *Yizker-bukh Koriv; sefer yizkor, matsevet zikaron la-ayaratenu Koriv* [yizkor book in memoriam of our hometown Kurow*]. Ed.: M. Grossman. Tel Aviv, Former Residents of Kurow in Israel, 1955. 1148 columns, ports., facsims. (Yiddish)

Kurzeniec (P). *Megilat Kurenits; ayara be-hayeha u-ve-mota* [The scroll of Kurzeniec; the town living and dead]. Ed.: A. Meyerowitz. Tel Aviv, Former Residents of Kurzeniec in Israel and in the USA, 1956. 335 p., ports. (Hebrew)

Kutno (P). *Kutno ve-ha-seviva* [Kutno and surroundings book*]. Ed.: D. Shtokfish. Tel Aviv, Former Residents of Kutno and Surroundings in Israel and the Diaspora, 1968. 591 p., ports., facsims. (Hebrew, Yiddish)

Kuty (P). *Kitever yizker-bukh* [Kitever memorial book]. Ed.: E. Husen. New York, Kitever Sick and Benevolent Society in New York, 1958. 240 p., ports. (Yiddish)

Kuzmir (P) see Kazimierz

Lachowicze (P). *Lachowicze; sefer zikaron* [Memorial book of Lachowicze]. Ed.: J. Rubin. Tel Aviv, Assoc. of Former Residents of Lachowicze, 1959. 395 p., ports. (Hebrew, Yiddish)

Lachwa (P). *Rishonim la-mered; Lachwa* [First ghetto revolt, Lachwa*]. Eds.: H. A. Malachi et al. Jerusalem, The Encyclopaedia of the Jewish Diaspora, 1957. 500 columns, ports., facsims. (Hebrew, Yiddish)

Lancut (P). *Lancut; hayeha ve-hurbana shel kehila yehudit* [Lancut; the life and destruction of a Jewish community*]. Eds.: M. Waltzer and N. Kudish. Tel Aviv, Associations of Former Residents of Lancut in Israel and USA, 1963. 465, lix p., ports., facsims. (Hebrew, Yiddish, English)

Lanovits (P) see Lanowce

Lanowce (P). *Lanovits; sefer zikaron le-kedoshei Lanovits she-nispu be-shoat ha-natsim* [Lanowce; memorial book of the martyrs of Lanowce who perished during the Holocaust]. Ed.: H. Rabin. Tel Aviv, Association of Former Residents of Lanowce, 1970. 440 p., ports. (Hebrew, Yiddish)

Lapichi (B) see under Bobruisk

Lask (P). *Lask; sefer zikaron* [Memorial book of Lask]. Ed.: Z. Tzurnamal. Tel Aviv, Assoc. of Former Residents of Lask in Israel, 1968. 737, 164 p., ports., facsims. (Hebrew, Yiddish, English).

Lask (P) see also under Pabianice

Latvia. *The Jews in Latvia*. Ed.: M. Bobe and others. Tel Aviv, Association of Latvian and Estonian Jews in Israel, 1971. 384 p., illus. (English)

Latvia. *Yahadut Latvia; sefer zikaron* [The Jews of Latvia; a memorial book]. Eds.: B. Eliyav, M. Bobe, A. Kramer. Tel Aviv, Former Residents of Latvia and Estonia in Israel, 1953. 458 p., ports., map (Hebrew)

Latvia. *Yidn in Letland* [Latvian Jewry*]. Ed.: Mendel Bobe. Tel Aviv, Reshafim, 1972. 368 p., illus. (Yiddish)

Leczyca (P). *Sefer Linshits* [Memorial book of Leczyca]. Ed.: J. Frenkel. Tel Aviv, Former Residents of Leczyca in Israel, 1953. 223 p., ports. (Hebrew)

Lemberg (P) see Lwow

Lenin (P). *Kehilat Lenin; sefer zikaron* [The community of Lenin; memorial book]. Ed.: M. Tamari. Tel Aviv, Former Residents of Lenin in Israel and in the USA, 1957. 407 p., ports. (Hebrew, Yiddish)

Leonpol (P) see under Druja (*Sefer Druja*)

Lesko (P). *Sefer yizkor; mukdash le-yehudei ha-ayarot she-nispu ba-shoa be-shanim 1939–44, Linsk, Istrik . . . ve-ha-seviva* [Memorial book; dedicated to the Jews of Linsk, Istrik . . . and vicinity who perished in the Holocaust in the years 1939–44]. Eds.: N. Mark and Sh. Friedlander. [Tel Aviv], Book Committee of the "Libai" Organization, [1965]. 516 p., ports. (Hebrew, Yiddish)

Levertev (P) see Lubartow

Lezajsk (P). *Lizhensk; sefer zikaron le-kedoshei Lizhensk she-nispu be-shoat ha-natsim* [Memorial book of the martyrs of Lezajsk who perished in the Holocaust]. Ed.: H. Rabin. Tel Aviv, Former Residents of Lezajsk in Israel, [1970]. 495 p., ports., facsims. (Hebrew, Yiddish)

Lida (P). *Sefer Lida* [The book of Lida*]. Eds.: A. Manor et al. Tel Aviv, Former

Residents of Lida in Israel and the Relief Committee of the Lida Jews in USA, 1970. 438, xvii p., ports., maps, facsims. (Hebrew, Yiddish, English)

Likeva (P) see Lukow

Linshits (P) see Leczyca

Linsk (P) see Lesko

Lipkany (R). *Kehilat Lipkany; sefer zikaron* [The community of Lipkany; memorial book]. Tel Aviv, Former Residents of Lipkany in Israel, 1963. 407 p., ports. (Hebrew, Yiddish)

Lipniszki (P). *Sefer zikaron shel kehilat Lipnishok* [Memorial book of the community of Lipniszki]. Ed.: A. Levin. Tel Aviv, Former Residents of Lipniszki in Israel, 1968. 206 p., ports. map (Hebrew, Yiddish)

Litevisk (Lutowiska) (P) see under Lesko

Lithuania. *Bleter fun yidish Lite* [Lithuanian Jews; a memorial book*]. Ed.: Jacob Rabinovitch. Tel Aviv, Hamenora, 1974. 289 p., illus. (Yiddish, Hebrew, English)

Lithuania. *Lite* [Lithuania], vol. I. Eds.: M. Sudarsky, U. Katzenelenbogen, J. Kissin. New York, Jewish-Lithuanian Cultural Society, 1951. 2070 columns, viii p., ports., maps. facsims. (Yiddish); [Lithuania], vol. II. Ed.: Ch. Leikowicz. Tel Aviv, I. L. Peretz, 1965. 894 columns, ports., facsims. (Yiddish)

Lithuania. *Yahadut Lita* [Lithuanian Jewry*], vol. I. Eds.: N. Goren, L. Garfinkel et al. Tel Aviv, Am-Hasefer. 1959. 648 p., ports., maps, facsims., music. Vol. II, 1972. (Hebrew); Vol. III. Eds.: R. Hasman, D. Lipec et al. Tel Aviv, Association for Mutual Help of Former Residents of Lithuania in Israel, 1967. 396 p., ports., maps (Hebrew)

Lizhensk (P) see Lezajsk

Lodz (P). *Lodzer yizker-bukh* [Lodzer yizkor book*]. New York, United Emergency Relief Committee for the City of Lodz, 1943. Various pagings, ports. (Yiddish)

Lodz (P). *Yiddish Lodz; a yiskor book*. Melbourne, Lodzer Center, 1974. 13, 243 p., illus. (Yiddish, English)

Lomza (P). *Lomza; ir oyfkum un untergang* [The rise and fall of Lomza]. Ed.: H. Sabatka. New York, American Committee for the Book of Lomza, 1957. 371 p., ports., facsims. (Yiddish)

Lomza (P). *Sefer zikaron le-kehilat Lomza* [Lomza—in memory of the Jewish community*]. Ed.: Y. T. Lewinski. Tel Aviv, Former Residents of Lomza in Israel, 1952. 337 p., ports., facsims. (Hebrew)

Lopatyn (P) see under Radziechow

Losice (P). *Loshits; lezeykher an umgebrakhte kehile* [Losice; in memory of a Jewish community, exterminated by Nazi murderers*]. Ed.: M. Shener. Tel Aviv, Former Residents of Losice in Israel, 1963. 459 p., ports., facsims. (Hebrew, Yiddish)

Lowicz (P). *Lowicz; ir be-Mazovia u-seviva, sefer zikaron* [Lowicz; a town in Mazovia, memorial book*]. Ed.: G. Shaiak. [Tel Aviv], Former Residents of Lowicz in Melbourne and Sydney, Australia, 1966. 395, xxii p., ports., facsims. (Hebrew, Yiddish, English)

Lubartow (P). *Khurbn Levartov* [The destruction of Lubartow]. Ed.: B. Tshubinski. Paris, Association of Lubartow, 1947. 117 p., ports., facsims. (Yiddish)

Lubcza. (P) *Lubtch ve-Delatich; sefer zikaron* [Lubtch ve-Delatich; in memory of the Jewish community*]. Ed.: K. Hilel. Haifa, Former Residents of Lubtch-Delatich in Israel, 1971. 480 p., ports., map, facsims. (Hebrew, Yiddish)

Lubenichi (B) see under Bobruisk

Lublin (P). *Dos bukh fun Lublin* [The memorial book of Lublin]. Paris, Former Residents of Lublin in Paris, 1952. 685 p., ports., facsims. (Yiddish)

Lublin (P). *Lublin* [Lublin volume*]. Eds.: N. Blumenthal and M. Korzen. Jerusalem, The Encyclopaedia of the Jewish Diaspora, 1957. 816 columns, ports., map, facsims. (Hebrew, Yiddish)

Luboml (P). *Sefer yizkor le-kehilat Luboml* [Yizkor book of Luboml*]. Ed.: Berl Kagan. Tel Aviv, 1974. 390, 18 p., illus. (Hebrew, Yiddish, English)

Lubraniec (P) see under Wloclawek

Luck (P). *Sefer Lutzk* [The memorial book of Lutzk]. Ed.: N. Sharon. Tel Aviv, Former Residents of Lutzk in Israel, 1961. 608 p., ports., facsims. (Hebrew, Yiddish)

Ludmir (P) see Wlodzimierz

Ludwipol (P). *Sefer zikaron le-kehilat Ludwipol* [Ludvipol-Wolyn; in memory of the Jewish community*]. Ed.: N. Ayalon. Tel Aviv, Ludvipol Relief Society of Israel, 1965. 335 p., ports., map, facsims. (Hebrew, Yiddish)

Lukow (P). *Sefer Lukow; geheylikt der khorev gevorener kehile* [The book of Lukow; dedicated to a destroyed community]. Ed.: B. Heller. Tel Aviv, Former Residents of Lukow in Israel and the USA, 1968. 652 p., ports., facsims. (Hebrew, Yiddish)

Luniniec (P). *Yizkor kehilot Luniniec/Kozhanhorodok* [Memorial book of the communities of Luniniec/Kozhanhorodok]. Eds.: Y. Zeevi (Wilk) et al. Tel Aviv, Assoc. of Former Residents of Luniniec/Kozhanhorodok in Israel, 1952. 268 p., ports. (Hebrew, Yiddish)

Lutowiska (P) see under Lesko

Lutsk (P) see Luck

Lvov (P) see Lwow

Lwow (P). *Lwow* [Lwow volume*], part I. Ed.: N. M. Gelber. Jerusalem, The Encyclopaedia of the Jewish Diaspora, 1956. 772 columns, ports., facsims. (Hebrew)

Lwow (P) see also Various (Miscellany) *Arim ve-imahot be-yisrael*, v. 1

Lyngmiany (P) see under Stolin

Lynki (P) see under Stolin

Lyntupy (P) see under Swieciany

Lyskow (P) see under Wolkowysk (*Volkovisker yizker bukh*)

Lyszkowice (P) see under Lowicz

Lyuban (B) see under Slutsk

Mad (H). *Ha-kehila ha-yehudit shel Mad, Hungaria* [The Jewish community of Maad, Hungary*]. Ed.: Arieh Lewy. Jerusalem, Mad Commemorative Committee, 1974. 154, 31 p., illus. (Hebrew, English, Hungarian)

Magyarlapos (R) see under Des

Makow-Mazowiecki (P). *Sefer zikaron le-kehilat Makow-Mazowiecki* [Memorial book of the community of Makow-Mazowiecki]. Ed.: J. Brat. Tel Aviv, Former Residents of Makow-Mazowiecki in Israel, 1969. 505 p., ports., facsims. (Hebrew, Yiddish)

Makow Podhalanski (P) see under Nowy Targ

Malecz (P) see under Pruzana

Margareten (R) see Margita

Margita (R). *Sefer yizkor le-kehilat Margareten ve-ha-seviva* [Memorial book of the community of Margareten and the surrounding region]. Ed.: Aharon Kleinmann. Jerusalem, Hayim Frank, 1979. 200, 275 p. (Hebrew, Hungarian)

Markuleshty (R). *Markuleshty; yad le-moshava yehudit be-Bessarabia* [Markuleshty; memorial to a Jewish colony in Bessarabia]. Eds.: Leib Kuperstein, Meir Kotik. Tel Aviv, Markuleshty Society, 1977. 272 p., illus. (Hebrew, Yiddish)

Markuszow (P). *Hurbana u-gevurata shel ha-ayara Markuszow* [The destruction and heroism of the town of Markuszow]. Ed.: D. Shtokfish. Tel Aviv, Former Residents of Markuszow in Israel, 1955. 436 p., ports. (Yiddish)

Marosvasarhely (R). *Korot yehudei Marosvasarhely ve-ha-seviva* [History of the Jews in Marosvasarhely]. [By] Yitzhak Perri (Friedmann). Tel Aviv, Ghetto Fighters House, Ha-Kibbutz ha-Meuhad, 1977. (Hebrew)

Marvits (Murawica) (P) see under Mlynow

Maytshet (P) see Molczadz

Medenice (P) see under Drohobycz

Melits (P) see Mielec

Mezritsh (P) see Miedzyrzec

Miava (C) see under Postyen

Michalovce (C) see Nagymihaly

Miechow (P). *Sefer yizkor Miechow, Charsznica, Ksiaz* [Miechov memorial book, Charshnitza and Kshoynge*]. Eds.: N. Blumenthal and A. Ben-Azar (Broshy). Tel Aviv, Former Residents of Miechov, Charshnitza and Kshoynzh, 1971. 314, [4] p., ports., facsims. (Hebrew, Yiddish)

Miedzyrzec (P). *Mezritsh; zamlbukh* [The Mezritsh volume]. Ed.: Y. Horn. Buenos Aires, Assoc. of Former Residents of Mezritsh in Argentina, 1952. 635 p., ports., facsims. (Yiddish)

Miedzyrzec (P). *Sefer Mezritsh; lezeykher di kdoyshim fun undzer shtot* [Mezritsh book, in memory of the martyrs of our city]. Eds.: Binem Heller, Yitzhak Ronkin. Israel, Mezritsh Societies in Israel and the Diaspora, 1978. 821 p., illus. (Hebrew, Yiddish)

Miedzryzec-Wolyn (P). *Mezeritsh Gadol be-vinyana u-be-hurbana* [Mezhiritch-Wolyn; in memory of the Jewish community*]. Ed.: B. H. Ayalon-Baranick. Tel Aviv, Former Residents of Mezhiritch, 1955. 442 columns, ports., facsims. (Hebrew, Yiddish)

Mielec (P). *Melitser yidn* [Mielec Jews]. [By] Schlomo Klagsbrun. Tel Aviv, Nay-Lebn, 1979. 288 p., illus. (Yiddish)

Mielnica (P) see under Kowel (*Pinkes Kowel*)

Mikepercs (H) see under Debrecen

Mikolajow (P) see under Radziechow

Mikulov (Nikolsburg) (C) see under Various (Miscellany) *Arim ve-imahot be-yisrael*, v. 4

Milosna (P) see under Rembertow

Minkovtsy (U) see under Kamenets-Podolskiy

Minsk (B). *Minsk; ir ve-em* [Minsk, Jewish mother city; memorial anthology*]. Ed.: Shlomo Even-Shushan. Israel, Minsk Society, Ghetto Fighters' House, ha-Kibbutz ha-Meuhad, 1975–v. 1; 692 p., illus. (Hebrew)

Minsk-Mazowiecki (P). *Sefer Minsk-Mazowiecki* [Minsk-Mazowiecki memorial book*]. Ed.: Ephraim Shedletzky. Jerusalem, Minsk-Mazowiecki Societies in Israel and Abroad, 1977. 6, 633 p., illus. (Hebrew, Yiddish, English)

Miory (P) see under Druja (*Sefer Druja*)

Mir (P). *Sefer Mir* [Memorial book of Mir]. Ed.: N. Blumenthal. Jerusalem, The Encyclopaedia of the Jewish Diaspora, 1962. 768, 62 columms, ports. (Hebrew, Yiddish, English)

Mizocz (P). *Mizocz; sefer zikaron* [The memorial book of Mizocz]. Ed.: A. Ben-Orni. Tel Aviv, Former Residents of Mizocz in Israel, 1961. 293, [24] p., ports., facsims. (Hebrew)

Mlawa (P). *Pinkas Mlawa* [Memorial book of Mlawa]. New York, World Assoc. of Former Residents of Mlawa, 1950. 483, 63 p., ports. (Yiddish)

Mlynow (P). *Sefer Mlynow-Marvits* [Mlynov-Muravica memorial book*]. Ed.: J. Sigelman. Haifa, Former Residents of Mlynov-Muravica in Israel, 1970. 511 p., ports. (Yiddish, Hebrew)

Modrzyc (P) see Deblin

Mogielnica (P). *Sefer Mogielnica-Bledow*. Ed.: Yisrael Zunder. Tel Aviv, Mogielnica and Bledow Society, 1972. 808 p., illus. (Hebrew, Yiddish)

Molczadz (P). *Sefer-zikaron le-kehilat Meytshet* [Memorial book of the community of Meytshet]. Ed.: Benzion H. Ayalon. Tel Aviv, Meytshet Societies in Israel and Abroad, 1973. 460, 12 p., illus. (Hebrew, Yiddish)

Monasterzyska (P). *Sefer Monastrishtz* [Monasterzyska; a memorial book*]. Ed.: M. Segal. Tel Aviv, Monasterzyska Association, 1974. 126 p., illus. (Hebrew, Yiddish, English)

Monastir (Y). *Ir u-shema Monastir* [A city called Monastir]. [By] Uri Oren. Tel Aviv, Naor, 1972. 167 p., illus. (Hebrew)

Mosty (P) see under Piaski

Mosty-Wielkie (P). *Mosty-Wielkie—Most Rabati, sefer zikaron* [Mosty-Wielkie memorial book*]. Ed.: Moshe Shtarkman, Abraham Ackner, A. L. Binot. Tel Aviv, Mosty Wielkie Societies in Israel and the United States, 1975–1977. 2 vols., illus. (Hebrew, Yiddish, English)

Motele (P) see Motol

Motol (P). *Hurban Motele* [The destruction of Motele]. [By] A. L. Poliak. Jerusalem, Council of Motele Immigrants, 1957. 87 p. (Hebrew)

Mszczonow (P) see under Zyrardow

Mukacevo (Munkacs) (C) see under Various (Miscellany) *Arim ve-imahot be-yisrael*, v. 1

Munkacs (C) see under Various (Miscellany) *Arim ve-imahot be-yisrael*, v. 1

Murawica (P) see under Mlynow

Myjava (Miava) (C) see under Postyen

Mysleniec (P) see under Wadowice

Myszyniec (P) see under Ostroleka

Nadarzyn (P) see under Pruszkow

Nadworna (P). *Nadworna; sefer edut ve-zikaron* [Nadworna, Stanislav district; memorial and records*]. Ed.: Israel Carmi (Otto Kramer). Tel Aviv, Nadworna Societies in Israel and the United States, 1975. 281, 67 p., illus. (Hebrew, Yiddish, English)

Nadzin (Nadarzyn) (P) see under Pruszkow

Nagybanya (R). *Nagybanya ve-ha-seviva* [Nagybanya and the surrounding region]. Ed.: Naftali Stern. Bne Brak, 1976. 245, 175 p., illus. (Hebrew, Hungarian)

Nagyilonda (R) see under Des

Nagymagyar (R) see under Dunaszerdahely

Nagymihaly (C). *Sefer Michalovce ve-ha-seviva* [The book of Michalovce*]. Ed.: M. Ben-Zeev (M. Farkas). Tel Aviv, Committee of Former Residents of Michalovce in Israel, 1969. 240, 64, 103 p., ports., facsims. (Hebrew, English, Hungarian)

Nagyszollos (C). *Sefer zikaron le-kehilat Selish ve-ha-seviva* [A memorial to the Jewish community of Sevlus (Nagyszöllos) & District*]. Ed.: Shmuel ka-Kohen Weingarten. Israel, Selish Society, 1976. 326 p., illus. (Hebrew)

Nagytapolcsany (C) see Topolcany

Naliboki (P). *Ayaratenu Nalibok, hayeha ve-hurbana* [Our town Nalibok, its existence and destruction*]. Tel Aviv, Former Residents of Nalibok, 1967. 239 p., ports., map (Hebrew, Yiddish)

Naliboki (P) see also under Stolpce

Narajow (P) see under Brzezany

Navaredok (P) see Nowogrodek

Naymark (P) see Nowy Targ

Nemirov (U) see under Various (Miscellany) *Arim ve-imahot be-yisrael*, v. 2

Nestilye (P) see Uscilug

Neumarkt (P) see Nowy Targ

Nevel (B) see under Vitebsk (*Sefer Vitebsk*)

Nieswiez (P). *Sefer Nieswiez*. Ed.: David Shtokfish. Tel Aviv, Nieswiez Societies in Israel and the Diaspora, 1976. 531 p., illus. (Hebrew, Yiddish)

Nieszawa (P) see under Wloclawek

Nikolsburg (C) see under Various (Miscellany) *Arim ve-imahot be-yisrael*, v. 4

Novograd-Volynskiy (U). *Zvhil-Novogradvolinsk*. Eds.: A. Ori, M. Bone. Tel Aviv, Association of Former Residents of Zvhil and the Environment, 1962. 354, 232, 16 p., ports. (Hebrew, Yiddish, English)

Novo Minsk (P) see Minsk Mazowiecki

Novyy Vitkov (Witkow Nowy) (P) see under Radziechow

Nowe Miasto (P) see under Plonsk

Nowogrod (P) see under Lomza (*Lomza; ir oyfkum un untergang*)

Nowogrodek (P). *Pinkas Navaredok* [Navaredok memorial book*]. Eds.: E. Yerushalmi et al. Tel Aviv, Alexander Harkavy Navaredker Relief Committee in the USA and . . . in Israel, 1963. 419 p., ports., maps, facsims. (Hebrew, Yiddish)

Nowo-Swieciany (P) see under Swieciany

Nowy Dwor (near Warszawa) (P). *Pinkas Nowy Dwor* [Memorial book of Nowy-Dwor]. Eds.: A. Shamri and D. First. Tel Aviv, Former Residents of Nowy-Dwor in Israel, USA, Argentina . . . , 1965. 556, xix p., ports., maps, facsims. (Hebrew, Yiddish, English)

Nowy Dwor (P) see under Szczuczyn (*Sefer zikaron le-kehilot Szczuczyn, Wasiliszki . . .*)

Nowy Sacz (P). *Sefer Sants* [The book of the Jewish community of Nowy Sacz*]. Ed.: R. Mahler. New York, Former Residents of Sants in New York, 1970. 886 p., ports., facsims. (Hebrew, Yiddish)

Nowy Targ (P). *Sefer Nowy Targ ve-ha-seviva* [Remembrance book Nowy Targ and vicinity*]. Ed.: Michael Walzer-Fass. Tel Aviv, Townspeople Association of Nowy Targ and Vicinity, 1979. 301 p., illus. (Hebrew, Yiddish, English)

Nowy Zagorz (P) see under Sanok

Odessa (U) see under Various (Miscellany) *Arim ve-imahot be-yisrael*, v. 2

Okuniew (P) see under Rembertow

Olkeniki (P). *Ha-ayara be-lehavot; sefer zikaron le-kehilat Olkenik pelekh Vilna* [Olkeniki in flames; a memorial book*]. Ed.: Sh. Farber. Tel Aviv, Association of Former Residents of Olkeniki and Surroundings, 1962. 287, [4] p., ports. (Hebrew, Yiddish)

Olkusz (P). *Olkusz (Elkish); sefer zikaron le-kehila she-huhehada ha-shoa* [Olkusz; memorial book to a community that was exterminated during the Holocaust]. Ed.: Zvi Yashiv. Tel Aviv, Olkusz Society, [1971/72]. 280 p., map, illus. (Hebrew, Yiddish)

Olshan (P) see Holszany

Olyka (P). *Pinkas ha-kehila Olyka; sefer yizkor* [Memorial book of the community of Olyka]. Ed.: Natan Livneh. Tel Aviv, Olyka Society, 1972. 397 p., illus. (Hebrew, Yiddish)

Opatow (P). *Apt (Opatow); sefer zikaron le-ir va-em be-Yisrael* [Apt; a town which does not exist anymore*]. Ed.: Z. Yasheev. Tel Aviv, The Apt Organization in Israel, USA, Canada and Brazil, 1966. 441, [3], 20 p., ports. (Hebrew, Yiddish, English)

Opatow (P) see also under Ostrowiec

Opole (P). *Sefer Opole-Lubelski* [Memorial book of Opole-Lubelski*]. Ed.: David Shtokfish. Tel Aviv, Opole Societies in Israel and the Diaspora, 1977. 467 p., illus. (Hebrew, Yiddish)

Orgeyev (R). *Orhayev be-vinyana u-be-hurbana* [Orhayev alive and destroyed]. Eds.: Y. Spivak et al. Tel Aviv. Committee of Former Residents of Orhayev, 1959. 216 p., ports. (Hebrew, Yiddish)

Orhei (R) see Orgeyev

Orlowa (P) see under Zoludek

Oshmena (P) see Oszmiana

Oshpitsin (P) see Oswiecim

Osiek (P) see under Staszow

Osipovichi (B) see under Bobruisk

Ostra (P) see Ostrog

Ostrog (P). *Ostrog*. [By] Judah Loeb Levin. Jerusalem–Tel Aviv, Yad Yahadut Polin, 1966. 111 p., map, ports., illus. (Hebrew)

Ostrog (P). *Pinkas Ostra; sefer zikaron* . . . [Ostrog-Wolyn; in memory of the Jewish community*]. Ed.: H. Ayalon-Baranick. Tel Aviv, Association of Former Residents of Ostrog, 1960. 640 columns, ports., maps, facsims. (Hebrew, Yiddish)

Ostrog (P) see also under *Arim ve-imahot be-yisrael*, v. 1

Ostrog (P). *Ven dos lebn hot geblit* [When life was blooming]. [By] M. Grines. Buenos Aires, 1954. 471 p., ports. (Yiddish)

Ostroleka (P). *Sefer kehilat Ostrolenka* [Book of kehilat Ostrolenka*]. Ed.: Y. Ivri. Tel Aviv, Association of Former Residents of Ostrolenka, 1963. 579 p., ports. (Hebrew, Yiddish)

Ostrowiec (P). *Ostrovtse; geheylikt dem ondenk . . . fun Ostrovtse, Apt* . . . [Ostrovtse; dedicated to the memory of Ostrovtse, Apt . . .]. Buenos Aires, Former Residents of Ostrovtse . . . in Argentina, 1949. 217 [3] p., ports. (Yiddish)

Ostrow Mazowiecka (P). *Ostrow Mazowiecka*. [By] Judah Loeb Levin. Jerusalem–Tel Aviv, Yad Yahadut Polin, 1966. 164 p., ports., illus. (Hebrew)

Ostrow-Mazowiecka (P). *Sefer ha-zikaron le-kehilat Ostrov-Mazovyetsk* [Memorial book of the community of Ostrow-Mazowiecka]. Ed.: A. Margalit. Tel Aviv, Association of Former Residents of Ostrów-Mazowieck, 1960. 653 p., ports. (Hebrew, Yiddish)

Ostryna (P) see under Szczuczyn (*Sefer zikaron le-kehilot Szczuczyn, Wasiliszki* . . .)

Oswiecim (P). *Sefer Oshpitsin* [Oswiecim-Auschwitz memorial book*]. Eds.: Ch. Wolnerman, A. Burstin, M. S. Geshuri. Jerusalem, Oshpitsin Society, 1977. 622 p., illus. (Hebrew, Yiddish)

Oszmiana (P). *Sefer zikaron le-kehilat Oshmana* [Oshmana memorial book*]. Ed.: M. Gelbart. Tel Aviv, Oshmaner Organization in Israel and the Oshmaner Society in the USA, 1969. 659, 109 p., ports. (Hebrew, Yiddish, English)

Otvotsk (P) see Otwock

Otwock (P). *Khurbn Otvotsk, Falenits, Kartshev* [The destruction of Otvotsk, Falenits, Kartshev]. [By] B. Orenstein. [Bamberg] Former Residents of Otvotsk, Falenits, and Kartshev in the American Zone in Germany, 1948. 87 p., ports. (Yiddish)

Otwock (P). *Yizker-bukh; Otvotsk-Kartshev* [Memorial book of Otvotsk and Kartshev*]. Ed.: Sh. Kanc. Tel Aviv, Former Residents of Otvotsk-Kartshev, 1968. 1086 columns, ports. (Hebrew, Yiddish)

Ozarow (P) see under Ostrowiec

Ozieran (P) see Jezierzany

Ozorkow (P). *Ozorkow*. [By] Judah Loeb Levin. Jerusalem, Yad Yahadut Polin, 1966. 128 p., illus. (Hebrew)

Pabianice (P). *Sefer Pabianice* [Memorial book of Pabianice]. Ed.: A. W. Yassni. Tel Aviv, Former Residents of Pabianice in Israel, 1956. 419 p., ports., facsims. (Hebrew, Yiddish)

Paks (H). *Mazkeret Paks* [Paks memorial book], vol. I. Ed.: D. Sofer. Jerusalem, 1962. [1972/73]. 3 vols., ports., facsims. Vol. II, 1966 (Hebrew)

Parafianowo (P) see under Dokszyce

Parichi (B) see under Bobruisk

Parysow (P). *Sefer Porisov* [Parysow; a memorial to the Jewish community of Parysow, Poland*]. Ed.: Y. Granatstein. Tel Aviv, Former Residents of Parysow in Israel, 1971. 625 p., ports. (Hebrew, Yiddish)

Perehinsko (P) see under Rozniatow

Petrikov (P) see Pictrkow Trybunalski

Piaski (P). *Pyesk ve-Most; sefer yizkor* [Piesk and Most, a memorial book*]. Tel Aviv, Piesk and Most Societies in Israel and the Diaspora, 1975. 657, 17, 52 p., illus. (Hebrew, Yiddish, English)

Piatnica (P) see under Lomza (*Lomza, ir oyfkum un untergang*)

Piesk (P) see Piaski

Piestany (C) see Postyen

Pilev (P) see Pulawy

Pinczow (P). *Sefer zikaron le-kehilat Pintshev; in Pintshev togt shoyn nisht* [A book of memory of the Jewish community of Pinczow, Poland*]. Ed.: M. Shener. Tel Aviv, Former Residents of Pinczow in Israel and in the Diaspora, 1970. 480 p., ports. (Hebrew, Yiddish)

Pinsk (P). *Pinsk sefer edut ve-zikaron le-kehilat Pinsk-Karlin* [Pinsk *]. Ed.: N. Tamir (Mirski). Tel Aviv, Former Residents of Pinsk-Karlin in Israel, 1966–77. 3 vols. ports., facsims. (Hebrew, Yiddish)

Pinsk (P). *Toyznt yor Pinsk; geshikhte fun der shtot, der yidisher yishev, institutsyes, sotsyale bavegungen, perzenlekhkeytn, gezelshaftlekhe tuer, Pinsk iber der velt* [A thousand years of Pinsk; history of the city, its Jewish community, institutions, social movements, personalities, community leaders, Pinsk around the world]. Ed.: B. Hoffman. New York, Pinsker Branch 210, Workmen's Circle, 1941. 15, 500 p., illus. (Yiddish)

Piotrkow Trybunalski (P). *Piotrkow Trybunalski ve-ha-seviva* [Piotrkow Trybunalski and vicinity*]. Eds.: Y. Melz and N. (Lavy) Lau. Tel Aviv, Former Residents of Piotrkow Tryb. in Israel, [1965], 1192, 1xiv p., ports., facsims. (Hebrew, Yiddish, English)

Pitshayev (P) see Poczajow

Plantsh (Polaniec) (P) see under Staszow

Plawno (P) see under Radomsko

Plintsk (P) see Plonsk

Plock (P). *Plotsk; toldot kehila atikat yomin be-Polin* [Plotzk; a history of an ancient Jewish community in Poland*]. Ed.: E. Eisenberg. Tel Aviv, World Committee for the Plotzk Memorial Book, 1967. 684, 96 p., ports., maps, facsims. (Hebrew, Yiddish, English)

Plock (P). *Yidn in Plotsk* [Jews in Plotzk*]. [By] S. Greenspan. New York, 1960. 325 p., ports. (Yiddish)

Plonsk (P). *Sefer Plonsk ve-ha-seviva* [Memorial book of Plonsk and vicinity]. Ed.: Sh. Zemah. Tel Aviv, Former Residents of Plonsk in Israel, 1963. 775 p., ports., map, facsims. (Hebrew, Yiddish)

Plotsk (P) see Plock

Poczajow (P). *Pitshayever yizker-bukh* [Memorial book dedicated to the Jews of Pitchayev-Wohlyn executed by the Germans*]. Ed.: H. Gelernt. Philadelphia, The Pitchayever Wohliner Aid Society, 1960. 311 p., ports. (Yiddish)

Poczajow (P) see also under Krzemieniec

Podbrodzie (P) see under Swieciany

Podhajce (P). *Sefer Podhajce*. Ed.: M. S. Geshuri. Tel Aviv, Podhajce Society, 1972. 295, 17 p., illus. (Hebrew, Yiddish, English)

Pogost (B) see under Slutsk

Pohost (Pogost) (B) see under Slutsk

Pokshivnitsa (P) see Koprzywnica

Poland. *Megilat Polin* [The scroll of Poland]. Part 5: Holocaust, vol. I. Jerusalem, Society of Religious Jews from Poland, 1961. 351 p., ports., facsims. (Hebrew, Yiddish)

Polaniec (P) see under Staszow

Poligon (P) see under Swieciany

Polonnoye (U) see under Novograd-Volynskiy

Porcsalma (H) see under Csenger

Porisov (P) see Parysow

Porozow (P) see under Wolkowysk (*Volkovisker yizker-bukh*)

Postawy (P) see under Glebokie

Postyen (C). *Gedenkbuch der Gemeinden Piestany und Umgebung.* [By] Sh. Grunwald. Jerusalem, 1969. 111, [10] p., ports., offset (German)

Pozsony (C) see Various (Miscellany) *Arim ve-imahot be-yisrael*, v. 7

Praga (P). *Sefer Praga; mukdash le-zekher kedoshei irenu* [Praga book; dedicated to the memory of the martyrs of our town]. Ed.: Gabriel Weisman. Tel Aviv, Praga Society, 1974. 563 p., illus. (Hebrew, Yiddish)

Premisle (P) see Przemysl

Pressburg (Pozsony) (C) see under Various (Miscellany) *Arim ve-imahot be-yisrael*, v. 7

Proshnits (P) see Przasnysz

Proskurov (U). *Khurbn Proskurov; tsum ondenken fun di heylige neshomes vos zaynen umgekumen in der shreklikher shkhite, vos iz ongefirt gevoren durkh di haydamakes* [The destruction of Proskurov; in memory of the sacred souls who perished during the terrible slaughter of the Haidamaks]. New York, 1924. 111 p., illus. (Yiddish, Hebrew)

Pruszkow (P). *Sefer Pruszkow, Nadzin ve-ha-seviva* [Memorial book of Pruszkow, Nadzin and vicinity]. Ed.: D. Brodsky. Tel Aviv, Former Residents of Pruszkow in Israel, 1967. 334 p., ports., facsims. (Hebrew, Yiddish)

Pruzana (P). *Pinkas me-hamesh kehilot harevot . . .* [Memorial book of five destroyed communities . . .]. Ed.: M. W. Bernstein. Buenos Aires, Former Residents of Pruzana . . . , 1958. 972 p., ports., facsims. (Yiddish)

Przasnysz (P). *Sefer zikaron kehilat Proshnitz* [Memorial book to the community of Proshnitz*]. Ed.: Shlomo Bachrach. Tel Aviv, Proshnitz Society, 1974. 273 p., illus. (Hebrew, Yiddish, English)

Przeclaw (P) see under Radomysl Wielki

Przedborz (P). *Przedborz—33 shanim le-hurbana* [Przedborz memorial book*]. Ed.: Shimon Kanc. Tel Aviv, Przedborz Societies in Israel and America, 1977. 84, 548 p., illus. (Hebrew, Yiddish, English)

Przedborz (P) see also under Radomsko

Przedecz (P). *Sefer yizkor le-kedoshei ir Pshaytsh korbanot ha-shoa* [Memorial book to the Holocaust victims of the city of Pshaytsh]. Ed.: Moshe Bilavsky et al. Tel Aviv, Przedecz Societies in Israel and the Diaspora, 1974. 400 p., illus. (Hebrew, Yiddish)

Przemysl (P). *Sefer Przemysl* [Przemysl memorial book*]. Ed.: A. Menczer. Tel Aviv, Former Residents of Przemysl in Israel, 1964. 552 p., ports., facsims. (Hebrew, Yiddish)

Przytyk (P). *Sefer Przytyk.* Ed.: David Shtokfish. Tel Aviv, Przytyk Societies in Israel, France and the U.S.A., 1973. 7, 461 p., illus. (Hebrew, Yiddish)

Pshaytsh (P) see Przedecz

Pshedbozh (P) see Przedborz

Pshemishl (P) see Przemysl

Pshetslav (Przeclaw) (P) see under Radomysl Wielki

Pshitik (P) see Prztyk

Pulawy (P). *Yizker-bukh Pulawy* [In memoriam—the city of Pulawy*]. Ed.: M. W. Bernstein. New York, Pulawer Yiskor Book Committee, 1964. 494 p., ports., maps, facsims. (Yiddish)

Pultusk (P). *Pultusk; sefer zikaron* [Pultusk memorial book]. Ed.: Yitzhak Ivri. Tel Aviv, Pultusk Society, 1971. 683 p., illus. (Hebrew, Yiddish)

Punsk (P) see under Suwalki

Rabka (P) see under Nowy Targ

Rachev (U) see under Novograd-Volynskiy

Raciaz (P). *Galed le-kehilat Raciaz* [Memorial book of the community of Racionz*]. Ed.: E. Tsoref. Tel Aviv, Former Residents of Raciaz, 1965. 446, 47 p., ports., facsims. (Hebrew, Yiddish, English)

Raczki (P) see under Suwalki

Radekhov (P) see Radziechow

Radom (P). *Radom* [Radom; a memorial to the Jewish community of Radom, Poland*]. Ed.: A. Sh. Stein. Tel Aviv, Former Residents of Radom in Israel and in the Diaspora, 1961. 346, lxxviii p., ports., facsims. (Hebrew, Yiddish)

Radom (P). *Sefer Radom* [Memorial book of Radom]. [By] Y. Perlow. Tel Aviv, Former Residents of Radom in Israel and the USA, 1961. 451, [23] p., ports. (Yiddish, English)

Radomsko (P). *Sefer yizkor le-kehilat Radomsk ve-ha-seviva* [Memorial book of the community of Radomsk and vicinity]. Ed.: L. Losh. Tel Aviv, Former Residents of Radomsk . . . , 1967. 603 p., ports., music, facsims. (Hebrew, Yiddish)

Radomysl Wielki (P). *Radomysl Rabati ve-ha-seviva; sefer yizkor* [Radomysl Wielki and neighbourhood; memorial book*]. Eds.: H. Harshoshanim et al. Tel Aviv, Former Residents of Radomysl and Surroundings in Israel, 1965. 1065, liii p., ports., map, facsims. (Hebrew, Yiddish, English)

Radoszkowice (P). *Radoshkovits; sefer zikaron* [Radoshkowitz; a memorial to the Jewish community*]. Eds.: M. Robinson et al. Tel Aviv, Former Residents of Radoshkowitz in Israel, 1953. 222 p., ports. (Hebrew)

Radzanow (P) see under Szransk

Radziechow (P). *Sefer zikaron le-kehilot Radikhov, Lopatyn, Witkow Nowy, Cholojow, Toporow, Stanislawczyk, Stremiltsh, Shtruvits, ve-ha-kefarim Ubin, Barylow, Wolica-Wygoda, Skrilow, Zawidcze, Mikolajow, Dmytrow, Sienkow, ve-od* [Memorial book of Radikhov, Lopatyn, Witkow Nowy, Cholojow, Toporow, Stanislawczyk, Stremiltsh, Shtruvits, and the villages Ubin, Baryow, Wolica-Wygoda, Skrilow (i.e., Sknilow?), Zawidcze, Mikolajow, Dmytrow, Sienkow, etc.]. Ed.: G. Kressel. Tel Aviv, Society of Radikhov, Lopatyn and Vicinity, 1976. 656 p., illus. (Hebrew, Yiddish)

Radzin (P). *Radzin 1939–1943*. Ed.: Y. Rosenkrantz. Tel Aviv, Committee of Former Residents of Radzin and Pudel in Israel. 17 p. (Hebrew), mimeo. (as previous)

Radzin (P). *Sefer Radzin* [The book of Radzin]. Ed.: I. Siegelman. Tel Aviv, Council of Former Residents of Radzin (Podolsky) in Israel, 1957. 358 p. (Hebrew, Yiddish)

Radziwillow (P). *Radziwillow; sefer zikaron* [A memorial to the Jewish community of Radziwillow, Wolyn*]. Ed.: Y. Adini. Tel Aviv, The Radziwillow Organization in Israel, 1966. 438, [15] p., ports., map, facsims. (Hebrew, Yiddish)

Radzymin (P). *Sefer zikaron le-kehilat Radzymin* [Le livre du souvenir de la communauté juive de Radzymin*]. Ed.: Gershon Hel. Tel Aviv, The Encyclopaedia of the Jewish Diaspora, 1975. 389 p., illus. (Hebrew, Yiddish, French)

Rakhov (P) see Annopol

Rakishok (L) see Rokiskis

Rakospalota (H). *Toldot kehilat Rakospalota* [History of the Rakospalota community]. [By] Rachel Aharoni. Tel Aviv, 1978. 52, 204 p., illus. (Hebrew, Hungarian)

Rakow (P) *Sefer zikaron le-kehilat Rakow* [Memorial book of the community of Rakow]. Ed.: H. Abramson. Tel Aviv, Former Residents of Rakow in Israel and the USA, 1959. 184, [13] p., ports, facsims. (Hebrew, Yiddish)

Ratno (P). *Yizker-bukh Ratne; dos lebn un umkum fun a yidish shtetl in Volyn* [Memorial book of Ratno; the life and destruction of a Jewish town in Wolyn]. Eds.: Y. Botoshansky and Y. Yanasovitsh. Buenos Aires, Former Residents of Ratno in Argentina and the USA, 1954. 806 p., ports., map (Yiddish)

Rawa Ruska (P). *Sefer zikaron le-kehilat Rawa Ruska ve-ha-seviva* [Rawa Ruska memorial book*]. Eds.: A. M. Ringel, I. Z. Rubin. Tel Aviv, Rawa Ruska Society, 1973. 468 p., illus. (Hebrew, Yiddish, English)

Raysha (P) see Rzeszow

Rembertow (P). *Sefer zikaron le-kehilot Rembertow, Okuniew, Milosna* [Yizkor book in memory of Rembertov, Okuniev, Milosna*]. Ed.: Shimon Kanc. Tel Aviv, Rembertow, Okuniew and Milosna Societies in Israel, the U.S.A., France, Mexico City, Canada, Chile and Brazil, 1974. 16, 465 p., illus. (Hebrew, Yiddish)

Retteg (R) see under Des

Rietavas (L). *Sefer Ritova; gal-ed le-zekher ayaratenu* [Memorial book: the Ritavas Community; a tribute to the memory of our town*]. Ed.: Alter Levite. Tel Aviv, Ritova Societies in Israel and the Diaspora, 1977. 37, 223 p., illus. (Hebrew, Yiddish, English)

Riskeva (R) see Ruscova

Rohatyn (P). *Kehilat Rohatyn ve-ha-seviva* [Rohatyn; the history of a Jewish community*]. Ed.: M. Amihai. Tel Aviv, Former Residents of Rohatyn in Israel, 1962. 362, [15], 62 p., ports., facsims. (Hebrew, Yiddish, English)

Rokiskis (L). *Yizker-bukh fun Rakishok un umgegnt* [Yizkor book of Rakishok and environs*]. Ed.: M. Bakalczuk-Felin. Johannesburg, The Rakishker Landsmanshaft of Johannesburg, 1952, 626 p., ports. facsim. (Yiddish)

Rokitno (P). *Rokitno (Volyn) ve-ha-seviva; sefer edut ve-zikaron* [Rokitno-Wolyn and surroundings; memorial book and testimony]. Ed.: E. Leoni. Tel Aviv, Former Residents of Rokitno in Israel, 1967. 459 p., ports., maps (Hebrew, Yiddish)

Romanova (B) see under Slutsk

Rotin (P) see Rohatyn

Rovno (P) see Rowne

Rowne (P). *Rowne; sefer zikaron* [Rowno; a memorial to the Jewish community of Rowno, Wolyn*]. Ed.: A. Avitachi. Tel Aviv, "Yalkut Wolyn"—Former Residents of Rowno in Israel, 1956. 591 p., ports., map, facsims. (Hebrew)

Rozan (P). *Sefer zikaron le-kehilat Rozan (al ha-Narew)* [Rozhan memorial book*]. Ed.: Benjamin Halevy. Tel Aviv, Rozhan Societies in Israel and the U.S.A., 1977. 518, 96 p., illus. (Hebrew, Yiddish, English)

Rozana (P). *Rozhinoy; sefer zikaron le-kehilat Rozhinoy ve-ha-seviva* [Rozana; a memorial to the Jewish community*]. Ed.: M. Sokolowsky. Tel Aviv, Former Residents of Rozhinoy in Israel, 1957. 232 p., ports. (Hebrew, Yiddish)

Rozanka (P) see under Szczuczyn (*Sefer zikaron le-kehilot Szczuczyn, Wasiliszki . . .*)

Rozhinoy (P) see Rozana

Rozniatow (P). *Sefer zikaron le-kehilat Rozniatow, Perehinsko, Broszniow, Swaryczow ve-ha-seviva* [Yizkor-book in memory of Rozniatow, Perehinsko, Broszniow, Swaryczow and environs*]. Ed.: Shimon Kanc. Tel Aviv, Rozniatow, Perehinsko, Broszniow and Environs Societies in Israel and the U.S.A., 1974, 58, 537 p., illus. (Hebrew, Yiddish, English)

Rozprza (P) see under Piotrkow Trybunalski

Rozwadow (P). *Sefer yizkor Rozwadow ve-ha-seviva* [Rozwadow memorial book*]. Ed.: N. Blumental. Jerusalem, Former Residents of Rozwadow in Israel . . . , 1968. 349 p., ports. (Hebrew, Yiddish, English)

Rozyszcze (P). *Rozyszcze ayarati* [Rozyszcze my old home*]. Ed.: Gershon Zik. Tel Aviv, Rozyszcze Societies in Israel, the United States, Canada, Brazil, and Argentina, 1976. 482, 76 p., illus. (Hebrew, Yiddish, English)

Rubeshov (P) see Hrubieszow

Rubiezewicze (P) see also under Stolpce

Rubiezewicze (P). *Sefer Rubizhevitsh, Derevne ve-ha-seviva* [Rubiezewicze and surroundings book*]. Ed.: D. Shtokfish. Tel Aviv, 1968. 422 p., illus. (Yiddish, Hebrew)

Rudki (P). *Rudki; sefer yizkor le-yehudei Rudki ve-ha-seviva* [Rudki memorial book; of the Jews of Rudki and vicinity*]. Ed.: Joseph Chrust. Israel, Rudki Society, 1978. 374 p., illus. (Hebrew, Yiddish, English)

Ruscova (R). *Sefer le-zikaron kedoshei Ruscova ve-Soblas, mehoz Marmarosh* [Memorial book of the martyrs of Ruscova and Soblas, Marmarosh District]. Ed.: Y.Z. Moskowits. Tel Aviv, Former Residents of Ruskova and Soblas in Israel and in the Diaspora, 1969. 126 p., ports., facsims. (Hebrew, Yiddish)

Ryki (P). *Yizker-bukh tsum fareybikn dem ondenk fun der khorev-gevorener yidisher kehile Ryki* [Ryki; a memorial to the community of Ryki, Poland*]. Ed.: Shimon Kanc. Tel Aviv, Ryki Societies in Israel, Canada, Los Angeles, France, and Brazil, 1973. 611 p., illus. (Hebrew, Yiddish)

Rypin (P). *Sefer Rypin* [Ripin; a memorial to the Jewish community of Ripin—Poland*]. Ed.: Sh. Kanc. Tel Aviv, Former Residents of Ripin in Israel and in the Diaspora, 1962. 942, 15 p., ports., facsims. (Hebrew, Yiddish, English)

Rytwiany (P) see under Staszow

Rzeszow (P). *Kehilat Raysha; sefer zikaron* [Rzeszow Jews; memorial book*]. Ed.: M. Yari-Wold. Tel Aviv, Former Residents of Rzeszow in Israel and the USA, 1967. 620, 142 p., ports., maps, facsims. (Hebrew, Yiddish, English)

Saloniki (G). *Saloniki; ir va-em be-yisrael* [Salonique, ville-mère en Israel*]. Jerusalem-Tel Aviv, Centre de recherches sur le Judaisme de Salonique, Union des Juifs de Grèce, 1967. 358, xviii p., ports., maps, facsims. (Hebrew, French)

Saloniki (G). *Zikhron Saloniki; gedulata ve-hurbana shel Yerushalayim de-Balkan* [Zikhron Saloniki; grandeza i destruyicion de Yeruchalayim del Balkan*]. Ed.: David A. Recanati. Tel Aviv, Committee for the Publication of the Saloniki Book, [1971/72]. Vol. 1: 16, 524, 56 p., illus. (Hebrew, Judezmo)

Sambor (P). *Sefer Sambor-Stary Sambor; pirkei edut ve-zikaron le-kehilot Sambor-Stary Sambor mi-reshitan ve-ad hurbanan* [The book of Sambor and Stari Sambor; a memorial to the Jewish communities of Sambor and Stari Sambor, the story of the two Jewish communities from their beginnings to their end*]. Ed.: Alexander Manor. Tel Aviv, Sambor/Stary Sambor Society, 1980. xlvi, 323 p., illus. (Hebrew, Yiddish, English)

Sammerein (Somorja) (C) see under Dunaszerdahely

Samorin (Somorja) (C) see under Dunaszerdahely

Sanok (P) see also under Dynow (*Khurbn Dynow*)

Sanok (P). *Sefer zikaron le-kehilat Sanok ve-ha-seviva* [Memorial book of Sanok and vicinity]. Ed.: E. Sharvit. Jerusalem, Former Residents of Sanok and Vicinity in Israel, 1970. 686 p., ports., facsims. (Hebrew, Yiddish)

Sants (P) see Nowy Sacz

Sarkeystsene (Szarkowszczyna) (P) see under Glebokie

Sarnaki (P). *Sefer yizkor le-kehilat Sarnaki* [Memorial book of the community of Sarnaki]. Ed.: D. Shuval. Haifa, Former Residents of Sarnaki in Israel, 1968. 415 p., ports. (Hebrew, Yiddish)

Sarny (P). *Sefer yizkor le-kehilat Sarny* [Memorial book of the community of Sarny]. Ed.: Y. Kariv. Tel Aviv, Former Residents of Sarny and Vicinity in Israel, 1961. 508, 32 p., ports., facsims. (Hebrew, Yiddish)

Sasow (P). *Mayn shtetl Sasow* [My town Sasow]. [By] Moshe Rafael. Jerusalem, 1979. (Yiddish)

Schodnica (P) see under Drohobycz

Schutt Szerdahely (C) see Dunaszerdahely

Secureni (R) see Sekiryany
Sedziszow (P) see under Wodzislaw
Sekiryani (R). *Sekurian (Bessarabia) be-vinyana u-be-hurbana* [Sekiryani, Bessarabia—alive and destroyed]. Ed.: Z. Igrat. Tel Aviv, [Committee of Former Residents of Sekiryani], 1954. 260 p., ports. (Hebrew)
Selib (Wsielub) (P) see under Nowogrodek
Selish (C) see Nagyszollos
Selts (Sielec) (P) see uner Pruzana
Semiatycze (P). *Kehilat Semiatycze* [The community of Semiatich*] . Ed.: E. Tash (TurSha-lom). Tel Aviv, Assoc. of Former Residents of Semiatich in Israel and the Diaspora, 1965. 449 p., ports., map, facsims. (Hebrew, Yiddish, English)
Sendishev (Sedziszów) (P) see under Wodzislaw
Serock (P). *Sefer Serotsk* [The book of Serock]. Ed.: M. Gelbart. Former Residents of Serock in Israel, 1971. 736 p., ports. (Hebrew, Yiddish)
Sevlus (C) see Nagyszollos
Shchedrin (B) see under Bobruisk
Shedlets (P) see Siedlce
Shelib (Wsielub) (P) see under Nowogrodek
Shidlovtse (P) see Szydlowiec
Shimsk (P) see Szumsk
Shkud (L) see Skuodas
Shpola (U). *Shpola; masekhet hayei yehudim ba-ayara* [Shpola; a picture of Jewish life in the town]. [By] David Cohen. [Haifa], Association of Former Residents of Shpola (Ukraine) in Israel, 1965. 307 p., ports. (Hebrew)
Shransk (P) see Szransk
Shtruvits (Szczurowice) (P) see under Radziechow
Siedlce (P). *Sefer yizkor le-kehilat Shedlets* [Memorial book of the community of Siedlce]. Ed.: A. W. Yassni. Buenos Aires, Former Residents of Siedlce in Israel and Argentina, 1956. xvi, 813 p., ports., facsims. (Hebrew, Yiddish)
Siedliszcze (P). *Sefer zikaron le-kehilat Siedliszcze ve-he-seviva* [Memorial book of the community of Siedliszcze and vicinity]. Ed.: B. Haruvi. Tel Aviv, Former Residents of Siedliszcze in Israel, 1970. 360 p., ports., facsims. (Hebrew, Yiddish)
Sielec (P) see under Pruzana
Sienkow (P) see under Radziechow
Sierpc (P). *Kehilat Sierpc; sefer zikaron* [The community of Sierpc; memorial book]. Ed.: E. Talmi (Wloka). Tel Aviv, Former Residents of Sierpc in Israel and Abroad, 1959. 603 p., ports., map, facsims. (Hebrew, Yiddish)
Sierpc (P). *Khurbn Sierpc 1939–1945; zikhroynes fun di ibergeblibene landslait vos gefinen zikh in der Amerikaner Zone in Daytshland* [The destruction of Sierpc 1939–1945; memories of the remnants of the community of Sierpc in the American Zone in Germany]. Eds.: A. Meirantz and H. Nemlich. Munich, Committee of the Former Residents of Sierpc in the American Zone in Germany, 1947. 55 p., ports. (Yiddish)
Siniawka (P) see under Kleck
Sislevitsh (P) see Swislocz
Skala (P). *Sefer Skala*. Ed.: Max Mermelstein (Weidenfeld). New York–Tel Aviv, Skala Benevolent Society, 1978. 98, 261 p., illus. (Hebrew, Yiddish, English)
Skalat (P). *Skalat; kovets zikaron le-kehila she-harva ba-shoa* [Skalat; memorial volume of the community which perished in the Holocaust]. Ed.: H. Bronstein. Tel Aviv, The Yaacov Krol School in Petah-Tikva and Former Residents of Skalat Israel, 1971. 160 p., ports., facsims. (Hebrew)

Skarzysko-Kamienna (P). *Skarzysko-Kamienna sefer zikaron* [The "yizchor" book in memoriam of the Jewish community of Skarzysko and its surroundings*]. Tel Aviv, Skarzysko Society, 1973. 260 p., illus. (Hebrew, Yiddish)

Skierniewice (P). *Sefer Skierniewice* [The book of Skierniewice]. Ed.: J. Perlow. Tel Aviv, Former Residents of Skierniewice in Israel, 1955. 722 p., ports., facsims. (Yiddish)

Sknilow (P) see under Radziechow

Skole (P) see under Galicia (*Gedenkbukh Galicia*)

Skuodas (L). *Kehilat Skhkud; kovets zikaron* [Memorial book of Skuodas]. Tel Aviv, Former Residents of Skuodas, 1948. 68 p., ports., facsims. (Hebrew, Yiddish)

Slonim (P). *Pinkas Slonim* [Memorial book of Slonim]. Ed.: K. Lichtenstein. Tel Aviv, Former Residents of Slonim in Israel, [1962–1979]. 4 vols., ports. (Hebrew, Yiddish, English)

Slupia (P) see under Ostrowiec

Slutsk (B). *Pinkas Slutsk u-benoteha* [Slutsk and vicinity memorial book*]. Ed.: N. Chinitz and Sh. Nachmani. Tel Aviv, Yizkor-Book Committee, 1962. 450 p., ports., maps, facsims. (Hebrew, Yiddish, English)

Sluzewo (P) see under Wloclawek

Smorgonie (P). *Smorgon mehoz Vilno; sefer edut ve-zikaron* [Smorgonie, District Vilna; memorial book and testimony]. [Tel Aviv], Assoc. of Former Residents of Smorgonie in Israel and USA, 1965. 584 p., ports., facsims. (Hebrew, Yiddish)

Smotrich (U) see under Kamenets-Podolskiy

Soblas (R) see under Ruscova

Sobota (P) see under Lowicz

Sochaczew (P). *Pinkas Sochaczew* [Memorial book of Sochaczew]. Eds.: A. Sh. Stein and G. Weissman. Jerusalem, Former Residents of Sochaczew in Israel, 1962. 843 p., ports. (Hebrew, Yiddish)

Sokal (P). *Sefer Sokal, Tartakow . . . ve-ha-seviva* [Memorial book of Sokal, Tartakow . . . and surroundings]. Ed.: A. Chomel. Tel Aviv, Former Residents of Sokal and Surroundings, 1968. 576 p., ports., facsims. (Hebrew, Yiddish)

Sokolka (P). *Sefer Sokolka* [Memorial book of Sokolka]. Jerusalem, The Encyclopaedia of the Jewish Diaspora, 1968. 767 p., ports., facsims. (Hebrew, Yiddish)

Sokolovka (Yustingrad) (U) see Yustingrad

Sokolow (P). *In shotn fun Treblinka (khurbn Sokolow-Podlaski)*. [In the shadow of Treblinka*]. [By] Symcha Polakiewicz. Tel Aviv, Sokolow-Podlaski Society, 1957. 167 p. (Yiddish)

Sokolow (P). *Mayn khorev shtetl Sokolow; shilderungen, bilder un portretn fun a shtot umgekumene yidn* [My destroyed town of Sokolow]. [By] Peretz Granatstein. Buenos Aires, Union Central Israelita Polaca en la Argentina, 1946. 188 p., illus. (Yiddish)

Sokolow (P). *Sefer ha-zikaron; Sokolow-Podlask* [Memorial book Sokolow-Podlask]. Ed.: M. Gelbart. Tel Aviv, Former Residents of Sokolow-Podlask in Israel and . . . in the USA, 1962. 758, [55] p., ports. (Yiddish, Hebrew)

Sokoly (P). *Sefer zikaron le-kedoshei Sokoly* [Memorial book of the martyrs of Sokoly]. Ed.: M. Grossman. Tel Aviv, Former Residents of Sokoly, 1962. 625 p., ports. (Yiddish)

Sokoly (P). *Sokoly—be-ma'avak le-hayim* [Sokoly—in a struggle for survival]. Translator and ed.: Shmuel Klisher. Tel Aviv, Sokoly Society, 1975. 438 p., illus. (Hebrew)

Sombor (Y) see Zombor

Somorja (C) see under Dunaszerdahely

Sonik (P) see Sanok

Sopockinie (P). *Korot ayara ahat; megilat ha-shigshug ve-ha-hurban shel kehilat Sopotkin* [Sopotkin; in memory of the Jewish community*]. [By] Alexander Manor (Menchinsky). [Tel Aviv], Sopotkin Society, 1960. 124 p., illus. (Hebrew)

Sopotkin (P) see Sopockinie

Sosnowiec (P). *Sefer Sosnowiec ve-ha-seviva be-Zaglembie* [Book of Sosnowiec and the surrounding region in Zaglebie]. Ed.: Meir Shimon Geshuri (Bruckner). Tel Aviv, Sosnowiec Societies in Israel, the United States, France, and other countries, 1973–1974. 2 vols., illus. (Hebrew, Yiddish)

Stanislawczyk (P) see under Radziechow

Stanislawow (P) see under Various (Miscellany) *Arim ve-imahot be-yisrael*, v. 5

Starachowice (P) see under Wierzbnik

Starobin (B) see under Slutsk

Starye Dorogi (B) see under Slutsk

Stary Sambor (P) see under Sambor

Staszow (P). *Sefer Staszow* [The Staszow book*]. Ed.: E. Erlich. Tel Aviv, Former Residents of Staszow in Israel . . . and in the Diaspora, 1962. 690 p., ports., facsims. (Hebrew, Yiddish, English)

Stavische (U). *Stavisht*. Ed.: A. Weissman. Tel Aviv, The Stavisht Society, New York, 1961. 252 columns, ports. (Hebrew, Yiddish)

Stawiski (P). *Stawiski; sefer yizkor* [Stawiski memorial book]. Ed.: I. Rubin. Tel Aviv, Stavisk Society, 1973. 379, 5 p., illus. (Hebrew, Yiddish, English)

Stepan (P). *Ayaratenu Stepan* [The Stepan story; excerpts*]. Ed.: Yitzhak Ganuz. Tel Aviv, Stepan Society, 1977. 4, 364 p., illus. (Hebrew, English)

Steybts (P) see Stolpce

Stiyanev (Stojanow) (P) see under Sokal

Stoczek-Wegrowski (P). *Pinkes Stok (bay Vengrov); matsevet netsah* [Memorial book of Stok, near Wegrow]. Ed.: I. Zudicker. Buenos Aires, Stok Societies in Israel, North America and Argentina, 1974. 654 p., illus. (Hebrew, Yiddish)

Stojaciszki (P) see under Swieciany

Stojanow (P) see under Sokal

Stok (P) see Stoczek-Wegrowski

Stolin (P). *Stolin; sefer zikaron le-kehilat Stolin ve-ha-seviva* [Stolin; a memorial to the Jewish communities of Stolin and vicinity*]. Eds.: A. Avatichi and Y. Ben-Zakkai. Tel Aviv, Former Residents of Stolin and Vicinity in Israel, 1952. 263 p., ports. (Hebrew)

Stolpce (P). *Sefer zikaron; Steibtz-Swerznie ve-ha-ayarot ha-semukhot* . . . [Memorial volume of Steibtz-Swerznie and the neighbouring villages . . . *]. Ed.: N. Hinitz. Tel Aviv, Former Residents of Steibtz in Israel, 1964. 537, xxiii p., ports., map, facsims. (Hebrew, Yiddish, English)

Stremiltsh (Strzemilcze) (P) see under Radziechow

Strusow (P) see under Trembowla

Stryj (P). *Sefer Stryj* [Memorial book of Stryj]. Eds.: N. Kudish et al. Tel Aviv, Former Residents of Stryj in Israel, 1962. 260, 68 p., ports., facsims. (Hebrew, Yiddish, English)

Strzegowo (P). *Strzegowo yizker-bukh* [Memorial book of Strzegowo]. New York, United Strzegower Relief Committee, 1951. 135, [18] p., ports., facsims. (Hebrew, Yiddish, English)

Strzemilcze (P) see under Radziechow

Strzyzow (P). *Sefer Strizhuv ve-ha-seviva* [Memorial book of Strzyzow and vicinity]. Eds.: J. Berglas, Sh. Yahalomi (Diamant). Tel Aviv, Former Residents of Stryzow in Israel and Diaspora, 1969. 480 p., ports., facsims. (Hebrew, Yiddish)

Stutshin (P) see Szczuczyn

Sucha (P) see under Wadowice

Suchocin (R) see under Plonsk

Suchowola (P). *Sefer Suchowola* [Memorial book of Suchowola]. Eds.: H. Steinberg et al.

Jerusalem, The Encyclopaedia of the Jewish Diaspora, 1957. 616 columns, [2] p., ports., map, facsims. (Hebrew, Yiddish)

Suwalki (P). *Yizker-bukh Suvalk* [Memorial book of Suvalk]. Ed.: B. Kahan. New York, The Suvalk and Vicinity Relief Committee of New York, 1961. 825 columns, ports., facsims. (Yiddish)

Swaryczow (P) see under Rozniatow

Swieciany (P). *Sefer zikaron le-esrim ve-shalosh kehilot she-nehrevu be-ezor Svintzian* [Svintzian Region; memorial book of twenty-three Jewish communities*]. Ed.: Sh. Kanc. Tel Aviv, Former Residents of the Svintzian District in Israel, 1965. 1954 columns, ports., maps, music, facsims. (Hebrew, Yiddish)

Swierzen (P) see under Stolpce

Swir (P). *Ayaratenu Swir* [Our townlet Swir*]. Ed.: Ch. Swironi (Drutz). Tel Aviv, Former Residents of Swir in Israel and . . . in the United States, 1959. 240 p., ports., map (Hebrew, Yiddish)

Swir (P). *Haya hayeta ayarat Swir; ben shtei milhamot ha-olam* [There once was a town Swir; between the two world wars]. [By] Herzl Vayner. [Israel], Swir Society, 1975. 227 p., illus. (Hebrew, Yiddish)

Swislocz (P). *Kehilat Swisiocz pelekh Grodno* [The community of Swisocz, Grodno District]. Ed.: H. Rabin. Tel Aviv, Former Residents of Swislocz in Israel, 1961. 159 p., ports. (Hebrew, Yiddish)

Swislocz (P) see also under Wolkowysk (*Volkovisker yizker-bukh*)

Szamosujvar (R). *Sefer zikaron shel kedoshei ayaratenu Számosujvar-Iklad ve-ha-seviva* . . . [Memorial book of the martyrs of our town Szamosjuvar-Iklad and surroundings]. Eds.: M. Bar-On and B. Herskovits. Tel Aviv, Former Residents of Szamosujvar-Iklad and Surroundings in Israel, 1971. 190, 90 p., ports., facsims. (Hebrew, Hungarian)

Szarkowszczyzna (P) see under Glebokie

Szczawnica (P) see under Nowy Targ

Szczekociny (P). *Pinkas Szczekociny* [A memorial book to the Jewish community of Szczekociny*]. Ed.: J. Schweizer. Tel Aviv, Former Residents of Szczekociny in Israel, 1959. 276 p., ports., facsims. (Hebrew, Yiddish)

Szczuczyn (District Bialystok) (P). *Hurban kehilat Szczuczyn* [The destruction of the community of Szczuczyn]. Tel Aviv, Former Residents of Szczuczyn in Israel and . . . , 1954. 151 p., ports. (Yiddish).

Szczuczyn (P). *Sefer zikaron le-kehilot Szczuczyn, Wasiliszki* . . . [Memorial book of the communities Szczuczyn, Wasiliszki . . .]. Ed.: L. Losh. Tel Aviv, Former Residents of Szczuczyn, Wasiliszki . . . , 1966. 456 p., ports., map, facsims. (Hebrew, Yiddish)

Szczurowice (P) see under Radziechow

Szereszow (P) see under Pruzana

Szikszo (H). *Nitsutsot—mi-kehilat Szikszo ve-mehoz Abauj-Turna she-nidmu; toldot hayehem ve-ad hurbanam* [Sparks; from the community of Szikszo and the region of Abauj Turna]. [By] Israel Fleishman; Bnei Brak, 1972. 96,374 p., illus. (Hebrew, Hungarian)

Szkudy (L) see Skuodas

Szransk (P). *Kehilat Szransk ve-ha-seviva; sefer zikaron* [The Jewish community of Szrensk and the vicinity; a memorial volume*]. Ed.: Y. Rimon (Granat). Jerusalem, [Former Residents of Szrensk in Israel], 1960. 518, 70 p., ports., maps, facsims. (Hebrew, Yiddish, English)

Szumsk (P). *Szumsk . . . sefer zikaron le-kedoshei Szumsk* . . . [Szumsk . . . memorial book of the martyrs of Szumsk . . .]. Ed.: H. Rabin. [Tel Aviv, Former Residents of Szumsk in Israel, 1968]. 477 p., ports., map, facsims. (Hebrew, Yiddish)

Szydlow (P) see under Staszow

Szydlowiec (P). *Shidlovtser yizker-bukh* [Yizkor book Szydowiec*]. Ed.: Berl Kagan. New York, 1974. 7, 912, 22 p., illus. (Yiddish, English)

Targowica (P). *Sefer Trovits* [Memorial book of Targovica*]. Ed.: I. Siegelman. Haifa, Former Residents of Targovica in Israel, 1967. 452 p., ports., map, facsims. (Hebrew, Yiddish)

Targu-Lapus (Magyarlapos) (R) see under Des

Targu-Mures (R) see Marosvasarhely

Tarnobrzeg (P). *Kehilat Tarnobrzeg-Dzikow (Galicia ha-ma'aravit)* [The community of Tarnobrzeg-Dzikow (Western Galicia)]. Ed.: Yaakov Yehoshua Fleisher. Tel Aviv, Tarnobrzeg-Dzikow Society, 1973. 379 p., illus. (Hebrew, Yiddish)

Tarnogrod (P). *Sefer Tarnogrod; le-zikaron ha-kehila ha-yehudit she-nehreva* [Book of Tarnogrod; in memory of the destroyed Jewish community]. Ed.: Sh. Kanc. Tel Aviv, Organization of Former Residents of Tarnogrod and Vicinity in Israel, United States and England, 1966. 592 p., ports. (Hebrew, Yiddish)

Tarnopol (P) *Tarnopol* [Tarnopol]. Ed.: Ph. Korngruen. Jerusalem, Encyclopaedia of the Jewish Diaspora, 1955. 474 columns, ports., facsims. (Hebrew, Yiddish, English)

Tarnow (P). *Tarnow; kiyuma ve-hurbana shel ir yehudit* [The life and decline of a Jewish city]. Ed.: A. Chomet. Tel Aviv, Association of Former Residents of Tarnow, 1954. xx, 928 p., ports., facsims. (Hebrew, Yiddish). Vol. II. Eds.: A. Chomel and Y. Kornilo, 1968. 433 p., map (Hebrew, Yiddish)

Tartakow (P) see under Sokal

Tasnad (R). *Tasnad; tei'ur le-zekher kehilat Tasnad (Transylvania) ve-ha-seviva ve-yeshivat Maharam Brisk, me-reshitan ve-ad le-aher y'mei ha-shoa* [Tasnád; description, in memory of the community of Tasnad (Transylvania) and the surrounding region, and the Brisk Yeshiva, from their beginnings until after the Holocaust]. [By] Avraham Fuks. Jerusalem, 1973. 276 p., illus. (Hebrew)

Teglas (H) see under Debrecen

Telechany (P). Telekhan [Telekhan memorial book*]. Ed.: Sh. Sokoler. Los Angeles, Telekhan Memorial Book Committee, 1963. 189, 15 p., ports., map (Hebrew, Yiddish, English)

Teplik (U). *Teplik, mayn shtetele; kapitlen fun fuftsik yor lebn* [My town Teplik; chapters from fifty years of life]. [By] Valentin Chernovetzky. Buenos Aires, El Magazine Argentino, 1946-50. 2 vols., illus. (Yiddish)

Terebovlya (P) see Trembowla

Ternovka (U). *Ayaratenu Ternovka; pirkei zikaron ve-matseva* [Our town Ternovka; chapters of remembrance and a monument]. [By] G. Bar-Zvi. Tel Aviv, Ternovka Society, 1972. 103 p., illus. (Hebrew)

Thessaloniki (G) see Saloniki

Tighina (R) see Bendery

Tiktin (P) see Tykocin

Timkovichi (B) see under Slutsk

Tishevits (P) see Tyszowce

Tlumacz (P). *Tlumacz-Tolmitsh; sefer edut ve-zikaron* [Memorial book of Tlumacz*]. Ed.: Shlomo Blond et al. Tel Aviv, Tlumacz Society, 1976. 187, 533 p., illus. (Hebrew, Yiddish, English)

Tluste (P). *Sefer Tluste* [Memorial book of Tluste]. Ed.: G. Lindenberg. Tel Aviv, Association of Former Residents of Tluste and Vicinity in Israel and USA, 1965. 289 p., ports., map, facsims. (Hebrew, Yiddish)

Tluszcz (P). *Sefer zikaron le-kehilat Tluszcz* [Memorial book of the community of Tluszcz]. Ed.: M. Gelbart. Tel Aviv, Association of Former Residents of Tluszcz in Israel, 1971. 340 p. (Hebrew, Yiddish)

Tomaszow-Lubelski (P). *Sefer zikaron shel Tomaszow-Lub.* [Memorial book of Tomaszow-Lubelski]. Ed.: Moshe Gordon. Jerusalem, 1972. 28, 549 p., illus. (Hebrew)

Tomaszow Lubelski (P). *Tomashover (Lubelski) yizker-bukh* [Memorial book of Tomaszow Lubelski]. New York, Tomashover Relief Committee, 1965. 912 p., ports., facsims. (Yiddish)

Tomaszow Mazowiecki (P). *Sefer zikaron le-kehilat Tomaszow Mazowiecki* [Tomashow-Mazowieck; a memorial to the Jewish community of Tomashow-Mazovieck*]. Ed.: M. Wajsberg. Tel Aviv, Tomashow Organization in Israel, 1969. 648 p., ports., map, facsims. (Hebrew, Yiddish, English, French)

Topolcany (C). *Korot mekorot le-kehila yehudit-Topolcany* [The story and source of the Jewish community of Topoltchany*]. [By] Yehoshua Robert Buchler. Lahavot Haviva, Topolcany Book Committee, 1976. 74, 64, 174 p., illus. (Hebrew, English, German)

Toporow (P) see under Radziechow

Torna (P) see Tarnow

Transylvania (Region R). *Toldot ha-kehilot be-Transylvania; perakim mi-sevalot ha-yehudim ve-nitsane ha-gevura bi-tekufat ha-shoa be-Hungaria* [History of the communities of Transylvania]. [By] Yehuda Shvartz. Hadera, Ha-Aguda Yad le-Kehilot Transylvania, [1976]. 293 p., illus. (Hebrew)

Trembowla (P). *Sefer yizkor le-kehilot Trembowla, Strusow ve-Janow ve-ha-seviva* [Memorial book for the Jewish communities of Trembowla, Strusow, Janow and vicinity*]. Bnei Brak, Trembowla Society, [198-]. li, 379 p., illus., maps (Hebrew, English)

Trisk (P) see Turzysk

Troki (P). *Troki* Tel Aviv, [1954]. 79 p., map (Hebrew)

Trovits (P) see Targowica

Trzebinia (P). *Kehilat Tshebin* [The community of Trzebinia*]. Eds.: P. Goldwasser et al. Haifa, Committee of Trzebinians in Israel, 1969. 21, 435, 35 p., ports., map, facsims. (Hebrew, English)

Tshebin (P) see Trzebinia

Tshekhanov (P) see Ciechanow

Tshekhanovets (P) see Ciechanowiec

Tshenstokhov (P) see Czestochowa

Tsheshanov (P) see Cieszanow

Tshizheva (P) see Czyzewo

Tshmelev (Cmielow) (P) see under Ostrowiec

Tuczyn (P). *Sefer zikaron le-kehilat Tuczyn-Krippe* [Tutchin-Krippe, Wolyn; in memory of the Jewish community*]. Ed.: B. H. Ayalon. Tel Aviv, Tutchin and Krippe Relief Society of Israel . . . , 1967. 383 p., ports., map, facsims. (Hebrew, Yiddish)

Turets (P) see Turzec

Turka (P). *Sefer zikaron le-kehilat Turka al nehar Stry ve-ha-seviva* [Memorial book of the community of Turka on the Stry River and vicinity]. Ed.: J. Siegelman. Haifa, Former Residents of Turka (Stry) in Israel, 1966. 472 p., ports., map, facsims. (Hebrew, Yiddish)

Turobin (P). *Sefer Turobin; pinkas zikaron* [The Turobin book; in memory of the Jewish community*]. Ed.: M. S. Geshuri. Tel Aviv, Former Residents of Turobin in Israel, 1967. 397 p., ports., map, facsims. (Hebrew, Yiddish)

Turzec (P). *Kehilot Turzec ve-Jeremicze; sefer zikaron* [Book of remembrance—Tooretz-Yeremitz*]. Eds.: Michael Walzer-Fass, Moshe Kaplan. Israel, Turzec and Jeremicze Societies in Israel and America, 1978. 114, 421 p., illus. (Hebrew, Yiddish, English)

Turzysk (P). *Pinkas ha-kehila Trisk; sefer yizkor* [Memorial book of Trisk]. Ed.: Natan Livneh. Tel Aviv, Trisk Society, 1975. 376 p., illus. (Hebrew, Yiddish)

Tykocin (P). *Sefer Tiktin* [Memorial book of Tiktin]. Eds.: M. Bar-Yuda and Z. Ben-Nahum. Tel Aviv, Former Residents of Tiktin in Israel, 1959. 606 p., ports., facsims. (Hebrew)

Tysmienica (P). *Tismenits; a matseyve oyf di khurves fun a farnikhteter yidisher kehile* [Tysmienica; a memorial book*]. Ed.: Shlomo Blond. Tel Aviv, Hamenora, 1974. 262 p., illus. (Hebrew, Yiddish)

Tyszowce (P). *Pinkas Tishovits* [Tiszowic book*]. Ed.: Y. Zipper. Tel Aviv, Assoc. of Former Residents of Tiszowic in Israel, 1970. 324 p., ports., facsims. (Hebrew, Yiddish)

Ubinie (P) see under Radziechow

Uhnow (P). *Hivniv (Uhnow); sefer zikaron le-kehila* [Hivniv (Uhnow); memorial book to a community]. Tel Aviv, Uhnow Society, 1981. 298, 83 p., illus.

Ujpest (H). *Sefer zikhronot shel k(ehila) k(edosha) Ujpest* [Memorial book of the community of Ujpest]. [By] Laszlo Szilagy-Windt; Hebrew translation: Menahem Miron. Tel Aviv, 1975. 27, 325 p., illus. (Hebrew, Hungarian)

Ukraine (U). *Yidn in Ukraine* [Jews in the Ukraine*]. Eds.: M. Osherovitch, J. Lestschinsky et al. New York, Association for the Commemoration of the Ukrainian Jews, 1961-67. 2 vols., 342 p., ports., maps, facsims. (Yiddish)

Ungvar (C) see under Various (Miscellany) *Arim ve-imahot be-yisrael*, v. 4

Urechye (B) see under Slutsk

Uscilug (P). *Kehilat Ustila be-vinyanau-be-hurbana* [The growth and destruction of the community of Uscilug]. Ed.: A. Avinadav. Tel Aviv, Association of Former Residents of Uscilug, [1961]. 334 p., ports. (Hebrew, Yiddish)

Ustila (P) see Uscilug

Ustrzyki Dolne (P) see under Lesko

Uzhorod (Ungvar) (C) see under *Arim ve-imahot be-yisrael*, v. 4

Uzlovoye (Cholojow) (P) see under Radziechow

Vamospercs (H) see under Debrecen

Vas (H). *Sefer zikaron mehoz Vas* [Memorial book of the region of Vas]. Ed.: Avraham Levinger. Israel, Vas Commemorative Committee, 1974. 214 p., illus. (Hebrew)

Vashniev (Wasniów) (P) see under Ostrowiec

Vasilishok (Wasiliszki) (P) see under Szczuczyn (*Sefer zikaron le-kehilot Szczuczyn, Wasiliszki. . . .*)

Vayslits (P) see Wislica

Velky Mager (Nagymagyar) (C) see under Dunaszerdahely

Vengrov (P) see Wegrow

Verbo (C) see under Postyen

Verzhbnik (P) see Wierzbnik

Vidz (Widze) (P) see under Swieciany

Vilna (P). *Bleter vegn Vilne; zamlbukh* [Pages about Vilna; a compilation]. Eds.: L. Ran and L. Koriski. Lodz, Association of Jews from Vilna in Poland, 1947. xvii, 77 p., ports., music, facsims. (Yiddish)

Vilna (P) see also under Lithuania and under Various (Miscellany) *Arim ve-imahot be-yisrael*, v. 1

Vilna (P). *Yerusholayim de-Lita* [Jerusalem of Lithuania, illustrated and documented*]. Collected and arranged by Leyzer Ran. New York, Vilna Album Committee, 1974. 3 vols., illus. (Hebrew, Yiddish, English, Russian)

Vinnitsa (U) see under Various (Miscellany) *Arim ve-imahot be-yisrael*, v. 4

Vinogradov (C) see Nagyszollos

Vishneva (P) see Wiszniew
Vishnevets (P) see Wisniowiec Nowy
Vishogrod (P) see Wyszogrod
Viskit (Wiskitki) (P) see under Zyrardow
Visooroszi (R) see Ruscova
Visotsk (P) see Wysock
Vitebsk (B). *Sefer Vitebsk* [Memorial book of Vitebsk]. Ed.: B. Karu. Tel Aviv, Former Residents of Vitebsk and Surroundings in Israel, 1957. 508 columns, ports., facsims. (Hebrew)
Vitebsk (B). *Vitebsk amol; geshikhte, zikhroynes, khurbn* [Vitebsk in the past; history, memoirs, destruction]. Eds.: G. Aronson, J. Lestchinsky, A. Kihn. New York, 1956. 644 p., ports. (Yiddish)
Vitkov (Novyy) (Witkow Nowy) (P) see under Radziechow
Vizna (B) see under Slutsk
Vladimir Volynskiy (P) see Wlodzimierz
Vladimirets (P) see Wlodzimierzec
Vloyn (P) see Wielun
Volozhin (P) see Wolozyn
Voronovo (P) see Werenow
Voydislav (P) see Wodzislaw
Vrbove (Verbo) (C) see under Postyen
Vurka (P) see Warka
Wadowice (P). *Sefer zikaron le-kehilot Wadowice, Andrychow, Kalwarja, Myslenice, Sucha* [Memorial book of the communities Wadowice . . .]. Ed.: D. Jakubowicz. Ramat Gan, Former Residents of Wadowice . . . and Masada, 1967. 454 p., ports., facsims. (Hebrew, Yiddish)
Warez (P) see under Sokal
Warka (P). *Vurka; sefer zikaron* [Vurka memorial book]. Tel Aviv, Vurka Societies in Israel, France, Argentina, England and the United States, 1976. 407 p., illus. (Hebrew, Yiddish)
Warsaw (P). *Pinkes Varshe* [Book of Warsaw]. Eds.: P. Katz et al. Buenos Aires, Former Residents of Warsaw and Surroundings in Argentina, 1955. 1351 columns, lvi p., ports., music, maps (Yiddish)
Warsaw (P) see also under Various (Miscellany) *Arim ve-imahot be-yisrael*, v. 3
Warsaw (P). *Warsaw* [Warsaw volume*]. Ed.: J. Gruenbaum. Jerusalem, The Encyclopaedia of the Jewish Diaspora, 1953–73. 3 vols., ports., maps, facsims. (Hebrew, Yiddish)
Warszawa (P) see Warsaw
Warta (P). *Sefer D'Vart*. Ed.: Eliezer Estrin. Tel Aviv, D'Vart Society, 1974. 567 p., illus. (Hebrew, Yiddish)
Wasiliszki (P) see under Szczuczyn (*Sefer zikaron le-kehilot Szczuczyn, Wasiliszki*)
Wasniow (P) see under Ostrowiec
Wegrow (P). *Kehilat Wegrow; sefer zikaron* [Community of Wegrow; memorial book]. Ed.: M. Tamari. Tel Aviv, Former Residents of Wegrow in Israel, 1961. 418 p., ports., facsims. (Hebrew, Yiddish)
Werenow (P). *Voronova; sefer zikaron le-kedoshei Voronova she-nispu ba-shoat ha-Nazim* [Voronova; memorial book to the martyrs of Voronova who died during the Nazi Holocaust]. Ed.: H. Rabin. Israel, Voronova Societies in Israel and the United States, 1971. 440 p., illus. (Hebrew, Yiddish)
Widze (P) see under Swieciany

Wieliczka (P). *Kehilat Wieliczka; sefer zikaron* [The Jewish community of Wieliczka; a memorial book*]. Ed.: Shmuel Meiri. Tel Aviv, The Wieliczka Association in Israel, 1980. 160, [9], 93 p., illus. (Hebrew, Yiddish, English, Polish)

Wielun (P). *Sefer zikaron le-kehilat Wielun* [Wielun memorial book*]. Tel Aviv, Wielun Organization in Israel and the Memorial Book Committee in USA, 1971. 534, 24 p., ports. (Hebrew, Yiddish, English)

Wieruszow (P). *Wieruszow; sefer yizkor* [Wieruszow; memorial book]. Tel Aviv, Former Residents of Wieruszow Book Committee, 1970. 907 p., ports., maps, facsims. (Hebrew, Yiddish)

Wierzbnik (P). *Sefer Wierzbnik-Starachowice* [Wierzbnik-Starachowitz; a memorial book*]. Ed.: Mark Schutzman. Tel Aviv, Wierzbnik-Starachowitz Societies in Israel and the Diaspora, 1973. 29, 399, 100, 83 p., illus. (Hebrew, Yiddish, English)

Wilejka (P). *Sefer zikaron kehilat Wilejka ha-mehozit, plakh Vilna* [Memorial book of the community of Vileika*]. Eds.: Kalman Farber, Joseph Se'evi. Tel Aviv, Wilejka Society, 1972. 12, 326 p., illus. (Hebrew, Yiddish, English)

Wilno (P) see Vilna

Wiskitki (P) see under Zyrardow

Wislica (P). *Sefer Vayslits; dos Vayslitser yizker-bukh* . . . [Book of Wislica]. Tel Aviv, Association of Former Residents of Wislica, 1971. 299 p., ports., map (Hebrew, Yiddish, Polish)

Wisniowiec Nowy (P). *Wisniowiec; sefer zikaron le-kedoshei Wisniowiec she-nispu be-shoat ha-Nazim* [Wisniowiec; memorial book of the martyrs of Wisniowiec who perished in the Nazi Holocaust]. Ed.: H. Rabin. [Tel Aviv], Former Residents of Wisniowiec. 540 p., ports. (Hebrew, Yiddish)

Wiszniew (P). *Vishneva, ke-fi she-hayta ve-enena od; sefer zikaron* [Wiszniew; as it was and is no more; memorial book]. Ed.: Hayyim Abramson. Tel Aviv, Wiszniew Society in Israel, 1972. 216 p., illus. (Hebrew, Yiddish)

Witkow Nowy (P) see under Radziechow

Wloclawek (P). *Wloclawek ve-ha-seviva; sefer zikaron* [Wlocawek and vicinity; memorial book*]. Eds.: K. F. Thursh and M. Korzen. [Israel], Assoc. of Former Residents of Wloclawek in Israel and the USA, 1967. 1032 columns, ports., facsims. (Hebrew, Yiddish)

Wlodawa (P). *Wlodawa; ner zikaron* [In memory of Wlodawa]. Ed.: D. Rovner. Haifa, 1968. 211 p., ports., facisms. (Hebrew, Yiddish, English, Polish), mimeo.

Wlodawa (P). *Yizker-bukh tsu Vlodave* [Yizkor book in memory of Vlodava and region Sobibor*]. Ed.: Shimon Kanc. Tel Aviv, Wlodawa Societies in Israel and North and South America, 1974. 1290, 128 p., illus. (Hebrew, Yiddish, English)

Wlodzimierz (P). *Pinkas Ludmir; sefer zikaron le-kehilat Ludmir* [Wladimir Wolynsk; in memory of the Jewish community*]. Tel Aviv, Former Residents of Wladimir in Israel, 1962. 624 columns, ports., facsims. (Hebrew, Yiddish)

Wlodzimierzec (P). *Sefer Vladimeretz* [The book of Vladimeretz]. Ed.: A. Meyerowitz. Tel Aviv, Former Residents of Vladimeretz in Israel, [196-]. 515 p., ports., map (Hebrew, Yiddish, English)

Wodzislaw (P). *Sefer Wodzislaw-Sedziszow*. Ed.: M. Schutzman. Israel, Community Council of Wodzislaw-Sedziszow Emigrants in Israel, 1979. 437 p., illus. (Hebrew, Yiddish)

Wojslawice (P). *Sefer zikaron Voislavitze* [Yizkor book in memory of Voislavize*]. Ed.: Sh. Kanc. Tel Aviv, Former Residents of Voislavitze, 1970. 515 p., ports., facsims. (Hebrew, Yiddish)

Wolborz (P) see under Piotrkow Trybunalski

Wolbrom (P). *Wolbrom irenu* [Our town Wolbrom]. Ed.: M. Geshuri (Bruckner). Tel

Aviv, Association of Former Residents of Wolbrom in Israel, 1962. 909 p., ports., map (Hebrew, Yiddish)

Wolica-Wygoda (P) see under Radziechow

Wolkowysk (P). *Hurban Wolkowysk be-milhemet ha-olam ha-sheniya 1939–1945* [The destruction of Wolkowysk during the Second World War 1939–1945]. Tel Aviv, Committee of Former Residents of Wolkovysk in Eretz-Israel, 1946. 96 p., ports. (Hebrew)

Wolkowysk (P). *Volkovisker yizker-bukh* [Wolkovisker yizkor book*]. Ed.: M. Einhorn. New York, 1949. 2 vols., 990 p., ports. (Yiddish)

Wolma (P) see under Rubiezewicze

Wolomin (P). *Sefer zikaron kehilat Wolomin* [Volomin; a memorial to the Jewish community of Volomin (Poland)*]. Ed.: Shimon Kanc. Tel Aviv, Wolomin Society, 1971. 600 p., illus. (Hebrew, Yiddish)

Wolozyn (P). *Wolozyn; sefer shel ha-ir ve-shel yeshivat "Etz Hayyim"* [Wolozin; the book of the city and of the Etz Hayyim Yeshiva*]. Ed.: E. Leoni. Tel Aviv, Former Residents of Wolozin in Israel and the USA, 1970. 679, 35 p., ports., map, facsims. (Hebrew, Yiddish, English)

Wolpa (P) see under Wolkowysk (*Volkovisker yizker-bukh*)

Wsielub (P) see under Nowogrodek

Wysock (near Rowne) (P). *Ayaratenu Visotsk; sefer zikaron* [Our town Visotsk; memorial book]. Haifa, Association of Former Residents of Visotsk in Israel, 1963. 231 p., ports., maps (Hebrew, Yiddish)

Wysokie-Mazowieckie (P). *Wysokie-Mazowieckie; sefer zikaron* [Visoka-Mazovietsk*]. Ed.: I. Rubin. Tel Aviv, Wysokie-Mazowieckie Society, 1975. 280 p., illus. (Hebrew, Yiddish, English)

Wyszkow (P). *Sefer Wyszkow* [Wishkow book*]. Ed.: D. Shtokfish. Tel Aviv, Association of Former Residents of Wishkow in Israel and Abroad, 1964. 351 p., ports., facsims. (Hebrew, Yiddish)

Wyszogrod (P). *Wyszogrod; sefer zikaron* [Vishogrod; dedicated to the memory . . . *]. Ed.: H. Rabin. [Tel Aviv], Former Residents of Vishogrod and . . . , [1971]. 316, 48 p., ports., facsims. (Hebrew, Yiddish, English)

Wyzgrodek (P) see under Krzemieniec

Yagistov (P) see Augustow

Yampol (U). *Ayara be-lehavot; pinkas Yampola, pelekh Volyn* [Town in flames; book of Yampola, district Wolyn]. Ed.: L. Gelman. Jerusalem, Commemoration Committee for the Town with the Assistance of Yad Vashem and the World Jewish Congress, 1963. [154] p. (Hebrew, Yiddish)

Yanova (L) see Jonava

Yanovichi (B) see under Vitebsk (*Vitebsk amol;*)

Yavoriv (P) see Jaworow

Yedintsy (R). *Yad le-Yedinitz; sefer zikaron le-yehudei Yedinitz-Bessarabia* [Yad l'Yedinitz; memorial book for the Jewish community of Yedintzi, Bessarabia]. Eds.: Mordekhai Reicher, Yosef Magen-Shitz. Tel Aviv, Yedinitz Society, 1973. 1022 p., illus. (Hebrew, Yiddish)

Yedwabne (P) see Jedwabne

Yekaterinoslav (U). *Sefer Yekaterinoslav-Dnepropetrovsk*. Eds.: Zvi Harkavi, Yaakov Goldburt. Jerusalem-Tel Aviv, Yekaterinoslav-Dnepropetrovsk Society, 1973. 167 p., illus. (Hebrew)

Yendrikhov (Andrychów) (P) see under Wadowice

Yendzheva (P) see Jedrzejow

Yustingrad (U). *Yustingrad-Sokolivka; ayara she-nihreva* [Yustingrad-Sokolivka; a town that was destroyed]. Kibbutz Mashabei Sadeh, 1972. 63, [17] p., ports., map, illus. (Hebrew)

Zablotow (P). *Ir u-metim; Zablotow ha-melea ve-ha-hareva* [A city and the dead; Zablotow alive and destroyed]. Tel Aviv, Former Residents of Zablotow in Israel and the USA, 1949. 218 p., ports. (Hebrew, Yiddish)

Zabludow (P). *Zabludow yizker-bukh* [Zabludowo; in memoriam*]. Eds.: Sh. Tsesler et al. Buenos Aires, Zabludowo Book Committee, 1961. 507 p., ports., map, facsims. (Yiddish)

Zaglebie (Region) (P). *Pinkes Zaglembye; memorial book.* Ed.: J. Rapoport. Melbourne, Zaglembie Society and Zaglembie Committee in Melbourne; Tel Aviv, Hamenorah, 1972. 82, 613 p., illus. (Yiddish, English)

Zakarpatskaya Oblast (C) see Karpatalja

Zakopane (P) see under Nowy Targ

Zaloshits (P) see Dzialoszyce

Zambrow (P). *Sefer Zambrow; Zambrove* [The book of Zambrov*]. Ed.: Y. T. Lewinsky. Tel Aviv, The Zambrover Societies in USA, Argentina and Israel, 1963. 627, 69 p., ports., facsims. (Hebrew, Yiddish, English)

Zamekhov (U) see under Kamenets-Podolskiy

Zamosc (P). *Pinkes Zamosc; yizker-bukh* [Pinkas Zamosc; in memoriam*]. Ed.: M. W. Bernstein. Buenos Aires, Committee of the Zamosc Memorial Book, 1957. 1265 p., ports., facsims. (Yiddish)

Zamosc (P). *Zamosc be-gnona u-be-shivra* [The rise and fall of Zamosc]. Ed.: M. Tamari. Tel Aviv, Former Residents of Zamosc in Israel, 1953. 327 p., ports., facsims. (Hebrew, Polish)

Zareby Koscielne (P). *Le-zikhron olam; di Zaromber yidn vos zaynen umgekumen al kidesh-hashem* [For eternal remembrance; the Jews of Zaromb . . .]. [New York], United Zaromber Relief, 1947. 68 p., ports., map, facsims. (Yiddish)

Zarki (P). *Kehilat Zarki; ayara be-hayeha u-ve-khilyona* [The community of Zarki; life and destruction of a town]. Ed.: Y. Lador. Tel Aviv, Former Residents of Zarki in Israel, 1959. 324 p., ports. (Hebrew, Yiddish)

Zaromb (P) see Zareby Koscielne

Zarszyn (P) see under Sanok

Zassow (P) see under Radomysl

Zastawie (P) see under Kamieniec Litewski

Zawidcze (P) see under Radziechow

Zawiercie (P). *Sefer zikaron; kedoshei Zawiercie ve-ha-seviva* [Memorial book of the martyrs of Zawiercie and vicinity]. Ed.: Sh. Spivak. Tel Aviv, Former Residents of Zawiercie and Vicinity, 1948. 570 p., ports. (Hebrew, Yiddish)

Zborow (P). *Sefer zikaron le-kehilat Zborow* [Memorial book of the community of Zborow]. Ed.: Eliyahu (Adik) Zilberman. Haifa, Zborow Society, 1975. 477 p., illus. (Hebrew, Yiddish)

Zdunska Wola (P). *Zdunska Wola* [The Zdunska-Wola book*]. Ed.: E. Erlich. Tel Aviv, Zdunska-Wola Associations in Israel and in the Diaspora, 1968. 718, 8, 55 p., ports., facsims. (Hebrew, Yiddish, English)

Zdzieciol (P). *Pinkas Zhetl* [Pinkas Zetel; a memorial to the Jewish community of Zetel*]. Ed.: B. Kaplinski. Tel Aviv, Zetel Association in Israel, 1957. 482 p., ports., facsims. (Hebrew, Yiddish)

Zelechow (P). *Yizker-bukh fun der Zhelekhover yidisher kehile* [Memorial book of the community of Zelechow]. Ed.: W. Yassni. Chicago, Former Residents of Zelechow in Chicago, 1953. 398, xxiv p., facsims. (Yiddish)

Zelow (P). *Sefer zikaron le-kehilat Zelow* [Memorial book of the community of Zelow]. Ed.: Avraham Kalushiner. Tel Aviv, Zelów Society, 1976. 447 p., illus. (Hebrew, Yiddish)

Zgierz (P). *Sefer Zgierz, mazkeret nezah le-kehila yehudit be-Polin* [Memorial book Zgierz*]. Ed.: David Shtokfish. Tel Aviv, Zgierz Society, 1975. 795 p., illus. (Hebrew, Yiddish)

Zhetl (P) see Zdzieciol

Zholkva (P) see Zolkiew

Zinkov (P). *Pinkas Zinkov* [Zinkover memorial book*]. Tel Aviv–New York, Joint Committee of Zinkover Landsleit in the United States and Israel, 1966. 239, 16 p., ports. (Hebrew, Yiddish, English)

Zloczew (Lodz) (P). *Sefer Zloczew* [Book of Zloczew]. Tel Aviv, Committee of the Association of Former Residents of Zloczew, [1971]. 432, [21] p., ports., facsims. (Hebrew, Yiddish)

Zloczow (P). *Sefer kehilat Zloczow* [The city of Zloczow*]. Ed.: Baruch Krua (Krupnik). Tel Aviv, Zloczow Society, 1967. 540, 208 columns, illus. (Hebrew, English)

Zolkiew (P). *Sefer Zolkiew (kirya nisgava)* [Memorial book of Zolkiew]. Eds.: N. M. Gelber and Y. Ben-Shem. Jerusalem, The Encyclopaedia of the Jewish Diaspora, 1969. 844 columns, ports., map, facsims. (Hebrew)

Zolochev (P) see Zloczow

Zoludek (P). *Sefer Zoludek ve-Orlowa; galed le-zikaron* [The book of Zoludek and Orlowa; a living memorial*]. Ed.: A. Meyerowitz. Tel Aviv, Former Residents of Zoludek in Israel and the USA, [n.d.] 329, [5] p., ports., map (Hebrew, Yiddish, English)

Zoludzk (P). *Ner tamid le-zekher kehilat Zoludzk* [Memorial book of the community of Zoludzk]. Ed.: A. Avinadav. Tel Aviv, Association of Former Residents of Zoludzk in Israel, 1970. 185, 3 p., ports., map (Hebrew, Yiddish)

Zombor (Y). *Kehilat Sombor be-hurbana; dapei zikaron le-kedoshei ha-kehila* [The Sombor community in its destruction; pages of commemoration to the martyrs of the community]. [By] E. H. Spitzer. Jerusalem, 1970. 29 p., ports. (Hebrew)

Zvhil (U) see Novograd-Volynskiy

Zwiahel (U) see Novograd-Volynskiy

Zwolen (P). *Zwoliner yizker-bukh* [Zwolen memorial book]. New York, Zwolen Society, 1982. 564, 112 p., illus. (Yiddish, English)

Zychlin (P). *Sefer Zychlin.* [The memorial book of Zychlin*]. Ed.: Ammi Shamir. Tel Aviv, Zychliner Organization of Israel and America, 1974. 4, 350 p., illus. (Hebrew, Yiddish, English)

Zyrardow (P). *Pinkas Zyrardow, Amshinov un Viskit* [Memorial book of Zyrardow, Amshinov and Viskit]. Ed.: M. W. Bernstein. Buenos Aires, Association of Former Residents in the U.S.A., Israel, France and Argentina, 1961. 699 p., ports., facsims. (Yiddish)

Various (Miscellany)

> *Arim ve-imahot be-yisrael; matsevet kodesh le-kehilot yisrael she-nehrevu bi-yedei aritsim u-tmeim be-milhemet ha-olam ha-aharona* [Towns and mother-cities in Israel; memorial of the Jewish communities which perished . . .]. Ed.: Y. L. Fishman (Maimon). Jerusalem, The Rav Kuk Institute (Hebrew)
>
> v. 1, 1947. 371 p., ports.
> v. 2, 1948. 354 p., ports.
> v. 3, *Warsaw.* [By] D. Flinker. 1948. 308 p., ports.
> v. 4, 1950. 313 p., ports.
> v. 5, *Stanislawow.* Eds.: D. Sadan and M. Gelerter. 1952. Ports., music.
> v. 6, *Brody.* [By] N. Gelber. 1956. 347 p., ports., map.
> v. 7, *Bratislava (Pressburg).* [By] Sh. Weingarten-Hakohen. 1960. 184 p., ports.

Various (Miscellany)

> *Pinkas ha-kehilot; entsiklopediya shel ha-yishuvim le-min hivasdam ve-ad le-aher shoat milhemet*

ha-olam ha-sheniya [Pinkas hakehillot: encyclopedia of Jewish communities*]. Jerusalem, Yad Vashem Martyrs' and Heroes' Remembrance Authority, 1969-
Romania. Eds.: Theodore Lavi, Aviva Broshni. v. 1: 1969. 224, 552 p., illus. (Hebrew); v. 2: 1980. Eds.: Jan Ancel, Theodore Lavi. 5,568 p., illus., maps. (Hebrew)
Germany: Bavaria. Ed.: Baruch Zvi Ophir. 1972. 12, 683, 40 p., illus. (Hebrew, English)
Hungary. Ed.: Theodore Lavi. 1975. 8,557 p., illus. (Hebrew)
Poland. v. 1: The communities of Lodz and its region. Eds.: Danuta Dabrowska, Abraham Wein. 1976. 15, 285, 15 p., illus. (Hebrew, English); v. 2: Eastern Galicia. Eds.: Danuta Dabrowska, Abraham Wein, Aharon Weiss. 1980. 31, 563 p., illus, maps (Hebrew, English)

Appendix II:
Geographical Index and Gazetteer

compiled by Zachary M. Baker

Compiler's note: This index includes all places within Poland as defined by its 1920–1939 boundaries that are mentioned in the text. (A few Lithuanian towns are also indexed.)* Place names are given in Yiddish (as used in the text) and in Polish or Lithuanian (in parentheses) wherever the official Polish forms of these names diverge from the text spellings. Page references are to pages in the text that refer to particular locales, whether or not they are mentioned explicitly. Short gazetteer entries on over seventy-five places receiving extensive mention within the text are also listed. These entries contain information pertaining to the precise location of these towns (within the pre–World War II political boundaries of Poland), their economic structure, population, and the development and destruction of their Jewish communities.

Amshinov (Mszczonow), 118
Antipolye (Antopol), 42
Apt (Opatow), 122, 123, 195
  Kielce prov., 35 mi. ESE of Kielce. Chemicals, cement, brushes. Jewish settlement from 16th century. Hasidic rebe: Abraham Joshua Heschel ("Apter"). Jewish pop.: 1856: 2,517 (65%); 1897: 4,138; 1939: approx. 5,200. Ghetto established Spring 1941; liquidated Oct. 1942 (Treblinka).
Baranovitsh (Baranowicze), 110
Beddin (Benzin), 4, 14, 80–81
  Kielce prov. (prewar), 30 mi. S of Czestochowa. Coal mining, quarrying, manufacturing, food processing. Jewish settlement from early 17th century. Large Jewish working-class pop.; center of socialist activity (1905). Jewish pop.: 1765: 446; 1856: 2,440 (59%); 1897: 10,839 (46%). 1921: 17,298 (62%). Deportations in May, Aug. 1942; ghetto liquidated Aug. 1943 (Auschwitz). Some armed resistance.
Belkhatov (Belchatow), 48–51, 216–18
  Lodz prov., 28 mi. S of Lodz. Textiles, tanning, sawmilling, cement. Jewish pop.: 1764: 7; 1897: 2,897 (75%); 1921: 3,688 (59%); after 1939: approx. 6,000. Jewish community liquidated Aug. 1942 (1,000 sent to Lodz ghetto; 5,000 to Chelmno).
Belz, 87
Belzhets (Belzec), 220
Bereze (Bereza Kartuska), 154
Berezene (Berezno), 26
Berezhnits (Bereznica), 26, 27
Bezoyn (Biezun), 206
  Warsaw prov., 70 mi. NW of Warsaw. Jewish pop.: 1765: 172; 1856: 790 (62%); 1921: 779.

*Places outside of Poland and Lithuania are excluded.

Bialystok, 47, 98, 131, 185
Capital, Bialystok prov., 105 mi. NE of Warsaw. Industrial city: textiles, sawmilling, woodworking, food processing. Rail junction. Center of Jewish labor movement. Violent pogrom June 13, 1906. 1921: 89% of industrial plants owned by Jews. Jewish pop.: 1765: 765; 1856: 9,547 (69%); 1895: 47,783 (76%); 1932: approx. 46,000 (50%). Ghetto established July 26, 1941; liquidated Aug. 16, 1943 (Treblinka, Majdanek). Armed resistance.

Bilgoray (Bilgoraj), 94–95, 215–16, 220–21
Lublin prov., 60 mi. S of Lublin. Mfg. of sieves, vegetable oil; flour- and sawmilling. Jewish settlement from mid-17th century; many perished 1648/49. Center of Hebrew printing. Childhood home of Israel Joshua Singer and Isaac Bashevis Singer. Jewish pop.: 1841: 1,637; 1897: 3,486; 1921: 3,715; 1939: approx. 5,000 (50%). Ghetto established June 20, 1940; liquidated Nov. 2, 1942 (Belzec).

Bolovitsh, 71–72

Brisk (Brzesc nad Bugiem; Brest Litovsk), 134, 154

Budzhin (Budzyn), 154

Bydgoszcz (Bromberg), 53

Cracow (Krakow), 25, 120, 172
Capital, Cracow prov. (W. Galicia), 155 mi. SSW of Warsaw, on Vistula R. Rail junction; trade and commercial center. Ancient Jewish community (from 13th century). 1495: Jews expelled to suburb of Kazimierz. Hebrew printing from 1534. Among rabbis: Moses Isserles, Yom Tov Lippman Heller. Late 18th century: center of both Hasidism and Enlightenment. Important Zionist center between World War I and World War II. Jewish pop.: 1900: 25,670 (28%); 1921: 45,229 (28%); 1938: approx. 60,000 (25%). Ghetto established March 21, 1941; liquidated March 1943 (Belzec, Auschwitz).

Danzig (Gdansk), 27

Disne (Dzisna), 146
Vilna prov., 140 mi. NE of Vilna, on W. Dvina R., at mouth of Dzisna R. (Now U.S.S.R.) Flax- and grain-trading center. Jewish pop.: 1847: 1,880; 1897: 4,617 (68%); 1921: 2,742 (62%); 1941: approx. 6,000. Ghetto established at end of 1941; liquidated June 14–15, 1942 (mass executions).

Dombrovits (Dabrowica; Dubrovitsa), 25–29
Polesie prov., 50 mi. SE of Pinsk, on Goryn R. (Now U.S.S.R.) Rail junction. Tanning, vegetable-processing, flour- and sawmilling. Old Jewish community (from 16th century). Hasidic influence from early nineteenth century. Jewish pop.: 1766: 404; 1847: 1,910; 1897: 2,868 (48%); 1921: 2,536.

Dubno, 145–46
Volyn prov., 75 mi. SE of Kowel, on Ikva R. (Now U.S.S.R.) Agricultural and food-processing. Tanning, sawmilling, tile and brick mfg. Jewish settlement from 16th century Home of Jacob Krantz ("Dubner Magid"). Jewish pop.: 1780: 2,325; 1847: 6,330; 1897: 7,108 (50%); 1941: approx. 12,000. Ghetto established April 1, 1942; liquidated Oct. 1942 (mass executions).

Falenits (Falenica), 85–86, 184

Frampol, 175–76
Lublin prov., 35 mi. S of Lublin. Jewish settlement from 18th century. Jewish pop.: 1856: 652 (78%); 1897: 1,251 (49%); 1921: 1,465; Jewish community liquidated Nov. 2, 1942 (Belzec).

Galicia, 98, 101, 152–53

Garbov (Garbow), 194

Garvolin (Garwolin), 60, 164
Gebeltov (Giebultow), 172–74
Ger (Gora Kalwaria), 87
Glayvits (Gleiwitz; Gliwice), 206
Glogov (Glogow), 31
Goray (Goraj), 175–76
Gostinin (Gostynin), 199
Govorove (Goworowo), 81–83
  Bialystok prov., 75 mi. WSW of Bialystok. Jewish community from 16th century.
  Jewish pop.: 1897: 1,844 (66%); 1921: 1,228.
Granastov, 103
Grobev (Grabow), 148–51
Grodno, 45–46
Gzhimalov (Grzymalow), 151
Hanusove, 101–102
Horodets (Horodec), 40–44
  Polesie prov., 40 mi. E of Brest-Litovsk. (Now U.S.S.R.) Jewish community from 16th
  century. Jewish pop.: 1847: 422; 1897: 648 (37%); 1921: 264. Ghetto established April
  1942; liquidated Oct. 15, 1942 (mass executions).
Horodok (Grodek), 45
Husiatyn, 151, 153
Kalushin (Kaluszyn), 1, 83–85, 118–19
  Warsaw prov., 34 mi. E of Warsaw. Mfg. of shingles; tanning, brewing, flour milling.
  Jewish settlement from early 17th century. Among Jewish enterprises: Talis-weaving,
  fur trade, tailoring, carpentry. Jewish pop.: 1827: 1,455 (80%); 1897: 6,419 (76%); 1921:
  5,033 (82%); 1939: approx. 6,500. Jewish community liquidated by Dec. 1942 (Tre-
  blinka).
Kamin-Koshirski (Kamien Koszyrski), 96–97, 136–37
  Polesie prov., 30 mi. NNE of Kowel, in Pripet Marshes. (Now U.S.S.R.) Jewish
  community from 17th century. Jewish pop.: 1847: 862; 1897: 1,189 (97%); 1921: 617.
  Ghetto established May 15, 1942; liquidated later that year (mass executions).
Kartshev (Karczew), 78, 85, 185–86
  Warsaw prov., 15 mi. SE of Warsaw. Jewish pop.: 1856: 855 (50%); 1897: 1,025 (36%);
  1921: 836. Jewish community liquidated Aug. 1942.
Kelts (Kielce), 120, 139, 215
  Capital, Kielce prov., 65 mi. NNE of Cracow. Rail junction, trade center, mfg.,
  brewing, tanning, flour- and sawmilling, food processing, quarrying. Jewish settlement
  prohibited until 1833. Jewish pop.: 1873: 974; 1897: 6,399; 1921: 15,530 (38%). 1939:
  approx. 25,000. Ghetto established March 31, 1941; liquidated Aug. 20–24, 1942 (Treblinka). More than 40 Holocaust survivors died in pogrom on July 4, 1946.
Khelm (Chelm), 51–53, 143–44
  Lublin prov., 40 mi. ESE of Lublin. Rail junction, trade center, mfg., brewing,
  distilling, flour- and sawmilling, brickworking. Ancient Jewish community (possibly
  dating from 12th century). Legendary site of humorous stories about "Chelm sages."
  Hasidic dynasty from 19th century. Jewish pop.: 1765: 1,500; 1857: 2,493 (68%); 1897:
  7,226 (56%); 1931: 13,537 (46.5%). Mass deportations May 21–23, 1942; final liquidation of Jewish community Nov. 6, 1942 (Sobibor).
Khmelnik (Chmielnik), 14, 126–30, 120–22
  Kielce prov., 18 mi. SSE of Kielce. Tanning, flour milling. Jewish settlement from 16th
  century. Hasidism strong in 18th–19th centuries. Jewish pop.: 1764: 1,445; 1897: 5,560

Krupe, 191–92
Kshanov (Chrzanow), 101
Kshepits (Krzepice), 134
Kshesivka (Krzeszowka), 174
Kshoynzh (Ksiaz Wielki), 172, 174
Kutno, 63–65
Warsaw prov. (pre–World War II), 33 mi. N of Lodz. Rail junction, trade and mfg. center; flour- and sawmilling, distilling, brewing. Old Jewish community (from early 15th century). Jewish pop.: 1765: 928; 1908: 8,978 (63%); 1921: 6,784 (42%); 1939: approx. 6,700. Ghetto established June 1940; liquidated March 1942 (Chelmno).
Lizhensk (Lezajsk), 39–40
Lwow prov., 24 mi. NE of Rzeszow. Brick- and cement-works, tanning, distilling. Jewish settlement from early 16th century. Wooden synagogue. Hasidic rebe: Elimelekh (1775). Jewish pop.: 1880: 1,868 (38%); 1900: 1,494 (28%); 1921: 1,575 (31%); 1939: over 3,000. Many Jews deported to Soviet zone in Oct. 1939; remainder concentrated in ghetto (liquidated in 1942).
Lodz, 2, 50, 54, 73, 118, 120, 139, 166
Capital, Lodz prov., 75 mi. WSW of Warsaw. Railroad junction, industrial center (textiles, clothing, machinery, food processing). Second largest city and Jewish community in Poland. Jews active in developing textile industry; center of Jewish labor movement and cultural life. Jewish pop.: 1820: 259 (34%); 1856: 2,886 (12%); 1897: 98,676 (32%); 1921: 156,155 (34.5%); 1939: approx. 233,000 (33%). Ghetto established Feb. 8, 1940; finally liquidated Sept. 1, 1944 (Chelmno, Auschwitz). Known as the "working ghetto," under Judenrat chairman Mordechai Chaim Rumkowski.
Logiv (Lagow), 195
Loshits (Losice), 105–106
Lublin prov., 70 mi. E of Warsaw. Jewish settlement from late 17th century. Jews active in horse trade. Jewish pop.: 1827: 654 (42%); 1897: 2,396 (71%); 1921: 2,708 (70%). Jewish community liquidated Aug. 22, 1942 (Treblinka).
Lublin, 12, 110, 139, 192, 197, 215, 221
Capital, Lublin prov., 105 mi. SE of Warsaw, on Bystrzyca R. Rail junction, trade and mfg. center. Ancient Jewish community (from 14th century). Hebrew printing from 1547. Massacres, 1648/49. Rabbinical center, Yeshiva "Hakhmei Lublin," fortress synagogue. Hasidic dynasties (18th-19th centuries). Jews active in leather industry. Jewish pop.: 1602: 2,000; 1787: 4,321; 1857: 8,747 (56%); 1897: 23,586 (51%); 1921: 37,337 (35%); beginning of 1941: approx. 45,000. Ghetto established March 1941; most Jews exterminated 1942 (Belzec, Majdanek). Final liquidation: July 1944.
Luninyets (Luniniec), 112
Polesie prov., 32 mi. ENE of Pinsk, in Pripet Marshes. (Now U.S.S.R.) Rail junction, agricultural center; tanning, flour milling. Jews permitted to settle, 1882. Jewish pop.: 1897: 283 (9%); 1921: 2,045 (25%). Ghetto liquidated Aug. 1942 (mass executions).
Lwow (Lvov; Lemberg), 52, 138, 139
Capital, Lwow prov. (Galicia), 200 mi. SE of Warsaw. (Now U.S.S.R.) Transportation and mfg. center. Ancient Jewish community (from before 14th century). Jews played a role in trade with Orient. Massacres 1648/49. Nineteenth century: center of both Hasidism and Enlightenment. Jewish pop.: 1550: 911; 1800: 18,302; 1869: 26,694; 1910: approx. 57,000 (28%); 1939: 109,500 (33%); 1941: approx. 150,000. Ghetto established Nov. 1941; liquidated June 1943 (Belzec, Janowska Rd.). Some armed resistance.
Markushov (Markuszow), 15
Matsyeyuv (Maciejowa), 174

(51%). Mass deportation Oct. 11–12, 1942 (Treblinka); forced labor camp established at Ostrowiec Oct. 1942, liquidated Aug. 3, 1944 (Auschwitz).

Otvotsk (Otwock), 78, 85, 87–88, 184
Warsaw prov., 14 mi. SE of Warsaw. Cement mfg., flour milling, health resort (tuberculosis). Medem Sanatorium for children. Hasidic dynasty. Jewish pop.: 1908: 2,356 (21%). 1921: 5,408. 1939: 14,200. Ghetto established Jan. 1941. Mass deportations Aug. 1942 (Treblinka), mass executions.

Ozhorov (Ozarow), 195
Pabyanets (Pabianice), 50
Partshits (Parcice), 133, 134
Pinsk, 28, 112
Polesie prov., 110 mi. E of Brest-Litovsk, in Pripet Marshes. (Now U.S.S.R.) Forested region. Fish and lumber-trading center. Mfg. (paper, matches, plywood, soap, candles, glass); tanning, distilling brewing, flour- and sawmilling. Jewish settlement from before 1506. Massacres 1648/49. Jews active in grain and lumber trade. Rabbinical center. Hasidic dynasty from 1760s (Pinsk-Karlin). Jewish pop.: 1566: 275 (7%); 1648: approx. 1,000 (20%); 1897: 21,819 (77%); 1921: 17,513 (75%); 1939: 20,200. Mass executions July 1941. Ghetto established April 1942; liquidated Oct. 28, 1942 (mass executions). Partisan activity.

Pintshev (Pinczow), 63
Plashuv (Plaszow), 172
Podolik (Podwilk), 102
Podvolotshisk (Podwoloczyska), 152
Polesie, 28
Pomyekhovek (Pomiechowek), 177
Povyatov (Powiatow), 134
Proskurov, 7
Pshemishl (Przemysl), 9, 17
Pshitik (Przytyk), 51
Pultusk, 62
Pushtshe (Puczyce), 220
Pyesk (Piaski), 71
Bialystok prov., 65 mi. ENE of Bialystok. (Now U.S.S.R.) Flour milling. Jewish community active in trade and crafts. Jewish pop.: 1847: 662; 1897: 1,615 (67%); 1921: 1,249.

Radom, 28, 51–52, 194
Rakov (Rakow), 127–30
Vilna prov., 85 mi. SE of Vilna. (Now U.S.S.R.) Tanning, flour milling, quarrying. Jewish settlement from 18th century. Jewish pop.: 1897: 2,168 (59.5%); 1921: 1,421.

Ratne (Ratno), 96
Raysha (Rzeszow), 32, 35
Rembertov (Rembertow), 177
Rozhan (Rozan), 13, 62, 130–32
Warsaw prov., 55 mi. NNE of Warsaw, on Narew R. Cement mfg., flour milling, tanning. Jewish settlement from 16th century. Jewish pop.: 1765: 173; 1856: 773 (58%); 1897: 1,698 (47%); 1921: 1,646.

Rozhinoy (Rozana), 107
Rudki, 9
Sabin (Sawin), 164

Lwow prov., 34 mi. S of Rzeszow. Mfg., flour- and sawmilling, brickworks. Old Jewish settlement (from 14th century). Jews active in wine and grain trade, and as furriers, tailors, tanners; also in oil production. Hasidism strong from late 18th century. Jewish pop.: 1800: 1,850 (40%); 1880: 2,129 (42%); 1910: 4,073 (38%); 1921: 4,067 (42%); 1939: approx. 5,000. Ghetto established 1941; most Jews deported Sept. 10, 1942 to Zaslaw, and from there to Belzec; remainder executed or deported.

Cracow prov., 45 mi. SE of Cracow. Rail junction, mfg. (agricultural tools, chemicals, cement products), food processing, tanning, lumbering, flour milling. Jewish settlement from mid-15th century. Hasidic dynasty (from first half of 19th century). Jews active in trade, tailoring, carpentry, shoemaking, engraving. Jewish pop.: 1880: 5,163 (46%); 1910: 7,990 (32%); 1921: 9,009 (34%). Ghetto established Aug. 1941; liquidated Aug. 24–28, 1942 (Belzec).

Kielce prov., 35 mi. SE of Kielce. Jewish settlement from 16th century. Jewish pop.: 1765: 430; 1856: 742 (37%); 1897: 867 (37%); 1921: 660.

Suburb of Kaunas, Lithuania. (Now U.S.S.R.) Site of famous yeshiva (founded 1882), under influence of Musar movement. Yeshiva active here until June 23, 1941.

Nowogrodek prov., 40 mi. SW of Nowogrodek, on Szczara R. (Now U.S.S.R.) Mfg. (agricultural machinery, matches, soap, candles, bricks, woolen textiles), tanning, distilling, flour- and sawmilling. Jewish settlement from late 16th century. Jews active in trade and crafts. Hasidic dynasty, yeshiva. Jewish labor movement active from late 19th century. Jewish pop.: 1766: 1,154; 1847: 5,700; 1897: 11,435 (78%); 1921: 6,917 (72%). Mass executions July 17, Nov. 14, 1941. Ghetto established Aug. 1941; liquidated July 1942. Partisan activity.

Lwow prov., 14 mi. SW of Rzeszow. Brewing, distilling, sawmilling, mfg. of cement products. Jewish community primarily active in trade. Jewish pop.: 1921: 1,104.

Bialystok prov., 70 mi. N of Bialystok. Rail junction, trade center, mfg. (chairs, stamps, knitwear, hosiery, gloves), flour milling, brewing, tanning. Jewish settlement from late 18th century. Jews active in trade and crafts, including talis mfg. Jewish emigration to U.S. from 1860s. Jewish pop.: 1827: 1,209 (32%); 1857: 6,587 (62%); 1897: 7,165 (40%); 1921: 5,747 (34%); 1939: approx. 6,000. Entire Jewish community deported Nov. 1939 to four other Polish towns, sharing the fate of Jews in those places.

Tarnogrod, 215–16, 220
    Lublin prov., 65 mi. S of Lublin. Distilling, brewing. Jewish settlement from 1580.
    Massacre 1648. Jewish pop.: 1827: 1,260 (32%). 1857: 1,673 (41%). 1897: 1,635 (32%).
    1921: 2,238 (47%). 1939: approx. 2,500. Jewish community liquidated Nov. 2, 1942
    (Belzec).
Telz (Telsiai), 110–11
Tiktin (Tykocin), 98
Torne (Tarnow), 6, 12, 75–76
    Cracow prov., 45 mi. E of Cracow. Rail junction, mfg. of machinery, flour- and
    sawmilling, lace and embroidery work, weaving, brickworks. Jewish settlement from
    15th century. Late 18th century: center of both Hasidism and Enlightenment. Jews
    active in garment mfg., hatmaking. Jewish pop.: 1772: 1,200 (34%); 1846: 7,914; 1890:
    11,677 (42%); 1910: 15,108 (41%); 1921: 15,608 (44%); 1939: approx. 25,000. Ghetto
    established March 1941; deportations June 11–13, Sept. 10, Nov. 15, 1942 (Belzec).
    Ghetto liquidated Sept. 2, 1943 (Plaszow, Auschwitz).
Tshartorisk (Czartorysk), 26
Tshastar (Czastary), 133
Tshekhanovits (Ciechanowiec), 69–71
    Bialystok prov., 42 mi. SW of Bialystok, on Nurzec R. Mfg. (cloth, liqueur, flour).
    Jewish settlement from 17th century. Jewish pop.: 1847: 2,054; 1897: 3,743 (67%); 1921:
    1,649 (50%). Ghetto liquidated Nov. 1942 (mass executions).
Tshenstokhov (Czestochowa), 4, 79–80, 124–26, 138, 139, 185, 186–88
    Kielce prov., 125 mi. SW of Warsaw, on Warta R. Rail junction, heavy industrial
    center (iron and steel), mfg. (bicycles, textiles, hats, paper, chemicals, glass), food
    processing, sawmilling. Jewish settlement from 18th century. Jews active in develop-
    ment of industry and commerce. Jewish pop.: 1827: 1,141 (18.5%); 1858: 2,976 (34.5%);
    1900: 11,764 (29.5%); 1921: 22,663; 1939: 28,486. Ghetto established April 9, 1941;
    deportations Sept. 23–Oct. 5, 1942 (Treblinka). Ghetto liquidated June 1943. Some
    armed resistance; some survivors of work camps at Czestochowa.
Tshervinsk (Czerwinsk), 178–79
Ulanov (Ulanow), 38
Uzhendov (Urzedow), 192–93
Vengerov (Wegrow), 91–94
    Warsaw prov., 45 mi. ENE of Warsaw. Tanning, mfg. (cement, shingles, parchment),
    food processing. Jewish settlement from early 16th century. Jews active in cattle trade,
    crafts, weaving, tanning. Active Jewish labor movment, 20th century. Jewish pop.:
    1827: 1,463 (48%); 1857: 2,343 (61%); 1897: 5,150 (62%); 1931: 5,227 (55%). Mass
    deportation Sept. 22, 1942 (Treblinka); thousands of escapees later rounded up and
    executed.
Vidava (Widawa), 75
Vilna (Wilno; Vilnius), 7, 25, 45, 112, 145, 185, 221
    Capital, Vilna prov., 240 mi. NE of Warsaw, on Wilja R. (Now U.S.S.R.) Cultural,
    commercial, industrial center. Rail junction, mfg., sawmilling, tobacco- and food pro-
    cessing. Jewish settlement from mid-16th century. "Jerusalem of Lithuania." Religious
    center (18th century: Elijah of Vilna ["Vilna Gaon"]). Printing of Vilna Talmud, 1854.
    Jewish Labor Bund founded here, 1897. Yiddish literary, educational, cultural center,
    late 19th–20th centuries (YIVO, 1925–1940). Jewish pop.: 1800: 6,917 taxpayers; 1897:
    63,831 (41.5%); 1921: 46,559 (36%); 1941: approx. 80,000. Mass executions at Ponary,
    summer 1941. Two ghettoes established Sept. 16, 1941; liquidated Sept. 23, 1943
    (Ponary, Majdanek, Estonia). Partisan activity.

Zembrove (Zambrow), 4, 97
Zhelekhov (Zelechow), 59–60, 164–66
    Lublin prov. (prewar), 50 mi. SE of Warsaw. Mfg. (shoes, vegetable oil), tanning, flour
    milling. Jewish settlement from 17th century. Levi Yitzhok of Berdichev (hasidic rebe)
    officiated here, 1772–1784. Jewish pop.: 1765: 1,464; 1856: 2,317; 1897: 4,930 (70%);
    1939: 5,500. Ghetto established autumn 1940; liquidated Sept. 30, 1942 (Treblinka).
Zhirardov (Zyrardow), 117–18
    Warsaw prov., 27 mi. WSW of Warsaw. Textile center, mfg. (railroad cars, clothing),
    tanning, brewing, distilling, flour milling. Jewish settlement from 1840s. Jews employed
    in textile factories, also in small trade and crafts. Jewish pop.: 1897: 2,310 (23%); 1921:
    2,547 (12%). Entire Jewish community expelled to Warsaw Feb. 1941, sharing the fate
    of Warsaw Jewry.
Zhulkin (Zolkinie), 182
Zlotshev (Zloczew), 73–75
    Lodz prov., 45 mi. SW of Lodz. Tanning, sawmilling, capmaking. Jewish pop.: 1856:
    922 (61%); 1897: 1,501 (65%); 1921: 1,959.
Zvyezhinets (Zwierzyniec), 215

Sources

Blackbook of localities whose Jewish population was exterminated by the Nazis (Jerusalem: Yad
    Vashem, 1965).
Cohen, Chester G. *Shtetl finder: Jewish communities in the 19th and early 20th centuries in the
    Pale of Settlement of Russia and Poland, and in Lithuania, Latvia, Galicia, and Bukovina, with
    names of residents* (Los Angeles: Periday, 1980).
The Columbia Lippincott Gazetteer of the World, ed. by Leon E. Seltzer (New York: Columbia
    University Press, 1962).
Encyclopaedia Judaica (Berlin: Eschkol, 1928–34). 10 vols. (A–L)
Encyclopaedia Judaica (Jerusalem: 1971–72). 16 vols. (A–Z)
Evreiskaia entsiklopediia [Jewish encyclopedia] (St. Petersburg: 1906–13). 16 vols. (A–Я)

BALTIC SEA

DANZIG

GERMA[N]

POMORZE

GERMANY

POZNAN

*Torun
• Biezun

Rozan •

WARSAW

Wyszkow
Kaluszyn

Poznan*

• Kolo

Nowy Dwor •

Warsaw*

• Kutno

LODZ

Zyrardow

Otwock •
• Karczew

*Lodz

Warka •

Kozienice •
Radom •

Piotrkow Trybunalski •

Wieruszow • • Belchatow
Zloczew •

KIELCE

Ostrowiec

*Kielce
•

Czestochowa •

Opatow •

• Chmielnik

Szydlow •

Katowice •

• Bedzin
• Miechow

SLASK

*Cracow

• Oswiecim

Tarnow •

CRACOW

Nowy Sacz •

CZECHOSLOVAKIA

POLAND (1921–1938)
*Provincial capitals

HUNGARY